The Best American Political Writing 2007

The Best American Political Writing 2007

Edited by Royce Flippin

Thunder's Mouth Press
New York

THE BEST AMERICAN POLITICAL WRITING 2007

Published by
Thunder's Mouth Press
An Imprint of Avalon Publishing Group, Inc.
245 West 17th St., 11th Floor
New York, NY 10011

www.thundersmouth.com

First printing October 2007

Library of Congress Cataloging-in-Publication Data is available.

ISBN-10: 1-56858-343-5
ISBN-13: 978-1-56858-343-3

Book design by Sue Canavan

10 9 8 7 6 5 4 3 2 1

Distributed by Publishers Group West

This book is dedicated to
the 110 journalists
who have been killed while reporting from Iraq.

CONTENTS

Acknowledgments

I'd like to thank all the writers featured in these pages, along with their agents and the permissions editors of their various publications, for allowing their articles to be reprinted here. Thanks, too, to Bill Strachan and Peter Jacoby of Avalon Publishing for their help in shepherding this year's edition into print, and to Mike Walters and the rest of the Avalon production team for their fine work on this book. Last but not least, a huge thank-you to my wife, Alexis Lipsitz Flippin, for her unwavering love and support.

Preface

What a difference a year makes! Since the previous edition of *The Best American Political Writing* was published, the Democrats have regained control of both houses of Congress (though by the barest of margins in the Senate); a growing number of Republicans have joined the Democrats in questioning the progress of the Iraq War; the Bush administration's political machinations have finally resulted in a pair of full-blown scandals, with the perjury conviction of Dick Cheney's former chief of staff I. Lewis "Scooter" Libby (on charges stemming from the investigation into the "outing" of CIA operative Valerie Plame), and revelations of the White House's involvement in the unprecedented midterm firings of nine U.S. attorneys (apparently because they were considered to be insufficiently loyal to the Bush agenda); and Secretary of State Condolleeza Rice is spearheading a belated attempt to inject some serious diplomacy into U.S. foreign policy. As a kicker, the American populace, including many leading corporations, seems to have reached a consensus that global warming is real and represents a major threat to our planet's future—despite the administration's seven-year effort to downplay any mention of the issue in its governmental reports.

Politically speaking, the past year was reality-check time—and, naturally, the nation's media has had a field day reporting on the right-to-left shift in the nation's political center of gravity. As readers of prior editions of this anthology know, however, the most astute political journalists have been predicting this shift for quite some time, based on the fact that ideology-driven government—the hallmark of the Bush White House and many of its staunchest allies—is an inherently self-limiting approach to running a country, especially one as large and diverse as the United States.

The Best American Political Writing 2007 continues in this tradition. The aim of this collection is, as always, to showcase articles and essays that not only cover the major political events of the past year, but also put these events into a broader political context. This year's edition features 26 of the nation's most insightful scholars, reporters, and commentators—a number of whom are making a repeat appearance in these pages, and a number of others who are being featured in this anthology for the first time. While the various selections encompass a wide range of topics and writing styles,

I think you'll find that they're uniformly eloquent, entertaining, and thought-provoking.

As in previous years, this edition is divided into several sections, according to the general subject matter of the pieces. Part One, "Politics in the Bush Era—Legacies and Lame Ducks," focuses on the continuing evolution of George W. Bush's presidency, starting with Carl Cannon's *Atlantic Monthly* piece "Untruths and Consequences," on how and why our nation's chief executives (including our current leader) prevaricate. Jeffrey Rosen's "A Unified Theory of Scandal," reprinted from the *New Republic,* attempts to fit the U.S. attorney firings into a broader push to expand executive power on the part of the administration. The *American Scholar* essay "Not Compassionate, Not Conservative," by political scientist Ethan Fishman, analyzes the underlying political philosophy of the Bush White House. Lastly, "The Washington Back Channel," by former *New York Times* executive editor Max Frankel, deconstructs the events leading up to the "Scooter" Libby trial as part of a larger discussion of Washington's time-honored culture of leaking to the press.

Part Two, "Republicans vs. Democrats—The 2006 Midterm Elections," examines the period before, during, and immediately after the watershed vote that brought the Democrats back into power on Capitol Hill. "Karl Rove's Split Personality," by *Vanity Fair*'s Todd Purdum, published in the runup to the election, revisits the man known as "Bush's Brain" on the eve of what promised to be his toughest electoral battle to date. Peter Boyer's "Southern Discomfort," which originally appeared in the *New Yorker,* provides an engrossing account of the wild and woolly Virginia Senate race between George Allen and James Webb. "The Worst Congress Ever" is exactly what it sounds like: a rant against the Republican rulers on Capitol Hill by *Rolling Stone*'s Matt Taibbi that's sure to resonate with anyone who's followed the myriad congressional scandals of recent years. The section's concluding piece, "Democrats: The Big Surprise," written by longtime Washington reporter Elizabeth Drew for *The New York Review of Books,* examines the forces behind the Democrats' remarkable victory on Election Day.

Part Three is devoted to the conflict in Iraq. It opens with "This is Baghdad. What could be worse?" a sad and evocative article by the *Washington Post*'s

Pulitzer-Prize-winning reporter Anthony Shadid on life in today's Iraq. "Survivor: The White House Edition," by Michael Wolff, which ran as a column in *Vanity Fair,* is a reflection on the inside-the-Beltway art of covering one's you-know-what in the late days of a failed military enterprise. "The Surge," by Peter Galbraith (author of the recent book *The End of Iraq: How American Incompetence Created a War Without End*), takes a pessimistic look at the prospects of the Bush adminstration's latest strategy for victory in Iraq. The last piece in this section, David Rose's "Neo Culpa" (also reprinted from *Vanity Fair*)—which made headlines when it first appeared—showcases the surprisingly frank regrets expressed by a number of leading neoconservatives about the progress of the Iraq War.

Part Four, "America in an Uncertain World," covers the broader scope of U.S. foreign policy. Military expert Thomas P.M. Barnett's "The State of the World," reprinted from *Esquire* magazine, is a must-read for anyone who wants to get up to speed quickly on the multiple global challenges that our country will be facing over the next few years. "The Redirection," by veteran reporter Seymour Hersh of the *New Yorker,* provides a fascinating insight into the Bush administration's latest strategy shift in its efforts to combat the threat of Islamic extremists. *Atlantic Monthly* correspondent James Fallows charts a new direction for the war on terror in "Declaring Victory," and Thomas Friedman of the *New York Times* urges America to become the world's environmental leader in "The Power of Green." This section ends on a psychological note with "Why Hawks Win," an essay that first appeared in the journal *Foreign Policy,* in which Nobel laureate Daniel Kahneman and coauthor Jonathan Renshon explain how a predilection for hawkish thinking is "built into the fabric of the human mind."

This year's anthology closes with a look ahead to next year's presidential election in Part Five, "The 2008 Presidential Race." The first three articles profile the top contenders for the Republican nomination: Chris Jones's intimate portrait of John McCain for *Esquire* ("One of Us"), a wry look at Rudy Giuliani's candidacy by *New York* magazine's Stephen Rodrick ("Rudy Tuesday"), and a *Boston Globe Magazine* article by staff writer Neil Swidey on how Mitt Romney has been influenced by his father George's run for the presidency thirty years ago ("The Lessons of the Father").

The concluding five pieces focus on the Democratic candidates. "The Starting Gate," by Jeffrey Goldberg, reports on the leading contenders' efforts to come up with coherent positions on the Iraq War. Next come articles on the three "top-tier" Democratic hopefuls: Chris Smith's *New York* magazine profile of Hillary Clinton ("The Woman in the Bubble"), *New Republic* editor Jason Zengerle's campaign snapshot of John Edwards ("The Accidental Populist"), and Larissa MacFarquhar's intriguing *New Yorker* profile of Barack Obama ("The Conciliator"). Finally, this year's anthology closes on an appropriate note—given that we're embarking on what promises to be the first-ever billion-dollar presidential contest—with "Money Chooses Sides," by *New York* magazine's John Heilemann, an inside look at the candidates' frenzied race to raise the millions needed to run for our nation's highest office.

Looking back is always easier than looking forward, of course. The next year is certain to bring increasing pressure to reduce our troop presence in Iraq—particularly with the Democrats now running Congress—and is also likely to see a fair amount of controversy involving the Roberts Supreme Court (as this is being written, the shock waves from the Court's recent 5-4 decision to outlaw partial-birth abortion are still reverberating). The U.S. has just opened its first diplomatic talks with Iran in decades, Congress is struggling to come up with a bill regulating immigration (now a hotter topic than ever) . . . plus, we're electing a new president next year! Stay tuned.

Royce Flippin
June 2007

The Best American Political Writing 2007

Part One:
Politics in the Bush Era—Legacies and Lame Ducks

Untruth and Consequences

Carl M. Cannon

The Atlantic Monthly | January/February 2007

Whether implying a connection between Saddam Hussein and Al Qaeda, or consistently editing government reports to downplay the scientific consensus regarding the reality of global warming, or hyping the benefits to middle-income earners of various tax-cut programs, the Bush administration has often indulged in rhetoric that, at best, can be described as misleading. But then again, as Carl Cannon points out in this Atlantic Monthly *essay, all presidents have prevaricated on occasion. "Bush's place in history," notes Cannon, ". . . will depend not on* whether *he lied . . . but* how *he lied, what consequences his lying unleashed, and how he ultimately responded to them."*

In 1944, Harry Truman was asked by his friend and Senate colleague Owen Brewster what Franklin Roosevelt was really like. Truman hadn't gotten to know his running mate very well, but the Democratic vice-presidential nominee had spent enough time around FDR to provide a succinct answer.

"He lies," Truman replied.

At that point, the most consequential issue the president was untruthful about was his health. Roosevelt was failing rapidly, as his physicians knew, and as those around the White House could not help but notice. With the Allies opening a second front in Europe and island-hopping across the Pacific, the commander in chief was working at most four hours a day, and sometimes as little as one or two. On March 28 that year, Dr. Howard G. Bruenn, Roosevelt's cardiologist, had given his diagnosis: hypertension, hypertensive heart disease, cardiac failure, and acute bronchitis. The president's condition, Bruenn later explained to Jan Kenneth Herman, editor of *Navy Medicine,* was "god-awful."

The American public, and the world, received a far different image: that of a jaunty, robust president preparing to crush Hitler and the Japanese empire while cruising to an unprecedented fourth term. Truman quickly became complicit in this deception. The Missouri senator—considered then and now a straight shooter—went to lunch at the White House on August 18 and told reporters afterward that Roosevelt "looked fine and ate a bigger lunch than I did."

But Truman provided a different account in the privacy of his Senate office. "I had no idea he was in such feeble condition," he confided to his military aide Harry Vaughan, noting that when the president poured cream into his coffee, more went into the saucer than into the cup. Winston Churchill had seen with his own eyes evidence of FDR's physical decline the year before, in 1943, but raised no objection to the American administration's deception—Roosevelt was too important to the war effort. That same year, at a conference in Tehran in which the Allies discussed opening new fronts against Nazi Germany, Churchill stressed the need to keep the Allies' plans secret. To Joseph Stalin, he said, "In wartime, truth is so precious that she should always be attended by a bodyguard of lies."

"Churchill's line is par for the course in wartime, when you have to keep your secrets to yourself," Sean Wilentz, a professor of history at Princeton, told me this summer when we discussed the morality, and the utility, of shading the truth in the White House. "Presidents lie for all kinds of reasons," he added. "Richard Nixon lied because he was trying to save his presidency, which was imperiled by his misdeeds. Franklin Delano Roosevelt misled the country over things like Lend-Lease in order to advance a policy he thought would save the world, but which he knew would be difficult to sell politically. Honesty doesn't necessarily make for an effective presidency . . . What the public has to judge is whether [presidents] are lying for the good of the country—or for their own good."

Wilentz's interest in this question is not entirely academic. In December 1998, he spoke passionately before the House Judiciary Committee against the articles of impeachment leveled against President Clinton, the most serious of which was lying under oath. Wilentz argued that Clinton's transgressions, stemming as they did from personal—not official—conduct, simply were not what the Founders envisioned when they gave Congress the remedy of impeachment. "As a historian," he told Congress, "it is clear to me the impeachment of President Clinton would do greater damage . . . to those institutions and to the rule of law, much greater damage, than the crimes of which President Clinton has been accused." Clinton initially staked his political survival on proving his veracity. When that was found wanting, his advocates successfully argued that perjury was too grave a charge to apply to purely private behavior.

In his second term, George W. Bush faces a credibility crisis of his own. And while the current president may not share his predecessor's earthy predilections, he also doesn't have the same excuse, a wish to protect his private life. Bush is accused of equivocating not about his personal life but about one of the most fundamental public-policy decisions a democracy can confront: the decision to take the nation to war.

For the past year and a half, a majority of Americans have expressed doubts that the president's reasons for ordering the military to invade Iraq were those he articulated publicly. An April 2005 Gallup Poll found that a majority of Americans believed Bush "deliberately misled the American public" about whether Iraq possessed weapons of mass destruction. In May 2006, 46 percent of respondents in an ABC News/*Washington Post* survey said they believed that the Bush administration had said "what it believed to be true" in making its case for Iraq, while 52 percent said that it had "intentionally misled the American public."

Bush loyalists have blamed the media for such perceptions, but even allowing for a heavy dose of anti-Bush feeling on the part of the networks, news outlets, and publishing houses, much of the American public has altered its opinion regarding the veracity of the man in the Oval Office. Bush's place in history, however, will depend not on *whether* he lied to the American people—every president, arguably, has succumbed to that temptation—but *how* he lied, what consequences his lying unleashed, and how he ultimately responded to them. Put bluntly, posterity will judge the current president not so much by whether he told the truth but by whether he recognized what the truth actually was.

Why do presidents lie? Do they lie more than most people? Are lies of omission essentially the same as lies of commission? What about presidents who convince themselves of things that are untrue—who are, we would say, "in denial"? Is this tantamount to lying? Can presidents be truly effective without lying—or are there times when they simply must engage in deception? If so, when? And how is the public to know whether presidents are abusing that prerogative?

The first question might be the easiest to answer: presidents lie because they are human.

"Everybody lies," says Charles Ford, a professor at the University of Alabama at Birmingham and the author of a book about the psychology of deceit. "It is part of human nature, ubiquitous in the animal kingdom.

However, some people lie compulsively, often when the truth would serve them better."

Admonitions against lying are as old as Western civilization itself, but the Ninth Commandment was applied to the presidency by the first presidential biographer—a parson named Mason Locke Weems, who not only launched the cult of the president-as-truth-teller but did so retroactively with that famous, but unverifiable, cherry-tree story. Ever since, historical revisionism notwithstanding, American schoolchildren have been raised on the standard of a U.S. president who didn't lie—couldn't lie—even as a six-year-old boy. Abraham Lincoln was said to have walked miles as an Illinois store clerk to return a few cents' change. His "Honest Abe" nickname, which predated his presidency, was an advantage that his opponent Stephen Douglas tried to erase by calling him "two-faced." (Lincoln's response: "I leave it to [my audience]. If I had another face, do you think I'd wear this one?") Mark Twain deadpanned that Americans held their presidents to a standard few mortals could meet. "I am different from [George] Washington," he would say. "I have a higher and grander standard of principle. Washington could not lie. I *can* lie, but I *won't*."

Presidents prevaricate for the reasons other people do: pathology, politeness, paternalism, convenience, shame, self-promotion, insecurity, ego, narcissism, and even, on occasion, to further a noble goal. Presidents also have burdens not felt by most of us—keeping the nation safe, for one. High-level statecraft requires a talent for telling divergent groups of people what they want to hear. This is not the best recipe for truth telling, particularly in times of war or national peril.

All lies, unlike all men, are not created equal. Philosophers from Aristotle to Niebuhr have made moral distinctions among falsehoods, whether "white lies" told for social convenience or to spare feelings, "excuses" that are only half true but that rationalize our own behavior, lies told during a crisis, lies told to liars, paternalistic lies told to protect those we care about, and lies told for the social good—also known as "noble lies." The presidential scholar Richard Norton Smith points out that Thomas Jefferson's own interpretation of the Constitution's limits on presidential power probably didn't allow for the Louisiana Purchase. Yet in office, having sworn to uphold that Constitution, Jefferson couldn't resist stretching the words and doubling America's size for a few million dollars. "And talk about a turnaround—it was Nixon who went to China," Smith added. "It's often the flip-flop, in pursuit of interests that transcend ideological consistency, that puts a president on Mount Rushmore."

Nor does the innocent social lie told by presidents—or on a president's behalf—usually get a president in trouble. Asked for President Reagan's reaction after winning a hard-fought 1981 vote in Congress authorizing the sale of AWACS planes to Saudi Arabia, the White House aide Michael Deaver told reporters the president exclaimed, "Thank God!" What Reagan actually said, according to someone in the room, was, "I feel like I've just crapped a pineapple."

The first cousin of the white lie is the idle boast—not quite so harmless, but not nefarious, either. The unkindest way of looking at the bio-lie is to say that presidents (and presidential candidates) tend to be braggarts. More charitably, one could conclude that the job description seems to demand some fiddling with one's pedigree or accomplishments as a way to bond with voters—to tell them, in effect, "I'm one of you." In 1840, William Henry Harrison campaigned as a rustic born in a log cabin and indulged crowds with Indian war whoops at his rallies. In reality, the Whig nominee was the scion of an elite colonial family (his father was a signer of the Declaration of Independence and a three-term governor of Virginia); a professional soldier, Harrison read the classics and enjoyed fine living.

That kind of personal embellishment was also at work when John F. Kennedy, courting the elites as well as the masses, told *Time* magazine's Hugh Sidey that he could read 1,200 words a minute (a figure JFK pulled out of the air); when Lyndon Johnson exclaimed to U.S. troops in Korea that his great-great-grandfather "died at the Alamo" (a great-great-uncle fought at San Jacinto, but wasn't killed); when Bill Clinton claimed he'd heard about the Iowa caucuses "since I was a little boy" (they didn't begin until he was in graduate school); and when Al Gore told a labor crowd that his mother used to lull him to sleep when he was a baby with "Look for the Union Label" (a ditty written in 1975, when Gore was twenty-seven years old). One bizarre whopper: Ronald Reagan told Israeli Prime Minister Yitzhak Shamir and the Nazi hunter Simon Wiesenthal, in separate Oval Office visits, that as a young soldier in the U.S. Army Signal Corps during World War II, he had filmed the liberation of Nazi death camps; Reagan never served in Europe at all, though his work involved handling footage shot by military cameramen and war correspondents. Covering the White House for the past dozen years, I've become something of a connoisseur of the presidential boast. My favorite was when Clinton told *The Des Moines Register* editorial board that he was the only president who knew anything about agriculture before coming to office—skipping over actual farmers like Washington, Jefferson, Truman, and Jimmy Carter, as well as the Iowa farm boy Herbert Hoover.

George W. Bush does this sort of thing, too. During a January 2002 visit to West Virginia, the president kibitzed with Bob Kiss, the Democratic speaker of that state's legislature, over something they had in common: twins. "I've been to war," Bush said. "I've raised twins. If I had a choice, I'd rather go to war." It was a funny line, except that Bush *did* have a choice to serve in a war—in Vietnam—and didn't.

As candidates seek to woo voters with promises of good things to come, truth is often the first thing jettisoned on the campaign trail. This phenomenon is not new. In the closing days of the 1932 campaign, Franklin Roosevelt promised a crowd in Pittsburgh that he'd balance the federal budget while cutting "government operations" by 25 percent. Wisely, he attempted neither, but four years later as he prepared for another campaign trip to western Pennsylvania, he asked his speechwriter Sam Rosenman what he should say if his earlier vow came up. "Deny you were ever in Pittsburgh," Rosenman replied.

Rosenman's quip is still funny. One could, of course, huffily demand absolute fealty to the truth, but one could also live in the real world and find comforting reassurance that neither a president nor his wordsmiths believe all their own public relations. We still should make distinctions. Some falsehoods—like many campaign lies—are relatively harmless; they may soil an opponent's résumé or polish one's own, but their consequences are slight. Deceptions to promote or protect a policy or presidential action—call them governing lies—are more consequential, and it is by their consequences that they should be judged, as the American public harshly judged the lies told about the Vietnam War and about Watergate. Over the course of a tumultuous decade, those consequences included not just the ignominious end of an unpopular war and the fall of a president but a profound change in how much deceit the public—and the media—would tolerate from the Oval Office.

Even before those twin traumas came to a head, the American public's trust in its leaders had frayed. David Wise, a former White House correspondent turned investigative reporter, tapped into widespread public disgust in his catalog of presidential untruths, *The Politics of Lying*, published in 1973. "By 1972 the politics of lying had changed the politics of America," he wrote. "In place of trust, there was widespread mistrust; in place of confidence, there was disbelief and doubt in the system and its leaders." Still to come were Watergate and the release of White House tapes on which Lyndon Johnson blurts out to Robert McNamara that he knows that the reason used to justify the massive buildup of troops in Vietnam—the supposed attack on U.S. Navy ships by North Vietnamese patrol boats in the Gulf of Tonkin—was fiction. By 1975, the year Saigon fell, 69 percent of Americans answered affirmatively to a poll question asking whether "over the last ten years this country's leaders have consistently lied to the people."

That widespread erosion of trust also prompted Sissela Bok, the daughter of the famed Nobel laureates Gunnar and Alva Myrdal and a professor, at the time, of philosophy and lecturer at Harvard Medical School, to write *Lying: Moral Choice in Public and Private Life*—a touchstone, since its 1978 publication, for those seeking to examine the morality and the social costs of lying. Bok argued that while there are rare occasions when a lie may be justified, these falsehoods (which range from harmless social lies to extreme scenarios like telling a would-be murderer you don't know where to find an intended victim) had contributed to a general disregard for truth telling. Bok's book, which sprang out of her own research on the ethics of administering medical placebos, did not focus on lying politicians, though they pop up here and there. But her deep concern about the decline of trust, and her call for political, corporate, and educational institutions to take the lead in demanding and rewarding truthfulness, resonated with the public.

Presidential candidates, even those with reputations for evasiveness, reacted to the growing focus on honesty the way you might expect: they accused their opponents of lying, while promising not to lie themselves. Richard Nixon had been elected president in 1968 after positioning himself as the peace candidate. As the phrase *credibility gap* gained currency in the context of Johnson's lies about the Vietnam War, the incoming White House communications director, Herbert Klein, vowed, "Truth will become the hallmark of the Nixon administration." But by the time Nixon left the White House, a new catchphrase had entered the lexicon: *What did the president know, and when did he know it?* Upon being sworn in to succeed Nixon, Gerald Ford pronounced truth "the glue that holds government together." Jimmy Carter went Ford one better, in his unequivocal promise to the American people: "I will never tell a lie. I will never make a misleading statement. I will never betray the confidence any of you has in me."

By many measures, the Carter administration was more open, transparent, and truthful than many of its predecessors—and successors as well. But Carter's monastic vow of absolute truthfulness also generated its own blowback, most memorably Steven Brill's stinging piece "Jimmy Carter's Pathetic Lies." One example: "If you ever have any questions or advice for me," Carter told audiences, "just put Jimmy Carter, Plains, Georgia, on the envelope . . . I open every letter myself, and read them all." This was an impossibility: the mail was forwarded, as it had to be, to Carter's campaign headquarters in Atlanta.

Such campaign exaggerations aside, Carter's commitment to truth telling did not wear well. "Humankind cannot bear very much reality," wrote T. S. Eliot, and after four years of Carter, the American electorate was no exception. Carter's revelatory form of communication (admitting to *Playboy* that he "looked on a lot of women with lust," for example, or bemoaning a national "crisis of confidence") was a poor substitute in voters' minds for executive-branch competence, or for leadership that could make Americans feel good about themselves. As Western Illinois University history professor George Hopkins sees it, all presidents lie for the simple reason that if they didn't, we wouldn't elect them. "So the problem is not them, it's us," Hopkins told me recently. "We should look in the mirror."

Thus, Carter was involuntarily retired by Reagan, who berated Carter for distorting his record but had a tendency himself to stretch the truth if it made for a good yarn. Witness a favorite Reagan story about his role in a football game in high school in which, he claimed, players for a rival school, Mendota, complained to the referees that Reagan, playing for Dixon High, had committed a penalty that was not called. The refs supposedly asked him about it. "I told the truth," Reagan later said. "The penalty was ruled, and Dixon lost the game." My father, the Reagan biographer Lou Cannon, investigated this claim. He discovered that there were no contemporaneous accounts of any such incident, and that Dixon lost to Mendota only once when Reagan was a member of the varsity team—by a score of 24-0. "The ironic point here is that Reagan seems to have told the story to demonstrate how truthful he was," notes George Mason University political scientist James Pfiffner, who has studied presidential lying. "Yet he was telling an untruth to make the point."

More infamously, in November 1986, Reagan told the American people that his administration had not traded weapons "or anything else" to Iran in return for American hostages captured in Lebanon. Three weeks later, in a radio address, the president softened this to "Let me just say it was not my intent to do business with [Ayatollah Ruhollah] Khomeini, to trade weapons for hostages." Three months after that, in an Oval Office address, Reagan confessed: "A few months ago I told the American people I did not trade arms for hostages. My heart and my best intentions still tell me that's true, but the facts and evidence tell me it is not." Reagan's presidency was winding down, but the not-yet-begun presidency of George H. W. Bush was already marred by his insistence that he was "out of the loop" on the Iran-Contra arms-for-hostages scandal. Special prosecutor Lawrence Walsh spent all four years of the first Bush presidency examining that alibi. Concluding that it was bogus, Walsh released documents three days before the 1992 election showing that Bush had attended crucial Iran-Contra meetings and approved the plan.

Bill Clinton's mendacity as president—or, depending on your politics, independent counsel Kenneth Starr's perjury trap—was the backdrop for the campaign in 2000 to find a new president. Once again, the public was looking for a relatively honest politician. As Sissela Bok wrote in the preface to an updated edition of *Lying*, released in 1999, "No matter how our own period comes to be judged . . . what is already certain is that we are all on the receiving end of a great many more lies than in the past." John McCain dubbed his campaign bus the "Straight Talk Express" and ended rallies by proclaiming that, as president, he would "tell the American people the truth—even if it's bad news." In the general election, George W. Bush stressed this theme, too. In his third debate with Al Gore, Bush said the country needed "somebody in office who will tell the truth." This was not a casual observation; it was a premeditated talking point for the Bush-Cheney campaign that night—and for the rest of the month of October.

By then, the story line of that campaign was framed as Al Gore's Bill Clinton–style exaggerations versus George W. Bush's Dan Quayle–style bloopers. Afterward, Bush assumed office with a reputation as a truth teller, even among Americans who didn't support his policies—or didn't think he was all that bright. Two months before 9/11, in an Opinion Dynamics poll, 69 percent of Americans—21 percent more than had voted for him—responded that they found Bush, who had campaigned on conservative themes, to be "honest and trustworthy." Only 20 percent of respondents disagreed with that sentiment.

How did Bush go in the public eye from truth teller to prevaricator in chief? He has now been pilloried, after all, not just by outspoken liberals—in books like David Corn's *The Lies of George W. Bush* and Al Franken's *Lies and the Lying Liars Who Tell Them,* in documentaries like Eugene Jarecki's *Why We Fight* and Michael Moore's *Fahrenheit 9/11,* and on countless Web sites—but also by an increasingly hostile mainstream media, including top national newspapers, *The New Yorker,* and this magazine, as well as high-profile books on the Iraq War like Thomas E. Ricks's *Fiasco,* Peter W. Galbraith's *The End of Iraq,* and *State of Denial,* the third volume in Bob Woodward's trilogy about this administration.

The critique that Bush isn't honest with the American people confounds many of those who have worked most closely with him. That includes two aides whose opinions and integrity I greatly respect: Michael J. Gerson, Bush's former chief speechwriter, who describes the president as a "compulsive truth teller," a man so guileless that he can't hide his boredom when making speeches he doesn't want to give; and Peter Wehner, director of the White House Office of Strategic Initiatives, who argues that the notion Bush "lied" about the presence of weapons of mass destruction in Iraq is absurd on its face—and that those accusing Bush of dishonesty are the ones deeply mistaken.

Yet Bush has gradually built a record of partial truths, half-truths, and untruths. Several cases in point:

- In his 2006 State of the Union address, Bush cited Iraq and Afghanistan as examples of "the great story of our time"—the advance of freedom. He proclaimed that the number of democracies in the world had increased from about two dozen at the end of 1945 to 122 today, but he didn't mention that neither Iraq nor Afghanistan was counted as such by the organization whose statistics he was touting.

- The president also asserted, accurately, that the U.S. economy had gained 4.6 million new jobs in the previous two and a half years, but he failed to note that it had lost 2.6 million jobs in his first two and a half years.
- In March 2003, Bush insisted that it was "a matter of fact" that the coalition he cobbled together for the invasion of Iraq included more nations than the alliance assembled by his father in 1991. In *Fiasco,* Ricks deconstructs this argument by pointing out that most of George W. Bush's partnering nations (with the notable exception of the British) were a reluctant bunch. The Poles fought, but resented being there. The Italians wouldn't get out of their vehicles on patrols. The Japanese wouldn't patrol at all and, in fact, wouldn't even guard their own perimeters—Dutch troops did it for them.
- In June 2004, when asked about Ahmad Chalabi, the Iraqi exile who'd done so much to encourage the U.S. invasion of Iraq, but who had fallen out of favor with U.S. military leaders, Bush acted as if he barely knew the man's name. "Chalabi? My meetings with him were very brief," Bush said. "I think I met with him at the State of the Union and just kind of working through the rope line, and he might have come with a group of leaders. But I haven't had any extensive conversations with him." Perhaps. But Chalabi wasn't confined behind a rope line at the 2004 State of the Union address. He was listed by the White House as a "special guest" of first lady Laura Bush and seated directly behind her.
- After the Democrats' victories in the 2006 midterm elections, the president allowed that "Democrats are going to support our troops just like Republicans will" and that the Democratic congressional leaders Nancy Pelosi and Harry Reid "care about the security of this country, like I do." Those gracious statements were at odds with his campaign rhetoric from just days before, when he had said, regarding Iraq, that if the Democrats' vision were to prevail, "the terrorists win and America loses." On November 8 at the White House, Bush suggested that it was the campaign talk that was disingenuous. But maybe it was the other way around—that Bush meant what he said in Texas, and was only being politic in the East Room.

- At the same press conference, Bush essentially admitted he'd lied to three White House correspondents who had asked him in an Oval Office interview the week before whether Defense Secretary Donald Rumsfeld was staying on. The president had assured the three reporters that Rumsfeld was remaining. Now, standing in the East Room, Bush was revealing the details of a different reality: he'd decided before the election to sack his Pentagon chief, and when asked the question, he was already focused on Rumsfeld's likely replacement. Bush provided dueling explanations: First, he maintained that he didn't "want to inject a major decision about this war" into the waning days of a campaign. Then he immediately added the more Clintonesque explanation that his answer hadn't really been dishonest, because he hadn't yet had his "final" conversation with Rumsfeld, and hadn't interviewed Robert Gates in person.

Presidents have rarely told the full truth in the midst of major military operations, and until Vietnam, Americans tended to cut them slack for the sake of the troops, if nothing else. During World War II, for example, the government launched an elaborate disinformation campaign to mask the details of D-Day—an episode that Sissela Bok cites (as a prime example of a lie commonly thought justifiable and one that was the precise context of Churchill's line to Stalin about protecting truth with a bodyguard of lies). Similar fabrications would fall under Bok's definition of "paternalistic lies." The everyday version would be a parent falsely reassuring a child that Mommy and Daddy are not fighting. Another presidential equivalent would be falsely reassuring the citizenry on issues of national security for their own protection. On December 9, 1941, two days after Pearl Harbor, President Roosevelt told Americans in a radio address that they were now in the war "all the way," while promising to share "together the bad news and good news." But FDR couldn't quite bring himself to reveal the extent of the losses in Hawaii, saying that he lacked "sufficient information," which was not exactly true.

Serious commentators on American public life have seldom questioned a president's right to lie in such circumstances. But they are starting to. Consider the media hand-wringing triggered by President Bush's surprise trip to Iraq in November 2003, when he and his aides lied about his Thanksgiving plans in an effort to preserve his safety and that of the troops he was to visit. As with the Vietnam War, the course of events in Iraq is prompting a reevaluation of truth telling for its own sake.

In *When Presidents Lie,* the liberal political journalist Eric Alterman attempts to raise the bar on when a commander in chief can dissemble. He argues that although wartime may be when presidents can get away with lying—and is perhaps even when they most feel the need to lie—recent American history suggests that it is also when the costs of a lie may be too high.

Alterman's thesis is that the lies told by Roosevelt during World War II, specifically those concerning the promises he made to Stalin at Yalta, helped set in motion the Cold War, and that unrealistic expectations in the West about the future of Eastern Europe fueled Soviet suspicions of America's motives. These suspicions, he argues, were stoked by Dwight Eisenhower's public denials about Francis Gary Powers's disastrous U-2 spy flight over the Soviet Union. The accompanying loss of U.S. credibility helped foment the Cuban missile crisis. In turn, the fiction that John F. Kennedy and his team of White House hagiographers spread about an uncompromising U.S. stance in October 1962 helped beget Vietnam: ever watchful of his political rival Robert Kennedy, Lyndon Johnson felt compelled to embrace the myth of a hard-line response to Communist adventure—never mind the truth that JFK had traded some NATO missiles in Turkey for Nikita Khrushchev's missiles in Cuba.

Alterman is considered an ideological man, which I am not, but I believe his revisionist argument is worth taking seriously. I say this not only because Alterman had the intellectual honesty to confront the record of liberal Democrats as well as conservative Republicans who have served as wartime commanders in chief, but also because the war in Iraq has shown the peril of taking a president's assertions at face value—even if that president believes he is telling the truth. But don't take it from me. Take it from Dwight Eisenhower. After he left office, Ike described the lies his administration had told about the U-2 incident as one of the biggest regrets of his presidency. "I didn't realize how high a price we were going to have to pay for that lie," Eisenhower told David Kraslow of Knight Newspapers. "And if I had to do it all over again, we would have kept our mouths shut."

But presidents have trouble resisting the short-term gain a lie can afford them. It was a Kennedy administration official who claimed the government's "right . . . to lie" to the public. He did so in the context of the Cuban missile crisis, which began with a little lie about Kennedy's health—press secretary Pierre Salinger announced that the president's trip to Chicago was being cut short because JFK had a cold. Salinger apparently never understood why anyone would question the cover story concocted to get Kennedy back to Washington in October 1962—just as Scott McClellan was taken aback by questions about the White House's deceptive statements on Bush's Thanksgiving trip to Iraq. "The trip certainly, I'm sure, gave a morale boost to the troops," David Wise told a wire-service reporter who asked his opinion. "The question is, should the government engage in lying in order to essentially . . . protect a photo op? The answer is, no it shouldn't. It's a serious business when government lies, and eventually it does hurt a government and a president's credibility."

Wise was prescient when he took on presidential honesty in the 1970s, but his expectations are probably too pure. I was president of the White House Correspondents' Association when Bush and his aides dissembled about the president's Thanksgiving plans and took only a small White House press pool to Iraq. I registered no protest upon their return. The security pressures must have been extreme, I reasoned. After all, Bush neglected to tell his own parents about the trip, although they were trekking to Crawford, Texas, for the holiday dinner. On the other hand, if going to Iraq was meant to be an evocative symbol, perhaps the ease with which the White House gave everyone the slip was emblematic as well.

It has been said about several recent U.S. presidents that they seem to believe what they are saying, even if what they are saying is not true. This explanation is offered as exculpation, as if presidents are Method actors who deserve credit for their "character motivation." Something like admiration was present in Bob Kerrey's description of Bill Clinton as "an unusually good liar."

Franklin Roosevelt practiced plausible deniability about his own declining health by ignoring his doctors. That's a profound kind of denial. Ronald Reagan was trained as a dramatic actor in a medium where shortcuts are taken with facts in order, supposedly, to get at a larger truth. Reagan's methods were internalized by aides who never set foot on a studio lot. In his memoir *A Different Drummer: My Thirty Years With Ronald Reagan,* Mike Deaver claims that he never once heard Reagan tell a lie, and that he believes it would have been "impossible" for Reagan to do so.

"Throughout the entire Iran Contra affair, Reagan believed what he did was right," Deaver wrote, "and that he was telling the truth to the American people."

George W. Bush's aides say similar things about him. Perhaps surprisingly, some of Bush's harshest critics do as well. David Corn, author of *The Lies of George W. Bush,* is a longtime acquaintance of mine, and I asked him to consider the following premises:

> a) That Bush considers himself a truth teller.
> b) That although statements made by Bush as president have proven to be untrue, Bush generally believed they were true when he made them.
> c) That even when Bush's words have been at odds with the facts, you could hook him up to a polygraph machine; he'd still tell you he was telling the truth—and he'd pass.

To me, Corn's book reads like an anti-Bush polemic, especially when it calls the president's veracity into question over issues that seem more about Bush's conservative governance. (Appointing John Ashcroft attorney general, for instance, made a "lie" of Bush's inaugural call for civility and national unity—under the theory that Ashcroft's archconservatism undermined any chance of détente with the Democrats.) Corn is scrupulous about the facts, however, and except for offering the caveat that Bush, like other politicians, has "stretched the truth" to help sell key policies of his presidency, Corn didn't much quarrel with the three postulates.

"So your question is, is it still lying anyway?" Corn said. "What Bush does is that he displays a kind of willful disregard for the truth, which is the moral equivalent of lying. He doesn't do any due diligence with the facts. Even if you believed something was true [at] the time you said it, it becomes a lie when you don't act on new information—or correct yourself when you've been proven wrong."

Whatever the president's original sincerity about his reasons for invading Iraq, he has never to this day really acknowledged his rhetorical excess. Two nights before launching the invasion, he gave this rationale: "Intelligence gathered by this and other governments leaves no doubt that the Iraq regime continues to possess and conceal some of the most lethal weapons ever devised." In his January 28, 2003, State of the Union address,

Bush had told the nation that U.S. intelligence agencies estimated that Saddam Hussein possessed more than 30,000 munitions capable of being armed with chemical agents, and that inspectors had turned up only sixteen of them. In May, two months into the invasion, Bush proclaimed simply: "We have found the weapons of mass destruction."

What the U.S. Army has unearthed in Iraq in three years are 500 rockets and artillery shells armed with mustard gas or the sarin nerve agent, some of them in degraded condition, buried in scattered bunkers around the country. The Army has found no evidence of an up-and-running Iraqi nuclear-weapons program. In *State of Denial,* Woodward quotes a December 11, 2003, recorded exchange between him and Bush in which it took the president five minutes and eighteen seconds to acknowledge the failure to find weapons of mass destruction.

Confronted later with their statements, Bush and other top officials in his government tend simply to reiterate them. Other times, they've simply denied making these statements, even though they are on film. For instance, when Bush was asked in May 2002 about the hunt for Osama bin Laden, he replied: "I don't know where he is. I repeat what I said. I truly am not that concerned about him." Yet on October 13, 2004, during Bush's third and final debate with John Kerry, the following exchange took place:

> **Kerry:** "Six months after he said Osama bin Laden must be caught dead or alive, this president was asked, 'Where is Osama bin Laden?' He said, 'I don't know. I don't really think about him very much. I'm not that concerned.'"
>
> **Bush:** "Gosh, I just don't think I ever said I'm not worried about Osama bin Laden. It's kind of one of those exaggerations."

In an ABC interview two weeks before the 2006 midterms, George Stephanopoulos asked Bush where the compromise might be on Iraq between the dueling political buzz phrases *stay the course* and *cut and run.* Bush's response: "Well, hey, listen, we've never been 'stay the course,' George . . ." Liberal bloggers quickly posted on YouTube a hilarious montage of Bush using that exact phrase repeatedly. "The president of the United States is not a fact-checker," White House communications director Dan Bartlett blurted out at a July 18, 2003, briefing about what the president knew, and when he knew it, regarding British intelligence reports of Saddam Hussein's agents prowling around Africa in search of enriched uranium.

No one expects him to be. What they do expect is that a president who takes the nation to war knows what he's talking about when he enumerates the reasons for that war. Which raises the central question about George W. Bush's tenure in the White House: Even giving him the benefit of the doubt on honesty, why doesn't the nation's first-ever M.B.A. president demonstrate a better command of the facts?

There are three popular theories about Bush's behavior: that the president is an intellectually incurious man who doesn't have or want enough information to make informed decisions; that his late-life embrace of religion has given him inner peace, but also a near-absolute level of certitude; and that his demand for total loyalty discourages the give-and-take a leader needs, because aides who proffer advice or information that doesn't jibe with administration policy are not viewed as team players.

Several White House aides, past and present, say it's simply wrong to suggest that people around Bush are afraid to bring him bad news or contrary opinions. "I was never intimidated," Michael Gerson told me. Former press secretary Ari Fleischer said the same thing. On July 2, 2003, when Bush made his infamous "Bring 'em on" taunt, Fleischer told the president pointedly as they walked out of the Roosevelt Room that this statement would offend a military mom with a child serving in Iraq. "I always found it easy to raise objections like that," Fleischer said. "Easy as a layup."

Yet Bush has somehow managed to be consistently surprised by events in the war of his own making. In the absence of any plausible explanation from his loyalists, it is his critics who are writing the history of this period. One consistent theme of these critics is that faith trumps fact for Bush when it comes to Iraq. There's ample supporting evidence for that belief, starting with Bush's bio-fib to Brit Hume in 2003 that he didn't read newspapers. Hume was rightly incredulous, and Laura Bush later refuted her husband in an exchange with Jay Leno. Yet in telling this particular lie, Bush may have been revealing an important truth about himself. What he was getting at, apparently, is that he doesn't read columns and editorials. The reason, he told me and other journalists, was his need to "stay optimistic."

There can be a thin line between optimism and delusion. During his

2004 reelection campaign, Bush went to a Boeing aerospace plant in Ridley Park, Pennsylvania, to put in a plug for the nation's fledgling missile-defense system, and asserted, "We say to those tyrants who believe they can blackmail America and the free world, 'You fire, we're going to shoot it down.'" Given the current technology, Bush's statement was a declaration of wishful thinking, not military reality. Bush had made an equally dubious assertion while running in 2000, after several highly publicized exonerations of men on death row had prompted nationwide soul-searching over capital punishment. "Everybody who's been executed [in Texas] is guilty of the crime of which they've been convicted," Bush said. He may have believed this, but in Austin, Bush presided over more executions than any other governor in modern history, and did so in a state that offers only rudimentary legal services for indigent defendants, enforces strict time limits for post-conviction appeals, and does little in the way of executive-branch or parole-board review of trial-court verdicts. Really, Bush had no way of knowing that what he *hoped* was true actually *was* true—and there were empirical reasons to wonder. This example has a recent echo in Bush's confident-sounding assurance in a September 6, 2006, East Room speech: "We have in place a rigorous process to ensure those held at Guantánamo Bay belong at Guantánamo."

This kind of blasé optimism has undergirded Bush's entire policy on Iraq, and its consequences have been grim. As Peter W. Galbraith, author of a new book critical of Bush's prosecution of the war, put it: "With regard to Iraq, President Bush and his top advisers have consistently substituted wishful thinking for analysis and hope for strategy." In May 2003, under that now-infamous MISSION ACCOMPLISHED banner aboard the U.S.S. *Lincoln,* Bush proclaimed, "Iraq is free" and "major combat operations in Iraq have ended." But almost four years later, scores of Iraqis are still dying every day, the country is in the throes of civil war, and American forces remain enmeshed in a conflict with no clear end. "The strategy was denial," wrote Woodward in the last paragraph of *State of Denial.* "With all Bush's upbeat talk and optimism, he had not told the American public the truth about what Iraq had become."

Bush's aides bristle at such words, but when asked why the president refuses to go back and correct his rhetorical mistakes—to level with the American people about where and why he was wrong—they falter or fall back on platitudes. Queried about Bush's failure to cite what he had ever done wrong, Fleischer answers: "It's the foolish politician who looks backwards and wallows in his difficulties. A good politician looks forward. It's the difference between a pessimist and an optimist, between a loser and a winner, between Jimmy Carter and George W. Bush." In his 2006 State of the Union address, the president voiced the same sentiment in addressing his Iraq War critics: "Hindsight alone is not wisdom," he said, "and second-guessing is not a strategy."

But optimism, while more appealing than its opposite number, is not a strategy, any more than hindsight. And it has the added drawback of not offering any Plan B. Regarding the failure to find weapons of mass destruction, Gerson said that the White House staff itself was never told what went wrong. "As opposed to being deceptive, when those weapons were not found I think people were shocked," he said. "I mean, it was beyond belief."

Now that the midterm elections are over, some speculate that the Administration will be more candid and less dogmatic about Iraq. Yet some results of this administration's self-deception are not reversible. While researching *Fiasco,* Thomas Ricks spoke to numerous battlefield commanders in Iraq who left thousands of tons of conventional weapons undisturbed as they raced toward Baghdad in the first heady days of the invasion. They didn't have enough troops to guard these caches of weapons, and they didn't dare destroy them, believing as they did that underneath might lie highly dangerous stockpiles of chemical and biological weapons. "So the bunkers were often bypassed and left undisturbed by an invasion force that was already stretched thin," Ricks wrote. "And the insurgents were able to arm themselves at leisure."

Of course, posterity rewards success, not truth. If D-Day had failed, FDR likely would have been remembered not as a heroic wartime president but as a tragic figure whose self-serving deceptions about his own health prolonged a savage war and jeopardized victory. And if Japan had not surrendered even after atomic bombs were dropped on the civilian populations of two of its cities, Truman might be recalled as a butcher. Conversely, if U.S. forces had found the fabled weapons of mass destruction in Iraq, would Bush's integrity be under question? Probably not. For presidents, consequences matter more than truth. Bush almost certainly understands this; it may inform his oft-expressed hope of being judged positively in the long sweep of history. Yet today he remains reluctant to reckon not only with his statements but also with their results. President Kennedy may have lied to the public about why the Russians removed their missiles from Cuba, but he knew the truth of the situation well enough to negotiate the compromise that led to their removal. Bush, on the other hand, seems unwilling to recognize that the reality of the situation in Iraq does not conform to his vision of it. The most dangerous lies a president can tell, it would seem, are the lies he tells himself.

A Unified Theory of Scandal: The Real Roots of the U.S. Attorney Firings

Jeffrey Rosen

the *New Republic* | April 23, 2007

President George W. Bush's administration has always been known for its tendency to blur politics and governance, but the recent uproar over Attorney General Alberto Gonzales's firing of nine U.S. attorneys in the middle of their four-year terms has brought this penchant into sharp focus. In this article, New Republic *legal affairs editor Jeffrey Rosen explains how the Justice Department firings are really just another example of the Bush team's embrace of the "unitary executive" concept—a legal theory that, taken to its furthest extent, imbues the presidency with virtually unlimited power over the U.S. government's executive branch.*

The ideological roots of the Justice Department scandal aren't buried in Karl Rove's office. They reside in a less likely place: the pages of *The Harvard Law Review.* More precisely, this scandal traces back to a 1992 article co-written by a founder of the Federalist Society, Steven Calabresi. A few years earlier, Calabresi had served as a special assistant to Ronald Reagan's attorney general, Ed Meese. During his time in government, Calabresi shared the Reaganite revulsion with the power wielded by EPA bureaucrats, Justice Department lawyers, and other obstreperous paper-pushers who populated the administrative state. These career denizens of government righteously trumpeted their commitment to objective analysis and the neutral application of the law. But these claims, conservatives argued, were merely guises for a liberal political agenda.

In his *Harvard Law* essay, Calabresi added an important new twist to this old critique. The power invested in the career bureaucrats wasn't just annoying: It was a constitutional impediment to the president's ability to control the executive branch. Accordingly, he proposed a constitutional justification for extending the president's political control over the entire bureaucracy, for making those bureaucrats submit to his will. He described his approach as the theory of the "unitary executive."

Calabresi's original formulation was not inherently radical or partisan. Indeed, Elena Kagan, a former Clinton administration official who is now the dean of Harvard Law School, wrote an influential article echoing Calabresi's call for presidential control over unelected bureaucrats. But, in her iteration of the argument—not to mention the actual practice of the Clinton administration and its Republican predecessors—there was the acknowledgment of a competing theory of governance, which dated back to the New Deal. This competing theory recognized a need to maintain some political independence for administrative and Cabinet agencies in order to protect detached expertise and neutral decision-making. Those paper-pushers may have resisted democratic accountability, but they were also important fonts of wonkish wisdom. According to Samuel Issacharoff of NYU Law School, "The best reading of the American political and legal tradition is that we want both of these visions at the same time, although, clearly, they are in tension with each other."

The George W. Bush administration, however, has turned the unitary executive theory in a new, dangerous direction. In foreign affairs, officials like John Yoo in the Office of Legal Counsel and David Addington, Vice President Cheney's chief of staff, used it to justify the radical claim that the president can ignore (or at least reinterpret) laws that infringe on his constitutional power as commander-in-chief. And, in domestic affairs, Bush tried to extend his political control over policy decisions far deeper into the Cabinet and administrative agencies than previous presidents had thought appropriate. He effectively declared war on the career officials in State and Justice, viewing them as untrustworthy. "Previous presidents had divided administrative power between the expert career people at the lower levels and the political appointees at the top, and the Bush administration tried to break this line down," says Issacharoff. "It became virtually impossible to be hired as a staff attorney at the Justice Department if you didn't have the proper Republican Party pedigree, and I saw students vetted for their political loyalty even when applying for career jobs much lower down the rung."

It should hardly be a surprise, therefore, that D. Kyle Sampson, former chief of staff to Attorney General Alberto Gonzales, e-mailed the Office of the White House Counsel calling for professional prosecutors to be replaced with "loyal Bushies." This was not just cronyism or a crude power grab, but the culmination of an ideological vision of unitary executive power that suffused the highest levels of the Justice Department and the White House counsel's office. "If indeed President Bush is doing something new and more aggressive than other presidents in terms of asserting control throughout the Justice Department, which I doubt," says Jack Goldsmith, former head of Bush's Office of Legal Counsel, "it's related to his vision of executive power."

In the enforcement of law, where are the places where politics doesn't belong? That's really the heart of this scandal, and the precedents set in the following months could hold for generations. Appearing before the Senate on March 29, Sampson hazarded an answer to this key question. He tried to distinguish proper and improper reasons for firing prosecutors: *Policy* disagreements were legitimate grounds for removal, he said, but it would be wrong for the president to try to influence a particular investigation for *partisan* ends. This attempt to define the category of improper rationale makes sense, as far as it goes. But Sampson went on to define policy disagreements very broadly, insisting that "the distinction between political and performance-related reasons for removing a United States attorney is, in my view, largely artificial." Sampson concluded, "A U.S. attorney who is unsuccessful from a political perspective . . . is unsuccessful." By "loyal Bushies," Sampson told the Senate, he meant nothing more than loyalty to Bush's "policies and the priorities [he] had laid out." In declaring war on the distinction between political and policy disagreements, however, Sampson, Gonzales, and Bush came close to the line of firing prosecutors for impermissibly partisan reasons.

Did Gonzales and Bush actually cross that line? To answer that question, it helps to examine historical antecedents. The most infamous example of an attempt by a president to twist executive power for partisan ends was Watergate. In the White House tape that brought him down,

Richard Nixon was heard telling H.R. Haldeman to instruct the FBI and CIA to stop the investigation into the hush funds set aside for the Watergate burglars. "That was the major item that broke Nixon's back," recalls Leonard Garment, who served as Nixon's White House counsel. "The agencies of the executive branch are not supposed to be personal weapons for the political use of the president."

In his testimony, Sampson confessed that, in a moment of Nixonian enthusiasm, he had impulsively suggested that White House Counsel Harriet Miers fire Patrick Fitzgerald in the middle of his investigation of the Valerie Plame leak. But this was so clearly beyond the pale that Sampson said he immediately regretted the suggestion, and Miers ignored it. Therefore, the most serious allegations against the Bush administration relate to the firings of Carol Lam in San Diego and David Iglesias in New Mexico. Let's consider each in turn.

Carol Lam was the U.S. attorney in San Diego, and the Senate wants to know whether she was fired because she was "hot on the trail," as Arlen Specter put it, of powerful Republicans alleged to have collaborated with former Representative Randy "Duke" Cunningham, who resigned from Congress in 2005 after pleading guilty to accepting more than $2 million in bribes from defense contractors. On May 10, 2006, Lam notified the Department of Justice that she was planning to seek search warrants for the home and CIA office of Kyle "Dusty" Foggo, who had resigned two days earlier as the number-three official at the agency under a cloud of Cunningham-related suspicion. The following day, Sampson sent an e-mail to the White House: "The real problem we have right now with Carol Lam . . . leads me to conclude that we should have someone ready to be nominated on 11/18, the day her 4-year term expires."

The Nixonian explanation of this e-mail is that Sampson was trying to obstruct Lam's investigation into an ally of the president because he feared that the corruption inquiry might hurt the White House. Sampson insists that he never knew about the search warrants and that the "real problem" he was referring to was Lam's less-than-enthusiastic prosecution of immigration offenses. Given the fact that Lam was commended for her immigration enforcement by the director of field operations for the San Diego office of U.S. Customs and Border Protection, this seems questionable. The administration's defenders also counter that Lam's firing was never intended to stifle the Foggo investigation. Foggo was, after all, indicted two days before Lam left office. Gonzales must have known that the investigation and prosecution of Foggo would continue regardless of who supervised the office, as indeed it has.

Choosing between the Nixonian and more charitable explanations turns on elusive questions of motives. If Gonzales fired Lam because he thought she wasn't a "team player," not because he was trying to shut down the Foggo investigation, the firing would be questionable but certainly not criminal. If he fired her to get her off the trail of powerful Republicans—like defense contractor Brent Wilkes, a friend of the vice president who was indicted with Foggo—it would be an impermissible attempt to influence the investigation for partisan advantage. Congress will need more facts to decide whether Gonzales crossed the line, but it already seems clear that he came close.

Now consider the firing of David Iglesias, whom Sampson alleges was insufficiently enthusiastic in his prosecution of alleged voter fraud committed by New Mexico Democrats. In voter fraud cases, it's even harder to distinguish between partisan politics and policy, because elections obviously have partisan consequences. Broadly speaking, as Issacharoff explains, "there is an undisguised political battle in this country about the right to vote." Democrats believe that voter intimidation is keeping many potential voters from voting. Republicans believe that Democrats are engaged in widespread countenance of voter fraud—encouraging improperly registered voters to cast ballots. Fortunately, there is little empirical evidence for either proposition. The most contested elections in recent U.S. history, including the mayoral election in Miami a decade ago, involve systematic attempts to destroy absentee ballots or to forge ballots after the election, not an attempt to encourage or prevent individual voters from casting votes before the election to affect the result. There appear to be very few instances, in other words, where voter fraud is pervasive enough to change the results of an election either way.

Nevertheless, in the controversy that led to the firing of Iglesias, House and Senate Republicans from New Mexico seem to have tried to influence the outcome of an election. As Iglesias recounted in a recent *New York Times* op-ed, he received phone calls just before the November 2006 elections from Representative Heather Wilson and Senator Pete

Domenici. Both asked whether he was planning to bring corruption charges against local Democrats before the election, and, when he said no, Domenici responded, "I'm very sorry to hear that." Soon after Wilson's call, Iglesias's name was added to Sampson's list of U.S. attorneys who were asked to resign. Iglesias convincingly argues that he took voter fraud allegations seriously. But, after he reviewed 100 allegations of voter fraud, he concluded that only one case warranted federal prosecution. Iglesias believes he was fired for not bringing charges in a case he considered without merit—that he was, in other words, "fired for not being political."

It's possible, in theory, to imagine a benign explanation for Iglesias's sacking. It would be fine for the attorney general to announce a general policy that all U.S. attorneys should vigorously prosecute voter fraud and then fire those who fail to bring prosecutions. As Jack Goldsmith told me, "The president can set the priority of demanding more voter fraud cases, appoint prosecutors he thinks will further his goals, and fire prosecutors who aren't pursuing his policies." The analogy here is to the Kennedy Justice Department in the 1960s: Robert Kennedy was free to fire recalcitrant Southern prosecutors who refused to bring civil rights prosecutions, even though he knew those prosecutions might indirectly help the Democratic Party among black voters. But there's a clear difference between insisting that prosecutors intervene in broad categories of cases and meddling in a particular case because you're trying to obtain partisan results. As Goldsmith acknowledges, "He can't press a prosecutor in a particular voter fraud case to intervene in order to influence the electoral result."

In this case, it seems likely that Iglesias was fired for not bringing dubious charges of voter fraud on the eve of an election. According to Issacharoff, "Voter fraud generally takes place on Election Day, and prosecutions tend to happen after the election took place. What was odd about this was the demand that Iglesias bring charges on the eve of an election. It was part of an electoral strategy, not a criminal justice strategy, and it rises to the level of trying to use the prosecution power for partisan advantage. It's a no-holds-barred effort to enlist every part of the federal government in an effort to reelect Republican candidates."

If this was indeed the administration's goal, it certainly crosses the line into impermissible partisanship. There are many federal laws, dating back to the Progressive era, that make it illegal to use the power of the federal government to affect the outcome of elections—from the Hatch Act to the Pendleton Act.

Deciding whether the Administration crossed the line in the voter fraud cases turns, once again, on elusive questions of motive. But these questions arise in the first place only because of the unitary executive theory that led the White House to blur the line between political and policy disagreements. By insisting that there is no distinction, as Sampson said, between "political and performance-related reasons" for firing a prosecutor, by demanding not only broad agreement with the president's policy goals but personal loyalty to his political agenda, Gonzales made it inevitable that voter fraud prosecutions would run the risk of being used as partisan weapons.

What should happen next? Some prominent Democrats have called for the appointment of a special prosecutor to investigate, but that would be a terrible idea. Even if administration officials did twist the prosecution power for partisan ends, it's hardly clear that they broke the narrow criminal laws regulating obstruction of justice. (Lying to Congress is another matter.) Special prosecutors, from Kenneth Starr to Patrick Fitzgerald, have been disasters when it comes to investigations that originate from violations of political norms, not criminal laws. Because there's no provable underlying crime, they always end up prosecuting the cover-up. Instead, Congress is doing the right thing by holding Gonzales and his aides accountable politically and should continue to hold hearings to determine precisely what happened.

The disrepute Gonzales has inflicted on the Justice Department stems from a heavy-handed embrace of the theory of the unitary executive. It was the failure to imagine the possibility that Republicans might not eternally hold all three branches of government that proved to be the undoing of Gonzales and his aides. The ease with which they extended their political control deep into the executive branch convinced them that it was politically wise to do so. Now it's up to congressional Democrats to show them why they were wrong.

Not Compassionate, Not Conservative

Ethan Fishman

the *American Scholar* | Winter 2007

In this fascinating essay, political-science professor Ethan Fishman explores the crucial distinction between conservative political thinking and what he calls "pseudo-conservatism"—a political attitude motivated primarily by economic dissatisfaction and cultural resentment, rather than by a defined philosophy of government. Fishman's analysis places the Bush White House squarely in this latter tradition, and goes on to note that, since the appeal of pseudo-conservatives is based on emotion rather than practical concerns ("a politics of the gut . . . rather than of the mind"), those seeking a logically coherent framework for Bush's policies are doomed to be disappointed.

In 1954 the celebrated American historian Richard Hofstadter offered his explanation for McCarthyism in an essay he contributed to *The American Scholar* titled "The Pseudo-Conservative Revolt." Looking back on his essay 11 years later, Hofstadter noted: "I have written nothing else of comparable brevity that aroused more attention or drew more requests for quotation or reprinting."

Seeking to understand the underlying social psychology of McCarthyism, Hofstadter borrowed the term pseudo-conservative from the philosopher Theodor Adorno to designate Americans who cloaked their "serious and restless dissatisfaction with American life, traditions and institutions" in the guise and rhetoric of conservatism. Hofstadter, who studied alternative explanations for political conduct, hypothesized that the dissatisfaction of 1950s pseudo-conservatives was based on a fear of loss of status common to open societies where social mobility is relatively fluid.

Compounding their fear in the McCarthy era was anxiety generated by the post–World War II nuclear arms race, which created a doomsday scenario in the minds of many Americans. In response to these fears, Hofstadter argued, alienated groups began describing themselves as conservative because the term appeared to identify them as being diametrically opposed to the forces they perceived were threatening both their lives and their social positions. As Hofstadter pointed out, however, from a strictly political perspective there was nothing authentically conservative about their arguments. In the first place, they were trying desperately to overturn the status quo of New Deal America—not to conserve it. Furthermore, they adhered to an ideology of anti-intellectualism, substituting feelings and emotions for the rational discourse that for millennia has characterized the history of Western conservative thought. "The pseudo-conservative tends to be more than ordinarily incoherent" about political issues, Hofstadter wrote. The result, he maintained, was a politics that emphasized unarticulated psychological impulses over reasonable analysis—a politics of the gut, in other words, rather than of the mind.

Another reason Hofstadter considered McCarthyism to be a form of pseudo-conservatism had to do with the rage with which it expressed its opposition to the American political system and with the reckless policies it supported. Conservatism as a political philosophy is analogous to conservatism as a personality trait. Both stress moderation, practicality, and prudence. "Look before you leap" and "a bird in the hand is worth two in the bush" might well be their credos. As Hofstadter reminded readers of *The American Scholar,* however, McCarthyism had virtually nothing "in common with the temperate and compromising spirit of true conservatism in the classical sense of the word."

Today another form of pseudo-conservatism threatens American institutions. Under the Administration of George W. Bush, our public policy has for six years been shaped by those who discount reason to practice a politics of largely inchoate sentiments.

In order to recognize the counterfeit quality of the pseudo-conservatism that Hofstadter identified, as well as the "compassionate conservatism" Bush sometimes espouses, one has only to turn to the political philosophies of Aristotle and Edmund Burke. It is in their works, notably Aristotle's *Politics* and *Nicomachean Ethics* and Burke's *Reflections on the Revolution in France* (1790), that the basic principles of the Western conservative tradition can be found. At the heart of Aristotle's and Burke's thinking is a belief in the existence of natural law, a set of moral ideals that gives meaning to such terms as honor, integrity, justice, and courage. Neither Aristotle nor Burke possessed much faith in the rationality and morality of human beings. They feared that without the guidance that natural law provides, humans would forfeit their opportunities to lead virtuous lives and establish just governments. Because Aristotle and Burke considered them to be universal, these moral ideas were meant to apply to every human relationship—including economics.

Aristotle and Burke supported private property and free enterprise on the basis of the distinguishing characteristic of human beings—the possession of a soul that makes it possible for us to exercise free will and become unique individuals. One of the advantages of private property, they taught, is that it helps us to develop and manifest our individuality as well as to express one of their most cherished ideals, generosity. If people did not own property to share, they pointed out, generosity would be a largely empty virtue. But Aristotle's and Burke's support for private property and free enterprise was not unlimited. The standards of natural law require owners to treat workers the same way they would like to be treated if the roles were reversed and challenge merchants to provide consumers with a fair product at a fair price.

From this perspective, what makes the Bush administration an example of pseudo-conservatism is its dogmatic commitment to laissez-faire policies that deny the relevance of universal ideals and that rely primarily on market forces to guide economic activities. In its pursuit of laissez-faire economic policies, the Bush administration has relaxed banking standards, introduced no-bid government contracts, allowed private corporations greater access to public lands, and refrained from limiting monopolistic practices. It has sought, furthermore, to reduce governmental responsibility for the welfare of its elderly citizens by advocating the privatization of Social Security accounts.

By assuming that some form of economic justice will result from the relatively unchecked selfishness of individuals and corporations, the policies of the Bush administration contradict Aristotle's and Burke's negative views of human behavior. Reinhold Niebuhr's *The Children of Light and the Children of Darkness* (1944) echoed Aristotle's and Burke's rejection of unlimited economic freedom for its smug optimism. Only people who think of themselves as "harmless egotists," Niebuhr remarked, could fail to understand that when the "economic process is left severely alone either the strong devour the weak, in which case monopoly displaces competition, or competition breeds chaos in the community."

Consistent in its inconsistency, the Bush administration celebrates economic freedom while acting to curtail other basic American freedoms, such as privacy, religion, speech, and press. The same government that hesitates to apply explicit moral standards to economic behavior has had few qualms about restricting the Fourth Amendment right against warrantless searches, loosening rules on the confidentiality of medical records, supporting faith-based initiatives that cause citizens to subsidize religions to which they do not belong, ordering librarians to divulge information on material checked out by patrons, and attempting to influence the content of National Public Radio and public television. Equally disturbing has been its approach to sexual issues. Among the manifestations of pseudo-conservatism that Hofstadter observed in 1954 was the vindictive quality of the policies it espoused. By opposing abortion as well as convenient access to birth control, the Administration has demonstrated a punitive attitude toward sexual conduct.

Another serious disconnect between the Bush administration and traditional Western political conservatism is its foreign policy. Although Aristotle and Burke believed in universal ideals, they were not idealists. Instead, they practiced a politics of prudence that seeks to adjust immutable natural laws to constantly changing situations and circumstances. The unique value of prudence, Aristotle wrote, is its ability to ensure that governments do the right thing at the right time "in the right way." Burke called prudence "the first of all virtues" because it alone can teach governments how to bring "power and right" into harmony. Indeed, Burke's famous criticism of the French Revolution was based upon his appreciation of political prudence.

Although Burke promoted the ideal of free government as the necessary political correlate to personal free will, his understanding of prudence taught him that societies are organisms that require great care in order to endure and flourish. They can be modified, consequently, only with considerable thought and patience. At the end of the 18th century, France had been living under feudal autocrats for centuries. When the revolutionaries ignored their past and tried to introduce a historically unprecedented level of "liberty, fraternity, and equality" into their society virtually overnight, Burke predicted that death and destruction beyond anything the French had ever experienced would soon transpire.

Burke favored the American Revolution, on the other hand, because he judged Americans, as former English men and women, to be seeking to adapt traditional English ideals of self-rule for their new home. He considered their goal to be a relatively moderate one that would serve to lay a firm foundation for the evolution of free government in the United States. Burke explained this in his *Reflections*:

> I flatter myself that I love a manly, moral, regulated liberty as well as any gentleman. But I cannot stand forward and give praise or blame to anything which relates to human actions, and human concerns, on a simple view of the object, as it stands stripped of every relation, in all the nakedness and solitude of metaphysical abstraction. Circumstances (which with some gentlemen pass for nothing) give in reality to every political principle its distinguishing colour and discriminating effect. The circumstances are what render every civil and political scheme beneficial or noxious to mankind.

By Aristotle's and Burke's theories of evolutionary change, the Bush administration's decisions to invade and occupy Iraq were clearly imprudent. A number of explanations have been offered to justify these policies. One was that Saddam Hussein possessed nuclear weapons. Another was that he was in league with Al Qaeda terrorists who attacked the United States on 9/11. The latest is that we need to remake Iraq into a democracy that will serve as a political role model for the rest of the Middle East. Although the first two explanations have been discredited by the thorough investigations of several bipartisan congressional committees and independent commissions, the Bush administration continues to stick by them. This strategy calls to mind Hofstadter's observation that pseudo-conservatives are suspicious of reasonable analysis and often rely on knee-jerk reactions to reach policy decisions.

As Bush's former Secretary of the Treasury Paul O'Neill revealed in Ron Suskind's book *The Price of Loyalty* (2004), the president in 2001—for reasons that were never explained fully and seemed like a snap judgment at the time—informed his cabinet that he was thinking seriously about overthrowing Saddam. It was especially shocking to O'Neill that Bush announced his convictions about Iraq only 10 days after his inauguration and a full eight months before 9/11. "Conviction is something you need in order to act," O'Neill said. "But your action needs to be proportional to the depth of evidence that underlies your conviction."

The third explanation is even more bewildering from a traditional conservative point of view. Iraq has never come close to being a democracy. The Iraqi people have never been free and rarely have shown an inclination to fight and die for freedom. In the context of Iraqi history, therefore, the administration's vision of a democratic Iraq is reminiscent of the mistakes made by the French revolutionaries. Both acted as if dreams can easily be translated into political reality. Both upheld the ideal of freedom, but neither was able to adapt that ideal to the specific circumstances they encountered. Both were unable to appreciate the staggering costs in human lives and property that are unavoidable when radical change is pursued over a very short period of time.

The Bush administration's attitudes toward the national debt and the environment represent another break with the Western conservative tradition. Aristotle's and Burke's writings remind today's generations that we have a moral responsibility to leave the world a better place for our descendants. This is why, Walter Lippmann explained in *Essays in the Public Philosophy* (1955), "young men die in battle for their country's sake and why old men plant trees they will never sit under." After six years of a supply-side economic policy that increases government spending but declines to pay the bills by increasing taxes, however, the Administration has left our children with a national debt of more than $8 trillion. By refusing to ratify the international Kyoto Protocol on global warming, deciding against requiring automobile manufacturers to raise fuel-efficiency ratings, withdrawing funds from the EPA, FEMA, and the Corps of Engineers, and discouraging wetlands-preservation projects, the Administration may have set the stage for future environmental catastrophes on the order of Hurricane Katrina. Our children will have to cope with these disasters.

Other similarities between Bush administration policies and Hofstadter's description of pseudo-conservatism include: hostility toward the United Nations; a penchant for amending the Constitution; an insistence on political conformity; an inability to make subtle distinctions between international players, which is required for effectiveness on the world political stage; and a reliance on the populist rhetoric of anti-intellectualism. John Bolton, Bush's U.N. ambassador, has taken the position that the institution is largely irrelevant. The Bush administration has supported amendments to the Constitution regarding flag burning and homosexual marriage. Americans who want to set a deadline for our troops' withdrawal from Iraq are described as traitorous "cut-and-runners." The failure of Senator McCarthy and his followers in 1954 to recognize that communist regimes in the Soviet Union, China, Yugoslavia, and Vietnam were different seems similar to the Bush administration's insistence that organizations such as Al Qaeda, Hezbollah, and Hamas are all part of a unified group of "Islamofascist" terrorists. Furthermore, the Bush administration's approach to such issues as creationism, placing replicas of the Ten Commandments in public places, and the Terri Schiavo debacle contains a good deal of anti-intellectual populist rhetoric.

Perhaps the most valuable aspect of Hofstadter's 1954 *American Scholar* essay is its ability to explain more than 50 years later why traditional conservatives tend to get so exasperated with the Bush administration. Traditional conservatives—of whom I am one—consider themselves loyal citizens who want to believe that their president knows what he is doing. So we keep trying, with little success, to appreciate the logic of his budget deficits, incoherent foreign policies, attacks on constitutional rights, anti-environmentalism, and puritanical attitude toward sex. What Hofstadter teaches us is that these policies were never meant to be understood logically in the first place. As he wrote in a later essay, "Pseudo-Conservatism Revisited—1965":

> As a rule, [pseudo-conservatism] does more to express emotions than to formulate policies. It is in fact hard to translate the claims of [its] policies into programs or concrete objectives . . . and for the most part the proponents of such politics, being less concerned with the uses of power than with its alleged misuse, do not offer positive programs to solve social problems. The operative content of their demands is more likely to be negative: they call on us mainly to prohibit, to prevent, to censor and censure, to discredit, and to punish.

Despite the brilliance of Hofstadter's analysis, there is a major difference between pseudo-conservatism and its traditional counterpart that he neglected to discuss. Aristotle's and Burke's pessimistic view of human nature, their belief in a system of natural law that sets moral parameters for human behavior, their development of a theory of prudence that appreciates the difficulties involved in translating morally preferable ideals into politically feasible policies, and their commitment to moderation and caution are major components of traditional conservatism's emphasis on doubt and limits. Traditional conservatives believe that the universe imposes profound restrictions on what individuals and governments can accomplish. They adhere, according to Noel O'Sullivan in his book *Conservatism* (1976), to a "philosophy of imperfection, committed to the idea of limits" that regards human beings as "imperfect, dependent" creatures who are "doomed to make the best of things by the more modest policies of compromise and accommodation."

The Bush administration, however, has not consistently recognized doubt and limitations. Despite the burgeoning national debt, the Administration declines to heed the advice of fiscal conservatives either to raise taxes or seriously reduce public spending. Despite the devastation caused by Hurricane Katrina, the Administration persists in ignoring the warnings of prominent scientists about the destructive effects of global warming. Despite former Army Chief of Staff Eric Shinseki's concern that we would need "several hundred thousand soldiers" in Iraq, the Administration went ahead with its preconceived plan for a diminished force. With a certainty bordering on arrogance, the Administration has behaved as if it believes the national debt somehow will disappear, nature will heal global warming on its own, and Iraqis will soon come to their senses, welcome Americans as their saviors, and conclude that democracy is preferable to secular or religious tyranny.

Certainty in the face of strong evidence to the contrary is the hallmark of ideological thinking. Ultimately, it is the ideological quality of Bush administration policies that classifies them as pseudo-conservative. Whereas ideologues advance one doctrinaire solution to every problem regardless of the circumstances, traditional conservatives expect political leaders to adjust their convictions to the situation at hand. Whereas ideologues prefer to deal with political abstractions, traditional conservatives seek to practice a more practical form of politics that operates, in Burke's words, on a level of "the more or less, the earlier or the later, and on a balance of advantage and inconvenience, of good and evil."

An especially troubling assault on traditional conservative limits and doubts has been the administration's adherence to a strategy for presidential leadership that it calls the "doctrine of the unitary executive." Among the people who participated in the formulation of this doctrine were Bush appointees Attorney General Alberto Gonzales and Justice Samuel Alito. Gonzales helped to develop it when he served as Bush's White House counsel; Alito, when he was a lawyer in Ronald Reagan's Justice Department. To the Administration the "doctrine of the unitary executive" means that the executive branch can interpret laws any way it wants—even if its interpretation differs markedly from the directives of Congress and the Supreme Court.

Although this doctrine represents an egregious violation of the separation of powers, the president has used it with impunity. Bush has claimed that he will disregard laws prohibiting warrantless wiretapping of domestic phone calls. He has said that he intends to ignore the provisions of the Patriot Act with which he disagrees. When Bush announced that he vehemently opposed the Military Commissions Act being considered by Congress, which would restrict his ability to detain and torture enemy combatants, Congress caved in to the president's pressure and virtually granted him the power to interpret the Geneva Convention as he sees fit.

With the two-term presidential limit in effect and the end of the Bush administration in sight, can we expect that pseudo-conservatism is about to run its course? Do the recent midterm election results indicate that moderate Americans have grown disillusioned with pseudo-conservative policies? Only for the time being, Hofstadter would maintain. Just as McCarthyism was followed by the presidential campaigns of Barry Goldwater and George Wallace, Richard Nixon's "Silent Majority," the Reagan presidency, and the current administration, it is inevitable that another version of pseudo-conservatism will appear on the American political scene.

As long as citizens remain fearful of their status in society and as long as Americans continue to dread attacks from powerful enemies committed to the destruction of their country, Hofstadter warned, the specter of pseudo-conservatism never will completely vanish. In 1954, he prophetically noted: "We do live in a disordered world . . . of enormous potential violence, that has already shown us the ugliest capacities of the human spirit. . . . These considerations suggest that the pseudo-conservative political style . . . is one of the long waves of [contemporary] American history and not a momentary mood."

The Washington Back Channel

Max Frankel

the *New York Times Magazine* | March 25, 2007

Last year's perjury trial and subsequent conviction of I. Lewis "Scooter" Libby, ex-chief of staff to Vice President Dick Cheney, made for gripping political theater, providing as it did a rare glimpse into the inner workings of the U.S. government and the media that covers it. Those who cheered Libby's downfall tended to overlook the fact that no one in the Bush administration was ever charged with leaking CIA covert operative Valerie Plame's name and position to the press—the supposed crime that triggered special prosecutor Patrick Fitzgerald's investigation in the first place.

In this article, New York Times *veteran Max Frankel (who as a Washington correspondent during the Vietnam War was involved personally in the controversy surrounding the famous leak of the Pentagon Papers), warns that the Libby prosecution may have hurt the cause of open government far more than it helped. By coercing reporters into revealing their sources, he worries that Fitzgerald's efforts may have put a permanent damper on the tradition of Washington officials selectively leaking information to the press. While such leaks are invariably self-serving, notes Frankel, they also serve a larger purpose. "[G]iven . . . the hoarding of information that always attends the lust for power," he writes, "a free, unregulated and unpunished flow of leaks remains essential to the sophisticated reporting of diplomatic and military affairs, a safeguard of our democracy."*

I.

So there I sat, watching the United States government in all its majesty dragging into court the American press (in all its piety), forcing reporters to betray confidences, rifling their files and notebooks, making them swear to their confused memories and motives and burdening their bosses with hefty legal fees—all for the high-sounding purpose, yet again, of protecting our nation's secrets. Top-secret secrets! In wartime!

To be sure, the defendant this time was not a journalist but a high-ranking official, I. Lewis Libby, the former chief of staff and national security adviser to Vice President Cheney and also a former assistant to President Bush—a pooh-bah courtier who knew virtually all government secrets worth knowing. Libby sat indicted, however, not as a critic of government who blew a whistle to correct an injustice but as an agent of government who lied and obstructed justice to protect the misuse of secrets. He was no Daniel Ellsberg, who gave the top-secret Pentagon Papers to *The New York Times* to expose the nation's devious drift into war in Vietnam. Libby peddled secrets with comparable fervor, but to defend misjudgments and misrepresentations on the path to war in Iraq.

The crosscurrents of this trial were particularly confusing. No one stood accused of spilling a secret; this was at best a proxy trial, with perjury substituting for an unreachable, perhaps even nonexistent crime. The issue was merely, Who knew what when and said what to whom and testified about it how? Then again, in many eyes, the Libby case, like the Pentagon Papers, amounted to a tortured trial of a current war, America's quaintly bitter way of assigning blame for a costly catastrophe.

And either way, reporters became central to the case. Their messy relations with officialdom were uncomfortably on display. We heard about celebrated correspondents routinely granting anonymity—better called irresponsibility—to government sources just to hear whispered propaganda and other self-serving falsehoods. We learned how our patriotic guardians of wartime secrets wantonly leak them to manipulate public opinion, protect their backsides or smear an adversary. And we learned again how clumsy are the criminal laws with which high-minded prosecutors try to discipline the politics of Washington.

Should we really be expending so much emotion crying over one spilled secret? Did Libby's lies really warrant the law's intrusion into reporters' dealings with government informants?

Sitting in court, I kept thinking back to 1971 and my effort to unwrap the mysteries of the capital's information traffic. I was *The New York Times*'s chief Washington correspondent when the Nixon administration asked the courts to halt our publication of the Pentagon Papers. Sensing then that even our own lawyers, like most judges, felt an urge to bow before the incantations of "national security," I wrote a memo that shared with them the ultimate secret about secrets in Washington: that "practically everything that our government does, plans, thinks, hears and contemplates in the realms of foreign policy is stamped and treated as secret—and then unraveled by that same government, by the Congress and by the press in one continuing round of professional and social contacts and cooperative and competitive exchanges of information."

My memorandum, duly attested, became an official affidavit and sailed with the case clear up to the Supreme Court. It continued:

> The governmental, political and personal interests of the participants are inseparable in this process. Presidents make "secret" decisions only to reveal them for the purposes of frightening an adversary nation, wooing a friendly electorate, protecting their reputations. . . . High officials of the government reveal secrets in the search for support of their policies, or to help sabotage the plans and policies of rival departments. . . . Though not the only vehicle for this traffic in secrets—the Congress is always eager to provide a forum—the press is probably the most important.

Libby's leaks fit this pattern, serving to protect his and Cheney's personal reputations as well as their interests of state. And Libby's lies were a ham-handed effort to evade responsibility for a possibly illegal betrayal, by his leaking, of a secret agent's identity. But since that offense was never established, was it wise for government to intrude so crudely into Washington's normal flow of secret information?

Libby's reasonable expectation that reporters would keep his confidences—and protect his perjury—was foiled by some weird mishaps and finally by the shrewd maneuvers of a passionate and politically independent prosecutor. The resulting trial produced a fascinating display of how information is harvested in Washington and how secrets are dripped out by officialdom. But I kept thinking that the compelled testimony about reporters and their sources would end up doing more damage than even the reckless violation of a CIA agent's cover. For given the cult of secrecy that enveloped our government during the cold war and the hoarding of information that always attends the lust for power, a free, unregulated and unpunished flow of leaks remains essential to the sophisticated reporting of diplomatic and military affairs, a safeguard of our democracy.

II.

Known for most of his 56 years as "Scooter," Libby is a man of slight build, warm disposition and prodigious intellect. For a quarter-century, he has been affiliated in and out of government with Dick Cheney, Paul Wolfowitz and Donald Rumsfeld, forming the nucleus of a neoconservative fraternity that wanted to project unchallengeable American power across the globe. The group aspired, even before its return to power with the second President Bush, to liberate Iraq from Saddam Hussein and turn it into a democratic bastion that might stabilize the Middle East and safeguard oil supplies and routes. When Cheney became vice president in 2001, he drew Libby to his side to coordinate policies with like-minded officials planted throughout the executive branch. The attacks of 9/11 gave the group its strategic opportunity to promote the invasion of Iraq on the ground that this would keep weapons of mass destruction out of the hands of Al Qaeda and other terrorist groups.

That misfired adventure, and the buyer's remorse of a press and public that accepted the war's pretext, lay at the root of Libby's perjury. For it was Cheney, with Libby's active help, who had sounded the loudest alarms about Hussein's "reconstituted" nuclear program, about his stores of chemical and biological weapons and supposed ties to Al Qaeda. When, mere weeks into the war in 2003, no such weapons could be found, it was Cheney and Libby whose reputations and influence were imperiled as much as the president's.

The Cheney office came to grief, however, not from any sober investigation of intelligence failures and misrepresentations. The crazy charm of the case of *United States v. I. Lewis Libby* was that misperceptions inside government about a retired American diplomat and his undercover wife became the inspiration of idle gossip and ugly smears that joined to produce an explosive chain reaction.

Thus, much as I regretted to see the press snagged again in the clutches of the law—and embarrassed by our susceptibility to government disinformation—I found myself deeply engrossed in this spectacle. A once-disciplined Bush administration was being forced to devour one of its most valued operatives. A nation's anger over an imperial debacle was being heaped upon a mainly symbolic defendant. A policy confounded by sectarian violence in Iraq was exposing fierce tribal warfare among the Potomac bureaucracies.

Paradox tumbled from paradox: Patrick J. Fitzgerald, a fastidious U.S. attorney with Democratic, Republican and Qaeda scalps on his wall, had to rely on the testimony of reporters he had bullied into his service, actually jailing Judith Miller, then of the *Times,* for 85 days. Conversely, Theodore V. Wells Jr., the expansive principal defense counsel, chose a strategy that required him to savage the character and skills of some of Libby's associates in government and also of his client's once-favored, "very responsible" media outlets—Miller and Tim Russert of NBC.

The final allure of the Libby trial was the hope that Fitzgerald had fully solved the underlying mystery that plagued the capital for four years: *Who outed Valerie Plame?* Also known as Valerie Wilson, she was a covert (and, as befits a spy story, comely) agent of the Central Intelligence Agency—so covert, in fact, that she had traveled in the guise of an energy consultant while recruiting spies abroad to track the traffic in weapons of mass destruction. Fatefully, she also became the wife of Joseph C. Wilson IV, a debonair diplomat who bravely shielded hundreds of Americans from Saddam Hussein when they were trapped in Baghdad during the first gulf war and who later developed broad contacts throughout Africa. Doctrinally, his approach to Iraq stood with the moderate center of both political parties, in favor of disarming Hussein with threats and diplomacy rather than militarily deposing him.

Except in the comics, of course, truth and justice do not often occupy the same realm. The Libby jury was never told the details about Valerie Plame's job and status; these were issues "beyond the scope" of the indictment and also judged too secret to air in public. Nor was the jury told about Libby's lawyerly knowledge that he could talk about Plame *to* reporters and still avoid violating the Intelligence Identities Protection Act by claiming to have learned about her *from* reporters. And of course the jury never heard a word about the deeper deception that had been the drumbeat for war.

The Bush administration's evidence of a revived nuclear weapons program in Iraq rested almost entirely on claims that Hussein had contracted to buy large amounts of yellowcake, a uranium concentrate, from Niger and shopped the world for aluminum tubes with which to enrich uranium for weapons fuel. Expert opinion at the United Nations and also inside the U.S. government insisted that the sought tubes were usable only in rockets, not nuclear weapons. And the supposed purchases of uranium were swiftly debunked by three investigations. Yet the intelligence about a uranium purchase, based on suspect and even forged information, acquired nine lives in Washington.

When in early 2002, Cheney and Libby came upon a fresh report about uranium sales, they insistently asked an already dubious CIA to check into it further. So with the assistance of Valerie Wilson, two of her colleagues in the agency's counterproliferation division invited Joseph Wilson, her husband, to seek out friends in Niger, where he quickly gathered proof that no such deal had been or could be made without being discovered.

Wilson's oral report to that effect and other findings persuaded the CIA's director, George Tenet, to remove any mention of uranium sales from a presidential speech in October 2002, but the Niger scare resurfaced three months later. Propelled by the winds of wishful thinking, it sailed clear into the president's prewar State of the Union address, becoming a notorious 16 Words: "*The British government has learned that Saddam Hussein recently sought significant quantities of uranium from Africa*." It was only one sentence among the pretexts for war, but because others were even less credible, it proved to be radioactive.

In April 2003, after the capture of Baghdad, with no nuclear or other mass weapon facilities in sight, Joe Wilson began to believe that the fishy Niger story, which he assumed his report had slain, had been the main prop under the president's rationale for war; and if so, he wondered, what other intelligence had been willfully misrepresented? With or without the benefit of some pillow talk with Valerie, Wilson grew particularly suspicious of Cheney and Libby, supposing that their request for a CIA inquiry into the Niger matter must have brought them knowledge of his negative finding. How then could the White House and State Department continue to defend the use of such discredited information?

Wilson aired his suspicions and Niger experience at a panel discussion on Iraq and agreed there to let Nicholas Kristof report them in his *Times* column on May 6, 2003, attributed only to a "former ambassador." That's how it's done by critics who want to appear modest or discreet and by writers who want a good story, whatever the terms.

Stung by that column's assertion that the vice president's office had inspired the diplomat's mission and knew of its result, Cheney and Libby asked the State Department to identify the ambassador. A search of the files at State brought up Wilson's name, but it also revealed the CIA as sponsor of his trip. Gratuitously, mistakenly and with a slight leer, the department reported back that "Wilson's wife, a CIA W.M.D. managerial type," had "convened" the meeting that sent him to Niger.

Now the pot began to bubble.

Libby's first reaction, as shown in trial testimony, was to badger the CIA to quickly absolve the vice president of any knowledge of the Wilson mission. The agency complied, but the press wolves kept howling about the missing W.M.D.'s and lusting to learn who wrote the already refuted 16 Words into the president's text. Condoleezza Rice, the national security adviser, pleaded ignorance, even scoffing that the negative Niger report must be languishing "in the bowels of" the CIA. That put-down brought forth a second column by Kristof, on June 13, still not naming Wilson. But it used provocative shorthand to say that the ambassador had gone to Niger "at the behest" of the vice president's office and added with provocative certainty that the office must have known that the Niger reports were forgeries.

III.

Here came the first freakish turn of events, not fully revealed until the trial testimony of Bob Woodward, *The Washington Post*'s hero of Watergate, protector of Deep Throat and supreme collector of capital leaks.

While chatting confidentially with Woodward on June 13, the day of Kristof's second column, Deputy Secretary of State Richard Armitage could not resist a huge dose of schadenfreude. Himself a skeptic about the war, Armitage had read his department's answer to Libby about the Wilson trip with a practiced bureaucratic eye. There was no way the State Department was going to take the blame for those 16 Words. And since he knew that Woodward was gathering information for a book rather than the next day's paper, he chortled crudely about the affair.

See how an official's boast of innocence fed a reporter's hunger for guilty knowledge, a combination that produced the very first leak concerning Wilson's wife. The audiotape played for the jury began with Armitage insisting that the saboteurs of the president's speech resided elsewhere:

> **Armitage:** We've got our documents on it. We're clean as a [expletive] whistle. And George [Tenet] personally got it out of the Cincinnati speech of the president.

Woodward: Oh, he did?

A: Oh, yeah. . . .

W: How come it wasn't taken out of the State of the Union then?

A: Because I think it was overruled by the types down at the White House. Condi doesn't like being in the hot spot. But she—

W: But it was Joe Wilson who was sent by the agency. I mean that's just—

A: His wife works in the agency.

W: Why doesn't that come out? Why does . . . that have to be a big secret? . . .

A: Yeah. And I know [expletive] Joe Wilson's been calling everybody. He's [expletive] off because he was designated as a low-level guy, went out [to Niger] to look at it. . . .

W: But why would they send him?

A: Because his wife's a [expletive] analyst at the agency.

W: It's still weird.

A: It—it's perfect. This is what she does, she is a W.M.D. analyst out there.

W: Oh, she is?

A: Yeah. . . .

W: She's the chief W.M.D.?

A: No, she isn't the chief, no.

W: But high enough up that she can say, "Oh, yeah, hubby will go"?

A: Yeah, "He knows Africa—" . . .

W: Was she out there with him?

A: No.

W: When he was ambassador?

A: Not to my knowledge. I don't know. I don't know if she was out there or not. But his wife is in the agency and is a W.M.D. analyst. How about that [expletive]!

That's how it's done, in barroom style: an official playing bureaucratic tennis, protecting his boss, Secretary of State Colin Powell; a reporter preying on the knowingness of his source. Woodward held the anecdote for possible follow-up questions and mentioned it to his *Post* colleague Walter Pincus, who did nothing with it.

It all sounded so familiar: government officials spreading secrets to shape a story and to advance their interests, large and small. Listening to Woodward, I found myself recalling the day Lyndon Johnson summoned me to his Texas ranch during a recess of his 1967 summit meeting with Aleksei Kosygin, the Soviet premier, in Glassboro, New Jersey. I was covering the conference for the *Times,* and the president, standing beside me waist-deep in his swimming pool, wanted me to know how well he was jousting with his guest and enjoying the discomfort of Kosygin's Kremlin colleagues. When I wondered casually how Kosygin was being second-guessed so readily, the president proudly revealed that, thanks to a global network of sophisticated intercepts, he could hear everything being said among the Soviet leaders then dispersed in different parts of the world. Like the reporters who appeared at the Libby trial, I received such information on my source's terms; I could use Johnson's observations to analyze the summit discussion without naming him, but I could not refer to his techniques of eavesdropping. Those were the rules of the game.

I knew the rules from the other side as well, from my experience as an Army private with newspaper connections. In early 1955, I was sent out from my desk in the Pentagon to Yucca Flat, Nevada, to squat in trenches with several hundred soldiers during three nuclear tests. As the mushrooms rose, we marched 1,000 yards to ground zero, pawns to prove that the infantry could safely fire atomic artillery shells.

Other government agencies at the tests were eager to prove the opposite —the great danger of these explosions. So to end the competing press briefings, the Atomic Energy Commission declared all the tests "top secret." Undaunted, the Army had me don civilian clothes and drive to Las Vegas to brief reporters I knew from the *Times* and the Associated Press about the maneuvers. Anonymous in the casinos, I told them atomic secrets.

IV.

Libby's interpretation of the Wilson challenge was much more sinister, and fateful, than anything implied in Armitage's gossip: someone at the CIA was trying to discredit the office of the vice president. Libby mentioned the Wilsons while complaining to the CIA that some of its analysts had been griping to reporters about being pressured into distorting intelligence during his and Cheney's frequent prewar visits to the agency. By the July 4 weekend, the suspicions in the vice president's office about a CIA vendetta—and the suspicions of its critics—hardened into angry resentment.

Provoked by Rice's dismissive claim that his Niger findings were languishing in obscurity, Wilson stormed into public view with a clarion *J'Accuse!* On July 6, he appeared simultaneously in the *Times* ("What I Didn't Find in Africa"), in a flattering *Washington Post* profile and as a last-minute guest on NBC's *Meet the Press.* He minced no words (only a punctuation mark) by opening the *Times*'s op-ed article with a question: "Did the Bush administration manipulate intelligence about Saddam Hussein's weapons programs to justify an invasion of Iraq?" He knew from experience, he added, that at least some of its information about nuclear weapons "was twisted to exaggerate the Iraqi threat."

I could easily imagine the calculations in Cheney's office. With just a touch of the paranoia produced by the war on terror, Cheney and Libby must have concluded that this relentless critic—connected by marriage to a resentful corner of the CIA—was leading a coordinated assault by analysts whose judgments they had either ignored or inflated to make the case against Hussein. I could almost sympathize, knowing (as the jury probably did not) that several analysts had indeed complained about excessive pressure to the CIA's ombudsman and that the news of their unhappiness had been leaked to the *Times* and *The Washington Post.* A similar restiveness had become evident at the Pentagon, where Cheney allies had pushed forward unproved claims of collaboration between Hussein and Al Qaeda over the objections of other intelligence analysts.

I also knew from experience how the highest officials, while publicly scorning the press, parsed its daily offerings with obsessive concern. Here was Cheney urgently underlining Kristof and scribbling a question to Libby atop Wilson's *Times* op-ed: "Do we ordinarily send people out pro bono to work for us?—Or did his wife send him on a junket?" A telltale word, that "junket"; it would soon flow from official lips that Libby swore he never tutored.

In fact, Libby told the FBI and the grand jury that he learned about Wilson's wife—as if for the first time—from Tim Russert on July 10 or 11. He insisted that he had totally forgotten discussing her during the preceding month with Cheney and with officials from State and the CIA. Libby's recollection of how he was "taken aback" by Russert's revelation stood at the heart of his indictment, and his meandering re-enactment of his talk with Russert would clinch the case for the jury.

The other, subsidiary counts charged that Libby lied by denying knowledge of Wilson's wife *before* the Russert conversation. And the sharpest contradiction was delivered by Ari Fleischer, the president's former press secretary. Fleischer began his last week on the job on July 7, one day after Joe Wilson's public attack, and lunched for the first time with Libby. You could hear a score being settled when Fleischer testified that Libby had rarely provided useful information for the press. But at this lunch they were chummy, discussing Fleischer's plans for private life, their bond as Miami Dolphins fans and that morning's White House press briefing, at which Fleischer assured the world that Cheney did not send Wilson to Niger. And that's when Libby told a man in touch with reporters all day long—"hush-hush, this is on the Q.T."—that Wilson was sent by his wife and that she worked at the CIA, and, Fleischer added, "I think he told me her name."

Did Libby mean simply to instruct Fleischer further about the affair? Or was he planting a seed that he hoped would germinate? He and Cheney knew that calling it a spousal perk would discredit Wilson's mission. Yet they surely also recognized the legal risk in exposing Valerie Plame's covert status—that the Intelligence Identities Protection Act prohibits anyone with authorized access to knowledge of a covert agent to intentionally disclose the agent's identity to persons not so authorized. Never forewarned that such a risk was involved in the Wilson case, Fleischer eventually spread the talk of a "boondoggle" to three reporters and would demand immunity from prosecution as the price of his testimony against Libby.

In the evening of July 7, Fleischer flew off with the president and other high officials to visit five African countries, but they worried that the Washington clamor about the 16 Words would drown out the journey's goodwill message. So Powell and Rice dictated a mealy surrender from Air Force One: Yes, the Niger tale was based on a forgery, and the remaining evidence for the 16 Words "did not rise to the level of inclusion in a presidential speech."

Instead of appeasing the press, however, that retraction provoked an even greater commotion: who pushed those false words into the president's mouth?

Libby persisted in building defenses for the vice president's office, not at all preoccupied, as his lawyers would argue, by the onslaught of foreign crises. On Tuesday, July 8, in what his normally detailed calendar listed only as a "private meeting," Libby spent two hours at breakfast with Judith Miller to enlist her help in countering Wilson's attack. He told the grand jury that he admired her reporting, on Al Qaeda and chemical and biological weapons, and presumably also her prewar articles lending credence to the administration's wild alarms about Iraqi W.M.D.'s—credulous articles that the *Times* eventually disowned.

Miller testified that Libby brought her selected excerpts from a top-secret National Intelligence Estimate (N.I.E.) to buttress his claim that long after Wilson's mission, the CIA still endorsed reports that Saddam Hussein had "vigorously" pursued uranium in Africa. This brought back memories of my own similar encounters—of President Kennedy allowing me to copy a secret transcript to prove how the Russians lied to him about missiles in Cuba; of Secretary of State Dean Rusk confiding that the Southeast Asia Treaty, later invoked in support of war in Vietnam, was "not worth the paper it's written on"; of Henry Kissinger casually bemoaning the anti-Semitism he experienced "in the highest places." The established Washington routine meant that such revelations could be reported, provided that they were attributed only to "senior administration officials." But on the subject of Joe Wilson and his wife, Miller's notes showed, Libby took the added precaution of asking to be identified as "a former Hill staffer." Though technically true, this was a devious dodge even by Washington's tortuous rules of engagement, and it should have led Miller to realize that the remedy for bad leaks is more leaks.

Miller said that she had gone to breakfast eager to learn why the intelligence reports she had swallowed had been so wrong but that she found Libby too much concerned with the 16 Words, with "who said what to whom, what I call inside baseball in Washington." The editor in me cringed at this justification for her not writing anything out of this interview. She could have been the first to recognize that the White House's denigration of the Wilsons betrayed a bitter feud during which Cheney was angrily pressuring Tenet to take sole responsibility for the bungled intelligence. By following the trail of Libby's leak back to CIA informants, she could have produced a pretty good yarn.

Miller's role in the case served no one very well. On cross-examination, she was rattled into multiple confessions of uncertainty, poor memory and wobbly note-taking. She had suffered nearly three months in jail to serve the principle that reporters had a duty to keep their promises of confidentiality to sources—but finally accepted Libby's longstanding offer to waive his protection as well as Fitzgerald's agreement to avoid asking her about other sources. The prosecutor, in turn, had to make do with Miller's tattered notes and testimony, for which he had fought a two-year battle clear up to the Supreme Court. As for Libby, his lawyers were so rough on Miller that the jury felt sympathy for her and her evidence.

The prosecutor did succeed in revealing the shameless ease with which top-secret information is bartered in Washington for political advantage. For example, Cheney and Libby claimed to have the president's authority for leaking self-serving quotes from the National Intelligence Estimate even while other high officials were still begging Tenet to agree to declassification. And we learned that not even the administration's best friends were spared the humiliation of falling for its ruses. To stimulate a supportive editorial in *The Wall Street Journal,* Libby enlisted Wolfowitz, the deputy defense secretary, whose relay of sensitive information was celebrated by the paper as especially credible because "it does not come from the White House."

Most reporters do not just lazily regurgitate such leaks; they use them as wedges to pry out other secrets. I remember once being shown the draft of a U.S. government "white paper" documenting the perfidies of the North Vietnam regime; a few more interviews found the news not in those accusations but in the fact that they were being assembled to justify the start of intensive bombing of that country. A few more questions following Libby's leak from the N.I.E. would have exposed it as a deeply flawed analysis, a cut-and-paste collection of stale reports. It had been thrown together in three weeks in September 2002 because Senate Democrats refused to authorize the Iraq war without evidence of W.M.D. activity. By mid-2003, intelligence experts were available to denounce the document as wrong on every important count, the worst N.I.E. ever produced and one obviously tailored to support a policy decision already made.

No wonder, then, that the White House tried to shift the blame for its embrace of such sour intelligence and to discredit Wilson for standing in its way. The claim that Wilson's mission to Niger had been an irrelevant junket arranged by his wife was duly conveyed, probably by Cheney, to Karl Rove, the president's top political aide and most practiced spinmeister.

And he promptly mobilized White House aides on July 8, observing that they were already late to the battle, "a day behind" in the pursuit of Wilson.

Reporters covering the president in Africa and some in Washington suddenly found themselves receiving broad hints to inquire about *who* had arranged the Wilson mission. And Robert Novak, a Rove favorite among conservative columnists, was the first to get an answer. After years of trying, he had obtained an interview with Armitage for July 8, at the end of which Armitage told him about Wilson's wife, Valerie, and her job at the CIA. It was a chatty, offhand comment, according to Armitage; it was a calculated leak that he was urged to print, Novak said. He did print it on July 14, causing the CIA to demand the criminal investigation of who illegally disclosed an agent's identity, and it resulted two years later in Libby's indictment.

When he finally described his role under oath, Novak said he had his own motives for asking Armitage about Wilson. Two days earlier, he overheard the ambassador making "obnoxious" comments about Bush in the green room before their separate appearances on *Meet the Press* and wondered why such a critic had been sent on an important mission. Novak said he used Rove—"a very good source, and I talked to him two or three times a week"—only to confirm the Armitage tip.

First Woodward, now Novak: why did Armitage dump on Wilson a second time? I suspect that he was half annoyed and half amused by the fuss an upstart diplomat had created—for other departments. But he may also have known of Rove's interest in spreading the junket tale. Whatever his motive, Armitage confessed his role to the FBI at the start of the criminal probe two months later and was spared prosecution, probably because he claimed ignorance of Valerie Wilson's covert status.

Knowing of Armitage's role, why didn't Fitzgerald fold his tent and return at once to his "day job" as U.S. attorney in Chicago? Because Libby's already evident lies to the FBI and Fleischer's multiple leaks in far-off Uganda convinced him that there had been more than a single careless source. He smelled an illegal White House smear campaign and thought Libby could help him crack the case. And if Libby persisted in his story before the grand jury, he would at least have a perjury case—if, against all precedent, he could force reporters to testify.

He overcame the press resistance with a clever strategy: shaming the reporters' known sources into waiving all claims of confidentiality, then persuading judges to jail reporters who still refused to talk. Miller held out because she doubted that Libby's waiver was truly voluntary, but the experience of prison and Libby's phone call eventually eased her conscience. Matthew Cooper, then of *Time* magazine, almost joined her in jail, but his bosses mooted resistance by turning over his notes. Cooper testified that he first learned about Wilson's wife from Rove, who mentioned her carefully as the subject of the imminent Novak column.

V.

As Fitzgerald's focus changed from leaking to lying, Tim Russert emerged as his key witness.

Russert hobbled into court with a crutch and a broken ankle to swear to what he had never said. Tight-lipped and ready for battle, he showed none of the cheerful ebullience with which he grills guests on *Meet the Press*. His confrontation with the impassive Libby, just 30 feet away, was especially striking because the vice president had so often used Russert's program to proclaim Saddam Hussein's nuclear ambitions; it was "our best format," Cathie Martin, Cheney's communications chief, testified, providing control of "our message." Symbiotically, the vice president was one of Russert's best, attention-winning guests.

But now Russert sat unyielding, denying and denying Libby's most important defense: that it was Russert who told *him* about Wilson's wife on Thursday or Friday of that fateful July week. Listening to eight hours of Libby's recorded grand-jury testimony, the petit jury heard a sometimes ingratiating, sometimes recoiling witness advancing this critical alibi:

"And then he said . . . Did you know that Ambassador Wilson's wife works at the CIA? And I was a little taken aback by that. I remember being taken aback by it. And I said—he may have said a little more but that was—he said that. And I said, No, I don't know that. And I said, No I don't know that intentionally because I didn't want him to take anything I was saying as in any way confirming what he said, because at that point in time I did not recall that I had ever known, and I thought this is something that he was telling me that I was first learning. And so I said, No, I don't know that because I want to be very careful not to confirm it for him, so that he didn't take my statement as confirmation for him.

"Now, I had said earlier in the conversation, which I omitted to tell you, that this—you know, as always, Tim, our discussion is off the record, if that's O.K. with you, and he said that's fine.

"So then . . . Mr. Russert said to me, Did you know that Ambassador Wilson's wife, or his wife, works at the CIA? And I said, No, I don't know that. And then he said, Yeah—yes, all the reporters know it. And I said, again, I don't know that. I just wanted to be clear that I wasn't confirming anything for him on this. And you know, I was struck by what he was saying in that he thought it was an important fact, but I didn't ask him any more about it because I didn't want to be digging in on him. . . ."

Never happened, Russert insisted—couldn't have happened, because he and NBC News never heard of Valerie Plame until Novak's column appeared the following Monday. He said Libby had called him in his role as NBC's Washington bureau chief to register a cussing complaint about Chris Matthews's attacks on Cheney and Libby. Russert said he referred Libby to Matthews's superiors and no other subject came up. The jury believed him, concluding that even if the wife had been brought up by Russert, Libby's claim of being "struck" and "taken aback" was simply incredible.

The defense's counterattack on this vital witness could aim only at Russert's character. It forced an embarrassed admission that Russert, a lawyer, had impulsively answered the FBI's questions without legal advice and without pleading the confidentiality he later invoked to contest a grand-jury summons. Russert also struggled to deny any animus toward the defendant, despite his giddy, celebratory comments on the *Today* and Don Imus shows on the morning of Libby's indictment. But he held firm, no doubt resolving to beware when next he wanders into unprepared forums.

VI.

Libby's main defense for misstatements was a bad memory. And the nine witnesses who disputed his accounts were treated by his lawyers as similarly impaired. Judge Reggie B. Walton insisted, however, that a "memory defense" required Libby to take the stand. Since neither Cheney nor Libby dared to submit to cross-examination, the defense used one of Libby's successors, John Hannah, to argue that burdensome crises weighed heavily on Libby in the summer of 2003. The jurors, judging by their written questions, were especially intrigued by Hannah's depiction of Libby as a simultaneously brilliant yet abysmally forgetful colleague.

Besides Novak, the defense presented five other reporters to whom Libby did *not* speak about Wilson's wife that July week. The most important was Walter Pincus of the *Post,* an early skeptic about W.M.D. claims, who revealed that he learned about Wilson's "boondoggle" and helpful wife "off the record" from Ari Fleischer, two days before the Novak column.

All the reporters told the jury that they could do their jobs only by subscribing to the convoluted code of conduct governing Washington interviews. "Off the record" information could not be published, but could guide research and perhaps be confirmed elsewhere; "deep background" material could be printed only if not attributed to anyone; "background" called for a circumlocution, like "senior administration official." Where no rules were explicit, the reporters protectively assumed some degree of confidentiality.

The system is sloppy and breeds confusion. Libby's press aide, Cathie Martin, said that he often spoke "off the record" when he really meant "deep background." Cheney by contrast was shown to have attached different degrees of anonymity to different parts of a single conversation—so much off the record, other items in various stages of "background." Novak explained that he and Rove "had a modus operandi, you might say, where I knew without him getting into a long dissertation, I knew when he was confirming something or rejecting something, or at least I felt that way. . . . When he said, 'Oh, you know that, too,' I took that as confirmation."

These rituals have been observed at least since World War II. As I put it in my 1971 affidavit, secrets are the coins of Washington reporting and of official briefings in the national security orbit:

> Learning always to trust each other to some extent, and never to trust each other fully—for their purposes are often contradictory or downright antagonistic—the reporter and the official trespass regularly, customarily, easily and un-self-consciously (even unconsciously) through what they both know to be official "secrets." The reporter knows always to protect his sources and is expected to protect military secrets about troop movements and the like. He also learns to cross-check his information and to nurse it until an insight or story has turned ripe. The official knows, if he wishes to preserve this valuable channel and outlet, to protect his credibility and the deeper purpose that he is trying to serve.

And Woodward gave voice to the universal understanding that while many sources speak confidentially "for very noble reasons," some do so "for less noble reasons."

VII.

Clearly, from the perspective of the public interest, there are and always have been both good and bad leaks, true and illuminating betrayals of secrets as well as false and conniving ones. On the path to war in Iraq, high officials of the Bush administration leaked classified but far from reliable information about W.M.D.'s, then pointed to its publication as "evidence" of its truth. When no W.M.D.'s were found, they used the same flawed secrets to justify their misrepresentations. But reporters could not expose this skullduggery until they obtained contradictory leaks from disheartened intelligence officials.

And while some leaks were destroying Valerie Wilson's career and endangering her associates around the world, the leaks of other secrets allowed reporters to uncover the inhuman treatment of prisoners in Iraq and Guantánamo, the illegal eavesdropping on Americans and the "rendition" of captives to distant dungeons. The "moral ambiguities" of all this contrapuntal leaking were fairly observed by Joseph Wilson in his memoir, *The Politics of Truth* (Carroll & Graf):

> I wondered: When is a leaker a true whistle-blower, risking his personal security to inform the citizenry and preserve the public's interest? When is a leaker a mendacious opportunist, out to advance the narrow interests of himself or his boss? When does a leaker become so appalled at the self-serving actions of his colleagues that he crosses the line to shine a light on them? Is there a reliable way to distinguish among the many varieties of that genus peculiarly indigenous to Washington, the leaker?

The answer, of course, is that there are no neat lines of distinction. Ambiguity can inhabit even a single leak, serving a selfish and public interest in one breath. Officials who leak secrets to ward off blame for policy failures may be disloyal and insubordinate, but they may also inspire constructive corrective action. Leaks that describe poor training and equipment for troops in Iraq may severely damage morale both at home and at the front, but they may also expose incompetence and save lives. The leaks in California about baseball players using steroids betrayed grand-jury secrecy and circulated unproved charges against players, but they also forced the baseball industry to confront its coverups of drug abuse and unfair competition.

An even greater cloud of ambiguity hovered over the Libby case after it failed to produce firm evidence of any crime. Valerie Wilson's exposure will be punished, if at all, only through the suit that she and her husband are bringing against Cheney, Libby, Armitage and Rove. Indeed, Libby's jurors expressed some regret that he alone faced their judgment, even as they pronounced him guilty on four of five counts.

VIII.

So was Libby's prosecution worth a four-year judicial and journalistic circus? Was it worth turning the White House into a defensive fortress? Was it worth invading newsroom files and alerting other sources that their chance of exposure has been significantly increased? Was tracking down one leak worth the risk that greater wrongdoing will go unreported in the future?

The damage to newsgathering, I believe, has been significant. Celebrity journalists like Bob Woodward and Tim Russert may not lose access to sources, but more vulnerable reporters and less-wealthy media outlets will surrender to the subpoenas and jail threats now descending on them in unprecedented numbers. Some will betray confidences; some will suppress articles whose defense would be costly. Others may avoid risky reporting altogether. Sensing danger, many investigative reporters have become highly circumspect, using what one judge sympathetically called the methods of drug dealers to protect themselves: resorting to disposable cellphones, meeting sources outdoors and avoiding e-mail and other computer communication.

Fitzgerald's strategy of prodding sources to waive confidentiality was a clever ploy that threatens other delicate relationships. In his separate capacity as U.S. attorney in Chicago, he has opened another route to uncovering sources without the media's cooperation: he won a battle to force telephone companies to reveal the call records of two *Times* reporters whose newsgathering may have forecast a government raid on an Islamic charity. Moreover, the Libby case has lost the media political support, on both the left and right flanks. Liberals were so eager to see Cheney and Libby exposed that they lost patience for reporters' claims of privilege. Conservatives, meanwhile, hoped that compelling reporters to reveal their sources was merely the start of legal actions to punish "unpatriotic" disclosures; they applaud the attorney general's threat to use the Espionage Act to punish both the receipt and publication of national-security secrets.

Government obviously needs to guard some secrets, especially those describing military tactics and intelligence sources and methods. That is why presidents struggle to impose discipline on their bureaucracies. President Johnson used to cancel promotions and other promised actions if his authority was undermined with premature leaks. President Nixon pursued leaks with lie detectors and "plumbers" who broke into adversaries' files, culminating in their hapless adventure at the Watergate. And Nixon's national security adviser, Henry Kissinger, withheld information from other government departments and tapped the phones of his aides as well as reporters. Yet these same leaders leaked freely to promote their personal and political agendas, no doubt unable, like Cheney and Libby, to distinguish between the two.

The Libby case, however, did not serve to enhance government discipline. If President Bush had truly wanted to find and fire the people who outed Valerie Wilson, as he vowed, he could have extracted confessions from the White House staffs in a single stern meeting. And the case did little to promote honesty among high officials; Libby, like the Iran-contra liars in the Reagan-Bush administration, will almost surely be pardoned and praised for taking a hit for the team.

Much as I enjoyed the human drama and revelations of the Libby case, I wound up regretting the rough ride of the law through the marketplace of information.

Fitzgerald may be forgiven his passionate defense of the integrity of grand-jury proceedings and FBI investigations. But attorneys general should resist the temptation to interfere with newsgathering or to delegate such a decision to a single-minded special counsel. When a White House leak is suspected, it is hard to avoid an independent prosecutor, but it's a pressure worth resisting. Nothing in the last four decades has altered my preference for the chaotic condition I described when I asked the courts not to fret over the lost secrets of the Pentagon Papers:

> For the vast majority of "secrets," there has developed between the government and the press (and Congress) a rather simple rule of thumb: The government hides what it can, pleading necessity as long as it can, and the press pries out what it can, pleading a need and right to know. Each side in this "game" regularly "wins" and "loses" a round or two. Each fights with the weapons at its command. When the government loses a secret or two, it simply adjusts to a new reality. When the press loses a quest or two, it simply reports (or misreports) as best it can. Or so it has been, until this moment.

It may sound cynical to conclude that tolerating abusive leaks by government is the price that society has to pay for the benefit of receiving essential leaks about government. But that awkward condition has long served to protect the most vital secrets while dislodging the many the public deserves to know.

As Justice Potter Stewart wrote after studying the unending contest between the government and the press during the cold war:

> So far as the Constitution goes . . . the press is free to do battle against secrecy and deception in government. But the press cannot expect from the Constitution any guarantee that it will succeed. . . . The Constitution itself is neither a Freedom of Information Act nor an Official Secrets Act. The Constitution, in other words, establishes the contest, not its resolution. . . . For the rest, we must rely, as so often in our system we must, on the tug and pull of the political forces in American society.

In loose translation: prosecutors of the realm, let this back-alley market flourish. Attorneys general and others armed with subpoena power, please leave well enough alone. Back off. Butt out.

Part Two: Republicans vs. Democrats— The 2006 Midterm Elections

Karl Rove's Split Personality

Todd S. Purdum

Vanity Fair | December 2006

Even with poll after poll predicting that the GOP would lose a significant number of congressional seats in 2006, there was a palpable nervousness among Democrats going into Election Day. The main reason could be summed up in two words: Karl Rove. The Republicans' top political strategist was a proven master at pulling off close victories, and no one doubted that he still had a few tricks up his sleeve.

In this insightful portrait, written during the run-up to the midterm elections, Vanity Fair's *national editor (and former* New York Times *correspondent) Todd Purdum examines the interplay between Rove's personality and his political methods. Purdum also suggests—correctly, it turns out—that, despite his past successes, Rove's tactics of cobbling together a majority by targeting narrow slices of the electorate "may have reached the limits of their effectiveness."*

I. The 34 Steps

In the five years my family has lived in a quiet corner of northwest Washington, our neighbors have included the secretary of homeland security, the executive editor of *The Washington Post,* the junior senator from Texas, a former White House chief of staff, the ambassador to the United Nations, and the general counsel of the Federal Communications Commission. But, as far as I know, only one of them has ever carried our newspapers up the 34 steps from the driveway to our front porch when we were away on vacation and forgot to stop delivery. His name is Karl Rove. And I know that he did so only because he made it his business to tell me.

"You have the second-most-expensive house on the block after Don Riegle," he said in an adenoidal bellow when he called me once about a story I was reporting, "and you can't pick up your own papers?" I have no idea whether this claim is true, or whether Rove came to his view by consulting tax records, real-estate listings, or simply his gut. But, in a single sentence, he marked me as a limousine liberal, associated me with a former senator caught up in an influence-peddling scandal, and suggested that I was a sloppy householder. It was friendly. Funny. But the unmistakable effect was to assert control: of the conversation, the situation, and me.

It turns out that the man who helped make micro-targeting of the electorate a winning art knows a lot about his neighbors. The instinct for categorization—for finding, probing, classifying, and ultimately harvesting voters according to minute gradations of preference—has made Karl Rove the power in politics that he is today, and he can't seem to help applying these methods to his own backyard. Most people pigeonhole their neighbors with a casual shorthand: we know them as teachers or lawyers, as tall or short, as pleasant or irascible. Rove is different. Talking with him one morning not long ago, I listened as he offered a household-by-household overview of the neighborhood, its residents broken down according to national origin, ethnicity, education, political affiliation, and career history. You or I might speak of "the Joneses at No. 42." Rove is more likely to refer to the Irish/Jordanian, Princeton/Oxford, pro-choice, World Bank–economist couple with the vacation home in the Shenandoahs, where they keep their battered second Volvo, the one with the Rehoboth Beach parking decal.

I'm exaggerating—a little. Rove is not quite the neighborhood's Professor Moriarty, at the center of the web, sensing every slight tremor of the distant filaments. But not much escapes his relentless, wire-rimmed eyes. Just around the corner there's the family with a Soap Box Derby car that caught Rove's attention last May. "Sir or Madam," Rove wrote to the occupants of that house on a White House note card, "I don't know if it was coincidence or intention, but I appear to share the name of your Derby car. May your path be fast and true, and may you arrive at the finish line well ahead of your competitors. Sincerely, Karl Rove. (Known in early years as 'Rover.')" Welles Orr, a Republican lobbyist whose firm made the car during a team-building retreat, told me that it had indeed been christened K-ROVE-R in honor both of Rove and of Washington's K Street corridor, where lobby shops and interest groups have their offices; the name is stenciled in block letters on the car's side. Orr was naturally surprised to get Rove's note, its envelope plastered with a hodgepodge of vintage stamps from his collection, including an eight-center with a stylized image of a bobsled, commemorating the Sapporo Olympics, in 1972. But the main cause for astonishment was this: "I kept thinking," Orr recalls, "How does he know? Because it's under heavy plastic tarp in our driveway."

For the past six years, Karl Christian Rove, senior adviser to the president, has asserted control over much of American politics, guiding George W. Bush to election, to re-election, and to highly atypical success in between, in the bitterly contested midterm elections of 2002. He has done so one demographic group, one wedge issue, sometimes virtually one block at a time. The big question this fall is whether he can do it again, in the midterm elections, for a Republican Party whose president has become one of the most unpopular and polarizing political figures in recent history. Predicting the outcome of dozens of individual congressional and Senate races is notoriously difficult—much harder than gauging the direction of a national presidential race—and this year's environment is unusually unsettled. The congressional-page scandal involving Representative Mark Foley, of Florida, and the failure of the Republican leadership to deal with it in a timely way, are dark clouds. So are the revelations in Bob Woodward's *State of Denial,* notably the assertion that, two months before 9/11, Condoleezza Rice brushed off warnings about an Al Qaeda attack, and the further substantiation that Bush and his aides have not leveled with the public about our failures in Iraq. If protecting voters and their values is the GOP's big sales pitch this fall, news like this is badly off message.

But substance aside, the midterm elections will also be a verdict on Rove's very methods. In politics, as in science, there are "lumpers" and "splitters"—those who consolidate, and those who discriminate; those who celebrate the inherent similarities among voles or voters, and those who relish the differences. Most of American politics is a story of divisions along existing fault lines: Hamiltonians versus Jeffersonians, Yankees versus Confederates, progressives versus mossbacks, internationalists versus isolationists. The nature of America's strong two-party system means that the electorate almost always *has* to split in two (and not into three, as in Britain, or into a dozen, as in Israel). But there have been moments when powerful forces and charismatic figures have combined to forge new coalitions that reconfigured prevailing party alignments and upended long-held assumptions. In the 20th century, Franklin D. Roosevelt was the greatest lumper of all, building a governing consensus that lasted for the better part of 50 years, until Ronald Reagan, another major-league lumper, came along and replaced it with a new coalition built in part on disaffected former Democrats like himself.

Karl Rove has always been a splitter. He doesn't have to think about it; it is the core of his being. In Rove's eyes, everyone is a micro-target. For his note to the neighbor with the sleek, competitive Soap Box Derby car, he went and found a stamp showing a sleek, competitive bobsled. For a note to the longtime *New York Times* reporter R. W. Apple Jr., a few months before his recent death from cancer, Rove used a 1976 stamp commemorating the newspaper's patriarch, Adolph Ochs. Early in his career, Rove became an expert in direct-mail techniques, fine-tuning just the right messages to move just the right voters at just the right time. As a political operative he has always played up to the line, if not over it. He has always found villains—gays, unions, trial lawyers, liberals, elitists, terrorists—that his candidates could use both to crack the electorate at a vulnerable spot and to define themselves in sharp relief. It was Rove who introduced the late Lee Atwater, his cutthroat colleague from their days as College Republicans, to the first President Bush, and it was Rove who played a decisive role in turning Texas into the solidly Republican state it is today. As much as anyone, it was Rove who made a once implausible governor of Texas into the president of the United States.

The 2006 midterm elections could well be Rove's last big campaign, and he has been running it true to form, with themes and tactics he has tested again and again. "I think the strategy is completely transparent," one rival Republican strategist says wearily. "I think you could literally have written this playbook in the run-up to the war in Iraq. It's a sort of classic leverage play: play upon the fears of the public, and leverage that into all the policies you've got that are unpopular. I've never seen a group of people who as consistently try to divide the public along the fault lines they already know exist, rather than try to unite it around something."

Up to now the strategy has always worked. And maybe it will work again, despite this year's unhappy portents. People close to Rove insist that as of mid-October he had yet to see any especially worrisome hard data. But the stakes for Rove go far beyond success or failure in this one midterm election. He has a larger dream, of a long-term "rolling re-alignment" of the American political system behind the Republican Party. This is the big idea, the brass ring, the grand ambition—the equivalent, for him, of what "remaking the Middle East" represents for a neoconservative hawk. And this is what may be slipping from his grasp. If it does, it would not be all his fault—looking around, he must see an administration, and a party, that has failed catastrophically on one issue after another. He may be the only senior administration official who actually knows how to do his job.

But if the dream should elude him, part of the blame will be his. Today's Republican coalition—of Main Street, Wall Street, Easy Street, and the Highway to Heaven—is less a natural alliance united behind broad principles than an unlikely aggregation pushed together by fear of the alternatives, skillfully stoked. That is how Rove has played it. But the very tactics that have worked for him in the short run may work against him in the long run.

II. The Napoleon of Insinuendo

"First of all," Rove told me one morning not long ago, sitting at his dining-room table, "the question is: is the election a choice or a referendum?" And he answered, "We're making it, as strong as we can, a choice."

We were in the midst of a conversation about the midterm elections, one that Rove had resisted for weeks, until suddenly, one Friday at summer's end, I was summoned to a leisurely Saturday breakfast at his home, the same three-story brick town house where he had held weekly strategy sessions for his staff during the 2004 presidential campaign. The menu was sliced tomatoes and eggs that Rove himself scrambled. The spicy venison sausage links had been rendered from a deer shot by his 17-year-old son, Andrew. The coffee was fresh French press, the sort of thing Rove might have mocked John Kerry for pouring. Score the first one for the NRA and the other for France—in GOP terms, a wash.

Rove's house is done in soft silks and elegant colors, seafoam and other pale-green shades. The long, harlequin-tiled kitchen opens onto a leafy backyard. This is presumably a testament to the good taste of Rove's wife, Darby, a graphic designer who once worked for his direct-mail firm. There are the usual Washington trophies—photos of the Roves with the famous and powerful—and a vintage picture in which a young Karl, with a shock of pale-blond hair and big horn-rimmed glasses, looks more like Andy Warhol than Elmer Fudd. There are unusual treasures, such as a framed collection of vintage campaign ribbons and political-convention badges. But the decorative element that dominates everything is Rove's vast collection of books.

They fill shelves in nearly every room and are organized by category with consummate care. Every subject has its niche.

The same can be said of Rove's work. For Rove, all politics is partitive, and there is almost nothing he can't explain by slicing up the electorate and slotting it into place. Divide and organize. Divide and categorize. Divide and conquer. As a College Republican in the early 1970s he advocated not only for precinct organizations on campus but also for dorm chairmen and even floor chairmen. He was an early computer nerd and number cruncher, and as a young Republican operative in still-Democratic Texas he helped develop the best voter lists, the best fund-raising lists, and the best political database in the state.

And always, everywhere, he won by splitting, using whatever he needed as a wedge. Rove's opponents have a way of ending up not just bruised but bloodied, assaulted by what used to be called "insinuendo." The attacks seldom, if ever, bear Rove's fingerprints, but his enemies usually believe they can discern his fine hand. Rove distilled his basic philosophy into a campaign memo he wrote more than 20 years ago, in which he quoted Napoleon on warfare: "The whole art of war consists in a well-reasoned and extremely circumspect defensive, followed by rapid and audacious attack." No one has ever proved that it was Rove who helped spread rumors that the late Ann Richards was a lesbian, during her 1994 gubernatorial race against George W. Bush in Texas (but a Bush-campaign official did complain to reporters about "avowed homosexual activists" in her administration). No one has ever proved that Rove had anything to do with the rumors that John McCain was gay, mentally unstable, and the father of a mixed-race child, which circulated during his South Carolina primary battle against Bush, in 2000 (but his allies almost certainly did spread those rumors).

It's nothing personal. It's all in service to the numbers, getting the electorate to divide in just the right way.

At breakfast Rove offered an example that illustrates how his mind works. Two days earlier, the lead story in *The Washington Post* had summed up the White House's fall electoral strategy with the headline BUSH TEAM CASTS FOES AS DEFEATIST. That same morning, the *Post*'s op-ed page carried a pungent essay by John Lehman, the Republican former navy secretary and member of the 9/11 commission, whose title delivered a counterpunch: "We're Not Winning This War." I asked Rove whether he was worried that Republicans might be restive because of Bush's handling of Iraq and his prosecution of the war on terror. "Not really," Rove said, as you would expect, but he then launched into a detailed analysis of the recent Connecticut primary, in which Senator Joseph Lieberman had narrowly lost the Democratic nomination to the liberal, anti-war insurgency of Ned Lamont. Lieberman's loss was being portrayed everywhere as a repudiation of the Bush administration's policies on Iraq. But Rove saw a hopeful pattern in the numbers. Sizing up the situation through the eyes of a splitter, he explained Lieberman's narrow loss in a way that came to seem like a harbinger of certain victory.

"We're talking about a pretty-blue Democratic primary, deep-blue Democratic primary," Rove began. "And Lieberman goes from being whatever it was—16 points behind—to 12, to 6, to 3½, in a matter of several weeks. Thirty-four percent of the state's electorate are Democrats. Forty percent of them turn out, so you've got about 14 percent of the state's electorate. As it gets close to Election Day, the question gets to be 'Do you want to win, or do you want to lose? Do you want America to prevail, or America to lose?' And just over 7 percent choose the candidate whose Election Night was punctuated by calls of 'Bring them home! Bring them home!' And just under 7 percent vote for the guy who says, 'Fight and win.' Now, if that happens inside a Democrat primary, what happens inside the electorate [as a whole] if the election gets crystallized as this guy says, 'It's tough, it's ugly, people are going to die, sacrifice is required, America needs to win,' and this crowd over here says, 'You can't win it. Get the hell out and we'll live with the consequences later'?" In other words, if even the bluest of the blue Democrats split nearly equally on the question, then the rest of America is bound to break Rove's way.

Rove's approach is coolly rational (and never mind that most of "this crowd over here" isn't actually arguing, "You can't win it. Get the hell out"). Polls show that voters agree with the Democratic rather than the Republican position on most issues, and the Republican coalition is far more fractious than Rove would like, with social conservatives unhappy at what they see as Bush's all-talk approach to issues such as gay marriage, fiscal conservatives angry at his expansion of the size of government, and libertarian conservatives appalled by his willingness to suspend civil liberties during the war on terror. Rove's—and Bush's—best hope of holding all those Republicans together, and beating back Democrats in a country that remains narrowly divided, lies in the tiny handful of issues that most sharply epitomize voters' deepest concerns.

To find and persuade those voters, Rove and his associates have developed a potent arsenal of tools and tactics for splitting the electorate, on both micro and macro levels. The micro is exemplified by the vast database that the Republican National Committee calls its "Voter Vault." Rove's protégé, the Republican National Committee chairman Ken Mehlman, has expanded an effort that began under the direction of Bush's pollster and strategist Matthew Dowd in the 2004 campaign, to gather detailed demographic and consumer data on Republican voters and potential Republican voters in the fashion of a consumer-oriented business. "We target voters the way that Visa targets credit-card customers," Mehlman says. "That's the difference from before. We used to target them based on their geography. We now target them based on what they do and how they live."

In 2004 the Bush team identified which Web sites its potential voters visited and which cable channels they watched. It spent its money accordingly, advertising on specialty cable outlets such as the Golf Channel and ESPN, whose audiences tilt Republican. In this way, Rove could reach out to potential Republican voters who lived in otherwise heavily Democratic neighborhoods, and who would once have been missed in get-out-the-vote efforts based on neighborhood or party registration alone. When the campaign learned that the sitcom *Will & Grace* was wildly popular with younger Republican and swing voters, especially young women, it larded the series with its commercials—473 of them in all. It was a neat trick: the Bush campaign managed to ratchet up turnout among one core group of voters by touting the president's proposal for a constitutional amendment banning gay marriage, and at the same time to attract another group of voters by running commercials on a television comedy that sympathetically portrayed urban gay life. It was another version of shoot-your-own sausage and French-press coffee.

Two years ago, in the presidential election, the Republicans used some form of these methods in 12 states; since then the party has spent $15 million to make the database available to all 50 states, and it has trained more than 10,000 party loyalists to use it. During a single week last September, as part of a grassroots effort called the "72 Hour Program," GOP activists knocked on the doors of one million potential Republican voters around the country. In theory, the Republicans now know more than ever about just where to position their chisel on the great marble block of the electorate so that the hammer of their macro-message will have the maximum effect when it is applied. That message itself could hardly be clearer—Democrats will raise your taxes and put you at risk; Republicans will lower your taxes and keep you safe—and the Republican Party openly acknowledges that in the final stretch it will spend the vast bulk of its money on negative advertising. The methods may be sophisticated, but the theme is anything but subtle. Position the chisel. Then hit it hard. There may even be votes just in the sharp and confident cracking sound it makes. Clarity gets attention. "People may not agree with you," Rove said at breakfast, "but if they know where you're coming from, they'll have respect for you that they will not have if they think you're weak and indecisive."

III. Wizard Without a Window

Democrats love to demonize Rove, but the truth is that many of them would hire him if they could. Senator Charles Schumer, the New York Democrat who chairs his party's Senate campaign committee, is emphatically one of the demonizers, but in a backhanded way he can't help giving the demon his due: "People think he's totally ruthless. There are few people who have come along who have, whatever the opposite of elevated is, who have helped politics descend by finding newer and nastier and more effective ways to practice it." Donna Brazile, who managed Al Gore's presidential campaign in 2000 and has shared occasional lunches with Rove in the years since, says, "I get blogged all the time for my, quote unquote, relationship with Karl Rove," adding, "Yes, he's hated. Yes, he's demonized. But I try to tell people, 'You should add another word: respected.' He knows how to play the game. I don't like the way Karl can go into a race and divide and conquer, but he has a maniacal focus on winning."

Still, these are not the easiest times for Rove. His belated acknowledgment that he was involved in 2003 in leaking the identity of Valerie Plame, the CIA operative whose husband, Ambassador Joseph Wilson, had emerged as one of the administration's sharpest critics on the Iraq war, hurt his credibility with the punditocracy and with the special prosecutor in the case, and perhaps—if one credits the report of the New York *Daily*

News's Thomas DeFrank, a Texan and one of the best GOP-sourced old hands in the Washington press corps—even angered the president he serves. The decision of the special prosecutor, Patrick Fitzgerald, not to indict Rove, and the recent confession by former deputy secretary of state Richard Armitage—presumably no fan of Rove's, and himself a skeptic on the war—that it was he, not Rove, who first casually leaked Plame's identity, led the dean of Washington's conventional wise men, *The Washington Post*'s David Broder, to declare that the town owed Rove an apology.

But the leak case was far from Rove's only problem. President Bush's original second-term agenda—from Social Security overhaul to tax reform—has been dead in the water for months, and the president's shaky performance in the aftermath of Hurricane Katrina led to Republican grumbling that Rove had lost his touch. Rove has also been grazed by the Jack Abramoff influence-peddling scandal; the convicted lobbyist turned out to have had seven lobbying contacts with Rove during a three-year period. Rove's executive assistant, Susan Ralston, had been an aide to Abramoff, and she resigned in early October after a congressional report found she had been a conduit between the two. Earlier this year the new White House chief of staff, Josh Bolten, stripped Rove of his formal responsibility for developing domestic policy (though not of his title of deputy chief of staff), and Rove was relegated to a smaller, windowless office in the West Wing, a few steps farther away from the Oval Office. It is not clear how much the staff shake-up actually diminished Rove's status or duties, and there is plenty of evidence that he remains every bit as powerful as Bolten when it comes to politics, if not more so. For instance, Rove accompanied Bush, Bolten, and Dick Cheney to Capitol Hill in September to argue for legislation clarifying the treatment and trial of suspected-terrorist detainees.

But those who know him say that the changes had to be a blow to a man as proud and prickly as Rove, who always "gets too much credit, and too much blame, and he loves it," as one fellow Republican strategist puts it. Since the 2004 campaign, there has also been some quiet but uncharacteristic grousing by allies of Mehlman and Dowd that Rove—who rides his staff hard and can be petty at times—was too quick to accept authorship of a re-election that was in fact a team effort. Some of them worry that his blunt rhetorical approach does not always serve the president well. "He pushes the envelope, communications-wise," one former colleague suggests, "just in being shrill."

Mehlman says he believes Republicans will prevail this fall—what else would an R.N.C. chairman say?—but he is quick to note that the three elections since 2000 were all close and hard-fought. And he adds, hedging further, that this is the sixth year of a presidential term, always a tough period. And on top of that, he goes on, there's the Iraq war, the biggest political challenge of all. "We know from history, from the Korean War in particular, that the American people judge the success of a war by the previous war they've fought," Mehlman explains. "So World War II made the Korean War seem like it wasn't successful, because it ended on the 38th parallel, as opposed to a surrender on the U.S.S. *Missouri.* It ended with a cease-fire, not a surrender, and it took the American people a while to figure out it was a success." It's probably safe to say that the American people have not yet had time to figure out that the Iraq war has been a success.

I asked Rove if he thought Bush would be better off if he had done more to emphasize the grueling realities that the Iraq war would entail. "I think he has, frankly," Rove said, but as he elaborated he in fact changed the subject, as the high-school debater he once was would have done. He spoke not of grueling realities but of abiding hopes, summoning the shades of wartime leaders past. "Go take a look at every one of those speeches," he said, invoking Churchill, "and there's an optimism about ultimately prevailing, which was there in all but a handful—you know, you have to go to April 1940 to get a speech in which there may be the hint of, you know, the night is descending on Britain. But there is an optimism in Roosevelt, there is an optimism in Churchill, there's an optimism in Bush. There's an optimism about winning the Cold War. I mean, very few people echo Whittaker Chambers, saying, 'We're choosing the wrong side, and we're gonna lose.' In fact, from Truman on, every president, with maybe one exception, has been continually optimistic about prevailing in that twilight struggle."

And that exception was Jimmy Carter?

"Yeah," Rove said, unable to suppress a smile, "and I'm probably saying that because I'm churlish and small about it."

IV. "I Say It Here, It Comes Out There"

It is late August, and a knot of protesters are gathered outside the manicured grounds of the Inverness Club, in Toledo, Ohio, brandishing signs that read, REPUBLICANS ARE SELLING OUT AMERICA and FIRE ROVE. Inside, Karl Rove is headlining a cocktail fund-raiser for Ohio's secretary of state, Kenneth Blackwell, the man responsible for the conduct of the 2004 election in Ohio, where some Democratic partisans suggest that voting irregularities and long lines in Democratic precincts may have lost the state for John Kerry and cost him the presidency. Now Blackwell is running for governor, and is his party's best hope of retaining the statehouse in a key swing state.

Rove is in his element. He will raise $165,000 at this event. In the past 18 months, he has been top-billed at more than 70 Republican fund-raisers around the country, raising more than $12 million—more than any Cabinet secretary or agency head, and about two-thirds of all the money raised by Bush-administration figures other than Dick Cheney and George and Laura Bush. He is in a playful mood, looking, for once, younger than his 55 years, and strikingly slimmer. When I ask, as he drives away from a handful of reporters, how many pounds he has lost, he shouts out, "Twenty-two." What's his secret? "Clean living, and avoiding you guys." (The other part of the secret turns out to be a liquid-protein diet, supervised by a doctor.)

The room looks very Republican, full of men in seersucker and blue blazers, and women in summer print dresses. Blackwell tells the crowd that Rove is "an ombudsman for the people and for the president, unafraid to pulse the system, challenge conventional thinking"—a man who is "not afraid to think bold ideas and then to act on them." Rove counters, making light of the tools of his trade and his reputation as a mastermind. "I know we've got polls, and we've got sophisticated databases, and we've got the Internet, and we've got television, and we've got radio, and we've got direct mail, and we've got micro-targeting—we've got all these sophisticated things in politics.

"But," he continues in a folksy-foxy tone, "politics really comes down to a little expression that a failed candidate in Illinois talked about as the key to politics in 1840. A tall, lanky fellow out of Springfield, a lawyer who went around the state of Illinois practicing law, wanted to serve more than one term in Congress but didn't get his wish. And he had a great expression. He said, to win the election 'we've got to make a perfect list of voters, ascertain with certainty for whom they will vote, have the undecideds talked to by someone that they hold in confidence, and on Election Day make certain that every Whig is brought to the polls.' And

Abraham Lincoln had it right: the key on that is to have the undecideds talked to by someone that they hold in confidence."

Rove sounds as if he's winding down, but he's really just getting started. He plunges into a vivid implicit preview of almost every speech the president will make in the weeks just after Labor Day, outlining the Republicans' fall campaign. It's not quite the ventriloquist's act of the brainy Albert Brooks in the movie *Broadcast News,* who marvels as he secretly prompts the blow-dried anchor played by William Hurt: "I say it here, it comes out there." But it's close. "We're at war with Islamic Fascists," Rove says. "Their goal is spelled out in the words and writings and sayings of Osama bin Laden . . . up to us to share with people what his goal is . . . establishment of a golden age of Islam . . . headquarters in the Middle East, probably in Baghdad . . . humiliate the Western world . . . utter destruction by whatever means necessary of the state of Israel . . . his plan is at the heart of the battle we're having in Iraq . . . central front in the war on terror."

A range of Islamic scholars and national-security experts might well quarrel with the particulars as Rove lays them out. They might point out, for instance, that Iraq is the central front in the war on terror because the United States has made it so. But Rove is off to the races with his main point, and rather than running away from the issue on which Bush is in the most trouble—the war in Iraq—Rove leans right into it, hard.

"The Democratic Party insists that it be taken seriously on national-security matters," he tells the Toledo crowd. "But after September 11, one of the party's leading grassroots organizations, Moveon.org, circulated a petition that called for 'justice, not escalating violence' against Afghanistan, for harboring the Taliban and harboring Osama bin Laden. Now, I don't question the patriotism of our opponents." The tone is sad, understanding. "Not a bit. These are hardworking public servants who are doing the best they can. The problem with these Democrats is that their policies would have consequences and their policies would make us more, not less, vulnerable. In war, weakness emboldens your enemies and is an invitation to disaster."

V. "Don't Believe a Single Word"

If Rove has ever displayed weakness to an enemy—or to a friend—the occasion went unrecorded. Even his wife once told a reporter that he knocked her croquet ball so hard on vacation that it made her cry. Rove has always led with his chin, and his trail is littered with former close friends turned bitter foes. When he was not yet ten, in Arvada, Colorado, he spoke up for Richard M. Nixon to a little girl who lived across the street and backed John F. Kennedy. She knocked him to the ground. He has since denied it, but his sister, Reba, told journalists that in the 1960s Rove hung a poster above his bed that demanded, WAKE UP, AMERICA!

Rove grew up in a home in which splitting in all its guises—discord, division, duality, departure—was the default mode. Louis Rove, the man Karl knew as his father, was a geologist, and the family bounced around the West, in Colorado, Nevada, and Utah. On Karl's 19th birthday—which was also Christmas Day—Louis Rove walked out on the family, and a short time later Karl learned that Louis was not actually his biological father. In 1997, Rove told the journalist Thomas Edsall that his mother, afterward, largely withdrew from family life. When Rove was in his mid-20s, she would sometimes ask to borrow money, and from time to time would send him packages with old magazines or broken toys. "It was like she was trying desperately to sort of keep this connection," Rove told Edsall, until finally, in 1981, she "drove out to the desert north of Reno and filled the car with carbon monoxide, and then left all of her children a letter saying, don't blame yourselves for this." It was, Rove thought, "the classic fuck-you gesture."

Rove never turned on or tuned in, but as you might expect of someone who went to a high school named Olympus, he grew up determined to take over. He found in Republican politics the promise of an order and stability that his family so conspicuously lacked, and he possessed a hard-earned, instinctive empathy with Richard Nixon's "silent majority." From the beginning of his career Rove used any weapon he could. While working for a U.S. Senate candidate from Illinois in 1970, he pretended to volunteer for a Democrat named Alan J. Dixon, who was running for state treasurer (and would himself later wind up in the Senate). Rove swiped some stationery from Dixon's office, wrote a flyer promising "free beer, free food, girls and a good time for nothing," and distributed a thousand copies at a commune, a rock concert, and a soup kitchen, and among drunks on the street; a throng showed up at Dixon's headquarters. Rove later dismissed the prank as a youthful misjudgment, but it has haunted him, because it suggests an early predilection to play dirty. Three years later, when Rove was locked in a disputed election to become national chairman of the College Republicans, Terry Dolan, who supported Rove's rival and would later go on to found the National Conservative Political Action Committee, leaked a tape to *The Washington Post* in which Rove and another College Republican were heard trading tales about campaign espionage. Eventually, the chairman of the Republican National Committee concluded that Rove had won the election. The chairman at the time was George Herbert Walker Bush.

Implausible as it sounds, some of the bad blood that has poisoned Rove's relations with the camp of George W. Bush's onetime rival John McCain dates back to College Republican feuds. As chairman of the Alabama chapter of the College Republicans, in the late 1970s, Rick Davis had been close to Rove. But then Davis dared to oppose Franklin Lavin, Rove's chosen candidate for national chairman and one of his closest friends, with a candidate of his own, who wound up winning. For 20 years Rove had virtually no contact with Davis, then unsparingly bad-mouthed him in front of reporters in the 2000 campaign, when Davis was McCain's campaign manager. "Karl has the thinnest skin of any person I've ever known," one of Davis's friends says.

Even more striking is Rove's estrangement from John Weaver, once such a close friend that Rove nearly went into business with him in Texas. But the two had a billing dispute, became rivals, and at some point Rove spread false rumors of personal misconduct on Weaver's part. After the 2000 campaign, when Weaver worked for McCain, Rove virtually blackballed him from Republican politics. Weaver went to work mostly for Democrats, though he is now masterminding McCain's presumed 2008 presidential campaign. Weaver and Rove had a much-publicized rapprochement during the 2004 presidential race, when Rove needed McCain to campaign hard for Bush, but the two have not talked in more than a year.

In a business in which give-and-take is the norm, Rove is strictly a disher-outer. He is never wrong, and in every encounter I have ever had with him, he has contrived to have the last word. Even his friends say it is the mark of the man, and he will call back, or keep a meeting going as long as he has to, in order to get it. On the one occasion when Rove has been in our house, at a large party for a *New York Times* editor, he stood apart from most of the crowd, near the bookshelves in the living room. Only later did we learn that he had pulled out a volume—*Bush's Brain: How Karl Rove Made George W. Bush Presidential*—and inscribed on the flyleaf: "Don't Believe a Single Word in This Piece of Trash. Karl Rove."

The book, by James Moore and Wayne Slater, recounts in fevered tones Rove's history as a rough-and-tumble campaigner, and Rove cooperated a bit in its writing. But Slater, a longtime reporter for *The Dallas Morning News* who has covered Rove for years, told me that before the book appeared "Karl, of course, being Karl, got a copy of the manuscript. Not the galleys, not the book, but the manuscript. He got it, and he called and said, 'Everything in this is wrong.' So he sent me 10 to 15 pages, single-spaced, that he faxed out of the White House, of corrections, or at least observations." Most were not so much factual corrections, Slater said, as "Karl's version of events."

By all accounts, Rove has been even more upset by Moore and Slater's latest effort, *The Architect: Karl Rove and the Master Plan for Absolute Power,* published this fall, and he evinces mock horror at the ludicrous subtitle, which he quotes in the portentous tones of old newsreel footage. In the book, the authors cite friends of Louis Rove's as saying that Louis was gay and lived out his days among openly gay friends in Palm Springs, where Karl would visit him. The two did indeed become close late in the elder Rove's life, often vacationing together and once making a pilgrimage to Norway, the ancestral Rove home. Rove has told people that he does not know whether his father was gay. He seems especially pained by the book's suggestion that there was no funeral and is no record of burial for his father. In fact, there was a memorial service and a scattering of ashes in precise accord with Louis Rove's wishes.

"It's very clear that the relationship between father and son was somehow made good later," Slater told me. But he added, "Your father is gay, and you have some people close to you who have an understanding of gay marriage, homosexuality, that is sophisticated, and yet at the same time you spend your political life using homosexuality as a wedge issue to elect people? And Karl has done that all his life."

VI. Rove's America, or Applebee's?

Rove's books fill row after row of built-in shelves in his house. In the living room, there is contemporary history and politics, and places for western writers, including Wallace Stegner and Paul Horgan. In his study, a big section on Lincoln and the Civil War. Another whole section on Churchill. Growing up, Rove was not the typical boy next door. He once described himself as a "strange kid" who morphed into a "big nerd, complete with the pocket-protector, briefcase, the whole deal." He still uses that old trove of stamps. Books were always Rove's solace. Politics seduced Rove so early that he never got around to finishing his undergraduate degree, at the University of Utah, but he is an autodidact of the highest order. His knowledge of political history runs wide and deep.

On the Thursday morning after the 2004 election, Rove called me, full of zip. He was mildly upset over an article I had co-authored about him in that morning's *New York Times*, which stated that his role model was Mark Hanna, the Ohio kingmaker and businessman who backed the career of William McKinley. McKinley's 1896 campaign had pioneered unusually sophisticated direct-mail efforts, with special appeals to Croatian-Americans, and a mass-produced publication in Yiddish.

Rove said he had not idolized Hanna, whom he described as merely "the Don Evans of the McKinley campaign," referring to George W. Bush's old oil-patch friend, leading fund-raiser, and first secretary of commerce. Instead, Rove cited a more intriguing idol, one hinting at grander ambition, erudition, and complexity. His real hero, he said, was another McKinley campaign strategist, Charles G. Dawes, who went on to become Calvin Coolidge's vice president and Herbert Hoover's ambassador to Britain. Dawes was a banker and utility executive who shared a Nobel Peace Prize for his efforts to rebuild Europe after World War I. ("But," Rove told me just before hanging up, "I'll never live up to his reputation!") Dawes also composed the music that—after his death—became the 1950s pop song whose opening words could be Karl Rove's motto: "Many a tear has to fall, but it's all in the game."

Few practical politicians know more about the history of polarization in American politics, and the swings between lumpers and splitters, than Rove does. In our breakfast conversation he rattled off dates: 1820, when James Monroe became the last president to be re-elected without effective opposition; 1860, when the country separated clean in two in the Civil War, but under Lincoln's leadership emerged more strongly united than ever; 1896, when McKinley invigorated the Republican coalition by drawing in formerly Democratic working-class and ethnic voters; 1932, when FDR built his own great coalition; 1980, when Reagan helped bury it. More often than not, the lasting re-alignments tend to be moments of coalition-building, not electorate-splitting. In fact, in 2000, Rove flirted with a lumping strategy himself, arguing that campaigns based on wedge issues such as patriotism, crime, and welfare represented "an old paradigm." Both George Bush and Al Gore ran toward the middle that year. But Bush's slender electoral victory (and indeed his loss of the popular vote) suggested that the path to re-election lay in splitting—in building and energizing Bush's natural base, not in rallying swing voters, of whom there were thought to be precious few left.

So I was interested in Rove's view of where the 2006 midterm election fits in history, what other election it might resemble. It's not like the 1974 midterms, when Democrats made big gains on a wave of post-Watergate revulsion. It is not, Rove said, like the 1966 midterms, when Republicans made gains in the middle of the Vietnam War. He argued that the GOP's success that year amounted simply to a natural pickup of close seats that had been lost in Lyndon Johnson's 1964 landslide.

Finally, Rove allowed, "You might be able to take 1950. You had Republicans as isolationists, 'Get out of Korea.'" In fact, the 1950 midterms were a classic splitter contest, just five months into a Korean conflict that Republicans were already denouncing as "Truman's war." Everett McKinley Dirksen, campaigning successfully for a Senate seat from Illinois, thundered, "All the piety of the Administration will not put any life into the bodies of the young men coming back in wooden boxes." The Democrats kept control of Congress, but Republicans gained 5 seats in the Senate and 28 in the House, presaging Dwight D. Eisenhower's Republican tide in 1952. Harry Truman drank so much bourbon on Election Night that he was visibly impaired—the only time his aides ever saw him so affected—and had difficulty making his way to bed aboard the presidential yacht *Williamsburg*.

But Rove registered a big caveat: Truman in 1950 barely campaigned against the Republicans, considering it beneath his dignity. No one will ever accuse George W. Bush of taking a similar approach.

The intriguing question this fall is not which party will prevail. Given the number of congressional seats that are considered safe, neither party has a chance of winning a big majority in either house. "It's either going to be two years of gridlock" if the Republicans retain control, says Kenneth Duberstein, the last chief of staff in the Reagan White House, "or two years of oversight, investigation, subpoena, and gridlock" if the Democrats take back one or both houses of Congress. The more important question is whether this election might hint at bigger changes to come, as in the 1978 midterms, in which the passage of Proposition 13, capping real-estate taxes in California, coupled with outrage over Jimmy Carter's signing of the Panama Canal treaty, helped pave the way for Ronald Reagan's revolution two years later.

Rove himself knows that this election could be messy for his party, and he takes some pains to insist—as he always has—that the Republican dominance he seeks cannot, by definition, be total. "It's never going to be permanent," he says. "That's not the nature of American politics. But is it going to be durable? You know, there are steps forward and steps back along the way." He notes that Martin van Buren, Andrew Jackson's chosen successor in the 1830s, lost after one term (as did Reagan's successor, the elder George Bush, in 1992). Woodrow Wilson won in a three-way race in 1912, creating a Democratic interregnum in the long Republican hold on the White House. In 1938, FDR and the Democrats suffered huge losses—governors, senators, congressmen—and so did Harry Truman in 1946.

Rove acknowledges that what he hopes will be a period of Republican dominance has not started with anything like the sharp thunderclaps of the Civil War or the New Deal. When I later asked Rove to elaborate on this, my request caught up with him on the road, and he immediately composed a mini-treatise on American political history, which an aide e-mailed from Air Force One. The salient point is this: "I believe we are entering a new political system—a new structure in which one party tends to dominate politics, as Democrats did in the New Deal system. We're entering this new political structure in a much different way than the sharp shifts we've seen before. You can see it not only in the presidential and Congressional elections, where reapportionment will strengthen the GOP in the coming years but also in the change in state legislatures. For the last several elections Republicans have been at or near the highest number of state legislative seats that we've had since the 1920s. And remember, in the '20s there were no Republicans in the South—literally a handful of Republican elected officials in Winston County, Alabama, eastern Tennessee, western North Carolina, the German hill country of Texas, and scattered remnants in West Virginia."

A powerful counter-thesis to Rove's comes from an unlikely source: Matthew Dowd, Bush's pollster and strategist in 2000 and 2004, who has just written a book, *Applebee's America,* with Douglas Sosnik, a former senior strategist in the Clinton White House, and Ron Fournier, a veteran political reporter for the Associated Press. "Conventional wisdom suggests that 2004 was the first of what will be a series of 'base elections,' with both parties catering only to their core voters," the book observes. "Supposedly, there is no longer a vital American middle." The authors pronounce this conventional wisdom wrong.

"The vast majority of the country is a mix," says Dowd. "If the country sees the parties only representing those segments on the outer edge, the middle is going to get more and more frustrated, and seek out somebody who has some ability to speak to a broader interest. And that's where I think we're headed. I think the successful people in the years ahead are going to be people who in the public's mind bring consensus, and are not ideologically driven, and have a desire to bring people together." Bush's vow in 2000 to be "a uniter, not a divider" had seemed to promise a new kind of politics, and it helped inspire Dowd, a former Democratic consultant, who had first gone to work for Bush in Texas. "It's one of the things I'm most disappointed in, as you look back, that it didn't happen," Dowd says.

There are many reasons it didn't happen, and one of the biggest of them is obviously Karl Rove. At almost every turn, when others in the White House or the Republican Party have counseled reaching out to larger constituencies, Rove has pushed the opposite course: consolidating and building the Republican base, but no more than that. Now that the war in Iraq has turned sour, and with public confidence in Bush's leadership badly shaken, Rove is sticking to what he knows. But Dowd's analysis suggests that these methods may have reached the limits of their effectiveness—for both parties. "I think as you look ahead," he says, "there is a continuing, rising desire for someone who says, 'We may have a disagreement about issues, but we can all be called to do something else bigger than ourselves.'"

VII. The Last Hurrah?

Practically no one, including Rove, seems to think he will serve again as chief strategist to any presidential candidate. What will he do next? He has taught in the past at the University of Texas, and friends suspect he may well want to teach again, perhaps at whatever academic institution winds up being affiliated with President Bush's presidential library. He and Darby have built a vacation house on the Florida Panhandle, and the strong indication is that it's her turn for some micro-targeted TLC. At the same time, Rove's effort to reshape American politics has been a project of 30 years, as has his friendship with the president he helped elect. If Bush asked him to help a candidate in 2008, it seems all but certain that he would.

Rove has always presented a complex and contradictory assortment of qualities. He is both ruthless and thin-skinned. He maintains an insider's aura of boundless confidence, but cannot quite mask the lingering insecurities and resentments of the outsider he once was. He affects disdain for the press, but hiked up 34 steps to deliver my paper anyway. He has shown no reluctance to destroy reputations, to cut people off at the knees. And yet in Ohio, before he addressed the country-club Republicans, I saw him stop and tenderly take the arm of an Iraq-war veteran whose severe injuries from a car bomb have left him disabled for life.

But the bedrock beneath everything is the boy with the books, the student of history. And no matter what the results of these midterm elections, this very smart student must already sense one larger truth: in the great sweep of American politics, skilled operatives may triumph in particular battles, but victory in the paradigm wars belongs to a rarer and different breed. "Is the election a choice or a referendum?" Rove had asked me. And he answered himself: "We're making it, as strong as we can, a choice." Choice is a small idea. Referendum is a big one. Great re-alignments have always been a lumper's legacy. In the long run, splitters never win.

Southern Discomfort: The Strangest Senate Race of the Year

Peter J. Boyer

the *New Yorker* | October 30, 2006

Of all the Senate races in 2006, the most riveting, hands down, was the Virginia contest between Republican ex-governor George Allen and his Democratic opponent, Vietnam veteran James Webb—which Webb won by a scant 7,000 votes. While Allen's infamous "macaca" moment was the media highlight of the campaign, there were plenty of other twists and turns along the way. In this entertaining

New Yorker *piece, Peter Boyer gives a blow-by-blow account of the race that turned Allen from a would-be presidential contender into a political has-been—and, in his first election ever, vaulted a hard-bitten ex-Marine into the U.S. Senate.*

The autumn political contest in Virginia began this year as it always does, with a Labor Day parade and festival in the Shenandoah Valley town of Buena Vista. The event featured appearances by the Democratic governor, Tim Kaine, and his predecessor, Mark Warner, another Democrat, who was then considering running for president in 2008. Senator George Allen, a Republican, who was also contemplating a presidential race, rode the parade route on a jumpy horse called Bubba, and forecast a victory in his current reelection campaign. Notably missing from the event was Allen's Democratic opponent, James Webb. To the consternation of some on his team, he had skipped the ritual opening of his first political campaign in favor of a private ritual, three hundred miles away.

At Camp Lejeune, North Carolina, members of the 1st Battalion, 6th Marine Regiment, were preparing for deployment to Iraq. Among them was Webb's only son, Lance Corporal James R. Webb, known as Jimmy. Two years earlier, Jimmy had interrupted his studies at Penn State and enlisted. His father could hardly protest; Jimmy was taking up the challenge posed by Webb in countless speeches, books, and articles. To Webb, himself once a distinguished member of the Marine Corps, military service was not just a patriotic gesture but part of a test of honor and courage, an essential rite of passage.

Webb had gone to Vietnam in 1969, unburdened by ambivalence at a time when the narrative of the Vietnam War had turned irretrievably toward tragedy. His first novel, *Fields of Fire,* published in 1978, was based on the war—"the finest of the Vietnam novels," according to Tom Wolfe—and Vietnam continued to be his point of reference, to the degree that even his friends wondered whether it had distorted his perspective. But Webb was shaped not so much by the war as by what he discovered when he returned.

The year 1969 was one of the bloodiest for Americans in Vietnam, with the weekly death toll averaging about two hundred and twenty-five. At home, it was the year of Woodstock, the takeover of the Harvard administration building by student radicals, the trial of the Chicago Eight, and the huge National Moratorium antiwar protest. It was also the year that President Richard Nixon used the term "silent majority" to describe those Americans who did not protest.

When Webb, debilitated by shrapnel wounds received in an action that earned him the Navy Cross, was forced to retire from the military, he enrolled at the Georgetown University Law Center, and stepped directly into the culture divide. He hated his time at Georgetown, largely because of his encounter with an attitude that caught him wholly unaware. It seemed to him that many of his classmates had been untouched by Vietnam (except for a gain in self-regard, accrued from opposition to what they deemed an immoral war). Webb concluded that they not only had figured out ways to avoid the risk and sacrifice of military service but had convinced themselves, as they proceeded along their education and career tracks, that theirs was the true heroism of the time. Inspired by his rage, he decided to write *Fields of Fire,* which included a series of withering cameo portrayals of Ivy League graduates who worked the system to avoid service. "Some day he will write speeches for great politicians," he wrote of one character. "Tim Forbes will confess his boondoggle, and we will admire his honesty. He only did what everybody else was doing." Webb could recite the minuscule number of men killed in Vietnam who, by his count, had matriculated at the elite colleges (Harvard, twelve; Princeton, six; M.I.T., two) compared with the vast numbers from public schools.

Webb returned to the subject repeatedly in his writing over the next twenty-five years, until he produced what amounted to his own ethnology. He saw himself as a creature of a pervasive but nearly invisible Scots-Irish subculture, descended from the warrior clans of Ulster who migrated to North America in large numbers in the eighteenth century. They came to live mostly in the Appalachian South—a stubborn, bellicose people, fiercely individualistic and egalitarian. They settled the frontiers, invented country music, and fostered a truly native form of American democracy. Most important, they bore the brunt of fighting the nation's wars. In 2004, Webb published *Born Fighting: How the Scots-Irish Shaped America.* He had found, he believed, the DNA of red-state America.

In Webb's world, manhood was a standing, to be earned. When he was a small boy, his father, a bomber pilot in the Second World War, would clench his fist and dare his son to strike it, taunting him to keep punching until the tears flowed. But Webb accepted that a father's highest duty was to prepare his son for manhood by teaching him to fight, to hunt, and to handle a weapon. He got his first gun when he was eight, and Jimmy did, too. In such a culture, going off to war is part of what Webb calls "the Redneck Bar Mitzvah."

During the week before Jimmy's deployment, Webb and his son were joined by José Ramirez, a former marine who is the boyfriend of Jimmy's sister Sarah, and Dale Wilson, a member of Webb's platoon in Vietnam, who is a triple amputee. Just before the departure of the transport bus that was taking the marines to the airfield from which they would leave for Kuwait, Jimmy and his father and their friends gathered in the parking lot. Webb had filled a Coke bottle with whiskey, which he poured into four cups. The three older men raised their cups to Jimmy, who offered the final toast: "To those who went before me. And to those who didn't come back. Now it's my time."

That afternoon, Webb, who is sixty, returned to Virginia, where he is running as an antiwar candidate, under the banner of the party of Hillary Clinton and the former protester John Kerry, whose handshake he refused for twenty years.

The unifying theme of Webb's fiction, his popular history of the Scots-Irish, and, especially, his opinion journalism has been that of put-upon people (the military, Southerners, white men) suffering the smug disregard of a hostile elite. In the Webb reckoning, much blame resides in nineteen-sixties-era liberalism, which has influenced the Democratic Party for a generation. That he now finds himself a Democratic candidate in a pivotal U.S. Senate race is a development that proceeds, by its own stubborn logic, from this insistent theme. Webb's candidacy is partly a quest to reclaim the Democratic Party for what he sees as a natural constituency

When Webb deployed to Vietnam as a raw second lieutenant, in 1969, he had no particular political leanings. His mission was to protect the tactical space in front of him, and to bring back as many of his men as possible. Returning home, he felt that he and others like him had been driven from a Democratic Party that had, he believed, sacrificed a broad populist tradition to the passions of the intemperate margins. Webb proved to be a natural polemicist. He denounced "the ones who fled" the war, and inveighed against the acts of the Watergate Congress, which, elected after Richard Nixon's disgrace, in 1974, halted funding to South Vietnam, hastening its doom. (The plight of the Vietnamese boat people came to have particular meaning for Webb. A girl named Hong Le was among those fished from the water by the U.S. Navy and transported to this country. She became a lawyer, practicing in Washington, and a year ago she became Webb's third wife. She travels with him on the campaign trail, and is expecting their first child in December.) Webb declared Jimmy Carter's blanket pardoning of draft resisters a rank betrayal and an abuse of presidential power. When President Clinton left office, he wrote, "It is a pleasurable experience to watch Bill Clinton finally being judged, even by his own party, for the ethical fraudulence that has characterized his entire political career."

Webb reserved a good portion of his pique for the "activist Left and cultural Marxists" and their efforts to effect "what might be called the collectivist taming of America, symbolized by the edicts of political correctness." He saw the Pentagon's prolonged investigation of the Navy Tailhook sexual-abuse scandal in the nineteen-nineties as a political witch hunt, driven by a radical-feminist agenda to undermine the masculine culture of the military. Affirmative action, he posited, quickly became a means of victimizing white men through "state-sponsored racism."

In *Born Fighting,* Webb developed the thesis that has become the rationale for his Senate run. Democrats, he argued, had foolishly written off the Southern white male, in the mistaken belief that it was a necessary cost of the Party's leadership in the civil-rights era. Southern rednecks thus became a convenient symbol of all that impeded progress. "And for the last fifty years," he wrote, "the Left has been doing everything in its power to sue them, legislate against their interests, mock them in the media, isolate them as idiosyncratic, and publicly humiliate their traditions in order to make them, at best, irrelevant to America's future growth." In alienating the South, Democrats ceded the region to Republican strategists, who took the trouble to cater to its culture. Webb, who had been a nominal Democrat in his youth, knew this from personal experience. According to Robert Timberg's book *The Nightingale's Song,* Webb was recruited into the Reagan administration by a Republican official who had once heard him being interviewed on the radio. The interviewer, talking to Webb about *Fields of Fire,* mentioned that Jane Fonda was in town and asked Webb whether he might wish to meet her. "Jane Fonda can kiss my ass," Webb replied. "I wouldn't go across the street to watch her slit her wrist." The Republican official, John Herrington, who later became Reagan's personnel chief, championed Webb's appointment, in 1984, as Reagan's Assistant Secretary of Defense for Reserve Affairs and, in 1987, as Secretary of the Navy.

Webb also believes from experience that the Republican hold on the South is not unshakable. His own political remigration began when he was working on *Born Fighting* and realized that his culture's natural home is the party of Andrew Jackson. His people don't hate the government; they hate governmental intrusion. It is the government's job to build dams and highways, not the perfect society.

"It's a bottom-up culture that has been manipulated," he told me one day. "Really, that's one of the big reasons that I decided to go ahead and do this—test the theory, because I believe it."

This is, of course, a thought that has occurred to other Democrats. It's what Howard Dean was trying to get at in 2003, while campaigning for the presidency, when he said, in a characteristic display of unfortunate phrasing, "I still want to be the candidate for guys with Confederate flags in their pickup trucks." Dean's point (and Webb's) is that Democrats cannot succeed in the South until the Party broadens its tent, becoming less insistent on such matters of current Party orthodoxy as abortion, gun control, and gay marriage. "You know, it's been a hard thing to get through the heads of many Democrats," Webb says. "They have to rethink a piece of something that's become fundamental to them, which has hurt them in ways they don't understand."

Webb's campaign adviser David (Mudcat) Saunders recalls a revealing exchange he had last spring at a retreat for Democratic senators in Philadelphia. "I had a very prominent U.S. senator come up to me and say, 'Mudcat, why are your people so stupid that they would vote against their own economic self-interest?' And I replied, 'Listen, we do vote against our own economic self-interest. We do that. But you say it's stupid. Do you ever consider that there might be a powerful force at work, and that it's driving these people to vote against their economic self-interest? I'm telling you, it's there. It's called culture.'"

Webb, who is licensed to carry a pistol, and whose campaign vehicles include a camouflaged Jeep, will not be mistaken by voters for Howard Dean—or for George Allen. No Southerner could confuse his strenuous opposition to the Iraq war with the reflexive antiwar attitude perceived by many in the South as a partisan wish for American failure. Before the first Gulf war, he testified in a 1990 Senate hearing that taking down Saddam

Hussein's regime would destabilize the region and empower Iran; he maintained that position through the inter-war decade, and points to the current situation as vindication of his view. He believes that the American military is fundamentally unsuited to a long-term occupation. ("It doesn't make a lot of sense to turn the greatest maneuver force in the world into one going around defending police stations.") But he does not advocate a sudden coalition pullout, or even a firm timetable for the withdrawal of troops. Rather, he argues for convening a conference of regional players, including Syria and Iran, and getting them invested in finding a resolution for Iraq. At some point, he says, American forces could be repositioned in nearby countries like Jordan and Kuwait, where they would be able to combat terrorism in Iraq with less American exposure.

On domestic matters, Webb's Democratic populism borrows from the "two Americas" theme that John Edwards struck during his vice-presidential campaign, emphasizing the widening gap between the very rich and everyone else. Webb urges strong border security, including the construction of a fence, coupled with strict enforcement of laws that will supposedly stop corporate exploitation of cheap illegal labor. He opposes the free-trade agreements ("Free trade is not fair trade"), and in this and other regards (such as his disdain for neoconservatives: "These guys are so far to the left you think they're on the right. It's right out of the Communist International—exporting ideology at the point of a gun") he almost seems a Pat Buchanan conservative. "I've been saying for a couple of years that we're going through a sea change, where the old labels just don't apply," he told me. "What does it mean to be a liberal? What does it mean to be a conservative?" (For Webb, the ambiguity meant that in Virginia's 1994 Senate race he endorsed the Democrat Chuck Robb over the Republican Oliver North; he then backed George Allen over Robb in 2000; and now he was running against Allen for that same seat.)

Webb's campaign is working hard to portray him as the kind of Democrat Ronald Reagan could trust. Webb's first television ad, called "Gipper," opened with a shot of Reagan giving the 1985 commencement address at the United States Naval Academy. "One man who sat where you do now," Reagan told the cadets, "is another member of our Administration, Assistant Secretary of Defense James Webb—the most decorated member of his class." Black-and-white photographs of a young Webb in uniform filled the screen, with Reagan's voice narrating. "James' gallantry as a Marine officer in Vietnam won him the Navy Cross and other decorations." An announcer's voice then intoned: "Soldier. Scholar. Leader. Now Jim Webb is running for Senate." Nowhere in the ad was the word "Democrat" mentioned.

When Webb's pollster, Pete Brodnitz, saw the ad, he said, "This is gonna make George Allen's head explode." Indeed, the Allen camp put a letter of protest from Nancy Reagan on its Web site and demanded that Webb take the ad off the air. Webb just laughed and said, "If George Allen can find a video of Ronald Reagan praising him, he's welcome to use it." The controversy guaranteed free airtime for the commercial in news broadcasts, and had precisely the effect that the Webb camp had hoped for. With the campaign entering its final stretch, the Democrat and the Republican were arguing over who had the greater claim to the legacy of Ronald Reagan.

To George Allen's critics, there is something manifestly ridiculous about his public personality—his cowboy boot and hat, his "howdy"s and "y'all"s, his lip pack of Copenhagen snuff and his spit cup. Allen, the son of the great football coach George Allen, Sr., grew up in Palos Verdes, California, a prosperous suburb of Los Angeles, and he did not move to Virginia until he was in college, when his father became the coach of the Washington Redskins. "WILL SEN. ALLEN'S COWBOY BOOTS FIT VIRGINIA VOTERS?" was the question asked recently in a *Washington Post* headline, over a story noting that Virginia "is far from cowboy country." The *Post* article, citing Allen "detractors" (Jim Webb's campaign strategist Steve Jarding), suggested, in an interrogatory tone, what liberal bloggers have long been declaring in the affirmative: George Allen is trying to fool voters into believing that he's a genuine country boy. A corollary irritant is the prospect that Allen might succeed in posing as his political hero, Ronald Reagan—or, more maddening, that he might even be another Reagan.

As Allen entered the race for a second term in the Senate, his reelection was considered a foregone conclusion. The bigger question in political circles was his positioning as a contender for the 2008 Republican presidential nomination. Allen, a popular governor of Virginia, who served from 1994 until 1998, had been remarkably successful in passing his conservative agenda—including welfare reform, required achievement standards in the public schools, the right to carry concealed weapons, and the abolition of prison parole—even though the state legislature was controlled by

Democrats. He has shown a formidable talent for electoral politics; he was the only Senate candidate to defeat a Democratic incumbent (Robb) in 2000, and, as chairman of the National Republican Senatorial Committee, he helped engineer a Republican gain in 2004, which included the defeat of the Senate Minority Leader, Tom Daschle. By the conventional calculations of presidential politics, Allen's record of conservative orthodoxy automatically made him a favorite in a nominating process that, in both parties, favors orthodoxy. A team of national political consultants, including Mary Matalin, had already signed on.

Such calculations matter, but so does personal chemistry—and that is where the association with Reagan applies. The cowboy-pol image, with its implied bedrock conservatism, is best presented in a sunny package. Reagan (who was born above a bank in Tampico, Illinois, a locale also far from cowboy country) was blessed with a natural amiability, and much of Allen's success in Virginia can be attributed to his determined good cheer and his slow, easy manner of speaking, the pauses always filled with a smile. It was true that his partisan rhetoric could sometimes get harsh (as when he declared, at a state Republican convention in 1994, "My friends . . . let's enjoy knocking their soft teeth down their whining throats"), but that could be written off as a vestige of an upbringing in a football environment. Astride his horse at the Labor Day parade, Allen was pressed by a reporter about the political wisdom of his cowboy routine during election season. He was wearing a hat, he said, because it was raining. Besides, he added, "kids like horses." It sounded almost like something Reagan would say.

It is precisely because geniality is an essential component of the George Allen proposition that a casual remark, tossed off at a lazy August campaign stop in a remote corner of Virginia, threatened to become his undoing.

Allen was addressing an outdoor gathering at the Breaks Interstate Park, near the Kentucky border. This is Allen country, staunchly conservative, and he was imploring his supporters to "motivate" for the stretch run when he was distracted by a ubiquitous presence. It was S. R. Sidarth, a twenty-year-old University of Virginia student, and a summer volunteer for the Webb campaign, who worked as a Webb "tracker"—following Allen along the campaign trail with a digital camcorder, hoping to capture some word or deed that might embarrass the Senator. (Allen has a tracker on Webb, too.) Chatting casually, his sleeves rolled up, Allen gestured toward Sidarth and introduced him to the crowd. "This fellow here, over here, with the yellow shirt," Allen said, "Macaca, or whatever his name is, he's with my opponent. He's following us around everywhere. And it's just great! We're going to places all over Virginia, and he's having it on film, and it's great to have you here, and you show it to your opponent"—presumably, he meant to say "candidate"—"because he's never been there and probably will never come." At this, there were cheers from the crowd, who understood that Allen was implicitly associating Webb with the urban liberals of the national Democratic Party. Recalling that Webb was in California, raising money, Allen turned again to Sidarth, and said, "His opponent"—again, meaning Webb—"actually, right now, is with a bunch of Hollywood movie moguls." Alluding, perhaps, to Webb's screenwriting ventures, Allen said, "We care about fact, not fiction. So, welcome, let's give a welcome to Macaca here. Welcome to America, and the real world of Virginia."

If Allen had any clue about what he'd just done, he didn't show it. Smiling, he turned from Sidarth and resumed his stump speech: "My friends, we're in the midst of a war on terror."

The Webb campaign had no trouble recognizing the opportunity presented by Allen's utterance. The incident occurred on a Friday. On Monday, Webb's staff posted Sidarth's video on YouTube, and mass-mailed the link to journalists and supporters. The next day, the *Washington Post* published a page-one story, the first of more than three dozen articles mentioning "Macaca" that the paper ran in the course of a month. The rest of the national press quickly followed, as did the television comedians, talk radio, and bloggers. "Macaca," a word that few Americans surely had ever heard, became the signature of the political season.

Three weeks later, Webb pulled into Roanoke at the end of a long day on the road to address supporters at the opening of his local campaign headquarters. He told them that the campaign accommodations (provided without charge by Mudcat Saunders, the landlord) were much nicer than the condemned building he was using in Arlington—a reminder that his campaign was continuing to struggle in the money race. But he also delivered some good news, which he'd learned that day. Earlier in the summer, he had trailed Allen by sixteen points; a new poll showed that the race had become a statistical dead heat.

I had accompanied Webb on the last leg of his journey to Roanoke, and as we made our way through the smoky rises and falls of the Blue Ridge he reflected on how his ancestors had crossed those mountains, after fleeing Ireland, only to take up new fights against new enemies—the Indians, the British, the Yankees, the Germans, the Vietcong. Webb's ruddy pugnacity does not easily accommodate the joviality demanded by his new calling in politics. He can arrive at a campaign event looking as if he were ready to leave, and he hardly disguises his dislike of the glad-handing, the bargaining, and, especially, the begging for money. At a campaign rally in Alexandria last month, he was preceded at the lectern by Jim Moran, a congressman who is a Massachusetts transplant and the consummate Irish pol, and who said of Webb, "I have to tell you, he's not all that comfortable in a political environment." He added, "But it's because he's genuine, he's real."

Moran was followed by Barack Obama, who spoke without consulting notes and cited Newt Gingrich's recommendation that the Democrats adopt the slogan "Had enough?" Obama continued, "Now, I don't quote Newt all the time, but I've got to say, ol' Newt is on to something right here. I don't know about you, but I have had enough of a can't do, won't do, won't even try style of government that we've been seeing in Washington." As Obama elaborated on the Administration's excesses and failures, the crowd took up the antiphonal chant and began cheering almost rapturously.

Then Webb stepped to the lectern. He praised Obama for the power of his words, and began reading, somewhat stiffly, his own speech—a carefully written address that included the observation "You know, back in another century, people like Marx and Engels talked about man being cut away from his land, his agricultural roots, and all the angst that followed from that. You know, today we risk being cut away from our government, from our democracy. The slash-and-burn politics of the Karl Rove era have too often obscured the real issues for America."

Bill Connelly, Jr., a politics professor at Washington and Lee University, in Lexington, Virginia, observes, "He looks like somebody who's making his first serious run for public office. He doesn't ask for votes. He's got to ask. There's an intimacy in local politics that is expected. Part of George Allen's appeal is that he's this down-home country guy with cowboy boots, chewing tobacco, glad-handing—a down-to-earth guy. Retail politics matters, and Webb is not as good at it."

But Webb did have one apparent edge—a warrior profile at a moment when the electorate was unnerved by Iraq and remained uncertain of the

Democrats' ability to take charge of national-security matters. The Webb campaign's strategy had been to run a race reflecting his biography, his sense of command. "We want the whole thing being about leadership," Pete Brodnitz, the campaign's pollster, said. The "Gipper" ad introduced Virginians to the Jim Webb who is still so highly regarded by his former platoon members that his radioman, Mac McGarvey (who lost his right arm in Vietnam), moved in with him for the duration of the campaign, working as his driver.

With George Allen's considerable advantage in amiability neutralized by the "Macaca" gaffe, there was a chance to move the focus of the contest to Webb. Instead, the campaign took an even weirder turn, which effectively pushed Webb off the stage. George Allen's family history became the only story

By mid-September, a month after Allen had welcomed "Macaca" Sidarth to "the real world of Virginia," the word still held a powerful fascination, its etymology probed, its sound repeated, until it assumed an odd familiarity in political discourse. The controversy meshed neatly with another lingering problem for Allen—his alleged racial insensitivity, deriving from a youthful interest in the Old Confederacy. It was reported last spring that Allen wore a Confederate pin in a high-school photograph, and that he'd once kept a Rebel battle flag in his home office. Now his use of a term seen as a slur seemed to confirm the suspicions of those willing to believe that he was a racist.

"Macaca" was still very much in the air when, on September 18th, Allen and Webb arrived at a Fairfax County hotel for a debate. The large ballroom was packed with members of the Chamber of Commerce, reporters, and political partisans. One of the debate panelists, a local television reporter named Peggy Fox, was dubious about Allen's claim that he hadn't intended to insult Sidarth and had invented the word on the spot. "But the word is a racial slur in French-influenced African nations, most notably Tunisia," Fox said. "Your mother's Tunisian. Are you *sure* you never heard the word?" No, Allen replied, he hadn't, and he apologized once again.

But Fox had opened another discomfiting line of inquiry—Allen's heritage on his mother's side. "It has been reported that her father, your grandfather Felix, whom you were given your middle name for, was Jewish," Fox said. "Could you please tell us whether your forebears include Jews"—there was a collective gasp in the room—"and, if so, at which point Jewish identity might have ended?"

The matter of Allen's ethnicity has lurked at the edges of his political career, largely because he has occasionally repeated a story that his mother, a French national who spent her childhood in North Africa, told him and his siblings: that her family had been hounded by the Nazis, and that her father, Felix Lumbroso, had been seized in the night and taken to prison. In August, the New York-based Jewish weekly *The Forward* published an article, by E. J. Kessler, revealing that the Lumbrosos were prominent Sephardic Jews in Tunisia; Felix Lumbroso, a wine importer, was also well known in the Sephardic community in France.

Allen had not discussed the matter with Kessler, and he physically recoiled at Fox's question. The audience booed her for asking it. After lecturing Fox on the First Amendment, Allen demanded, "I would like to ask you, why is that relevant, my religion, Jim's religion, or the religious beliefs of anyone out here?"

That got cheers, but Allen's ethnicity became the next pressing issue of the campaign. The bloggers and the opinion writers questioned his apparent bemusement on the subject, and wondered whether he was trying to hide his Jewishness. "If it was discovered that Allen knew this family history, but attempted to keep it under wraps for whatever reason, it could do great harm to any political campaign," John Mercurio, an analyst with the political tip sheet *Hotline,* said.

Overnight, Allen was transformed from a closet Confederate to a self-hating Jew. And things grew stranger still.

Having stumbled after "Macaca," Allen now acted quickly. He issued a statement declaring, "I embrace and take great pride in every aspect of my diverse heritage, including my Lumbroso family line's Jewish heritage, which I learned about from a recent magazine article and my mother confirmed." He indicated that he had not owned up to his Jewishness at the debate earlier that week out of respect for his mother's privacy. (He also told a reporter for the *Richmond Times-Dispatch,* "I still had a ham sandwich for lunch.") And then Allen made a remarkable appearance on CNN's political show *Situation Room,* with the anchor, Wolf Blitzer, playing the role of Oprah. Allen told of visiting his mother in California in August and confronting her with the story of their family that had been laid out in *The Forward*.

"I was with my mother across the table," he said. "And I asked her. I said, 'You know, there's these rumors flying around here that you're Jewish or, you know, Jewish bloodlines and so forth.' And I asked her, 'Is this—is there anything to this?' And I saw her reaction. And she said, 'Yes, there are.' And I said, 'Well, why didn't you ever tell?' 'I didn't want to tell you. Do you love me? You won't love me as much.' I said, 'Oh, Ma, why would that make—I love you even more. I respect you even more.' When I heard of why she had hid this, for fear of retribution, of stigma, and how that would harm not just her but my father and her children—she was protecting her children. And I said, 'Well, Ma, this just doesn't matter. You know, the Nazis are gone. And it just doesn't matter.'"

Allen has now claimed to embrace his Jewish identity. His discovery, he told Blitzer, had lent him new purpose. "I have been a leader for fighting against anti-Semitism and intolerance," he said. "But now it's personal. And I'm going to use my time here on Earth to continue to fight for freedom and justice, and to make sure intolerance never rears its ugly head in this country or anywhere else in the world."

But Allen was immediately confronted by another surprise. On September 24th, the online magazine *Salon* published a story in which a former teammate of Allen's on the University of Virginia football team alleged that the young Allen had been a rank racist who routinely used the term "nigger." The teammate, a North Carolina radiologist named Ken Shelton, also told a bizarre story of a long-ago hunting trip with Allen. After the hunting party killed a doe, Shelton said, Allen severed the dead animal's head and stuffed it in the mailbox of an African-American family.

The *Times* and the *Washington Post* quickly picked up the story, adding a new allegation. Christopher Taylor, now a professor at the University of Alabama-Birmingham, said he'd once visited Allen's farm and was shocked by something Allen said. The two men had been discussing the problematically large population of turtles in Allen's pond, Taylor claimed, when he asked Allen why he didn't just kill the turtles and eat them. "We don't eat them," Allen was quoted as replying. "The niggers eat them."

Allen again issued angry denials ("ludicrously false"), and his former wife, Anne Waddell, was among those who came forward to defend him. Yes, she said, Taylor had visited the farm, and there were turtles who fed on the Allens' beloved goslings. She herself had fished the predatory turtles from the pond. "The person who ate the turtles," she said, "was our *neighbor*."

Allen now made appearances with African-American leaders; he spoke of his own awakening on racial matters on a pilgrimage to the civil-rights battlefields, such as Selma; he apologized so thoroughly for his misunderstanding of the pain caused by the symbols of the Confederacy that the Sons of Confederate Veterans demanded their own apology from him.

The common wisdom in the political commentariat was that George Allen was finished, at least as a national candidate. Conservative commentators were among the first to jump ship, including *The Weekly Standard* ("Forget the Presidential Campaign. Can he still win the Senate race?"), William F. Buckley, Jr., and the neoconservative writer John Podhoretz, who tagged Allen with a new name: Felix Macacawitz.

Throughout this curious drama, which unfolded in the crucial final weeks of the campaign, Jim Webb might as well have been on vacation. "We'd be just as happy to see it all go away," Pete Brodnitz said. "We're looking forward to beating Allen on the issues, and his lack of leadership." When Webb was finally summoned back to the stage, it was not in the manner he might have wished. Inevitably, he was asked if he had ever uttered what the press, in one of its strained conventions of delicacy, called "the 'n' word." He answered in a way that made it pretty clear that he had. "I don't think that there's anyone who grew up around the South that hasn't had the word pass through their lips at one time in their life," he told a reporter for the *Richmond Times-Dispatch*. That statement prompted demands for clarification, which came, in a fashion, from Webb's spokeswoman, Kristian Denny Todd. Webb didn't want to issue any blanket denial regarding the offensive word, as Allen had, she said. "Jim has not used the word directed at another person. He's never used it himself as a racial slur."

When October arrived, bringing with it the fresh scandal of the Florida congressman Mark Foley's sexual exploitation of House pages, the frenzy in Virginia finally ended, with the race still being considered a toss-up. One possible outcome is that Allen, should he hold his Senate seat, will emerge as an even stronger national candidate, having weathered scrutiny of an intensity usually reserved for presidential nominees.

As for Jim Webb, he seemed, by the ending days of the campaign, to be something less than the Happy Warrior. He had come into the race as a

Democratic iconoclast, hoping to advance the debate on Iraq while broadening the Party, but he had found himself taken captive by George Allen's controversies. He'd shown no taste for this sort of political knife fight, and one sensed that if this first campaign also proved to be his last he would survive the disappointment.

On the other hand, he has made some new friends. As an underdog challenger, running against an incumbent with deep pockets, Webb would inevitably have to come to terms with the Democratic Party's two biggest stars. In late summer, he met privately with Hillary Clinton. "I went into the meeting not really expecting that I would necessarily like her, or that she would like me," he recalled. "But I've got to tell you, I was impressed." Last week, on the day George Allen brought President Bush to Virginia, James Webb and Bill Clinton held a fund-raiser of their own. When the two men met with reporters, Clinton said, "I'm encouraged for my country that we're here together," and he thanked his fellow-Democrat for the "sheer audacity" of his decision to make the race.

The Worst Congress Ever

Matt Taibbi

Rolling Stone | November 11, 2006

It's a generally accepted truth that whatever idealism the Newt Gingrich-led revolutionaries brought with them when the Republicans took control of Congress in 1994 has long since vanished in the moneyed swamp of Washington politics. When Representative Mark Foley resigned in September 2006 for allegedly having inappropriate contact with underage congressional pages, it was just the latest in a series of GOP scandals, including the conviction and imprisonment of Representatives Randy "Duke" Cunningham (for accepting bribes from defense contractors) and Bob Ney (who pled guilty to charges of conspiracy and making false statements in connection with the Jack Abramoff lobbying scandal) as well as the resignation of House majority leader Tom DeLay (after being indicted for the alleged misuse of campaign funds in Texas). In this uproariously indignant essay, published shortly before the 2006 midterm elections, Rolling Stone's *Matt Taibbi enumerates these and the many other sins of the 109th Congress. "They aimed far lower than any other Congress has ever aimed," observes Taibbi, "and they nailed their target."*

There is very little that sums up the record of the U.S. Congress in the Bush years better than a half-mad boy-addict put in charge of a federal commission on child exploitation. After all, if a hairy-necked, raincoat-clad freak like Rep. Mark Foley can get himself named co-chairman of the House Caucus on Missing and Exploited Children, one can only wonder: What the hell else is going on in the corridors of Capitol Hill these days?

These past six years were more than just the most shameful, corrupt and incompetent period in the history of the American legislative branch. These were the years when the U.S. parliament became a historical punch line, a political obscenity on par with the court of Nero or Caligula—a stable of thieves and perverts who committed crimes rolling out of bed in the morning and did their very best to turn the mighty American empire into a debt-laden, despotic backwater, a Burkina Faso with cable.

To be sure, Congress has always been a kind of muddy ideological cemetery, a place where good ideas go to die in a maelstrom of bureaucratic hedging and rank favor-trading. Its whole history is one long love letter to sleaze, idiocy and pigheaded, glacial conservatism. That Congress exists mainly to misspend our money and snore its way through even the direst political crises is something we Americans understand instinctively. "There is no native criminal class except Congress," Mark Twain said—a joke that still provokes a laugh of recognition a hundred years later.

But the 109th Congress is no mild departure from the norm, no slight deviation in an already-underwhelming history. No, this is nothing less than a historic shift in how our democracy is run. The Republicans who control this Congress are revolutionaries, and they have brought their revolutionary vision for the House and Senate quite unpleasantly to fruition. In the past six years they have castrated the political minority, abdicated their oversight responsibilities mandated by the Constitution, enacted a conscious policy of massive borrowing and unrestrained spending, and installed a host of semipermanent mechanisms for transferring legislative power to commercial interests. They aimed far lower than any other Congress has ever aimed, and they nailed their target.

"The 109th Congress is so bad that it makes you wonder if democracy is a failed experiment," says Jonathan Turley, a noted constitutional scholar and the Shapiro Professor of Public Interest Law at George Washington Law School. "I think that if the Framers went to Capitol Hill today, it would shake their confidence in the system they created. Congress has become an exercise of raw power with no principles—and in that environment corruption has flourished. The Republicans in Congress decided from the outset that their future would be inextricably tied to George Bush and his policies. It has become this sad session of members sitting down and drinking Kool-Aid delivered by Karl Rove. Congress became a mere extension of the White House."

The end result is a Congress that has hijacked the national treasury, frantically ceded power to the executive, and sold off the federal government in a private auction. It all happened before our very eyes. In case you missed it, here's how they did it—in five easy steps:

Step One: Rule by Cabal

If you want to get a sense of how Congress has changed under GOP control, just cruise the basement hallways of storied congressional office buildings like Rayburn, Longworth and Cannon. Here, in the minority offices for the various congressional committees, you will inevitably find exactly the same character—a Democratic staffer in rumpled khakis staring blankly off into space, nothing but a single lonely "Landscapes of Monticello" calendar on his wall, his eyes wide and full of astonished, impotent rage, like a rape victim. His skin is as white as the belly of a fish; he hasn't seen the sun in seven years.

It is no big scoop that the majority party in Congress has always found ways of giving the shaft to the minority. But there is a marked difference in the size and the length of the shaft the Republicans have given the Democrats in the past six years. There has been a systematic effort not only to deny the Democrats any kind of power-sharing role in creating or refining legislation but to humiliate them publicly, show them up, pee in their faces. Washington was once a chummy fraternity in which members of both parties golfed together, played in the same pickup basketball games, probably even shared the same mistresses. Now it is a one-party town—and congressional business is conducted accordingly, as though the half of the country that the Democrats represent simply does not exist.

American government was not designed for one-party rule but for rule by consensus—so this current batch of Republicans has found a way to work around that product design. They have scuttled both the spirit and the letter of congressional procedure, turning the lawmaking process into a backroom deal, with power concentrated in the hands of a few chiefs behind the scenes. This reduces the legislature to a Belarus-style rubber stamp, where the opposition is just there for show, human pieces of stagecraft—a fact the Republicans don't even bother to conceal.

"I remember one incident very clearly—I think it was 2001," says Winslow Wheeler, who served for twenty-two years as a Republican staffer in the Senate. "I was working for [New Mexico Republican] Pete Domenici at the time. We were in a Budget Committee hearing and the Democrats were debating what the final result would be. And my boss gets up and he says, 'Why are you saying this? You're not even going to be in the room when the decisions are made.' Just said it right out in the open."

Wheeler's very career is a symbol of a bipartisan age long passed into the history books; he is the last staffer to have served in the offices of a Republican and a Democrat at the same time, having once worked for both Kansas Republican Nancy Kassebaum and Arkansas Democrat David Pryor simultaneously. Today, those Democratic staffers trapped in the basement laugh at the idea that such a thing could ever happen again. These days, they consider themselves lucky if they manage to hold a single hearing on a bill before Rove's well-oiled legislative machine delivers it up for Bush's signature.

The GOP's "take that, bitch" approach to governing has been taken to the greatest heights by the House Judiciary Committee. The committee is chaired by the legendary Republican monster James Sensenbrenner Jr., an ever-sweating, fat-fingered beast who wields his gavel in a way that makes you think he might have used one before in some other arena, perhaps to beat prostitutes to death. Last year, Sensenbrenner became apoplectic when Democrats who wanted to hold a hearing on the Patriot Act invoked a little-known rule that required him to let them have one.

"Naturally, he scheduled it for something like 9 A.M. on a Friday when Congress wasn't in session, hoping that no one would show," recalls a Democratic staffer who attended the hearing. "But we got a pretty good turnout anyway."

Sensenbrenner kept trying to gavel the hearing to a close, but Democrats again pointed to the rules, which said they had a certain amount of time to examine their witnesses. When they refused to stop the proceedings, the chairman did something unprecedented: He simply picked up his gavel and walked out.

"He was like a kid at the playground," the staffer says. And just in case anyone missed the point, Sensenbrenner shut off the lights and cut the microphones on his way out of the room.

For similarly petulant moves by a committee chair, one need look no further than the Ways and Means Committee, where Rep. Bill Thomas—a pugnacious Californian with an enviable ego who was caught having an affair with a pharmaceutical lobbyist—enjoys a reputation rivaling that of the rotund Sensenbrenner. The lowlight of his reign took place just before midnight on July 17th, 2003, when Thomas dumped a "substitute" pension bill on Democrats—one that they had never read—and informed them they would be voting on it the next morning. Infuriated, Democrats stalled by demanding that the bill be read out line by line while they recessed to a side room to confer. But Thomas wanted to move forward—so he called the Capitol police to evict the Democrats.

Thomas is also notorious for excluding Democrats from the conference hearings needed to iron out the differences between House and Senate versions of a bill. According to the rules, conferences have to include at least one public, open meeting. But in the Bush years, Republicans have managed the conference issue with some of the most mind-blowingly juvenile behavior seen in any parliament west of the Russian Duma after happy hour. GOP chairmen routinely call a meeting, bring the press in for a photo op and then promptly shut the proceedings down. "Take a picture, wait five minutes, gavel it out—all for show" is how one Democratic staffer described the process. Then, amazingly, the Republicans sneak off to hold the real conference, forcing the Democrats to turn amateur detective and go searching the Capitol grounds for the meeting. "More often than not, we're trying to figure out where the conference is," says one House aide.

In one legendary incident, Rep. Charles Rangel went searching for a secret conference being held by Thomas. When he found the room where Republicans closeted themselves, he knocked and knocked on the door, but no one answered. A House aide compares the scene to the famous "Land Shark" skit from *Saturday Night Live,* with everyone hiding behind the door afraid to make a sound. "Rangel was the land shark, I guess," the aide jokes. But the real punch line came when Thomas finally opened the door.

"This meeting," he informed Rangel, "is only open to the coalition of the willing."

Republican rudeness and bluster make for funny stories, but the phenomenon has serious consequences. The collegial atmosphere that once prevailed helped Congress form a sense of collective identity that it needed to fulfill its constitutional role as a check on the power of the other two branches of government. It also enabled Congress to pass legislation with a wide mandate, legislation that had been negotiated between the leaders of both parties. For this reason Republican and Democratic leaders traditionally maintained cordial relationships with each other—the model being the collegiality between House Speaker Nicholas Longworth and Minority Leader John Nance Garner in the 1920s. The two used to hold daily meetings over drinks and even rode to work together.

Although cooperation between the two parties has ebbed and flowed over the years, historians note that Congress has taken strong bipartisan action in virtually every administration. It was Sen. Harry Truman who instigated investigations of wartime profiteering under FDR, and Republicans Howard Baker and Lowell Weicker Jr. played pivotal roles on the Senate Watergate Committee that nearly led to Nixon's impeachment.

But those days are gone. "We haven't seen any congressional investigations like this during the last six years," says David Mayhew, a professor of political science at Yale who has studied Congress for four decades. "These days, Congress doesn't seem to be capable of doing this sort of thing. Too much nasty partisanship."

One of the most depressing examples of one-party rule is the Patriot Act. The measure was originally crafted in classic bipartisan fashion in the Judiciary Committee, where it passed by a vote of thirty-six to zero, with famed liberals like Barney Frank and Jerrold Nadler saying aye. But when the bill was sent to the Rules Committee, the Republicans simply chucked the approved bill and replaced it with a new, far more repressive version, apparently written at the direction of then-Attorney General John Ashcroft.

"They just rewrote the whole bill," says Rep. James McGovern, a minority member of the Rules Committee. "All that committee work was just for show."

To ensure that Democrats can't alter any of the last-minute changes, Republicans have overseen a monstrous increase in the number of "closed" rules—bills that go to the floor for a vote without any possibility of amendment. This tactic undercuts the very essence of democracy: In a bicameral system, allowing bills to be debated openly is the only way that the minority can have a real impact, by offering amendments to legislation drafted by the majority.

In 1977, when Democrats held a majority in the House, 85 percent of all bills were open to amendment. But by 1994, the last year Democrats ran the House, that number had dropped to 30 percent—and Republicans were seriously pissed. "You know what the closed rule means," Rep. Lincoln Diaz-Balart of Florida thundered on the House floor. "It means no discussion, no amendments. That is profoundly undemocratic." When Republicans took control of the House, they vowed to throw off the gag rules imposed by Democrats. On opening day of the 104th Congress, then-Rules Committee chairman Gerald Solomon announced his intention to institute free debate on the floor. "Instead of having 70 percent closed rules," he declared, "we are going to have 70 percent open and unrestricted rules."

How has Solomon fared? Of the 111 rules introduced in the first session of this Congress, only twelve were open. Of those, eleven were appropriations bills, which are traditionally open. That left just one open vote—H. Res. 255, the Federal Deposit Insurance Reform Act of 2005.

In the second session of this Congress? Not a single open rule, outside of appropriation votes. Under the Republicans, amendable bills have been a genuine Washington rarity, the upside-down eight-leafed clover of legislative politics.

When bills do make it to the floor for a vote, the debate generally resembles what one House aide calls "preordained Kabuki." Republican leaders in the Bush era have mastered a new congressional innovation: the one-vote victory. Rather than seeking broad consensus, the leadership cooks up some hideously expensive, favor-laden boondoggle and then scales it back bit by bit. Once they're in striking range, they send the fucker to the floor and beat in the brains of the fence-sitters with threats and favors until enough members cave in and pass the damn thing. It is, in essence, a legislative microcosm of the electoral strategy that Karl Rove has employed to such devastating effect.

A classic example was the vote for the Central American Free Trade Agreement, the union-smashing, free-trade monstrosity passed in 2005. As has often been the case in the past six years, the vote was held late at night, away from the prying eyes of the public, who might be horrified by what they see. Thanks to such tactics, the 109th is known as the "Dracula" Congress: Twenty bills have been brought to a vote between midnight and 7 A.M.

CAFTA actually went to vote early—at 11:02 P.M. When the usual fifteen-minute voting period expired, the nays were up, 180 to 175. Republicans then held the vote open for another forty-seven minutes while GOP leaders cruised the aisles like the family elders from *The Texas Chainsaw Massacre,* frantically chopping at the legs and arms of Republicans who opposed the measure. They even roused the president out of bed to help kick ass for the vote, passing a cell phone with Bush on the line around the House cloakroom like a bong. Rep. Robin Hayes of North Carolina was approached by House Speaker Dennis Hastert, who told him, "Negotiations are open. Put on the table the things that your district and people need and we'll get them." After receiving assurances that the Administration would help textile manufacturers in his home state by restricting the flow of cheap Chinese imports, Hayes switched his vote to yea. CAFTA ultimately passed by two votes at 12:03 A.M.

Closed rules, shipwrecked bills, secret negotiations, one-vote victories. The result of all this is a Congress where there is little or no open debate and virtually no votes are left to chance; all the important decisions are made in backroom deals, and what you see on C-Span is just empty theater, the world's most expensive trained-dolphin act. The constant here is a political strategy of conducting congressional business with as little outside input as possible, rejecting the essentially conservative tradition of rule-by-consensus in favor of a more revolutionary strategy of rule by cabal.

"This Congress has thrown caution to the wind," says Turley, the constitutional scholar. "They have developed rules that are an abuse of majority power. Keeping votes open by freezing the clock, barring minority senators from negotiations on important conference issues—it is a record that the Republicans should now dread. One of the concerns that Republicans have about losing Congress is that they will have to live under the practices and rules they have created. The abuses that served them in the majority could come back to haunt them in the minority."

Step Two: Work as Little as Possible—and Screw Up What Little You Do

It's Thursday evening, September 28th [2006], and the Senate is putting the finishing touches on the Military Commissions Act of 2006, colloquially known as the "torture bill." It's a law even Stalin would admire, one that throws habeas corpus in the trash, legalizes a vast array of savage interrogation techniques and generally turns the president of the United States into a kind of turbo-charged Yoruba witch doctor, with nearly unlimited snatching powers. The bill is a fall-from-Eden moment in American history, a potentially disastrous step toward authoritarianism—but what is most disturbing about it, beyond the fact that it's happening, is that the senators are *hurrying* to get it done.

In addition to ending generations of bipartisanship and instituting one-party rule, our national legislators in the Bush years are guilty of something even more fundamental: They suck at their jobs.

They don't work many days, don't pass many laws, and the few laws they're forced to pass, they pass late. In fact, in every year that Bush has been president, Congress has failed to pass more than three of the eleven annual appropriations bills on time.

That figures into tonight's problems. At this very moment, as the torture bill goes to a vote, there are only a few days left until the beginning of the fiscal year—and not one appropriations bill has been passed so far. That's why these assholes are hurrying to bag this torture bill: They want to finish in time to squeeze in a measly two hours of debate tonight on the half-trillion-dollar defense-appropriations bill they've blown off until now. The plan is to then wrap things up tomorrow before splitting Washington for a month of real work, i.e., campaigning.

Sen. Pat Leahy of Vermont comments on this rush to torture during the final, frenzied debate. "Over 200 years of jurisprudence in this country," Leahy pleads, "and following an hour of debate, we get rid of it?"

Yawns, chatter, a few sets of rolling eyes—yeah, whatever, Pat. An hour later, the torture bill is law. Two hours after that, the diminutive chair of the Defense Appropriations Subcommittee, Sen. Ted Stevens, reads off the summary of the military-spending bill to a mostly empty hall; since the members all need their sleep and most have left early, the "debate" on the biggest spending bill of the year is conducted before a largely phantom audience.

"Mr. President," Stevens begins, eyeing the few members present. "There are only four days left in the fiscal year. The 2007 defense appropriations conference report must be signed into law by the president before Saturday at midnight. . . ."

Watching Ted Stevens spend half a trillion dollars is like watching a junkie pull a belt around his biceps with his teeth. You get the sense he could do it just as fast in the dark. When he finishes his summary—$436 billion in defense spending, including $70 billion for the Iraq "emergency"—he fucks off and leaves the hall. A few minutes later, Sen. Tom Coburn of Oklahoma—one of the so-called honest Republicans who has clashed with his own party's leadership on spending issues—appears in the hall and whines to the empty room about all the lavish pork projects and sheer unadulterated waste jammed into the bill. But aside from a bored-looking John Cornyn of Texas, who is acting as president pro tempore, and a couple of giggling, suit-clad pages, there is no one in the hall to listen to him.

In the Sixties and Seventies, Congress met an average of 162 days a year. In the Eighties and Nineties, the average went down to 139 days. This year, the second session of the 109th Congress will set the all-time record for fewest days worked by a U.S. Congress: ninety-three. That means that House members will collect their $165,000 paychecks for only three months of actual work.

What this means is that the current Congress will not only beat but shatter the record for laziness set by the notorious "Do-Nothing" Congress of 1948, which met for a combined 252 days between the House and the Senate. This Congress—the Do-Even-Less Congress—met for 218 days, just over half a year, between the House and the Senate *combined.*

And even those numbers don't come close to telling the full story. Those who actually work on the Hill will tell you that a great many of those "workdays" were shameless mail-ins, half-days at best. Congress has arranged things now so that the typical workweek on the Hill begins late on Tuesday and ends just after noon on Thursday, to give members time to go home for the four-day weekend. This is borne out in the numbers: On nine of its "workdays" this year, the House held not a single vote—meeting for less than eleven minutes. The Senate managed to top the House's feat, pulling off three workdays this year that lasted less than one minute. All told, a full 15 percent of the Senate's workdays lasted less than four hours. Figuring for half-days, in fact, the 109th Congress probably worked almost two months less than that "Do-Nothing" Congress.

Congressional laziness comes at a high price. By leaving so many appropriations bills unpassed by the beginning of the new fiscal year, Congress forces big chunks of the government to rely on "continuing resolutions" for their funding. Why is this a problem? Because under congressional rules,

CRs are funded at the lowest of three levels: the level approved by the House, the level approved by the Senate or the level approved from the previous year. Thanks to wide discrepancies between House and Senate appropriations for social programming, CRs effectively operate as a backdoor way to slash social programs. It's also a nice way for congressmen to get around having to pay for expensive-ass programs they voted for, like No Child Left Behind and some of the other terminally underfunded boondoggles of the Bush years.

"The whole point of passing appropriations bills is that Congress is supposed to make small increases in programs to account for things like the increase in population," says Adam Hughes, director of federal fiscal policy for OMB Watch, a nonpartisan watchdog group. "It's their main job." Instead, he says, the reliance on CRs "leaves programs underfunded."

Instead of dealing with its chief constitutional duty—approving all government spending—Congress devotes its time to dumb bullshit. "This Congress spent a week and a half debating Terri Schiavo—it never made appropriations a priority," says Hughes. In fact, Congress leaves itself so little time to pass the real appropriations bills that it winds up rolling them all into one giant monstrosity known as an Omnibus bill and passing it with little or no debate. Rolling eight-elevenths of all federal spending into a single bill that hits the floor a day or two before the fiscal year ends does not leave much room to check the fine print. "It allows a lot more leeway for fiscal irresponsibility," says Hughes.

A few years ago, when Democratic staffers in the Senate were frantically poring over a massive Omnibus bill they had been handed the night before the scheduled vote, they discovered a tiny provision that had not been in any of the previous versions. The item would have given senators on the Appropriations Committee access to the private records of any taxpayer—essentially endowing a few selected hacks in the Senate with the license to snoop into the private financial information of all Americans.

"We were like, "What the hell is this?'" says one Democratic aide familiar with the incident. "It was the most egregious thing imaginable. It was just lucky we caught them."

Step Three: Let the President Do Whatever He Wants

The Constitution is very clear on the responsibility of Congress to serve as a check on the excesses of the executive branch. The House and Senate, after all, are supposed to pass all laws—the president is simply supposed to execute them. Over the years, despite some ups and downs, Congress has been fairly consistent in upholding this fundamental responsibility, regardless of which party controlled the legislative branch. Elected representatives saw themselves as beholden not to their own party or the president but to the *institution* of Congress itself. The model of congressional independence was Sen. William Fulbright, who took on McCarthy, Kennedy, Johnson and Nixon with equal vigor during the course of his long career.

"Fulbright behaved the same way with Nixon as he did with Johnson," says Wheeler, the former Senate aide who worked on both sides of the aisle. "You wouldn't see that today."

In fact, the Republican-controlled Congress has created a new standard for the use of oversight powers. That standard seems to be that when a Democratic president is in power, there are no matters too stupid or meaningless to be investigated fully—but when George Bush is president, no evidence of corruption or incompetence is shocking enough to warrant congressional attention. One gets the sense that Bush would have to drink the blood of Christian babies to inspire hearings in Congress—and only then if he did it during a nationally televised State of the Union address and the babies were from Pennsylvania, where Senate Judiciary chairman Arlen Specter was running ten points behind in an election year.

The numbers bear this out. From the McCarthy era in the 1950s through the Republican takeover of Congress in 1995, no Democratic committee chairman issued a subpoena without either minority consent or a committee vote. In the Clinton years, Republicans chucked that long-standing arrangement and issued more than 1,000 subpoenas to investigate alleged administration and Democratic misconduct, reviewing more than 2 million pages of government documents.

Guess how many subpoenas have been issued to the White House since George Bush took office? Zero—that's right, zero, the same as the number of open rules debated this year; two fewer than the number of appropriations bills passed on time.

And the cost? Republicans in the Clinton years spent more than $35 million investigating the Administration. The total amount of taxpayer funds spent, when independent counsels are taken into account, was more than $150 million. Included in that number was $2.2 million to investigate former HUD secretary Henry Cisneros for lying about improper payments he made to a mistress. In contrast, today's Congress spent barely half a million dollars investigating the outright fraud and government bungling that followed Hurricane Katrina, the largest natural disaster in American history.

"Oversight is one of the most important functions of Congress—perhaps more important than legislating," says Rep. Henry Waxman. "And the Republicans have completely failed at it. I think they decided that they were going to be good Republicans first and good legislators second."

As the ranking minority member of the Government Reform Committee, Waxman has earned a reputation as the chief Democratic muckraker, obsessively cranking out reports on official misconduct and incompetence. Among them is a lengthy document detailing all of the wrongdoing by the Bush administration that should have been investigated —and would have been, in any other era. The litany of fishy behavior left uninvestigated in the Bush years includes the manipulation of intelligence on Saddam Hussein's weapons of mass destruction, the mistreatment of Iraqi detainees, the leak of Valerie Plame's CIA status, the award of Halliburton contracts, the White House response to Katrina, secret NSA wiretaps, Dick Cheney's energy task force, the withholding of Medicare cost estimates, the administration's politicization of science, contract abuses at Homeland Security and lobbyist influence at the EPA.

Waxman notes that the failure to investigate these issues has actually hurt the president, leaving potentially fatal flaws in his policies unexamined even by those in his own party. Without proper congressional oversight, small disasters like the misuse of Iraq intelligence have turned into huge, festering, unsolvable fiascoes like the Iraq occupation. Republicans in Congress who stonewalled investigations of the Administration "thought they were doing Bush a favor," says Waxman. "But they did him the biggest disservice of all."

Congress has repeatedly refused to look at any aspect of the war. In 2003, Republicans refused to allow a vote on a bill introduced by Waxman that would have established an independent commission to review the false claims Bush made in asking Congress to declare war on Iraq. That same year, the chair of the House Intelligence Committee, Porter Goss, refused to hold hearings on whether the Administration had forged evidence of the nuclear threat allegedly posed by Iraq. A year later the chair of the Government Reform Committee, Tom Davis, refused to hold hearings on new evidence casting doubt on the "nuclear tubes" cited by the

Bush administration before the war. Sen. Pat Roberts, who pledged to issue a Senate Intelligence Committee report after the 2004 election on whether the Bush administration had misled the public before the invasion, changed his mind after the president won re-election. "I think it would be a monumental waste of time to re-plow this ground any further," Roberts said.

Sensenbrenner has done his bit to squelch any debate over Iraq. He refused a request by John Conyers and more than fifty other Democrats for hearings on the famed "Downing Street Memo," the internal British document that stated that Bush had "fixed" the intelligence about the war, and he was one of three committee chairs who rejected requests for hearings on the abuse of Iraqi detainees. Despite an international uproar over Abu Ghraib, Congress spent only twelve hours on hearings on the issue. During the Clinton administration, by contrast, the Republican Congress spent 140 hours investigating the president's alleged misuse of his Christmas-card greeting list.

"You talk to many Republicans in Congress privately, and they will tell you how appalled they are by the administration's diminishment of civil liberties and the constant effort to keep fear alive," says Turley, who testified as a constitutional scholar in favor of the Clinton impeachment. "Yet those same members slavishly vote with the White House. What's most alarming about the 109th has been the massive erosion of authority in Congress. There has always been partisanship, but this is different. Members have become robotic in the way they vote."

Perhaps the most classic example of failed oversight in the Bush era came in a little-publicized hearing of the Senate Armed Services Committee held on February 13th, 2003—just weeks before the invasion of Iraq. The hearing offered senators a rare opportunity to grill Secretary of Defense Donald Rumsfeld and top Pentagon officials on a wide variety of matters, including the fairly important question of whether they even had a fucking plan for the open-ended occupation of a gigantic hostile foreign population halfway around the planet. This was the biggest bite that Congress would have at the Iraq apple before the war, and given the gravity of the issue, it should have been a beast of a hearing.

But it wasn't to be. In a meeting that lasted two hours and fifty-three minutes, only one question was asked about the military's readiness on the eve of the invasion. Sen. John Warner, the committee's venerable and powerful chairman, asked Gen. Richard Myers if the U.S. was ready to fight simultaneously in both Iraq and North Korea, if necessary.

Myers answered, "Absolutely."

And that was it. The entire exchange lasted fifteen seconds. The rest of the session followed a pattern familiar to anyone who has watched a hearing on C-Span: The members, when they weren't reading or chatting with one another, used their time with witnesses almost exclusively to address parochial concerns revolving around pork projects in their own districts. Warner set the tone in his opening remarks; after announcing that U.S. troops preparing to invade Iraq could count on his committee's "strongest support," the senator from Virginia quickly turned to the question of how the war would affect the budget for Navy shipbuilding, which, he said, was not increasing "as much as we wish." Not that there's a huge Navy shipyard in Newport News, Virginia, or anything.

Other senators followed suit. Daniel Akaka was relatively uninterested in Iraq but asked about reports that Korea might have a missile that could reach his home state of Hawaii. David Pryor of Arkansas used his time to tout the wonders of military bases in Little Rock and Pine Bluff. When the senators weren't eating up their allotted time in this fashion, they were usually currying favor with the generals. Warner himself nicely encapsulated the obsequious tone of the session when he complimented Rumsfeld for having his shit so together on the war.

"I think your response reflects that we have given a good deal of consideration," Warner said. "That we have clear plans in place and are ready to proceed."

We all know how that turned out.

Step Four: Spend, Spend, Spend

There is a simple reason that members of Congress don't waste their time providing any oversight of the executive branch: There's nothing in it for them. "What they've all figured out is that there's no political payoff in oversight," says Wheeler, the former congressional staffer. "But there's a big payoff in pork."

When one considers that Congress has forsaken hearings and debate, conspired to work only three months a year, completely ditched its constitutional mandate to provide oversight and passed very little in the way of meaningful legislation, the question arises: What do they do?

The answer is easy: They spend. When Bill Clinton left office, the nation had a budget surplus of $236 billion. Today, thanks to Congress, the budget is $296 billion in the hole. This year, more than 65 percent of all the money borrowed in the entire world will be borrowed by America, a statistic fueled by the speed-junkie spending habits of our supposedly "fiscally conservative" Congress. It took forty-two presidents before George W. Bush to borrow $1 trillion; under Bush, Congress has more than doubled that number in six years. And more often than not, we are borrowing from countries the sane among us would prefer not to be indebted to: The U.S. shells out $77 billion a year in interest to foreign creditors, including payment on the $300 billion we currently owe China.

What do they spend that money on? In the age of Jack Abramoff, that is an ugly question to even contemplate. But let's take just one bill, the so-called energy bill, a big, hairy, favor-laden bitch of a law that started out as the wet dream of Dick Cheney's energy task force and spent four long years leaving grease-tracks on every set of palms in the Capitol before finally becoming law in 2005.

Like a lot of laws in the Bush era, it was crafted with virtually no input from the Democrats, who were excluded from the conference process. And during the course of the bill's gestation period we were made aware that many of its provisions were more or less openly for sale, as in the case of a small electric utility from Kansas called Westar Energy.

Westar wanted a provision favorable to its business inserted in the bill—and in an internal company memo, it acknowledged that members of Congress had requested Westar donate money to their campaigns in exchange for the provision. The members included former Louisiana congressman Billy Tauzin and current Energy and Commerce chairman Joe Barton of Texas. "They have made this request in lieu of contributions made to their own campaigns," the memo noted. The total amount of Westar's contributions was $58,200.

Keep in mind, that number—fifty-eight grand—was for a *single* favor. The energy bill was loaded with them. Between 2001 and the passage of the bill, energy companies donated $115 million to federal politicians, with 75 percent of the money going to Republicans. When the bill finally passed, it contained $6 billion in subsidies for the oil industry, much of which was funneled through a company with ties to Majority Leader Tom DeLay. It included an exemption from the Safe Drinking Water Act for companies that use a methane-drilling technique called "hydraulic fracturing"—one of the widest practitioners of which is Halliburton. And it included billions in subsidies for the construction of new coal plants and billions more in loan guarantees to enable the coal and nuclear industries to borrow money at bargain-basement interest rates.

Favors for campaign contributors, exemptions for polluters, shifting the costs of private projects on to the public—these are the specialties of this Congress. They seldom miss an opportunity to impoverish the states we live in and up the bottom line of their campaign contributors. All this time—while Congress did nothing about Iraq, Katrina, wiretapping, Mark Foley's boy-madness or anything else of import—it has been all about pork, all about political favors, all about budget "earmarks" set aside for expensive and often useless projects in their own districts. In 2000, Congress passed 6,073 earmarks; by 2005, that number had risen to 15,877. They got better at it every year. It's the one thing they're good at.

Even worse, this may well be the first Congress ever to lose control of the government's finances. For the past six years, it has essentially been writing checks without keeping an eye on its balance. When you do that, unpleasant notices eventually start appearing in the mail. In 2003, the inspector general of the Defense Department reported to Congress that the military's financial-management systems did not comply with "generally accepted accounting principles" and that the department "cannot currently provide adequate evidence supporting various material amounts on the financial statements."

Translation: The Defense Department can no longer account for its money. "It essentially can't be audited," says Wheeler, the former congressional staffer. "And nobody did anything about it. That's the job of Congress, but they don't care anymore."

So not only does Congress not care what intelligence was used to get into the war, what the plan was supposed to be once we got there, what goes on in military prisons in Iraq and elsewhere, how military contracts are being given away and to whom—it doesn't even give a shit what happens to the half-trillion bucks it throws at the military every year.

Not to say, of course, that this Congress hasn't made an effort to reform itself. In the wake of the Jack Abramoff scandal, and following a public uproar over the widespread abuse of earmarks, both the House and the Senate passed their own versions of an earmark reform bill this year. But when the two chambers couldn't agree on a final version, the House was left to pass its own watered-down measure in the waning days of the most recent session. This pathetically, almost historically half-assed attempt at reforming corruption should tell you all you need to know about the current Congress.

The House rule will force legislators to attach their names to all earmarks. Well, not all earmarks. Actually, the new rule applies only to *nonfederal* funding—money for local governments, nonprofits and universities. And the rule will remain in effect only for the remainder of this congressional year—in other words, for the few remaining days of business after lawmakers return to Washington following the election season. After that, it's back to business as usual next year.

That is what passes for "corruption reform" in this Congress—forcing lawmakers to put their names on a tiny fraction of all earmarks. For a couple of days.

Step Five: Line Your Own Pockets

Anyone who wants to get a feel for the kinds of beasts that have been roaming the grounds of the congressional zoo in the past six years need only look at the deranged, handwritten letter that convicted bribetaker and GOP ex-congressman Randy "Duke" Cunningham recently sent from prison to Marcus Stern, the reporter who helped bust him. In it, Cunningham—who was convicted last year of taking $2.4 million in cash, rugs, furniture and jewelry from a defense contractor called MZM—bitches out Stern in the broken, half-literate penmanship of a six-year-old put in time-out.

"Each time you print it hurts my family And now I have lost them Along with Everything I have worked for during my 64 years of life," Cunningham wrote. "I am human not an Animal to keep whiping [sic]. I made some decissions [sic] Ill be sorry for the rest of my life."

The amazing thing about Cunningham's letter is not his utter lack of remorse, or his insistence on blaming defense contractor Mitchell Wade for ratting him out ("90% of what has happed [sic] is Wade," he writes), but his frantic, almost epic battle with the English language. It is clear that the same Congress that put a drooling child-chaser like Mark Foley in charge of a House caucus on child exploitation also named Cunningham, a man who can barely write his own name in the ground with a stick, to a similarly appropriate position. Ladies and gentlemen, we give you the former chairman of the House Subcommittee on Human Intelligence Analysis and Counterintelligence:

"As truth will come out and you will find out how liablest [sic] you have & will be. Not once did you list the positives. Education Man of the Year . . . hospital funding, jobs, Hiway [sic] funding, border security, Megans law my bill. Tuna Dolfin [sic] my bill . . . and every time you wanted an expert on the wars who did you call. No Marcus you write About how I died"

How liablest you have & will be? What the fuck does that even mean? This guy sat on the Appropriations Committee for years—no wonder Congress couldn't pass any spending bills!

This is Congress in the Bush years, in a nutshell—a guy who takes $2 million in bribes from a contractor, whooping it up in turtlenecks and pajama bottoms with young women on a contractor-provided yacht named after himself (the "Duke-Stir"), and not only is he shocked when he's caught, he's too dumb to even understand that he's been guilty of anything.

This kind of appalling moral blindness, a sort of high-functioning, sociopathic stupidity, has been a consistent characteristic of the numerous Republicans indicted during the Bush era. Like all revolutionaries, they seem to feel entitled to break rules in the name of whatever the hell it is they think they're doing. And when caught breaking said rules with wads of cash spilling out of their pockets, they appear genuinely indignant at accusations of wrongdoing. Former House Majority Leader and brazen fuckhead Tom DeLay, after finally being indicted for money laundering, seemed amazed that anyone would bring him into court.

"I have done nothing wrong," he declared. "I have violated no law, no regulation, no rule of the House." Unless, of course, you count the charges against him for conspiring to inject illegal contributions into state elections in Texas "with the intent that a felony be committed."

It was the same when Ohio's officious jackass of a (soon-to-be-ex) Congressman Bob Ney finally went down for accepting $170,000 in trips from Abramoff in exchange for various favors. Even as the evidence piled high, Ney denied any wrongdoing. When he finally did plead guilty, he blamed the sauce. "A dependence on alcohol has been a problem for me," he said.

Abramoff, incidentally, was another Republican with a curious inability to admit wrongdoing even after conviction; even now he confesses only to trying too hard to "save the world." But everything we know about

Abramoff suggests that Congress has embarked on a never-ending party, a wild daisy-chain of golf junkets, skybox tickets and casino trips. Money is everywhere and guys like Abramoff found ways to get it to guys like Ney, who made the important discovery that even a small entry in the Congressional Record can get you a tee time at St. Andrews.

Although Ney is so far the only congressman to win an all-expenses trip to prison as a result of his relationship with Abramoff, nearly a dozen other House Republicans are known to have done favors for him. Rep. Jim McCrery of Louisiana, who accepted some $36,000 from Abramoff-connected donors, helped prevent the Jena Band of Choctaw Indians from opening a casino that would have competed with Abramoff's clients. Rep. Deborah Pryce, who sent a letter to Interior Secretary Gale Norton opposing the Jena casino, received $8,000 from the Abramoff money machine. Rep. John Doolittle, whose wife was hired to work for Abramoff's sham charity, also intervened on behalf of the lobbyist's clients.

Then there was DeLay and his fellow Texan, Rep. Pete Sessions, who did Abramoff's bidding after accepting gifts and junkets. So much energy devoted to smarmy little casino disputes at a time when the country was careening toward disaster in Iraq: no time for oversight but plenty of time for golf.

For those who didn't want to go the black-bag route, there was always the legal jackpot. Billy Tauzin scarcely waited a week after leaving office to start a $2 million-a-year job running PhRMA, the group that helped him push through a bill prohibiting the government from negotiating lower prices for prescription drugs. Tauzin also became the all-time poster boy for pork absurdity when a "greenbonds initiative" crafted in his Energy and Commerce Committee turned out to be a subsidy to build a Hooters in his home state of Louisiana.

The greed and laziness of the 109th Congress has reached such epic proportions that it has finally started to piss off the public. In an April poll by CBS News, fully two-thirds of those surveyed said that Congress has achieved "less than it usually does during a typical two-year period." A recent Pew poll found that the chief concerns that occupy Congress—gay marriage and the inheritance tax—are near the bottom of the public's list of worries. Those at the top—education, health care, Iraq and Social Security—were mostly blown off by Congress. Even a Fox News poll found that 53 percent of voters say Congress isn't "working on issues important to most Americans."

One could go on and on about the scandals and failures of the past six years; to document them all would take . . . well, it would take more than ninety-three fucking days, that's for sure. But you can boil the whole sordid mess down to a few basic concepts. Sloth. Greed. Abuse of power. Hatred of democracy. Government as a cheap backroom deal, finished in time for thirty-six holes of the world's best golf. And brains too stupid to be ashamed of any of it. If we have learned nothing else in the Bush years, it's that this Congress cannot be reformed. The only way to change it is to get rid of it.

Fortunately, we still get that chance once in a while.

Democrats: The Big Surprise

Elizabeth Drew

the *New York Review of Books* | January 11, 2007

With the Republicans beset by scandals and "Bush fatigue," the Democratic party went into the 2006 midterm elections hoping for the best, but steeled for yet another disappointment. When the dust finally cleared, they found they'd gotten all they could have wished for, and then some: The Dems gained thirty seats in the House, leaving them with a thirty-one-seat majority, and won a series of close races to pick up six seats in the Senate, giving them a 51-49 edge over the GOP in the upper chamber (a margin that included independent Senators Joe Lieberman of Connecticut and Bernie Sanders of Vermont, both of whom had announced they would caucus with the Democrats).

The nationwide popular vote was even more telling, with the Democrats posting a 52-45.6 percent edge over the Republicans in the overall votes cast for House members, and a 53.6-42.4 percent edge in votes cast for Senate nominees. In this New York Review of Books *article, veteran Washington correspondent Elizabeth Drew analyzes how the Democrats swept to victory, and reviews their first days as the new majority power in Congress.*

Perhaps, just perhaps, the 2006 midterm elections will give pause to the "long-term trend" school—industry, actually—of American politics. For years, pundits have been telling us, and it became the received wisdom, that the Republicans have been and will continue to be dominant in American politics. We have been through this many times: Richard Nixon, with the advice of the young political analyst Kevin Phillips, was building a "New American Majority." That lasted eight years at the most. Then, during the Reagan years, we had the "Republican lock" on the Electoral College—the theory that Republican domination of Southern and noncoastal Western states gave them a permanent edge in the Electoral College vote. (Inconveniently, Democratic presidents interrupted these "trends.")

More recently, political commentators have bombarded us with the theory that George W. Bush's guru (or "architect") Karl Rove had designed a successful strategy to achieve lasting Republican dominance. This strategy was more thorough, if not more cold-blooded, than earlier ones—building a new base of right-wing conservatives and Christian evangelicals combined with the money-raising power of K Street lobbyists, and the companion efforts to assure Republican rule by such enforcers as Grover Norquist, the president of Americans for Tax Reform.

In fact, K Street will not change a great deal even though the Democrats are in charge on Capitol Hill and Tom DeLay is gone. Democrats have their own K Street connections, and the lobbying firms, anticipating a Democratic win in November, had already begun recruiting more Democrats, and raising more money for the Democratic Party. The Republican lobbyists have no lack of business: they will now devote their efforts to trying to block new Democratic legislation that their clients oppose, such as lower drug prices in the prescription drug program, or elimination of tax breaks. The question is whether, like the Republicans, the Democrats will allow their own lobbyist allies to have the run of Capitol Hill, even letting them write bills there.

Another question is how strong Bush's base will continue to be, against other forces in the electorate. After the 2000 election Bush and Rove concluded that the way to preserve power was to build a conservative base that would turn out in force the next time. They courted the Christian right by opposing stem-cell research using human embryos; calling for a constitutional amendment banning gay marriage; signing a law against "partial birth abortion"; and putting conservative, apparently anti-abortion judges on the Supreme Court and the lower courts as well. Bush also set up in 2001 the White House Office of Faith-Based and Community Initiatives, from which both its first head as well as a deputy head later resigned, saying that it was being exploited for political purposes.[1] (David Kuo, the former deputy, has written that it was used in 2004 to target evangelical voters in twenty races.[2]) From Ronald Reagan on, Republicans have appealed for support from Christian right organizations, but now the Christian right has become not only an integral part of the Republican Party but also the party's main constituency. In an interview, the astute Republican lobbyist and activist Vin Weber said of the Christian conservatives, "They really are to the Republican party what labor or African-Americans are to the Democrats—similar in numbers and impact." Weber told me, "The evangelical vote is simply larger than that of other Republican constituencies."

The Rove "genius," his daunting get-out-the-vote machinery mobilizing Republican activists on the ground, as well as his ability to frame issues from gay marriage to fighting terrorism in a way that puts Democrats on the defensive, added to the mystique of Republican invincibility. But Rove's real innovation was to develop a far more sophisticated "targeting" operation —figuring out, for example, where the Christian right and evangelical voters are to be found, and making sure they get to the polls.

Rove's vaunted targeting operation, first notable in 2002, wasn't enough this time. Mechanics alone can't win elections. The embrace of Christian conservatives had helped push the Republican Party far to the right, leaving more centrist and independent voters up for grabs. In the 2006 elections, 59 percent of independents voted for Democrats—up from 49 percent in 2004. Immigration was supposed to be a "hot-button" issue for Republicans this year, but at best it was a dud. Even the loudmouth J.D. Hayworth, an Arizona congressman who exploited the opposition to immigration that was supposedly rampant, lost his seat. Democrats made strong gains among Hispanics. Bush's position against federal funding for stem-cell research using human embryos actually helped some Democratic candidates, such as Claire McCaskill, who won a narrow victory over the Republican incumbent in the Missouri Senate race.

The long-term trend theories fail to foresee the ways events can affect an election: a disastrous war, a botched response to a devastating hurricane, an economy that isn't working for the middle class. They also don't anticipate an eruption of scandals—this time the ethics violations of Republicans who had dealings with Jack Abramoff, and, toward the end of the campaign, the discovery that Florida Republican congressman Mark Foley had been sending highly suggestive messages to Capitol Hill pages, which the Republican House leadership apparently had been covering up.

In fact, the last two presidential elections had already shown that the electorate is closely divided, a conclusion reinforced by the 2006 midterm elections. There is also the plain fact that some candidates are better politicians than others, and that some may stumble. In Virginia, for example, starting well before the Senate race began, it was the wisdom among the Washington consultants, journalists, and politicians who all talk to one another that George Allen, an amiable man not known for his intellect, was a shoo-in for reelection and a likely and even potent candidate for president in 2008. But Allen's goofs—starting with his "macaca" moment, which put him under closer scrutiny—caused his own defeat, albeit narrowly. (He even lost the southern Virginia district, known as "red-neck" territory, where he had been so offensive to S.R. Sidarth, a young American of Indian descent.)

For the 2006 midterm elections, Rove and Bush reached back for the same playbook they used in the 2002 midterm elections. The basic strategy both times was to paint the opposition party as weak on protecting the country. Rove signaled its return with a speech to the Republican National Committee in January 2006 that was eerily similar to the one he had given to the same group four years earlier: both times, his message was that the Republicans should raise questions about the patriotism of the Democrats, their ability to protect America and to understand the threats the country faces. ("We now hear a loud chorus of Democrats who want us to cut and run," Rove said this year.)

Then Bush exploited the fifth anniversary of the September 11 attacks by shamelessly turning the solemn national event into a defense of his policy in Iraq, and for several days thereafter he campaigned on the "war on terror" and, among other things, misrepresented the efforts of many Democrats to make his illegal NSA wiretapping program adhere to the law. He said that the Democrats were "opposed to listening in on terrorists' conversations," and that in their (and, as it happened, several Republicans') opposition to his policy of detaining suspected terrorists indefinitely and permitting interrogation techniques amounting to torture, "they oppose letting the CIA detain and question the terrorists." Bush's standing in the polls began to rise. In the first part of September, it appeared that his strategy was working.

But then something happened. By late September, most of the public had come to realize that the war in Iraq was an entirely separate matter from the "war on terror." In the past, Bush, Vice President Dick Cheney, and other administration figures had, with considerable success, tried to conjoin the two issues. Iraq, Bush said repeatedly, was the "central front in the war on terror." But the highly respected pollsters Peter Hart and Bill McInturff, in their surveys for NBC and *The Wall Street Journal,* found that there was a dramatic shift in the public's thinking in September. From September 8 through 11, the polling team asked registered voters the question "Do you think the war in Iraq is helping the United States in its ability to win the war on terrorism?" The result was 33 percent thought it was helping; 32 percent thought it was hurting; and 32 percent thought it wasn't making a difference. (These results have a margin of error of 3.1 percentage points.)

When asked the same question at the end of the month, however, 32 percent said it was helping; 46 percent said it was hurting, and the rest said it wasn't making any difference. Also at the end of September, the pollsters asked whether America's safety from terrorism depended on success in the war in Iraq; 37 percent said that it did, and 57 percent said that it didn't. Hart attributes this shift of attitude to the fact that during September a large part of the public figured out that it had been sold a bill of goods: that the increasingly costly and unsuccessful war in Iraq wasn't part of the war on terrorism, as Bush and Cheney had been asserting that it was.

Bush's, Cheney's, and Donald Rumsfeld's claims of progress in Iraq sharply contrasted with the rising American casualties and the increasing carnage that people were seeing daily on their television screens. Though Bush, Cheney, and Rove tried the same sales pitch that they had been using for four years, the public stopped buying. They had tried to "nationalize" the congressional elections—that is, base them on national rather than local issues—and that strategy came back to bite them.

So strong was the rebellion against Bush and the House Republican leadership that several moderate Republicans—including Jim Leach of Iowa and Charles Bass of New Hampshire—were swept away. It wasn't that the voters rejected these men and their records as such, but that they came to understand that a vote for a Republican was a vote to retain Republican control of the House or the Senate. A similar fate befell the independent-minded Rhode Island Republican Lincoln Chafee, who had opposed Bush on the Iraq war. David Price, a Democratic congressman from North Carolina and one of the more thoughtful members of the House, told me, "The election was much more a referendum on Bush and Iraq and the Republican stewardship of the House than a response to what we said. It wasn't that we had such an inspiring program."

In a speech he gave to a dinner in New York on November 15, Bill Clinton said that the midterm elections were in large part a rejection of unthinking ideology—the Iraq war, extremism on social issues, rancid rhetoric about illegal immigrants. Clinton said that the voters had "elected us to think"—to consider the facts, even inconvenient ones—before acting. He also argued that the Democrats had been given "not a mandate but an opportunity."

Many Republicans seem not to have fully realized what happened to them. The conservative columnist David Brooks lamented on *The NewsHour* on November 8 that the Republican leaders were in denial: that they were telling each other that things were going well until "the Foley scandal" or "the Abramoff scandal." Some Republicans argue that they lost because they hadn't been conservative enough. But that wasn't what Pennsylvanians said when they rejected the highly conservative Rick Santorum. A large number of Republicans also blame Bush, and are angry that, among other things, he waited until after the election to fire Donald Rumsfeld.

Rove, meanwhile, has tried to spin his way out of the fact that the Republicans lost, in particular the House. His view—sent out through Fox News and friendly columnists—is that, you see, the Republicans didn't really lose the election because Rahm Emanuel, who ran the Democratic House campaign, deliberately recruited some candidates who were social conservatives, such as Heath Shuler from North Carolina, a former NFL football star and evangelical Christian who opposes abortion, and who went on to defeat an eight-term incumbent; or military heroes such as Joe Sestak of Pennsylvania, a highly decorated retired vice-admiral, who defeated a ten-term incumbent by a fourteen-point margin. But, as the *Washington Post* columnist E.J. Dionne wrote, every new Democrat elected was well to the left of the Republican whom he or she defeated. And several Democrats ran as conservatives on social issues such as abortion but as economic populists when it came to eliminating some of the tax cuts for the rich, or opposing trade agreements.

More recently Rove has been telling White House allies that the new strategy is to "reach out" to members on both sides of the aisle. But this might of necessity be limited to conservative Democrats: other Bush goals are to go back to "Republican basics"—stop the Democrats from undoing some of Bush's tax cuts, be tough on spending (Bush hasn't yet vetoed any appropriations bills), and resist changes to his "anti-terrorist" programs. And, puzzlingly, Rove has been saying that Bush will again press for Social Security reform—an effort that quickly collapsed in 2005. Bush in fact may well push for broad reform of entitlement programs.

Limited as the vote for a Democratic revolution may have been in November—and however limited or extensive the legislative results will be—the turnover to the Democrats in both chambers will have some profound effects. There are expected to be extensive investigations as well as oversight of how programs are being carried out (there have been none under the Republicans). Henry Waxman, the new chairman of the House Government Reform Committee, will begin with hearings on "waste, fraud and abuse of the taxpayers' money," an approach that will allow him to justify investigation of many issues as being in the broad public interest. The Democrats will also try to pass legislation modifying the prescription drug program to bring drug prices down and to raise the minimum wage; they will also show more interest in passing, and enforcing, strong ethics rules. But there is also a real opportunity for the Democrats to challenge Bush's dangerous power grab of the last six years. The elevation of Patrick Leahy, a strong civil libertarian, to be chairman of the Senate Judiciary Committee, replacing Arlen Specter, has large implications for Bush's claims to virtually unlimited executive power that have until now been supported almost automatically by the Republican Congress. After talking tough about making the NSA wiretapping conform to the law, Specter negotiated with Cheney, who had been working against any restrictions on the program, and in effect sold out, agreeing to new rules that were so vague that the resulting bill didn't amount to any substantial limitations on the president's powers.

Dianne Feinstein, another Judiciary Committee member, called Specter's compromise "worse than no bill at all." Leahy has vowed not to let it pass the Senate. In the next Congress, he will work with the new chairman of the Intelligence Committee, Jay Rockefeller, who replaces Pat Roberts. Unlike Roberts, who was complaisant toward the Administration and the CIA, Rockefeller will ask a lot of questions about the NSA wiretapping program and he and Leahy will likely write new legislation restricting the administration's power to conduct it. (Rockefeller had complained in a letter to Cheney about the administration's withholding information about it from the committee.)

Leahy's new position could also affect the new Military Commissions Act, which he has called "flagrantly unconstitutional" and "a dangerous bill." The final bill was the result of a "compromise" struck with the Administration by John McCain, Lindsey Graham, and John Warner, the chairman of the Armed Services Committee. They had at first objected on principle to the powers that the Administration was still claiming in the treatment of detainees, thereby denying the Administration enough votes to pass its own proposal. But the new "compromise" bill leaned very much toward the administration's position. It stripped the right of habeas corpus not only from foreign suspects arrested abroad, who may or may not have been "enemy combatants" (which had already been part of the law as the result of an amendment offered by Graham in 2005), but now also from millions of permanent or long-term foreign residents in the United States whom the government alleges are abetting terrorist causes.

The final bill also circumvented the Supreme Court's ruling, in the *Hamdan* case in June 2006, that the detention and treatment of prisoners captured in the administration's war on terror were governed by Common Article 3 of the Geneva Convention (which includes limits on torture). Instead of unilaterally amending, or nullifying, Common Article 3, as the Administration had advocated, it slipped the Bush administration's defiance of the Geneva Convention into another section of the bill. This narrowed the War Crimes Act—a 1996 law that defines a war crime under U.S. law to include a "grave breach of the Geneva Conventions"—so as to give the Administration more leeway on the detention and torture of detainees.

(In any event, the Bush administration has never prosecuted anyone under the War Crimes Act.) McCain suggested that waterboarding and confinement at freezing temperatures would be banned, but the Administration has refused to be specific about what limits on torture it will observe.

This sleight-of-hand was another form of "whack-a-mole," a term McCain had used to describe the moving about of U.S. troops in Iraq from one trouble spot to another. At Bush's insistence—apparently to meet a demand of CIA interrogators—the final version of the bill also gave retroactive immunity to those in the military and the CIA who had abused prisoners. (It did strike a compromise with McCain and his allies over their objection that the Administration bill denied detainees access to any evidence that would be used against them; in the end, the bill allowed the evidence to be presented to the detainees' attorneys if the presiding judge approved.) McCain's support for the final version of the detainees bill gave it legitimacy. This was further evidence that the former free-spirited maverick who campaigned for the 2000 Republican nomination for president on the "Straight Talk Express" was morphing into just another panderer—to Bush and the Republican Party's conservative base.

Leahy was particularly outraged by the provision of the Military Commissions Act expanding the denial of habeas corpus. Along with Specter, he had sought but failed to obtain any jurisdiction for the Judiciary Committee over the provision, and then offered an amendment to strip it from the bill, which lost on a narrow vote of 48–51. He and Specter recently proposed legislation to repeal this provision of the military commissions bill, which was rammed through Congress before the election so that Bush could claim it as an achievement in his war on terror. Now Leahy will work with Carl Levin of Michigan, the new chairman of the Senate Armed Services Committee, to reconsider a broad range of issues involving the treatment of detainees. Similar changes in House committee chairmanships will help to bring these changes about.

The president has certainly been weakened, but he will not be without power in the next Congress. Not only are the Democratic majorities narrow, but Bush has sometimes been able to win support from centrist Democrats for some of his proposals, including tax cuts and his nomination of John Roberts to the Supreme Court. Since overruling the president's veto requires a vote of two thirds of both houses of Congress, Bush will likely be able to block almost any legislation he opposes. Another limit on the Democrats' power is that, in effect, sixty votes are necessary in the Senate to get most things done, since senators may filibuster most legislation they oppose.

The Democrats' euphoria over their congressional victories was suddenly punctured when, over the weekend after the election, Nancy Pelosi, the next House speaker, made the large, and puzzling, misstep of throwing her support for majority leader to John Murtha of Pennsylvania, an outspoken critic of the war in Iraq, who was making a bid for the job against Steny Hoyer of Maryland, who was next in line for the position. Murtha, a decorated former Marine, was the first significant figure in Congress to call for a quick pullout of U.S. troops in Iraq. The agreeable Hoyer is popular with fellow Democrats, and has been an effective party whip. Pelosi made the mistake of acting on a grudge she held against him: when Hoyer ran against her in 2001 for majority whip, Pelosi took his challenge personally, even though competition for congressional leadership is routine. Moreover, Murtha had managed Pelosi's campaign for the post, and Pelosi was also grateful to him for providing cover for other Democrats to speak out against the war.

That Pelosi threw herself into this fight without any reason to believe that she would have enough votes to win raised questions about her judgment, and also exposed divisions among the House Democrats. The higher people climb in power, the more careful they have to be about indulging the petty grudges, jealousies, and rivalries that are endemic in Washington politics. The new speaker of the House lost her first, ill-considered fight two to one.

Pelosi was within her rights to pass over Jane Harman of California as chairman of the House Intelligence Committee—Harman was not "entitled" to the job, which is the choice of the leadership, and her term on the committee was expiring. Pelosi felt that Harman hadn't been tough enough on the Administration—she had okayed the NSA wiretapping program—but it was clear that she was also acting out of personal dislike for her, creating the unfortunate impression of a catfight. The lengthy search for Harman's replacement, during which both the black and Hispanic caucuses championed one of their own, also exposed the fact that the House Democrats are more a collection of ethnic and ideological groups than a unified party. (She chose a Hispanic, Silvestre Reyes, third in seniority on the committee, after the second-in-line, Alcee Hastings, a black, was seen as having too many ethics problems—he'd been impeached as a federal judge.) Since many of the newly elected Democrats come from districts that voted strongly for Bush in 2004, there is no guarantee that these seats will remain in Democratic hands when Bush is no longer in office. The skill of congressional leaders may be critical to their survival in the next election.

The national vote against the Iraq war only intensified the question of what Bush and Congress would do about it. This fall, the Administration finally made a show of facing up to the fact that things were going badly in Iraq. Even some of the neocons, including Richard Perle and Kenneth Adelman, who were among the most ardent supporters of overthrowing Saddam and spreading democracy in the Middle East, began to express doubts about the war—blaming the calamity that ensued on the Bush administration's incompetence and on the Iraqis who failed to capitalize on their glorious new opportunity—but not questioning their own earlier assumptions about the happy outcome of such a venture. Bush ordered up a rethink before the election and studies have been taking place in the Pentagon and the National Security Council.

Some of this, of course, was in anticipation of the report by the Iraq Study Group led by James Baker and Lee Hamilton—a strange "commission" that really wasn't officially authorized by anyone. It derived from an idea put forward by Frank Wolf, a Republican congressman from Virginia, who upon his return from his third discouraging trip to Iraq, in September 2005, decided that what was needed was a panel of "wise men" to look at the problem with "fresh eyes." This was, of course, a way of putting pressure on an administration that didn't seem to know what to do and a president who didn't seem to recognize the extent of the problem.

Wolf lined up some important allies on Capitol Hill, including the then Armed Services Committee chairman John Warner, and enlisted the help of some Washington think tanks, in particular the United States Institute of Peace, an independent organization funded by Congress, and he got $1 million from Congress for his vaguely defined project. The leaders chosen to head the project and pick the other commissioners were not surprising: Lee Hamilton, a co-chair of the 9/11 Commission, is everyone's idea of a wise, and safe, Democrat; and James Baker is not only a former secretary of state but is one of the canniest operators Washington has seen. While Washington has enjoyed the spectacle of "Poppy" Bush's pals coming to the rescue of the son who messed up, there were other reasons for choosing Baker, who made sure that the president approved of his being co-chairman. (Baker has been talking to George W. throughout the year, but for three years, his father's people had been shut out.) Nonetheless, the commission marked the return of the "realists" so disparaged by the neocons as they pursued their dream of establishing democracy throughout the Middle East.

The result was, inevitably, a panel of establishment figures who could be counted upon to be critical but not to go too far. The leaders wanted unanimity, to give the report more strength, but to get unanimity, of course, the members of the commission had to engage in horse-trading, which went on until just before the report was issued; for example, Democrats wanted to include a timetable for the withdrawal of troops, and Baker, not wanting to include proposals that the president would dismiss out of hand, opposed a precise schedule. They compromised by making a unanimous recommendation that most combat troops "could" be withdrawn by the first quarter of 2008. Many Washingtonians were surprised by the report's scathing criticism of the administration's policies and by its recommendation for withdrawal of combat troops. A Republican senator described the call for withdrawal from a respected bipartisan group "a breakthrough." As expected, the commission also recommended that the U.S. rely more on diplomacy and engage with Syria and Iran. Baker has made it clear that he believes the U.S. should have been talking to them all along. But it is far from clear how helpful they will be in the case of Iraq.

The Baker-Hamilton commission proposal on withdrawing troops is remarkably close to, if more open-ended than, a proposal offered in June by Democratic senators Jack Reed of Rhode Island and Carl Levin of Michigan, which called for a beginning of redeployment in four to six months and received the votes of thirty-nine Democratic senators; Lincoln Chafee was the only Republican to vote for it. Reed and Levin say numerous Republicans told them that they agreed with the proposal but couldn't abandon the president at that point. Now some are expected to be more willing. Members of the new Democratic Congress are itching to propose a specific date for the beginning of the redeployment. But they want such a proposal to have bipartisan backing, and to avoid having the blame for a bad outcome in Iraq shifted from Bush to them.

Almost everyone in Washington understands, even if they don't say it, that there is no real solution to what now seems to be the most disastrous foreign policy decision in American history. It's now a matter of how to bring America's involvement to an end with the fewest bad consequences. Despite all the studies and reports and amendments, events in Iraq itself will likely define the outcome.

—December 13, 2006

Notes

[1] See Garry Wills, "A Country Ruled by Faith," *The New York Review,* November 16, 2006.

[2] See David Kuo, *Tempting Faith: An Inside Story of Political Seduction* (Free Press, 2006).

Part Three: The Iraq War

This is Baghdad. What could be worse?

Anthony Shadid

the *Washington Post* | October 29, 2006

One of the more surreal aspects of the Iraq conflict has been the ongoing debate in America over what the actual state of affairs is in that war-torn country. Is daily life getting better, as many proponents of the war continue to insist (including, most recently, Senator John McCain, who toured a Baghdad marketplace surrounded by a military cordon, then tried to pass it off as an ordinary Sunday stroll), or is Iraq spiraling ever deeper into civil war? When journalists have filed reports that imply the latter, Bush administration officials have frequently tried to portray these reporters as timid souls, too hotel-bound to seek out the "good news" stories of Iraqi progress. Meanwhile, as of this writing, the death toll of newspeople killed on the job in Iraq is now 110, according to the Committee to Protect Journalists.

In this Washington Post *article, reporter Anthony Shadid—who was awarded the Pulitzer Prize for International Reporting in 2004 for "his extraordinary ability to capture, at personal peril, the voices and emotions of Iraqis as their country was invaded, their leader toppled and their way of life upended"—returns to Baghdad in an attempt to assess the conditions there, three and a half years after the U.S. invasion.*

Baghdad

There was an almost forgettable exchange earlier this month in the Iraqi National Assembly, itself on the fringe of relevance in today's disintegrating Iraq. Lawmakers debated whether legislation should be submitted to a committee to determine if it was compatible with Islam. Ideas were put forth, as well as criticism. Why not a committee to determine whether legislation endorses democratic principles? one asked. In stepped Mahmoud Mashadani, the assembly's speaker, to settle the dispute.

"Any law or decision that goes against Islam, we'll put it under the kundara!" he thundered.

"God is greatest!" lawmakers shouted back, in a rare moment of agreement between Sunni and Shiite Muslims.

Kundara means shoe, and the bit of bluster by Mashadani said a lot about Baghdad today.

It had been almost a year since I was in the Iraqi capital, where I worked as a reporter in the days of Saddam Hussein, the U.S.-led invasion in 2003, and the occupation, guerrilla war and religious resurgence that followed. On my return, it was difficult to grasp how atomized and violent the 1,250-year-old city has become. Even on the worst days, I had always found Baghdad's most redeeming quality to be its resilience, a tenacious refusal among people I met over three years to surrender to the chaos unleashed when the Americans arrived. That resilience is gone, overwhelmed by civil war, anarchy or whatever term could possibly fit. Baghdad now is convulsed by hatred, paralyzed by suspicion; fear has forced many to leave. Carnage its rhythm and despair its mantra, the capital, it seems, no longer embraces life.

"A city of ghosts," a friend told me, her tone almost funereal.

The commotion in the streets—goods spilling across sidewalks, traffic snarled under a searing sun—once prompted the uninitiated to conclude that Baghdad was reviving. Of course, they were seeing the city through a windshield, the often angry voices on the streets inaudible. Today, with traffic dwindling, stores shuttered and streets empty by nightfall, that conceit no longer holds.

Even the propaganda, once ubiquitous and often incongruous, is gone. One piece I recalled from two years ago: a map of Iraq divided into three colored bands. In white, it read, "Progress." In red, "Iraq." In white again, "Prosperity." The promises are now more modest: "However strong the wind," reads a new poster of a woman clutching her child, "it will pass." More indicative of the mood, perhaps, was one of the old banners still hanging. Faded and draped over a building scarred with craters from the invasion, it was an ad for the U.S.-funded Iraqi network, al-Iraqiya. In Arabic, its slogan reads, "Prepare your eyes for more."

As I spoke to friends, some for the first time in more than a year, that was their fear: more of the kundara.

"When anyone is against you, when anyone has differences with me, I will put a kundara in his mouth, I will shove a kundara down his throat, I will hit him with a kundara, and so on," another friend told me.

"We live in a kundara culture today."

I had first met Karima Salman during the U.S. invasion. She was a stout Shiite Muslim matriarch with eight children, living in a three-room apartment in the working-class district of Karrada. Trash was piled at her entrance, a dented, rusted steel gate perched along a sagging brick sidewalk. When I visited last year, the street, still one of the safer ones in Baghdad, exuded a veneer of normalcy. Makeshift markets overflowed with goods piled on rickety stands: socks imported from China, T-shirts from Syria and stacks of shoes, sunglasses and lingerie. Down the street were toys: plastic guns, a Barbie knockoff in a black veil, and a pirate carrying an AK-47 and a grenade. There was a "Super Mega Heavy Metal Fighter" action figure and a doll that, when squeezed, played "It's a Small World."

On this day, the metal stands were empty, as were the streets.

"Praise God," Karima said as I asked how she was. In a moment, her smile faded as she realized the absurdity of her words. "Of course, it's not good," she said, shaking her head. "There's nothing that's ever happened like what's happening in Iraq."

On June 23, 2005, three car bombs detonated in Karrada, outside her home, wrecking the Abdul-Rasul Ali mosque and spraying shrapnel that sliced into the forearm of one of her five daughters, Hiba. Friends at school nicknamed her "Shrapnel Hiba." Two months ago, yet another bomb hurled glass through their window, cutting the head of Hiba's twin sister, Duaa. Four stitches sealed the wound. Over that time, Karima lost her job as a maid at the Palm Hotel, where she had earned about $33 a month.

"People are too scared to come," she said matter of factly.

Next to her sat her son Mohammed. During the invasion, Mohammed, an ex-convict, had joined a motley unit of a dozen men patrolling Baghdad's streets as part of the Baath Party militia. Now he had entered the ranks of the Mahdi Army, a Shiite militia loyal to a young cleric, Moqtada al-Sadr, and blamed for many of today's sectarian killings in Baghdad. Karima's son-in-law Ali had been an officer in the American-equipped police force, earning $300 a month. He quit after receiving a death threat. Now he, too, had joined the Mahdi Army.

"Not all of them are good," Karima told me, casting a glance at her son.

Stocky and a little surly, Mohammed smiled. "Who else is going to protect Iraq?" he asked.

They debated the causes of the violence that, these days, is the topic of almost every conversation. Radical Sunnis, the Americans, Iranian agents, other militias. "Even the Egyptians," Karima offered. "And the Sudanese," Mohammed added.

"Brothers are killing their brothers," she said.

Stories poured forth: a bomb amputating the arm of a 10-year-old neighbor; another killing Marwan, the barber.

"If they brought the Israelis, the Jews, and they ruled Iraq, it would be better," said Karima, her face framed by a black veil. Sunlight bathed the room; electricity, as usual, was cut off. "It would be a million times better than a Sunni, a million times better than a Shiite."

Her first grandchild, 2-month-old Fahd, sat next to her. His expression was rare in Baghdad: eyes expectant, fearless.

"Is it not a pity to bring a baby in a world like this?" she asked. "It's a shame."

Her eldest daughter, Fatima, looked on.

"One-third of us are dying, one-third of us are fleeing and one-third of us will be widows," she said.

"This is Iraq," Karima added.

The last time I had visited Faruq Saad Eddin, he and his wife, Muna, had argued over whether their eldest son should have left the country. We sat in Jihad, a neighborhood so dangerous now that a stranger risks death by entering it. A generator droned in the background; occasional bomb blasts thundered in the distance, probably homemade mines targeting U.S. patrols. An urbane former diplomat, Faruq had been upset. He worried about what would become of his ancient land if its capable fled.

"You can't just cut out and run away," he told me. "This is our country and sooner or later our children will come back. The resilience of the people, that's what 11,000 years means," he said. "Someone who has 11,000 years, 100 years to lose here or there is not that much."

On April 17, Faruq and Muna left Iraq at the insistence of their son, who had paid a year's rent for an apartment in Jordan. A month later, a car bomb detonated outside their Baghdad home, shattering the windows in the room where we once had shared bitter coffee.

On a cool morning in the Amman neighborhood of Umm al-Summaq, Faruq shook his head at the arbitrariness of fate.

"We would have been killed, no doubt about it," he said.

"We are all stranded, here and there, Iraqis," he added.

A friend once compared the elderly who are reluctant to leave Baghdad to the blind. Take them away from the familiarity of their home, garden and street, and they become lost and disoriented. Faruq has sought new routines:

morning strolls, e-mails to friends, a voracious appetite for news and late-night updates on his favorite baseball team, the St. Louis Cardinals. His apartment overlooked the rolling hills of Amman, glowing in the morning's soft sun; his granddaughter Mayasa played giddily next to him with a stuffed toy.

"I should feel happy," he said.

He shook his head again, a gesture that meant he wasn't.

"We have a heavy heart, really," he said after a few moments of silence. "Just knowing what's happening makes us grieve."

I had come to know Wamidh Nadhme in 2002, before the invasion. A professor of political science at Baghdad University, he was a forthright voice in those tense, uneasy days when Hussein was still in power. He tried to speak with complete honesty despite the possible consequences of doing so in a police state. With an ever-present Dunhill cigarette, he would slowly field questions back then, reasoning out every intricate response, surrounded by his French-style furniture, worn Persian carpets and a framed piece of papyrus from Egypt, where he had spent time in exile as a young activist. But on this visit, reason eluded him, as did explanation.

"I find myself unable to understand what's going on," he said.

Wamidh had settled into what he called "withdrawal." He still visited the university once a week, but Baghdad was simply too dangerous to venture outside. After nightfall, the streets of his neighborhood of Adhamiya look like they might an hour or so before dawn: dark, without traffic, and menacing. As we talked, helicopters rumbled overhead. Gunfire burst almost continuously.

"You feel like the country is exploding," he said.

We traded stories. One I had heard from a friend: Insurgents stopped a driver at a checkpoint. They opened his trunk. "Why do you have a spare tire?" the insurgent asked solemnly. "You don't have trust in God?"

Well into 2005, Wamidh has bristled at the notion of a sectarian divide, even as the very geography of Baghdad began to transform into Shiite and Sunni halves divided by the Tigris River. Like many Iraqis, he blamed the Americans for naively viewing the country solely through that sectarian prism before the war, then forging policies that helped make it that way afterward. He ran through other "awful mistakes": the carnage unleashed by Sunni insurgents affiliated with Al Qaeda, the assassination of a Shiite ayatollah in 2003 who may have bridged differences, the devolution of Sadr's movement today into armed, revenge-minded mobs.

As Wamidh finished, he flashed his customary modesty. "Perhaps you could correct me?" he offered.

I asked him whether it would become worse if the American military withdrew.

He looked at me for a moment without saying anything, as though he were a little confused.

"What could be worse?" he asked, knitting his brow.

I saw Wamidh again a week later, and the question had lingered with him. "I sometimes wonder what I would do if I were the Americans," he said over a traditional Ramadan dinner. His answer seemed to hurt him. "I have no idea, really."

"It's like a volcano that has erupted. How do you stop that?"

On April 9, 2003, Firdaus Square became the lasting image of the U.S. entry into Baghdad. In its center was a metal statue of Hussein in a suit, his arm outstretched in socialist realist fashion. Like an arena of spectators, columns of descending height encircled him, each bearing the initials "S.H." on their cupolas. By early afternoon that day, hundreds of Iraqis swarmed around the statue with one task in mind: bring it down. It marked the fall. A year later, amid uprisings by Sunni insurgents in Fallujah and Sadr's militia in Baghdad and the south, it spoke of occupation. The square was deserted, guarded by U.S. tanks whose barrels read, "Beastly Boy" and "Bloodlust." Soldiers, edgy, had orders to shoot anyone with a weapon. At times, music blared over speakers on a Humvee.

One song: "Ring of Fire," by Johnny Cash.

As I stood in Firdaus Square this day, after invasion, liberation and occupation, I wondered what word described Baghdad.

"This is a civil war now," Harith Abdel-Hamid, a psychiatrist, had told me, trying to diagnose the madness. "When you see hundreds of people killed every day, corpses of people tortured in the streets every day, what else does it mean?"

"Call it what you will," he said, "but it is a civil war."

Perhaps. But I felt as though I was witnessing something more: the final, frenzied maturity of once-inchoate forces unleashed more than three years ago by the invasion. There was civil war-style sectarian killing, its echoes in Lebanon a generation ago. Alongside it were gangland turf battles over money, power and survival; a raft of political parties and their militias fighting a zero-sum game; a raging insurgency; the collapse of authority;

social services a chimera; and no way forward for an Iraqi government ordered to act by Americans who themselves are still seen as the final arbiter and, as a result, still depriving that government of legitimacy.

Civil war was perhaps too easy a term, a little too tidy.

I looked out on the square. On one side were rows of concrete barricades and barbed wire, having faded almost organically into the landscape. In another direction, a billboard read: "Terrorism has no religion." Across the street, a poster portraying Iraqi police pleaded: "We are the heroes fighting for the sake of Baghdad." In the middle of the square, on the stone perch where Hussein's statue once stood, were torn scraps of other posters: "Your voice," "the nation," "patriotism," "dialogue," "building the future." The words were isolated, without context, like fragments of a clay tablet.

Sirens soon pierced the square. Two armed police escorts, headed in opposite directions, rushed along the street. Each frantically waved at the other to pull over. Guns dangling from the window, they fired volleys into the air to intimidate each other.

In time, the one with fewer rifles and fewer men let the other pass. They were playing by the rules of the kundara.

In the square, Salam Ahmed sat with a friend, Saad Nasser, under the statue, looking out at the scene.

"They died under Saddam, and they're dying now," Salam said.

Unshaven, wearing a baseball cap, Saad looked at the ground. He was grim, angry and dejected.

"No one can stop it but God," he said. "Only God has the power."

Survivor: The White House Edition

Michael Wolff

Vanity Fair | December 2006

Watching the Washington establishment's weight of opinion turn slowly but steadily against the Iraq War has been a fascinating sociological exercise. The transition is exemplified by the change of tone in each successive volume of Bob Woodward's best-selling trio of books on the Bush administration's handling of the

Afghanistan and Iraq conflicts—his fairly laudatory Plan of Attack, *its more equivocal sequel,* Bush at War, *and his most recent volume, the highly critical* State of Denial. *In this* Vanity Fair *column, media critic Michael Wolff keeps score as Woodward and the rest of the nation's movers and shakers position themselves for the Iraq endgame. Along the way, Wolff brilliantly elucidates a key rule of political survival in our nation's capital: In times of shifting consensus, it never pays to be too far ahead of the curve.*

Bush fires Cheney and names McCain as the replacement V.P.—although it is not yet entirely clear to me who tells Bush to fire Cheney, if not Cheney. The war in Iraq, except for the shooting, is so over. But between now and when, as the president has no doubt accurately described it, we "cut and run," when there's a final helicopter lifting from a Green Zone rooftop, there's a whole third act to play.

In Vietnam the third act began more or less with the Tet offensive, in 1968—when, with Saigon and the U.S. Embassy nearly overrun, it became clear that not only were we not winning, we were not going to win—and went on, encompassing the downfall of Lyndon Johnson, the election of Richard Nixon, the rise of Henry Kissinger, the dubious invasion of Cambodia, and, ultimately, Watergate (one proposed article of impeachment involved Nixon's deception of Congress in bombing Cambodia), until 1975 and the final helicopter scene from the rooftop of the American Embassy in Saigon.

In the third act of a failing war—when, in Vietnam, most of the American casualties actually occurred—much of the off-site drama involves how the panicky people involved with the mess manage their own public relations. The goal, obviously, is to not be blamed, and even, perchance, to emerge heroically. (John Kerry became an anti-war activist in the third act of Vietnam, and was celebrated for it; most others in the military, not so sensitive to the *Zeitgeist,* plodded on, and came home more or less ignominiously. In part, the Swift-boat episode during the last election was the revenge of the less adroit.)

It's the Walter Cronkite moment. Far from being remembered as a detached narrator of a situation that, for three years, had been wildly spiraling out of control, Cronkite is remembered as the man who, suddenly, in 1968, told truth to power (though, in fact, he was the power) and exposed the hopelessness of the whole misadventure.

Bob Woodward, the nation's most famous journalist—a wooden and sanctimonious television presence, as well as an author of books and a reporter for *The Washington Post*—is a reasonable equivalent of Cronkite. If he's going in another direction, the world has changed. He's the power barometer. And broker. If he's no longer sucking up to you, you better get out of town in a hurry.

You've lost if you've lost Woodward.

With the publication of *State of Denial,* Woodward's peeling away of the flesh of the Bush national-security team, the third act is under way.

Woodward is hardly the only turn of the screw. There's Bill Clinton (there's always Bill Clinton). The once and future leader, who's been building himself a global career as, in part, the other president, has taken a more or less righteous position on virtually every global issue—health, environment, economics—except the war elephant in the room. Now, as the third act begins, he seizes the opportunity and is suddenly in high dudgeon about who is or is not to be blamed for the terror mess, not just defending his pursuit of Osama bin Laden but accusing the Bush administration of idleness and negligence. Fair enough, perhaps. But 9/11 was an age ago. How come we had to wait for this most fundamental discussion?

And there's *The New York Times*, which, after nearly five years of highly politic treatment of virtually anything that the White House coupled with the war on terror, is now, as the press critic Michael Massing recently characterized it, "the voice of the opposition." Here in the third act, there's Colin Powell—who prides himself on his soldier's loyalty except when he's whispering to reporters—playing the martyr. There's the chairman of the Senate Armed Services Committee, Virginia Republican John Warner, saying that the U.S. might have to consider "a change of course"—translation: run, run, run for the hills. (The chairwoman of the Senate Homeland Security and Governmental Affairs Committee, Maine Republican Susan Collins, added, for good measure: "When Chairman Warner, who has been a steadfast ally of this administration, calls for a new strategy, that is clearly significant.") Via Woodward, there's Andrew Card, the president's former chief of staff, adjusting his position; Jay Garner, the Bush administration's haplessly selected first proconsul in Iraq, telling his revisionist tale of gross mismanagement in the war zone; George Tenet, the former CIA director, taking the dramatic opportunity of the third act to, finally, drop responsibility for 9/11 onto the White House; Powell's number two, Richard Armitage, dumping all over just about everything; and, indeed, even Laura Bush, wringing her hands.

Such re-inventions and rationalizations and self-justifications and personal P.R. game plans will continue until the responsibility for Iraq has been reduced to Bush, Cheney, and Rumsfeld—the troika.

Everybody's positioning himself for the end.

The plot structure of the war, and how it reaches its conclusion, is determined less, at this point, by events in Iraq (although the *Times* gamely reported a few weeks ago on the front page that the military was *really, truly* honing a new counter-insurgency strategy) than by the involvement of so many drama queens with their super-awareness of crisis and timing.

The basic facts, after all, are three years old: no W.M.D., no connection between Iraq and Al Qaeda, not enough troops, no planning, and, obviously, no idea about how to deal with an ever growing insurgency.

But patience is key. Richard Clarke, the terrorism expert of both the Clinton and first Bush administrations, went public more than two years ago with his harsh critique of the Bush terror war, and, to many, seemed like a bitchy Cassandra, which is not necessarily the perfect career face. Clarke seemed to think he could precipitate the dénouement, but the drama has its own rhythms. It's only in the third act that you get the big reversals and tough truths—we're finally ready.

Knowing when we're ready is the important skill set—the higher media talent.

Early in the war, a network correspondent and I were debating the troop-casualty/president-approval-rating calculus. I said, naïvely, anything beyond the death toll of the first Gulf war would seem like a worrisome deficit to me. The network correspondent speculated that the war could support the same number of people killed on 9/11—a number we are, in fact, about to reach. I bring this up not to say I, or necessarily anyone, really know when the worm actually turns, but to make the point that the calculation of when too much is too much is ever present, and even something of a moral guide in the mind of the media.

Hence, Woodward's deliberate, steady, committed, even quite intelligent troika of the first two volumes of his war trilogy (*Bush at War* and *Plan of Attack*—in the first book our protagonists come to moral attention; in the second they take managerial action and responsibility) turn into the three crazy buggers in the third, when everything collapses. From even-tempered managers to narcissistic stooges. (What reader would believe such a stark reversal not just of the facts and circumstances but of character? But then, I don't think Woodward or his publishers expect us to read all three volumes together. Woodward isn't Churchill.)

This is, I suppose, a terrible thing to suggest: that Woodward might have been overly attentive to the president's soaring approval ratings, and to what was then considered the likelihood that we'd get out of this Iraq war with some efficiency; that he might have seen a picture of illogic and disarray in the White House (the picture, based at least in part on reporting he did while writing the previous book, that he is painting now), but instead rendered a picture of conviction and even occasional sagacity, because that was the canny and commercial way to tell the story, and because these were the terms on which he got his intimate access. But now, suddenly, like everybody else, including his great cast of highly placed characters, he sees it all going south, and smells the blood . . . hmm.

And yet you don't really believe he could be *that* mercenary (perhaps he was just obtuse or clinically unself-aware).

Well, give him the first two volumes—let's assume his admiration was genuine, his sucking up a professional habit and technique.

But since then, given that Woodward has gotten all his access, and given that he now understands that the war is a historic calamity, I'd have sure liked to know, among other things, that Kissinger (Kissinger!) was advising this White House, as he had advised the Nixon White House on Vietnam, as soon as Woodward found out about it. (It's important to know when the drama turns surreal.) Also, it would have been useful to know that George Tenet had told the White House in July of 2001 that a terror attack was imminent, that, as he later described it, "the system was blinking red," as soon as Woodward knew it. But Woodward, even though on the payroll of a daily newspaper, held his tongue. Why? Well . . . I guess for dramatic effect. (We've been here recently: Woodward had the key to the Valerie Plame leak mystery—it turned out he was at the very nexus of who said what to whom—but kept it hidden.) And, indeed, few books in the history of publishing have been received like this one (all right, Solzhenitsyn's

Gulag Archipelago, emerging out of the Soviet prison camps)—Woodward's sense of the dramatic is really something.

He's writer and director, pushing his actors to their appointed moment. It must be an extraordinary backstage drama, too. It's Woodward trying to figure out if Bush is really cooked, if the war is really toast. And it's everybody else trying to figure out what Woodward has figured out. Because you want to be in step with Woodward. You want to give the director what the director wants. And then, Woodward, because in a sense he's the producer too, has to hold it all together—has to somehow bind his people not to blow the ending (not to leak what they've leaked to him). Indeed, a new biography of Colin Powell, *Soldier: The Life of Colin Powell,* written by *Washington Post* associate editor Karen DeYoung and excerpted in *The Washington Post*'s Sunday magazine, further positioning Powell as distinct from the mess, confirming his special if tragic wisdom, appeared only just as Woodward's book did—reality is *so* managed and negotiated.

Anyway, why Cheney makes his exit . . . The third act may be the most historically memorable part of any war because this is when so many of the books are written. (It's odd and quaint that books still seem to be the medium of final account.) And, indeed, for the past year, the troika (I don't mean to exclude Condi Rice here, but she does seem to be, at least as Woodward sees her, not too substantial—Rummy doesn't return her calls) has more and more found itself on the nether side of an ever growing library which disputes the most fundamental aspects of why and how the war has been waged. It must be confusing for Karl Rove—that master of repetition and keeping it simple, stupid—to have to fight against these thousands of pages, this ferocious welter of detail (do they have people in the White House reading and summarizing?).

This information divide itself—between those who have read these books and those who haven't, or, anyway, those who have read about these books—becomes a crucial element of the third act. In some sense, it was the third act of Vietnam that defined these dual constituencies: part of the country, which followed the information trend, came to believe the war was unwinnable and suspect, while the other part, more remote from the information, continued to believe in the simpler, standard patriotic assumptions. This is the same divide that we now analyze ideologically as blue and red, but in so many aspects it might just be reduced to the smarts and the stupids, or the on-the-makes and the always-out-of-its.

It involves not only information (i.e., knowing that Saddam and Osama were not partners in the same law firm) but opportunity too—or opportunism. This is one reason the smarts have such a bad reputation among the stupids, because so many of them, including the Democrats in Congress, the news media, and Woodward himself, as well as the many people who once helped give the president his 80 or 90 percent approval rating, were stupids when that was advantageous. And because so many of them, like Woodward, and the editors of *The New York Times*, and the Clintons, did not make the break across the information divide until they were confident that they'd be in good company.

Indeed, the Woodward book gives a pretty clear picture of the time lag between when the smarties knew the war was a loser and when they decided to strategically alter and broadcast their own positions with regard to it. In some sense, the book goes back to Woodward's career theme: who knew what when. First there's the cover-up and then the unraveling.

Colin Powell, currently working so hard on salvaging his reputation, knew that the war was a hopeless calamity pretty much 2,500 bodies ago.

Woodward (never, in the book, acknowledging his own personal time line of apparent support and doubt about the war) reports that in September 2005 he told Senator Carl Levin, the ranking Democrat on the Senate Armed Services Committee, that he "thought Powell was in anguish about what had happened in Iraq, with 130,000 American troops still stuck there, facing an ever-growing insurgency."

"I don't want to hear about his anguish," Woodward has Levin responding. "I don't have the stomach to hear his anguish. He is so smart and his instincts are so decent and good that I can't just accept his anguish. I want more than anguish. I expected more than anguish. . . . I don't want to read a year later or two years later saying that this is the worst moment of his life or something."

Richard Armitage was, inside the Administration, one of its most caustic and astute critics—Cheney and Rumsfeld can't stand him. Perhaps to his credit, he was a great leaker. But he takes his public stand only now, making himself a moral stalwart, only because Woodward gives him cover (likewise, if he hadn't appeared, Woodward might have easily made him into a moral coward).

In the aftermath of the publication of *State of Denial,* the White House has most furiously gone after George Tenet, a man Bush gave the Presidential Medal of Freedom to. This is partly because if he really did tell them in the summer of 2001 that an attack was imminent, then that changes the Bush narrative in a really dicey way. But they're also going after him because he's so desperate not to be blamed himself. He may be right, the White House is, oddly, in essence saying, but he's dirty, too—remember, he's one of us.

Jay Garner, the first Iraq administrator, has chosen not to write a book (the next guy in the job, Paul Bremer, who, according to both Woodward and Garner, was a terrifyingly arrogant dope, wrote his own, majorly self-justifying book, *My Year in Iraq*) and instead gave Woodward his story about, sure enough, the mismanagement three years ago of the occupation. Even Woodward taunts him a bit for not at least trying to lay this out for the president when he had the chance.

The time just wasn't right, Garner says.

Timing.

The point here is about the pendulum swinging. Count on it: all the characters in Woodward's book—Powell, Armitage, Garner, Tenet, Card, et al.—along with Woodward himself, and the Clintons, and the people at *The New York Times*, and Senate Armed Services Committee chairman Warner, and Senate Homeland Security and Governmental Affairs Committee chairwoman Collins, say "tipping point" several times a day, at least.

They all have had their fingers in the wind.

The interesting thing is that Bush, Cheney, and Rumsfeld are as concerned about their reputations—for them, it's called their "place in history"—as all the other pathological careerists who surround them.

Hence, Kissinger in the White House. Kissinger, to whom, according to Woodward, it is not clear "the president really knew how to run the government," is, nevertheless, "the most regular and frequent outside adviser to Bush on foreign affairs."

"Of the outside people that I talk to in this job," Cheney tells Woodward, "I probably talk to Henry Kissinger more than I talk to anybody else."

Now, it cannot be that the Bush team so thoroughly admires the way

Kissinger handled Vietnam—that remarkable success. But it is not unlikely that they are well aware that he is the only primary player in the Vietnam War to have emerged with his reputation not in tatters (indeed, he thrived for many years and still, it seems, is at it). He survived the third act, not to mention several Woodward books.

The similarities between now and then are stark. By the end in Vietnam, the media and the smarties, the makers and breakers of reputations, had deserted the war. Nixon and Kissinger had to go on fighting with only the support of the stupids. Likewise, the only group foursquare in the Bush camp at this point are the people who wait patiently for news of the discovery of W.M.D. and who continue to believe that Saddam and Osama were once lovers. Even the neocons and *Weekly Standard* crowd, the very people who invented the war, have a new line: the war was right, but the people running it are hopeless.

What Kissinger is telling the troika, as they perhaps waver (who wouldn't waver?) in their resolve, is that you can continue, as he and Nixon did, fighting a war with the support only of the morons—there are that many of them—for a long time. In the process, you can invade Cambodia, or Laos, or Iran (Kissinger has always believed in raising the stakes). But you can't just cut off the smarties, see them as the enemy, as Nixon did, and as, for instance, Cheney obviously does—but as Kissinger didn't. Whereas the troika was united in snubbing Woodward for this most recent book, Kissinger was always talking, selling Nixon out.

The third act is ever so complicated—who knows this better than Kissinger? People must pay, blame must be apportioned. Not everybody gets out alive. Your own party—everyone eager to avoid blame—turns against you. (Actually, even your own father turns against you: Woodward reports that George Bush Sr. is, according to his close friend and former national-security adviser, Brent Scowcroft, "in 'agony,' 'anguished' and 'tormented' by the war.")

Rummy, for instance—"enigmatic, obstructionist, devious, never know what his game is" Rummy (as Woodward has Scowcroft describe him)—is, let's face it, dead. He's gone at any moment. Indeed, as Woodward points out, he's managed to hold on only because intransigent Cheney intransigently supports him.

Cheney. "Cheney was the worst," Woodward says, again using Scowcroft as his moral guide. Kissinger, the architect of the bloodiest and most catastrophic phase of the Vietnam War, emerged as well as he did (for sure, a war criminal to some, but to many, a man of renown) because most of the ill will got heaped on Nixon. Kissinger was the contrast gainer. Next to Nixon, he seemed . . . human.

So, yes, Cheney is the new Nixon.

It's Kissinger, it's got to be Kissinger, who tells Bush what he's got to do with Cheney.

Cheney, in this respect, is such a gift. Born to be hated. He might even willingly—given his dystopian personality—take the fall. He resigns—his hundred heart attacks could be the gentle cover. But it's clear: the war's on him. It's his mistake. (Since we've regarded him as a virtual president anyway, we ought to accept his leave-taking as a virtual impeachment and removal.) McCain is nominated to replace Cheney as V.P. The Republicans go wild because they have a presidential contender in the White House (likewise, the Democrats might not be so unhappy to have McCain suddenly stuck with Iraq). The smarty-media pendulum swings (or at least hesitates) because McCain is McCain and because he might be the next president. A big conference of Arabs is convened. McCain heads a blue-ribbon delegation to Iraq (Powell comes back for this), which determines that the Iraqis are ready to handle their own security. We cut and run, declaring victory.

And Bush can go to China, or North Korea. With Kissinger.

The end in Iraq may not yet be near, but it is ordained.

The Surge

Peter W. Galbraith

the *New York Review of Books* | March 15, 2007

Most analysts now agree that the U.S. occupation of Iraq has been hampered from the start by an inadequate American troop presence. Late in 2006, the Bush administration announced a new strategy involving a "surge" of 20–30,000 additional U.S. troops, many of them to be deployed in small outposts scattered throughout the neighborhoods of Baghdad—a strategy that, as of late spring 2007, had reduced the civilian death rate in Baghdad somewhat, but had also resulted in some of the deadliest months of the entire war for American forces. In this New York Review of Books *essay, Peter W. Galbraith, author of the book* The End of Iraq: How American Incompetence Created a War Without End, *analyzes the Bush administration's last-ditch effort to contain the violence in Iraq—noting that, among other things, it represents a "reckless escalation" of the U.S. mission there.*

On January 10, 2007, President Bush presented his new Iraq plan in a nationally broadcast address from the White House library. "The most urgent priority for success in Iraq," he explained, "is security, especially in Baghdad." He announced that he was sending more than 20,000 additional troops to Baghdad and Anbar Province. Baghdad would be divided into nine districts and U.S. forces would be embedded with the Iraqi army and police in each of those districts. These forces would monitor the Iraqi units operating in Baghdad, support them with additional firepower, and provide training.

By reducing the violence, Bush hopes to open the door to political reconciliation between Shiites and Sunnis. He said he would hold the Iraqi government to a program of national reconciliation that included disarming Shiite militias, a petroleum law guaranteeing the regions of Iraq a fair share of revenues, and a relaxation of penalties for service in the Baath Party. But unlike the Iraq Study Group report, Bush proposed no penalty if the Iraqi government failed to comply.

Bush aimed his toughest language at Iran and Syria, charging that they were allowing terrorists to move in and out of Iraq. The Iranians, he said, were providing material support for attacks on U.S. troops, which he vowed to disrupt. To underscore his determination, he announced the deployment of an aircraft carrier to the Persian Gulf, and a few days after the speech, U.S. special forces staged a raid on the Iranian liaison office in Erbil and arrested six Iranian intelligence operatives.

Bush's strategy is the polar opposite of that proposed by James Baker and Lee Hamilton in their Iraq Study Group report. Where they recommended the withdrawal of combat troops, Bush announced an escalation. Where they urged a diplomatic opening to Iran and Syria, Bush issued threats.

Bush's plan is laden with ironies. Four years ago, military and diplomatic professionals warned that the U.S. was embarking on a war with insufficient troops and inadequate planning. President Bush never listened to this advice, choosing to rely on the neoconservative appointees who assured him that victory in Iraq would be easy.

In devising his new strategy, Bush again turned to the neoconservatives. The so-called surge strategy is the brainchild of Frederick Kagan, a military historian at the neoconservative American Enterprise Institute who has never been to Iraq. And once again, President Bush dismissed the views of his military advisers. General George Casey and General John Abizaid, the commanders in the field, doubted that additional troops would make any difference in Iraq. They were replaced by surge advocates, including Lieutenant General David Petraeus, now the top commander in Iraq.

Petraeus, on whom so much now rests, served two previous tours in Iraq. As the American commander in Mosul in 2003 and 2004, he earned adulatory press coverage—including a *Newsweek* cover story captioned "Can This Man Save Iraq?"—for taming the Sunni-majority city. Petraeus ignored warnings from America's Kurdish allies that he was appointing the wrong people to key positions in Mosul's local government and police. A few months after he left the city, the Petraeus-appointed local police commander defected to the insurgency while the Sunni Arab police handed their weapons and uniforms over en masse to the insurgents.[1] Neither this episode nor the evident failure of the training programs for the Iraqi army and police which he ran in his next assignment seemed to have damaged the general's reputation.

In view of the role of neoconservatives in producing the Iraq fiasco, Bush's continued reliance on them was, even more than the proverbial second marriage, the triumph of hope over experience. In so doing, Bush apparently, and uncharacteristically, swallowed his pride. In a *Vanity Fair* article released just before the mid-term elections, the main neoconservative proponents of the war, including the AEI's Richard Perle and David Frum, trashed Bush as an incompetent. Perle, a noted Washington defense hawk who was among the most vociferous advocates of the war, said that in retrospect, the invasion was a mistake. Frum, who wrote the most famous phrase of the Bush presidency, "the axis of evil," provided a comment that neatly encapsulated the president's governing style and the neoconservatives' belief that ideas trump the practical:

> I always believed as a speechwriter that if you could persuade the president to commit himself to certain words, he would feel himself committed to the ideas that underlay those words. And the big shock to me has been that, although the president said the words, he just did not absorb the ideas. And that is the root of, maybe, everything.

In his speech and in interviews that followed, Bush said he would take responsibility for the mistakes made in the Iraq war. But when asked if he owed the Iraqi people an apology for not doing a better job of providing security after the invasion, he quickly deflected the responsibility to the Iraqis:

> Well I don't, that we didn't do a better job or they didn't do a better job? . . . I think I am proud of the efforts we did. We liberated that country from a tyrant. I think the Iraqi people owe the American people a huge debt of gratitude. That's the problem here in America. They wonder whether or not there is a gratitude level that's significant enough in Iraq.

Bush's obliviousness to his own failure contributed to the overwhelmingly negative public and congressional reaction to his plan. According to a Gallup poll taken immediately after the speech, 70 percent of Americans disapproved of Bush's handling of the Iraq war and his overall approval ratings fell to the lowest of his presidency. Aside from Connecticut senator Joe Lieberman, no Democrat supported the new Bush plan. At the Senate Foreign Relations Committee the day after the speech, Republican senators—and in particular those up for reelection in 2008—were among the fiercest critics as Secretary of State Condoleezza Rice tried to defend the new strategy.

President Bush's plan has no chance of actually working. At this late stage, 21,500 additional troops cannot make a difference. U.S. troops are ill prepared to do the policing that is needed to secure Baghdad. They lack police training, knowledge of the city, and requisite Arabic skills. The Iraqi troops meant to assist the effort are primarily Kurdish peshmerga from two brigades nominally part of the Iraqi army. These troops will have the same problems as the Americans, including an inability to communicate in Arabic.

Bush's strategy assumes that Iraq's Shiite-led government can become a force for national unity and that Iraqi security forces can, once trained, be neutral guarantors of public safety. There is no convincing basis for either proposition. The Bush administration's inability to grasp the realities of Iraq is, in no small measure, owing to its unwillingness to acknowledge that Iraq is in the middle of a civil war.

As everyone except Bush seems to understand, Iraq's Shiite-led government has no intention of transforming itself into an inclusive government of national unity. The parties that lead Iraq define themselves—and the state they now control—by their Shiite identity. For them, Saddam's overthrow and their electoral victory is a triumph for Islam's minority sect that has been 1,300 years in the making and a matter of historic justice. They are not going to abandon this achievement for the sake of a particular Iraqi identity urged by an American president.

Sunni Arabs are implacably opposed to an Iraq ruled by Shiites who want to define their country by the religion of the majority. Most see the current Iraqi government as alien and disloyal to the Iraq the Sunni Arabs built. (On the gallows, Saddam spoke for many Sunni Arabs when he warned against the Americans and "the Persians," by which he clearly meant Iraq's Shiite rulers.) The Sunni Arabs will not be reconciled with what they see as small measures, such as a guaranteed share of petroleum, a relaxation of de-Baathification laws, or constitutional amendments. They object to the very things that are quintessential to the claims of the Shiites, namely Shiite rule and the Shiite character of the new Iraq.

Bush's strategy depends on the Iraqi police and army eventually taking over from U.S. forces. Somehow the president imagines that Iraq's army and police are exempt from the country's sectarian and ethnic divisions. In reality, both the army and police are as polarized as the country itself. U.S. training will not make these forces neutral guarantors of public security but will make them more effective killers in Iraq's civil war. It is hard to see how this is in the U.S. interest. The execution of Saddam—in which, as Iraqi officials subsequently admitted, members of Moqtada al-Sadr's Mahdi Army participated—illustrated just how pervasive is the militia penetration of Iraq's security services. Since the advocates of the president's surge strategy have had no idea about how to make Iraq's police and army committed to an inclusive Iraq, they simply pretend the problem does not exist.

At best, Bush's new strategy will be a costly postponement of the day of reckoning with failure. But it is also a reckless escalation of the military mission in Iraq that could leave U.S. forces fighting a powerful new enemy with only marginally more troops than are now engaged in fighting the Sunni insurgency. The strategy also risks extending Iraq's civil war to the hitherto peaceful Kurdish regions, with no corresponding gain for security in the Arab parts of the country.

Until now, U.S. forces in Iraq have been fighting, almost exclusively, the Sunni Arab insurgency. Bush's new plan calls for the U.S. military to initiate operations against the Mahdi Army (and related militias) as well, a measure that could mean U.S. forces will become embroiled in all-out urban warfare throughout Baghdad, a city of more than five million. In addition, the Mahdi Army has members throughout southern Iraq, in the Diyala Governorate northeast of Baghdad, and in Kirkuk. While many Shiites do not support al-Sadr (the Mahdi Army has had armed clashes with the Badr Organization belonging to the Supreme Council for the Islamic Revolution, or SCIRI, one of the two main Shiite parties), the Mahdi Army is a formidable force comprising as many as 60,000 armed men.[2] With Bush ratcheting up the rhetoric against Iran, the Iranian government may see a broad-based Shiite uprising against the coalition as its best insurance against a U.S. military strike. It has every incentive to encourage—and assist—the Mahdi Army in organizing such an uprising. Iran has sufficient influence with Iraqi Shiite groups—including SCIRI—to ensure at least their neutrality in a clash with the Mahdi Army.[3]

At the core of the Iraq fiasco has been Bush's unwillingness to send forces adequate to accomplish the mission. Now the president proposes a military strategy to confront twice as many foes with just 15 percent more troops. The Mahdi Army may choose to wait out the Americans by taking a low profile for the duration of the surge. If so, this will be helpful to U.S. troops, but, of course, it will have done nothing to break the power of the Shiite militias. President Bush's public statements indicate no awareness of the risks of escalating America's mission in Iraq. Democrats have concentrated almost exclusively on the escalation in troop numbers, giving the president a free ride on the far more dangerous escalation of the mission itself.

So far, the Kurds have largely sat out Iraq's civil war. Although their constituents want as little connection with the Iraqi nation as possible, Iraq's

Kurdish president and Kurdish ministers often appear to be the only senior figures in Baghdad serious about national unity and national reconciliation. President Jalal Talabani has worked tirelessly to reach out to Sunni Arabs, including the insurgents. Barham Salih, once again Iraq's deputy prime minister, promoted an Iraq-wide development strategy and has gotten the Kurdistan government to agree to share revenues from (but not control of) new oil fields, even though the constitution assigns such revenues to the producing region

Latif Rashid, the Kurd who has been minister of water resources since his appointment by L. Paul Bremer in 2003, has put most of his efforts into restoring the marshes in southern Iraq, in an attempt to reverse Saddam Hussein's draining of them, which resulted in an ecological catastrophe. The rebirth of some marshes is, perhaps, the biggest achievement of the "new Iraq," but one largely unnoticed by the press and, oddly, little mentioned by the Bush administration. Hoshyer Zebari, the Kurd who has been Iraq's foreign minister since 2003, has proved a powerful voice for the entire country, both internationally and at pan-Arab conclaves. The Kurdish leaders have been able to pursue a national agenda precisely because their actions do not affect Kurdistan's separate status.

But Bush's plan could change that. As of this writing it is not clear how the Kurdish troops will be used in Baghdad, but any deployment runs a serious risk of enlarging Iraq's civil war. If the Kurdish troops are used against Sunni Arabs, insurgents may respond by escalating attacks on Kurds living in close proximity to Sunni areas. The most endangered population consists of the Kurds living in mostly Kurdish east Mosul. The Kurdish political parties will respond militarily to an escalation of the attacks on Mosul's Kurds and this could transform Mosul from a place of low-level ethnic conflict to full-scale civil war.

Even more risky, the U.S. military may use Kurdish troops to fight the Mahdi Army. Iraq's Shiite-led government obstructed past U.S. moves against the Mahdi Army and Shiite troops have been mostly unwilling to fight their coreligionists. This leaves Kurdish troops as the only indigenous force that the U.S. could plausibly deploy against the Mahdi Army.

Iraq's government is a partnership between a coalition of Shiite religious parties and the two main Kurdish nationalist parties. The Shiite coalition is itself evenly split between a faction led by SCIRI and a faction heavily influenced by supporters of Moqtada al-Sadr. The Kurdish parties have a close relationship with SCIRI that goes back decades in the struggle against Saddam and is built around a shared commitment to a highly decentralized Iraqi state. By contrast, Moqtada al-Sadr, with his political support coming heavily from Shiite east Baghdad, opposes federalism and Kurdish claims to Kirkuk. Like the Sunni Arabs, he objects to the constitutional mandate for a referendum to determine Kirkuk's status and has sent the Mahdi Army there to fight the peshmerga on behalf of Kirkuk's Shiite Arabs. (Kirkuk's indigenous Arab population is Sunni and Kirkuk is adjacent to Iraq's Sunni Arab govenorates. As part of his plan to make Kirkuk more Arab and less Kurdish and Turcoman, Saddam settled Shiites from the south in the homes of Kurds and Turcomans who were killed or expelled. Many of these Shiite settlers want to return south but those who wish to stay are a fertile pool for Mahdi Army recruits.)

A battle for Baghdad between the Mahdi Army and Kurdish troops could spill over to Kirkuk. If the Shiite coalition stays together, it could fracture the Kurdish–Shiite alliance. Or the Shiite coalition could itself fracture, making Iraq's civil war a three-way affair among Sunni Arab insurgents, the Mahdi Army and its allies, and a SCIRI–Kurdish alliance. Neither outcome will make resolving Iraq's problems any simpler. The Kurds, of course, are aware of the risks. Their decision to send troops at America's behest reflects their deep commitment to their American ally in spite of a history that would suggest they are more likely to be double-crossed than to have their support reciprocated.

There is near-unanimous opposition in Kurdistan to sending troops to Baghdad. Although the Kurdish troops are nominally part of the Iraqi army, Kurdish leaders understand that Arab Iraqis will see the Kurdish troops as peshmerga; and, indeed, their loyalty is to Kurdistan and not Iraq. They only began moving to Baghdad after getting approval from the Kurdish political leaders. Even so, many Kurdish troops deserted rather than go to Baghdad. The actual number of Kurds deployed is more likely to be two thousand than the anticipated four thousand. Kurdish leaders have told their troops to stay out of Sunni–Shiite sectarian fighting.

Scholars who study civil wars observe that they generally last a long time—a decade is the mean since 1945—and they end, in 85 percent of the cases, with one side winning a military victory. If Iraq's civil war is fought to the end, there can be little doubt that the Shiites will prevail. They are three times as numerous as the Sunnis, are in control of the armed apparatus of the Iraqi state, and have a powerful ally in neighboring Iran. While Arab states, including Saudi Arabia, talk about supporting the Sunni Arabs, those that border Iraq are relatively small, militarily weak, and separated from Iraq's population centers by vast tracts of desert.

The three-state solution I have outlined in my book would protect the Sunni Arabs from military annihilation—and its attendant humanitarian consequences—by giving them their own self-governing region with defined borders.[4] The alternative to promoting this kind of power-sharing arrangement is to let the civil war take its course. In late 2006, Vice President Cheney floated a trial balloon dubbed the "80 percent solution." In starkest terms, the 80 percent solution would write off reconciliation with the Sunni Arabs on the grounds that they are intractable and focus on supporting the 80 percent of Iraqis who are Shiite or Kurdish. In essence, the United States would take the Shiite side in the Sunni–Shiite civil war.

This is a plausible, if cruel, strategy. But it would not result in a democratic, unified, or stable Iraq. The common ground between Shiites and Kurds is their shared commitment to the partition plan embodied in the Iraqi constitution. An 80 percent solution is, in effect, a two-state solution with Kurdistan and a Shiite-dominated Arab Iraq. It becomes all the more difficult to achieve if Bush administration efforts to involve the Kurds in the civil war shatter the Shiite coalition or break up the Kurdish–Shiite alliance.

George W. Bush has said he will leave the problem of Iraq to the president elected in 2008. Rather than acknowledge failure in Iraq—and by extension a failed presidency—Bush has chosen to postpone the day of reckoning. It is a decision that will cost many American and Iraqi lives, will leave the United States weaker, and will prolong the decline in American prestige abroad caused by the mismanaged Iraq war. And it will not change the truth that the president so desperately wishes to escape: George W. Bush launched and lost America's Iraq war.

—February 15, 2007

Notes

[1] In a coordinated assault in November 2004, Sunni insurgents overran all of Mosul's Sunni-led police stations, while every Kurdish police station successfully defended itself.

[2] When the Mahdi Army last fought the coalition on a large scale in April and May 2004, it severely disrupted U.S. supply lines from Kuwait and took over several U.S. installations. It is a more potent force in 2007 than it was then.

[3] In 2004, SCIRI was neutral in the battle between the coalition and the Mahdi Army, in spite of attacks by the latter on SCIRI's militiamen.

[4] See "How to Get Out of Iraq," *The New York Review,* May 13, 2004, and my book *The End of Iraq: How American Incompetence Created a War Without End* (Simon and Schuster, 2006), to be reissued in June with an afterword from which this article is drawn.

Neo Culpa

David Rose

Vanity Fair | January 2007

The following article sent shock waves through the political establishment when Vanity Fair *first posted excerpts from it on the magazine's Web site, just before the 2006 midterm elections. "Victory has a hundred fathers," John Kennedy famously remarked after the Bay of Pigs fiasco, "and defeat is an orphan." By that standard, the leading neoconservative thinkers interviewed by David Rose for this piece are clearly putting the Iraq War up for adoption. As Rose notes, several of his interviewees subsequently claimed that their words had been misinterpreted. Still, the underlying message of his article is clear: A number of those who lobbied most intensely for the Iraq invasion are now taking pains to distance themselves from the conflict, while at the same time pointing a finger of blame at the White House and the Pentagon for grossly mismanaging the whole enterprise.*

I. About That Cakewalk . . .

I remember sitting with Richard Perle in his suite at London's Grosvenor House hotel and receiving a private lecture on the importance of securing victory in Iraq. "Iraq is a very good candidate for democratic reform," he said. "It won't be Westminster overnight, but the great democracies of the world didn't achieve the full, rich structure of democratic governance overnight. The Iraqis have a decent chance of succeeding."

In addition to a whiff of gunpowder, Perle seemed to exude the scent of liberation—not only for Iraqis, but for all the Middle East. After the fall of Saddam Hussein, Perle suggested, Iranian reformers would feel emboldened to change their own regime, while Syria would take seriously American demands to cease its support for terrorists.

Perle had spent much of the 1990s urging the ouster of Saddam Hussein. He had co-founded the Project for the New American Century, a neoconservative think tank that agitated for Saddam's removal, and he had helped to engineer the 1998 Iraq Liberation Act, which established regime change as formal U.S. policy. After the accession of George W. Bush, in 2001, Perle was appointed chairman of the Pentagon's Defense Policy Board Advisory Committee, and at its first meeting after 9/11—attended by Defense Secretary Donald Rumsfeld; his deputy, Paul Wolfowitz; and Rumsfeld's No. 3, Douglas Feith—Perle arranged a presentation from the exiled Iraqi dissident Ahmad Chalabi. Perle wanted to shut down terrorist havens—not only in Afghanistan but also in Iraq. When we spoke at Grosvenor House, it was late February 2003, and the culmination of all this effort—Operation Iraqi Freedom—was less than a month away.

Three years later, Perle and I meet again, at his home outside Washington, D.C. It is October 2006, the worst month for U.S. casualties in Iraq in nearly two years, and Republicans are bracing for what will prove to be sweeping losses in the upcoming midterm elections. As he looks into my eyes, speaking slowly and with obvious deliberation, Perle is unrecognizable as the confident hawk I once knew. "The levels of brutality that we've seen are truly horrifying, and I have to say, I underestimated the depravity," Perle says, adding that total defeat—an American withdrawal that leaves Iraq as an anarchic "failed state"—is not yet inevitable, but is becoming more likely. "And then," he says, "you'll get all the mayhem that the world is capable of creating."

According to Perle, who left the Defense Policy Board in 2004, this unfolding catastrophe has a central cause: devastating dysfunction within the Bush administration. The policy process has been nothing short of "disastrous," he says. "The decisions did not get made that should have been. They didn't get made in a timely fashion, and the differences were argued out endlessly. At the end of the day, you have to hold the president responsible. . . . I think he was led to believe that things were chugging along far more purposefully and coherently than in fact they were. I think he didn't realize the depth of the disputes underneath. I don't think he realized the extent of the opposition within his own administration, and the disloyalty."

Perle goes as far as to say that, if he had his time over, he would not advocate an invasion of Iraq: "I think if I had been delphic, and had seen where we are today, and people had said, 'Should we go into Iraq?,' I think now I probably would have said, 'No, let's consider other strategies for dealing with the thing that concerns us most, which is Saddam supplying weapons of mass destruction to terrorists.' . . . I don't say that because I no longer believe that Saddam had the capability to produce weapons of mass destruction, or that he was not in contact with terrorists. I believe those two premises were both correct. Could we have managed that threat by means other than a direct military intervention? Well, maybe we could have."

Having spoken with Perle, I wonder: What do the rest of the war's neoconservative proponents think? If the much-caricatured "Prince of Darkness" is now plagued with doubt, how do his comrades-in-arms feel? I am particularly interested in finding out because I interviewed some of the neocons before the invasion and, like many people, found much to admire in their vision of spreading democracy in the Middle East.

I expect to encounter disappointment. What I find instead is despair, and fury at the incompetence of the Bush administration many neocons once saw as their brightest hope.

David Frum, the former White House speechwriter who co-wrote Bush's 2002 State of the Union address, accusing Iraq of being part of an "axis of evil," says it now looks as if defeat may be inescapable, because "the insurgency has proven it can kill anyone who cooperates, and the United States and its friends have failed to prove that it can protect them. If you are your typical, human non-hero, then it's very hard at this point to justify to yourself and your family taking any risks at all on behalf of the coalition." This situation, he says, must ultimately be blamed on "failure at the center."

Kenneth Adelman, a longtime neocon activist and Pentagon insider who has served on the Defense Policy Board, wrote a famous op-ed article in *The Washington Post* in February 2002, arguing, "I believe that demolishing

Hussein's military power and liberating Iraq would be a cakewalk." Now he says, "I am extremely disappointed by the outcome in Iraq, because I just presumed that what I considered to be the most competent national-security team since Truman was indeed going to be competent. They turned out to be among the most incompetent teams in the postwar era. Not only did each of them, individually, have enormous flaws, but together they were deadly, dysfunctional."

Fearing that worse is still to come, Adelman believes that neoconservatism itself—what he defines as "the idea of a tough foreign policy on behalf of morality, the idea of using our power for moral good in the world"—is dead, at least for a generation. After Iraq, he says, "it's not going to sell." And if he, too, had his time over, Adelman says, "I would write an article that would be skeptical over whether there would be a performance that would be good enough to implement our policy. The policy can be absolutely right, and noble, beneficial, but if you can't execute it, it's useless, just useless. I guess that's what I would have said: that Bush's arguments are absolutely right, but you know what? You just have to put them in the drawer marked CAN'T DO. And that's very different from LET'S GO."

James Woolsey, another Defense Policy Board member, who served as director of the CIA under President Clinton, lobbied for an Iraq invasion with a prodigious output of articles, speeches, and television interviews. At a public debate hosted by *Vanity Fair* in September 2004, he was still happy to argue for the motion that "George W. Bush has made the world a safer place." Now he draws explicit parallels between Iraq and Vietnam, aghast at what he sees as profound American errors that have ignored the lessons learned so painfully 40 years ago. He has not given up hope: "As of mid-October of '06, the outcome isn't clear yet." But if, says Woolsey, as now seems quite possible, the Iraqi adventure ends with American defeat, the consequences will be "awful, awful. . . . It will convince the jihadis and Al Qaeda-in-Iraq types as well as the residual Ba'thists that we are a paper tiger, and they or anybody they want to help can take us on anywhere and anytime they want and be effective, that we don't have the stomach to stay and fight."

Professor Eliot Cohen of Johns Hopkins University's School of Advanced International Studies, yet another Defense Policy Board member and long-time advocate of ousting Saddam Hussein, is even more pessimistic: "People sometimes ask me, 'If you knew then what you know now, would you still have been in favor of the war?' Usually they're thinking about the

W.M.D. stuff. My response is that the thing I know now that I did not know then is just how incredibly incompetent we would be, which is the most sobering part of all this. I'm pretty grim. I think we're heading for a very dark world, because the long-term consequences of this are very large, not just for Iraq, not just for the region, but globally—for our reputation, for what the Iranians do, all kinds of stuff."

II. Let the Finger-Pointing Begin

I turn in my piece on Thursday, November 2—five days before the midterm elections. The following day, the editors phone to say that its contents—especially the comments by Perle, Adelman, and Frum—are so significant and unexpected that they have decided to post an excerpt that afternoon on the magazine's Web site, vanityfair.com.

The abridged article goes up at about 4:45 P.M., eastern standard time. Its impact is almost immediate. Within minutes, George Stephanopoulos confronts Vice President Dick Cheney with Perle's and Adelman's criticisms during an on-camera interview. Cheney blanches and declines to comment, other than to say that the Administration remains committed to its Iraq policy and will continue to pursue it, "full speed ahead." By the next morning, news of the neocons' about-face has been picked up by papers, broadcasters, and blogs around the world, despite a White House spokesperson's attempt to dismiss it as "Monday-morning quarterbacking."

Some of my interviewees, Richard Perle included, protest in a forum on *National Review Online* that they were misled, because they believed that their words would not be published until *V.F.*'s January issue hit newsstands—after the midterms. Posting a preview on the Web, they say, was a "partisan" attempt to score political points. In response, the magazine issues a statement: "At a time when Vice President Dick Cheney is saying that the Administration is going 'full speed ahead' with its policy in Iraq and that 'we've got the basic strategy right,' and the president is stating that Defense Secretary Rumsfeld's job is secure, we fell that it was in the public's interest to hear now, before the election, what the architects of the Iraq war are saying about its mission and execution."

Some of the neocons also claim that the Web excerpt quotes them out of context—implying, perhaps, that in other parts of their interviews they had praised the performance of Bush and his administration. That charge is untrue. Meanwhile, not all the neocons are unhappy. On Wednesday,

November 8, with news of the Democratic takeover of Congress still fresh and Rumsfeld's resignation still hours away, I receive an e-mail from Adelman. "I totally agree with you," he writes. "Why keep Issue #1 behind closed doors until the American people have a chance to vote? That's why I was (among the only ones) not giving any 'rebuttal' to the [Web] release, despite being asked and pressured to do so, since I think it's just fine to get word out when it could make a difference to people.

"Plus I personally had no rebuttal. I thought the words I read from you were fair and right on target."

A cynic might argue that, since the Iraqi disaster has become so palpably overwhelming, the neocons are trashing what is left of Bush's reputation in the hope of retaining theirs. Given the outcome of the midterms, it also seems likely that these interviews are the first salvos in a battle to influence how history will judge the war. The implications will be profound—not only for American conservatism but also for the future direction and ambitions of American foreign policy. The neocons' position in this debate starts with an unprovable assertion: that when the war began, Iraq was "a doable do," to use a military planner's phrase cited by David Frum. If not for the administration's incompetence, they say, Saddam's tyranny could have been replaced with something not only better but also secure. "Huge mistakes were made," Richard Perle says, "and I want to be very clear on this: they were not made by neoconservatives, who had almost no voice in what happened, and certainly almost no voice in what happened after the downfall of the regime in Baghdad. I'm getting damn tired of being described as an architect of the war. I was in favor of bringing down Saddam. Nobody said. 'Go design the campaign to do that.' I had no responsibility for that."

Some of those who did have responsibility, and were once the most gung-ho, are also losing heart. In December 2005, I spoke with Douglas Feith, the former undersecretary of defense for policy, whose Office of Special Plans was reportedly in charge of policy planning for the invasion and its aftermath. He told me then, "I have confidence that in 20 to 30 years people will be happy we removed Saddam Hussein from power and will say we did the right thing. They will look back and say that our strategic rationale was sound, and that through doing this we won a victory in the war on terror."

When we talk again, in October 2006, Feith sounds less certain. It is beginning to seem possible that America will withdraw before Iraq achieves stability, he says, and if that happens his previous statement would no longer be justified. "There would be a lot of negative consequences," he says, adding that America's enemies, including Osama bin Laden, have attacked when they perceived weakness. Leaving Iraq as a failed state, Feith concludes, "would wind up hurting the United States and the interests of the civilized world." In 2005, Feith thought failure unimaginable. Now he broods on how it may occur, and envisions its results.

At the end of 2003, Richard Perle and David Frum published a book, *An End to Evil: How to Win the War on Terror.* Neoconservatives do not make up an organized bloc—much less a "cabal," as is sometimes alleged—but the book ends with a handy summary of their ideas. Foreign policy, write Perle and Frum, should attempt to achieve not only the realist goals of American wealth and security but also less tangible ends that benefit mankind. The neoconservative dream, they say, is similar to that which inspired the founders of the United Nations after World War II: "A world at peace; a world governed by law; a world in which all peoples are free to find their own destinies." But in Perle and Frum's view, the UN and similar bodies have failed, leaving "American armed might" as the only force capable of bringing this Utopian world into being. "Our vocation is to support justice with power," they write. "It is a vocation that has earned us terrible enemies. It is a vocation that has made us, at our best moments, the hope of the world."

Although Perle was one of the first to frame the case for toppling Saddam in realist terms of the threat of W.M.D.—in a letter he sent to Clinton in February 1998 whose 40 signatories included Rumsfeld, Wolfowitz, and Feith—he insists that the idealist values outlined in his book shaped the way he and his allies always believed the war should be fought. At the heart of their program was an insistence that, no matter how Saddam was deposed, Iraqis had to be allowed to take charge of their destiny immediately afterward.

In the 1990s, the neocons tried to secure American air and logistical support for an assault on Saddam by a "provisional government" based in Kurdistan—a plan derided by former CentCom chief General Anthony

Zinni as a recipe for a "Bay of Goats." After 9/11, as America embarked on the path to war in earnest, they pushed again for the recognition of a provisional Iraqi government composed of former exiles, including Chalabi. In addition to acting as a magnet for new defectors from the Iraqi military and government, they argued, this government-in-exile could assume power as soon as Baghdad fell. The neocons, represented inside the Administration by Feith and Wolfowitz, also unsuccessfully demanded the training of thousands of Iraqis to go in with coalition troops.

The failure to adopt these proposals, neocons outside the Administration now say, was the first big American error, and it meant that Iraqis saw their invaders as occupiers, rather than liberators, from the outset. "Had they gone in with even just a brigade or two of well-trained Iraqis, I think things could have been a good deal different," James Woolsey tells me at his law office, in McLean, Virginia. "That should have been an Iraqi that toppled that statue of Saddam." Drawing a comparison to the liberation of France in World War II, he recalls how "we stood aside and saw the wisdom of having [the Free French leaders] de Gaulle and Leclerc lead the victory parade through Paris in the summer of '44." The coalition, he says, should have seen the symbolic value of allowing Iraqis to "take" Baghdad in 2003. He draws another historical parallel, to the U.S. campaigns against Native Americans in the 19th century, to make another point: that the absence of Iraqi auxiliaries deprived coalition soldiers of invaluable local intelligence. "Without the trained Iraqis, it was like the Seventh Cavalry going into the heart of Apache country in Arizona in the 1870s with no scouts. No Apache scouts. I mean, hello?"

If the Administration loaded the dice against success with its pre-war decisions, Kenneth Adelman says, it made an even greater blunder when Saddam's regime fell. "The looting was the decisive moment." Adelman says. "The moment this administration was lost was when Donald Rumsfeld took to the podium and said, 'Stuff happens. This is what free people do.' It's not what free people do at all: it's what barbarians do. Rumsfeld said something about free people being free to make mistakes. But the Iraqis were making 'mistakes' by ruining their country while the U.S. Army stood there watching!" Once Rumsfeld and General Tommy Franks failed to order their forces to intervene—something Adelman says they could have done—several terrible consequences became inevitable. Among them, he tells me over lunch at a downtown-D.C. restaurant, was the destruction of Iraq's infrastructure, the loss of documents that might have shed light on Saddam's weapons capabilities, and the theft from Iraq's huge munitions stores of tons of explosives "that they're still using to kill our kids." The looting, he adds, "totally discredited the idea of democracy, since this 'democracy' came in tandem with chaos." Worst of all, "it demolished the sense of the invincibility of American military power. That sense of invincibility is enormously valuable when you're trying to control a country. It means, 'You fuck with this guy. you get your head blown off.' All that was destroyed when the looting began and was not stopped."

According to Frum, there was a final ingredient fueling the wildfire spread of violence in the second half of 2003: intelligence failures that were, in terms of their effects, even "grosser" than those associated with the vanishing weapons. "The failure to understand the way in which the state was held together was more total," he tells me in his office at the neoconservative think tank the American Enterprise Institute (AEI). America assumed it was invading a functional, secular state, whose institutions and lines of control would carry on functioning under new leadership. Instead, partly as a result of the 1990s sanctions, it turned out to be a quasi-medieval society where Saddam had secured the loyalty of tribal sheikhs and imams with treasure and SUV's. Here, Frum says, another disadvantage of not having an Iraqi provisional government made itself felt: "There's no books, there's no treasury, and he's distributing. One guy gets a Land Rover, another guy gets five Land Rovers, somebody else gets a sack of gold. . . . That is information that only an Iraqi is going to have, and this is something I said at the time: that Iraq is going to be ruled either through terror or through corruption. Saddam knew how to do it through terror. Ahmad Chalabi would have known how to do it through corruption. What we are now trying to do, in the absence of the knowledge of who has to be rewarded, is to do a lot of things through force." The state had ceased to "deliver" rewards to loyalists, and in that vacuum the insurgency began to flourish.

III. The Trouble with Bush and Rice

As *V.F.* first revealed, in the May 2004 issue, Bush was talking about invading Iraq less than two weeks after 9/11, broaching the subject at a private White House dinner with British prime minister Tony Blair on September 20, 2001. With so much time to prepare, how could the aftermath have begun so badly? "People were aware in February or March of 2003 that the planning was not finished," Frum says. "There was not a coherent plan, and in the knowledge that there was not a coherent plan, there was not the decision made to wait." The emphasis here needs to be on the word "coherent." In fact, as Frum points out, there were several plans: the neocons' ideas outlined above, a British proposal to install their client Iyad Allawi, and suggestions from the State Department for a government led by the octogenarian Adnan Pachachi. To hear Frum tell it, the State Department was determined to block the neocons' anointed candidate, Ahmad Chalabi, and therefore resisted both Iraqi training and a provisional government, fearing that these measures would boost his prospects.

It would have been one thing, the neocons say, if their plan had been passed over in favor of another. But what really crippled the war effort was the Administration's failure, even as its soldiers went to war, to make a decision. Less than three weeks before the invasion, Bush said in a rousing, pro-democracy speech to the AEI, "The United States has no intention of determining the precise form of Iraq's new government. That choice belongs to the Iraqi people." But with the Administration unable to decide among Allawi, Pachachi, and Chalabi, the Iraqis ultimately were given no say. Instead, L. Paul Bremer III soon assumed almost unlimited powers as America's proconsul, assisted by a so-called Governing Council, which he was free to ignore and which, to judge by Bremer's memoir, he regarded as a contemptible irritant.

The place where such interagency disputes are meant to be resolved is the National Security Council, chaired during Bush's first term by Condoleezza Rice, who was national security adviser at the time. AEI Freedom Scholar Michael Ledeen—whose son, Gabriel, a lieutenant in the Marines, recently returned from a tour of duty in Iraq—served as a consultant to the NSC under Ronald Reagan and says the council saw its role as "defining the disagreement" for the president, who would then make up his mind. "After that, we'd move on to the next fight." But Rice, says Ledeen, saw her job as "conflict resolution, so that when [then secretary of state Colin] Powell and Rumsfeld disagreed, which did happen from time to time, she would say to [then deputy national-security adviser Stephen] Hadley or whomever, 'O.K., try to find some middle ground where they can both agree.' So then it would descend at least one level in the bureaucracy, and people would be asked to draft new memos." By this process, Ledeen complains, "thousands of hours were wasted by searching for middle ground, which most of the time will not exist." Sometimes—as with the many vital questions about postwar Iraq—"it may well have been too late" by the time decisions emerged.

"The National Security Council was not serving [Bush] properly," says Richard Perle, who believes that the president failed to tackle this shortcoming because of his personal friendship with Rice. "He regarded her as part of the family." (Rice has spent weekends and holidays with the Bushes.) The best way to understand this aspect of the Bush administration, says Ledeen, is to ask, Who are the most powerful people in the White House? "They are women who are in love with the president: Laura [Bush], Condi, Harriet Miers, and Karen Hughes." He cites the peculiar comment Rice reportedly made at a dinner party in 2004, when she referred to Bush as "my husb—" before catching herself. "That's what we used to call a Freudian slip," Ledeen remarks.

Whatever the NSC's deficiencies, say the neocons, the buck has to stop with the president. "In the Administration that I served," says Perle, who was an assistant secretary of defense under Reagan, there was a "one-sentence description of the decision-making process when consensus could not be reached among disputatious departments: 'The president makes the decision.'" Yet Bush "did not make decisions, in part because the machinery of government that he nominally ran was actually running him." That, I suggest, is a terrible indictment. Perle does not demur: "It is." Accepting that, he adds, is "painful," because on the occasions he got an insight into Bush's thinking Perle felt "he understood the basic issues and was pursuing policies that had a reasonable prospect of success." Somehow, those instincts did not translate into actions.

On the question of Bush, the judgments of some of Perle's ideological allies are harsher. Frank Gaffney also served under Reagan as an assistant secretary of defense; he is now president of the hawkish Center for Security Policy, which has close ties with the upper echelons of the Pentagon. Gaffney describes the Administration as "riven," arguing that "the drift, the incoherence, the mixed signals, the failure to plan this thing [Iraq] rigorously were the end product of that internal dynamic." His greatest disappointment has been the lack of resolution displayed by Bush himself: "This president has tolerated, and the people around him have tolerated, active, ongoing, palpable insubordination and skulduggery that translates into subversion of his policies. . . . He doesn't in fact seem to be a man of principle who's steadfastly pursuing what he thinks is the right course," Gaffney says. "He talks about it, but the policy doesn't track with the rhetoric, and that's what creates the incoherence that causes us problems around the world and at home. It also creates the sense that you can take him on with impunity."

In 2002 and '03, Danielle Pletka, a Middle East expert at the AEI, arranged a series of conferences on the future of Iraq. At one I attended, in October 2002, Perle and Chalabi were on the platform, while in the audience were a Who's Who of Iraq policymakers from the Pentagon and the vice president's office. Pletka's bitterness now is unrestrained. "I think that even though the president remains rhetorically committed to the idea of what he calls his 'freedom agenda,' it's over," she says. "It turns out we stink at it. And we don't just stink at it in Iraq. We stink at it in Egypt. And in Lebanon. And in the Palestinian territories. And in Jordan. And in Yemen. And in Algeria. And everywhere else we try at it. Because, fundamentally, the message hasn't gotten out to the people on the ground. . . . There is no one out there saying, 'These are the marching orders. Follow them or go and find a new job.' That was what those fights were about. And the true believers lost. Now, that's not to say had they won, everything would be coming up roses. But I do think that we had a window of opportunity to avert a lot of problems that we now see."

For Kenneth Adelman, "the most dispiriting and awful moment of the whole administration was the day that Bush gave the Presidential Medal of Freedom to [former CIA director] George Tenet, General Tommy Franks, and Jerry [Paul] Bremer—three of the most incompetent people who've ever served in such key spots. And they get the highest civilian honor a president can bestow on anyone! That was the day I checked out of this administration. It was then I thought, There's no seriousness here. These are not serious people. If he had been serious, the president would have realized that those three are each directly responsible for the disaster of Iraq."

The most damning assessment of all comes from David Frum: "I always believed as a speechwriter that if you could persuade the president to commit himself to certain words, he would feel himself committed to the ideas that underlay those words. And the big shock to me has been that, although the president said the words, he just did not absorb the ideas. And that is the root of, maybe, everything."

IV. Was Rumsfeld Lousy? You Bet!

Having started so badly, the neocons say, America's occupation of Iraq soon got worse. Michael Rubin is a speaker of Persian and Arabic who worked for Feith's Office of Special Plans and, after the invasion, for the Coalition Provisional Authority (CPA), in Baghdad. Rubin, who is now back at the AEI, points to several developments that undermined the prospects for anything resembling democracy. First was the decision to grant vast powers to Bremer, thus depriving Iraqis of both influence and accountability. "You can't have democracy without accountability," says Rubin, and in that vital first year the only Iraqi leaders with the ability to make a difference were those who controlled armed militias.

The creation of the fortified Green Zone, says Rubin, who chose to live outside it during his year in Baghdad, was "a disaster waiting to happen." It soon became a "bubble," where Bremer and the senior CPA staff were almost completely detached from the worsening realities beyond—including the swelling insurgency. "The guys outside—for example, the civil-affairs officers, some of the USAID [United States Agency for International Development] workers, and so forth—had a much better sense of what was going on outside, but weren't able to get that word inside," Rubin says. Because Bremer was their main source of information, Rumsfeld and other administration spokesmen were out of touch with reality and soon "lost way too much credibility" by repeatedly claiming that the insurgents were not a serious problem.

Meanwhile, waste, corruption, and grotesque mismanagement were rife. Perle tells me a story he heard from an Iraqi cabinet minister, about a friend who was asked to lease a warehouse in Baghdad to a contractor for the Americans in the Green Zone. It turned out they were looking for someplace to store ice for their drinks. But, the man asked, wouldn't storing ice in Iraq's hot climate be expensive? Weren't the Americans *making* ice as and when they needed it? Thus he learned the extraordinary truth: that the ice was trucked in from Kuwait, 300 miles away, in regular convoys. The convoys, says Perle, "came under fire all the time. So we were sending American forces in harm's way, with full combat capability to support them, helicopters overhead, to move goddamn ice from Kuwait to Baghdad."

Perle cites another example: the mishandling of a contract to build 20 health clinics. While it is certainly "a good thing for the U.S. to be building clinics, and paying for it," Perle says, "the prime contractor never left the

Green Zone. So there were subcontractors, and the way in which the prime contractor superintended the project was by asking the subcontractors to take videos of their progress and send them into the Green Zone. Now, you've got to expect projects to go wrong if that's the way you manage them, and indeed they did go wrong, and they ran out of money, and the contract was canceled. A complete fiasco." He knows, he says, "dozens" of similar stories. At their root, he adds, is America's misguided policy of awarding contracts to U.S. multi-nationals instead of Iraqi companies.

To former CIA director Woolsey, one of this saga's most baffling features has been the persistent use of military tactics that were discredited in Vietnam. Since 2003, U.S. forces have "fought 'search-and-destroy' instead of 'clear-and-hold,'" he says, contrasting the ineffective strategy of hunting down insurgents to the proven one of taking territory and defending it. "There's never been a successful anti-insurgency campaign that operated according to search-and-destroy, because bad guys just come back in after you've passed through and kill the people that supported you," Woolsey explains. "How the U.S. government's post-fall-of-Baghdad planning could have ignored that history of Vietnam is stunning to me." But Rumsfeld and Bush were never willing to provide the high troop levels that Woolsey says are necessary for clear-and-hold.

Adelman's dismay at the handling of the insurgency is one reason he now criticizes Rumsfeld so severely. He is also disgusted by the former defense secretary's claims that the mayhem has been exaggerated by the media, and that all the war needs is better PR. "The problem here is not a selling job. The problem is a performance job," Adelman says. "Rumsfeld has said that the war could never be lost in Iraq; it could only be lost in Washington. I don't think that's true at all. We're losing in *Iraq*."

As we leave the restaurant together, Adelman points to an office on the corner of Washington's 18th Street Northwest where he and Rumsfeld first worked together, during the Nixon administration, in 1972. "I've worked with him three times in my life. I have great respect for him. I'm extremely fond of him. I've been to each of his houses, in Chicago, Taos, Santa Fe, Santo Domingo, and Las Vegas. We've spent a lot of vacations together, been around the world together, spent a week together in Vietnam. I'm very, very fond of him, but I'm crushed by his performance. Did he change, or were we wrong in the past? Or is it that he was never really challenged before? I don't know. He certainly fooled me."

V. "A Huge Strategic Defeat"

Though some, such as James Woolsey, still hope against hope for success in Iraq, most of the neocons I speak with are braced for defeat. Even if the worst is avoided, the outcome will bear no resemblance to the scenarios they and their friends inside the Administration laid out back in the glad, confident morning of 2003. "I think we're faced with a range of pretty bad alternatives," says Eliot Cohen. "The problem you're now dealing with is sectarian violence, and a lot of Iranian activity, and those I'm not sure can be rolled back—certainly not without quite a substantial use of force that I'm not sure we have the stomach for. In any case, the things that were possible in '03, '04, are no longer possible." Cohen says his best hope now is not something on the way toward democracy but renewed dictatorship, perhaps led by a former Ba'thist: "I think probably the least bad alternative that we come to sooner or later is a government of national salvation that will be a thinly disguised coup." However, he adds, "I wouldn't be surprised if what we end up drifting toward is some sort of withdrawal on some sort of timetable and leaving the place in a pretty ghastly mess." And that, he believes, would be "about as bad an outcome as one could imagine. . . . Our choices now are between bad and awful."

In the short run, Cohen believes, the main beneficiary of America's intervention in Iraq is the mullahs' regime in Iran, along with its extremist president, Mahmoud Ahmadinejad. And far from heralding the hoped-for era of liberal Middle East reform, he says, "I do think it's going to end up encouraging various strands of Islamism, both Shia and Sunni, and probably will bring destabilization of some regimes of a more traditional kind, which already have their problems." The risk of terrorism on American soil may well increase, too, he fears. "The best news is that the United States remains a healthy, vibrant, vigorous society. So, in a real pinch, we can still pull ourselves together. Unfortunately, it will probably take another big hit. And a very different quality of leadership. Maybe we'll get it."

Frank Gaffney, of the Center for Security Policy, is more pessimistic. While defeat in Iraq is not certain, he regards it as increasingly likely. "It's not a perfect parallel here, but I would say it would approximate to losing the Battle of Britain in World War II," he says. "Our enemies will be emboldened and will re-double their efforts. Our friends will be demoralized and disassociate themselves from us. The delusion is to think that the war is confined to Iraq, and that America can walk away. Failure in Iraq would be a huge strategic defeat." It may already be too late to stop Iran from acquiring nuclear weapons, Gaffney says, pointing out that the Manhattan Project managed to build them in less than four years from a far smaller base of knowledge. "I would say that the likelihood of military action against Iran is 100 percent," he concludes. "I just don't know when or under what circumstances. My guess is that it will be in circumstances of their choosing and not ours."

Richard Perle is almost as apocalyptic. Without some way to turn impending defeat in Iraq to victory, "there will continue to be turbulence and instability in the region. The Sunni in the Gulf, who are already terrified of the Iranians, will become even more terrified of the Iranians. We will be less able to stop an Iranian nuclear program, or Iran's support for terrorism. The Saudis will go nuclear. They will not want to sit there with Ahmadinejad having the nuclear weapon." This is not a cheering prospect: a Sunni-Shia civil war raging in Iraq, while its Sunni and Shia neighbors face each other across the Persian Gulf armed with nukes. As for the great diplomatic hope—that the Iraq Study Group, led by George Bush Sr.'s secretary of state James Baker III, can pull off a deal with Syria and Iran to pacify Iraq—Perle is dismissive: "This is a total illusion. Total illusion. What kind of grand deal? The Iranians are not on our side. They're going to switch over and adopt our side? What can we offer them?"

If the neocon project is not quite dead, it has evidently suffered a crippling blow, from which it may not recover. After our lunch, Adelman sends me an e-mail saying that he now understands the Soviet marshal Sergei Akhromeyev, who committed suicide in the Kremlin when it became clear that the last-ditch Communist coup of 1991 was going to fail. A note he left behind stated, "Everything I have devoted my life to building is in ruins." "I do not share that level of desperation," Adelman writes. "Nevertheless, I feel that the incompetence of the Bush team means that most everything we ever stood for now also lies in ruins."

Frum admits that the optimistic vision he and Perle set out in their book will not now come to pass. "One of the things that we were talking about in that last chapter was the hope that fairly easily this world governed by law, the world of the North Atlantic, can be extended to include the Arab and Muslim Middle East," he says. "I think, coming away from Iraq, people are going to say that's not true, and that the world governed by law will be only a portion of the world. The aftermath of Iraq is that walls are going to go up, and the belief that this is a deep cultural divide is going to deepen." This is already happening in Europe, he adds, citing the British government's campaign against the wearing of veils by women and the Pope's recent critical comments about Islam. As neoconservative optimism withers, Frum fears, the only winner of the debate over Iraq will be Samuel Huntington, whose 1996 book famously forecast a "clash of civilizations" between the West and Islam.

Reading these interviews, those who always opposed the war would be justified in feeling a sense of vindication. Yet even if the future turns out to be brighter than the neocons now fear, the depth and intractability of the Iraqi quagmire allow precious little room for Schadenfreude. Besides the soldiers who continue to die, there are the Iraqis, especially the reformers, whose hopes were so cruelly raised. "Where I most blame George Bush," says the AEI's Michael Rubin, "is that, through his rhetoric, people trusted him, people believed him. Reformists came out of the woodwork and exposed themselves." By failing to match his rhetoric with action, Bush has betrayed them in a way that is "not much different from what his father did on February 15, 1991, when he called the Iraqi people to rise up, and then had second thoughts and didn't do anything once they did." Those who answered the elder Bush's call were massacred.

All the neocons are adamant that, however hard it may be, stabilizing Iraq is the only option. The consequences of a precipitous withdrawal, they say, would be far worse. Listening to them make this argument, I cannot avoid drawing a deeply disturbing conclusion. One of the reasons we are in this mess is that the neocons' gleaming pre-war promises turned out to be wrong. The truly horrifying possibility is that, this time, they may be right.

Part Four:
America in an Uncertain World

The State of the World
Thomas P.M. Barnett

Esquire | May 2007

Global geopolitics is a staggeringly complex business, especially as seen from the perspective of the quote-unquote world's only remaining superpower. For the average person, simply trying to keep all the world's actors straight can be a mind-scrambling exercise. Luckily, former Naval War College professor Thomas P.M. Barnett does the heavy lifting for us in this Esquire *piece—his third article on international affairs to appear in this anthology—as he attempts to surmise what the future will hold for American foreign policy. Whether or not you agree with his conclusions, you're sure to find Barnett's tour of the world's flashpoints both engaging and illuminating in the extreme.*

Now that the Bush presidency is over, it's time those of us left behind assess the damage and seize the opportunities. There's plenty of both. But there's no time to waste, so let's get started: the good news, the bad news, and the news that could change everything.

001
Iran: The Coming Distraction

Good News: Mahmoud Ahmadinejad suffered a worse midterm election than George Bush, with his political allies losing metro elections all over the country and his mullah mentors failing to grab seats in the crucial Assembly of Experts, a college-of-cardinals body that'll pick Grand Ayatollah Ali Khamenei's successor. With the supreme leader on a Francisco Franco-like deathwatch, Ali Akbar Rafsanjani's stunning resurrection (crushed by Ahmadinejad in the '05 presidential election, now he's the Assembly's deputy mullah) suggests our latest Muslim "Hitler" is nothing more than a Persian Newt Gingrich. And over the next two years, we're looking at a potential wholesale swap-out of the senior leadership, and if the result isn't more pragmatism, expect supremely pissed-off college students to do more than just chant "Death to the dictator," like they did recently during an Ahmadinejad speech. Iran is crumbling from within, economically and socially, much like the late-Brezhnevian Soviet Union. In any post-Khamenei scenario, Rafsanjani could easily play Andropov (patron) to the rise of some would-be reformer (like the currently ascending mayor of Tehran) who'd likely try to restructure (perestroika, anyone?) the failed revolutionary system as a going concern in the global economy. Bush's recent full-court press—UN sanctions, moving a carrier battle group into the Persian Gulf, arresting Iranian operatives in Iraq—has put the mullahs on the defensive and might end up being very clever. But the president's got to be careful. The minute he gets violent, Beijing and Moscow are outta here, not to mention the American public.

Bad News: Iran is successfully spreading its influence throughout the region, with significant regime-bonding investment strategies unfolding in southern Lebanon, Syria, Iraq, and Afghanistan. But since that's intimately tied to the price of oil, Iran's strategy is subject to Saudi containment. Tehran's mullahs may put a muzzle on Ahmadinejad now and dump him in two years, but they still want the bomb (and no, that's not an irrational desire after we toppled regimes to their east and west). As far as they're concerned, America's wars to date have left Iran the regional kingpin, and they're right. So Tehran might as well start acting like it while taking the necessary precautions against an inevitable downstream military confrontation with Washington. (Did I mention that the Persians gave us chess?) Iran's shown itself to be a crafty asymmetrical warrior, using proxies Hamas and Hezbollah to demonstrate that it can conflate the region's conflicts at will, so it is not to be underestimated. The mullahs get deterrence all right, as well as preemptive war. If you're unconvinced, talk to Israel as it continues to lick its wounds from last summer.

Wild Card: As Tehran nears the bomb, Israel may well strike first, convinced the second Holocaust is imminent due to Ahmadinejad's skill at turning phrases. A signal of the end times to many believers, it may well be Dick Cheney's plan all along. The problem is, Israel's not up for much more than a token strike (unless it goes preemptively nuclear, at which point all bets are off), so having Israel try and fail conventionally may be a necessary precursor for Bush's—and the Saudis'—final solution. But don't expect Iran's pragmatic mullahs to sit on their hands in the meantime. They recognize a losing hand when they see one and may well trade off on Lebanon and Shiite Iraq if Israel's push comes to Bush's shove. At that point, everyone will recognize that Riyadh—and not Tehran—really won the Iraq war.

002
Middle East: The Big Bang Theory

Good News: It's not as dead as you may think—or pray. Cynically expressed, the Big Bang strategy was always about speeding the killing necessary to trigger systemic change, so the worse Iraq becomes, the more the process picks up speed. I mean, you can't get to the punch line any faster than by forcing the House of Saud to deal directly with an Al Qaeda hornet's nest right next door in the Sunni Triangle (the Saudis' first choice was a security fence on the border—go figure!) while simultaneously triggering Riyadh's proxy war with Tehran in Baghdad. Toss in some Israeli nukes and finally the neocons have really got this party started, because those are the three knockdown fights they believe need to unfold before any serious restructuring of the region's power relationships can occur. A lesser variant has Washington prying Damascus away from Tehran, holding down the fort in Baghdad, and getting Riyadh's tacit approval for Israel's preemptive war on Iran in exchange for a supported solution on Palestine, but that almost seems boring in comparison.

Bad News: It's not as dead as you may think—or pray. Bush and the neocons never had a clue about what was naturally coming on the heels of Saddam's fall (i.e., the Shiite revival) any more than they had a plan about Iraq's postwar occupation. Their in-progress Iranification of the Long War against the global jihadist movement makes even less sense than Bush's poorly planned decision to invade Saddam's secularized Iraq. The Salafist jihad spearheaded by Al Qaedá is exclusively Sunni derived, so why add into the mix their hated enemies, the Shiites? Bush is like the barroom brawler who enters the joint and declares, "I'm taking all of you bastards on"—read: axis of evil—"right here and now!" His administration has committed the fatal mistake that Clinton deftly avoided in the Balkans: They've let the conflicts accumulate instead of tackling them sequentially. The White House's unfolding Iran strategy is nothing more than an ass-covering exercise on Iraq and Afghanistan—a third splendid little war to divert attention from the two previous failures.

Wild Card: If there was ever a time for Al Qaeda to cripple Saudi Arabia's oil infrastructure, now is it. Delivered with the right fingerprints, Al Qaeda might be able to get just enough unity among the United States, Saudi Arabia, and Israel for a full-blown war with Iran. Nothing would set China on a more aggressive course regarding its long-term access to energy in the region, and therein lies Osama bin Laden's best hope for setting "rising Asia" against an aging West in the Persian Gulf.

003
Globalization: Life During Wartime

Good News: The world has never enjoyed a bigger and more dynamic global economy than the one we're riding high on right now, with unprecedented amounts of poverty reduction concentrated in China and India alone. Advanced economies are expanding steadily in the 2 to 3 percent range, while emerging markets dash along in the 7 to 8 percent range, giving us a stunning—and steady—global growth rate of roughly 5 percent. Rising Asia will add upwards of a billion new consumers (i.e., people with disposable income) in the coming years, providing the biggest single impulse the global economy has ever experienced. Financial flows in 2005 hit $6 trillion, more than double the total in 2002. If terrorists are running the world, nobody has told the global financial markets.

Bad News: There's plenty to be nervous about, especially if you're a white-collar worker who's always assumed your job can't be outsourced. (Hint: If your graduate degree involved tons of memorizing facts, you're in the crosshairs.) But with financial panics becoming far less frequent and damaging (e.g., a recent scare in Thailand passed without turning contagious), the biggest dangers now are political. Trade protectionism is on the rise (keep an eye on our Democratic Congress), and the World Trade Organization's Doha Development Round is going nowhere because the West refuses to reduce agricultural subsidies. But neither trend surprises, as a rising tide lifts everybody's demands when it comes to trade deals.

Wild Card: A supply shock in the maxed-out oil industry, which faces a persistently rising long-term global demand due overwhelmingly to skyrocketing requirements in emerging markets led by China and India. "Peak oil" predictions are overblown, focusing exclusively on easily extracted, known conventional reserves. If prices remain high, then the shift to exploiting unconventional reserves and alternative energy sources will grow exponentially. But timing is everything, so a shock to the system could have the lasting effect of moving us down the hydrocarbon chain faster toward hydrogen, nuclear, and renewables. When that happens, it won't be just Al Gore sticking out his chest in pride—we'll all be able to breathe more easily.

004
Al Qaeda: The Global Brand

Good News: We have killed or captured a good portion of Al Qaeda's senior brain trust, meaning the generational cohort of leaders who built up the transnational network to the operational peak represented by the 9/11 strikes. As a result, Al Qaeda's network is a lot more diffuse and dispersed, with the surviving leadership's role trimmed back largely to inspirational guidance from above on strategy and tactics. Yes, Al Qaeda now takes credit for virtually every terrorist act across the globe, but the truth is that its operational center of gravity remains southwest Asia—specifically Iraq's Sunni Triangle and the Afghanistan-Pakistan border region. As worldwide revolutionary movements go, this one is relatively contained and successful only in terms of generating local stalemates against intervening external powers, meaning we get to pick the fight and keep it consistently an "away game." As the Middle East "middle-ages"—demographically speaking—over the next quarter century, time is definitely on our side, since jihadism, like all revolutionary movements, is a young man's game.

Bad News: Al Qaeda's operational reach may now be effectively limited to the same territory (southwest Asia and extending to adjacent areas) as were the classic Middle Eastern terrorist groups of the 1970s and 1980s, but that just means America's efforts to date have made us safer at the expense of allies in Europe, Asia, and Africa. In short, we've turned back the clock but made no strategic headway, plus we've created a dual cause célèbre in Iraq and Afghanistan that will stoke Al Qaeda's recruitment efforts for the long haul. Neither winning nor losing, the Bush administration has merely engineered a back-to-the-future operational stalemate at an unsustainably high cost in blood and treasure, effectively isolating America from the world in the process. Strategically speaking, we've reached a dead end.

Wild Card: Al Qaeda's pursuit of a weapon of mass destruction (think biological, not nuclear) is unrelenting, meaning eventually we will face this threat, and ultimately one side in this Long War will need to break out of the strategic stalemate. The key question, then, is, Which side is more energized and which is more exhausted? With the majority of Gulf oil now flowing to Asia and that trend only increasing with time, won't the American public eventually revolt at the notion that it's their oil and our blood? Osama sure hopes that one more strategic bitch-slap does the job.

005
Iraq: The Quagmire

Good News: The Kurdish areas are secure and thriving economically. Then again, they've been in the nation-building business ever since America started that no-fly zone in the early 1990s. The insurgency is still centered primarily in the Sunni Triangle, so many parts of the Shiite-controlled southeast are surviving okay, thanks in part to significant Iranian investment. Though the central government remains weak, it has forged some important compromises, like a deal to share oil revenue. Following our last best effort on the "surge," the inevitable U.S. drawdown—and "drawback" from combat roles—will look like Vietnam in reverse: We shift from direct action to advising locals. With any luck, Iraq's not much more of a fake state than Pakistan or Lebanon is, and America's military presence can retreat behind the wire of permanent bases in the Kurdish areas or Kuwait, where we currently keep about twenty-five thousand troops. By increasing our naval presence in the region, America can return somewhat to its historic role as offshore balancer in the region. And by participating in the regional peace conference on Iraq, it seems Bush may have finally discovered diplomacy in the Middle East. About time.

Bad News: Baghdad itself is an unmitigated disaster, and the Sunni Triangle has become a no-go zone for all but the most heavily armed outsiders. The horrific social toll of constant violence and massive unemployment is measured in dog years, meaning Bush's surge strategy is far too little and way too late. There is no "Iraq" any more than there was a "Yugoslavia," so America will have to accept this Humpty Dumpty outcome for what it is: a Balkans done backward. The Iraq Study Group rejected partitioning, saying it would be impossible to divide up major cities. Too bad the locals didn't get the word, because that low-grade "ethnic cleansing" proceeds rather vigorously—neighborhood by neighborhood—fueled by rising sectarian violence that outside interested parties (Iran, Saudi Arabia) clearly feed. America cannot stem this tide; only a combined effort by the neighbors can.

Wild Card: The right wrong move by embryonic Kurdistan could trigger a military intervention from anxious Turkey, especially after the highly contested oil-rich city of Kirkuk votes to join "free Kurdistan." Also looming is a Saudi-Iranian proxy war within Iraq itself, just as the persecution and targeting of restive Shiite minorities by entrenched Sunni regimes hits an inflection point regionwide—nudge-nudge, wink-wink from the White House. For now, the Saudis seem content to 1) limit Iran's oil revenue by ramping up their production and 2) curb Iran's influence in Lebanon by funding Hezbollah's opponents. The regional peace conference on Iraq puts everyone at the same table, but if Sy Hersh is correct that Bush has already "redirected" on Iran, that parley might just be for show.

006
The Long War: The Theater-After-Next

Good News: As we squeeze the Persian Gulf-centric radical Salafi jihadist movement, that balloon can expand in two directions over the near term: north into Central Asia or south into Africa. For now, Central Asia is relatively quiet, and local authoritarian regimes—with the consent and support of all interested outside parties—aim to keep it that way. Simply put, there are just too many untapped energy reserves in that region for neighboring great powers (e.g., Russia, Turkey, India, China, and even Shiite Iran) to let radical Sunni terror networks establish significant beachheads. Remember, China and Russia set up the Shanghai Cooperation Organization way before 9/11, so calling our recent arrival (now down to just one military base in Kyrgyzstan) the resumption of the "great game" is a bit much. The Chinese and Russians are basically watching our backs on this one, and we should continue to let them do so because . . .

Bad News: . . . This fight's headed south into sub-Saharan Africa over the long haul. The recent rise and fall of the Islamic courts in Somalia was but a preview of coming attractions. Don't believe? Then check out similar north-versus-south (i.e., Muslim versus Christian) fights simmering across a wide swath of middle Africa (basically where the desert meets the grasslands and forests), because it might not surprise you to find out that the cowboy and the farmer still can't be friends. Al Qaeda, according to our Defense Intelligence Agency, recently brokered an alliance with the Algerian Group for Salafist Preaching and Combat and has famously issued threats regarding any potential Western intervention in Sudan's Darfur region to stem the genocidal war being waged by the invasive Arab *janjaweed* against indigenous black Africans. Success in the Long War will not be marked by less violence or less resistance but by a shift in the geographic center of gravity out of the Gulf region and into Africa. Egypt, with its looming succession from Mubarak father to son (Hosni to Gamal), will continue to either fulfill or fail in its role as continental bulwark, much the way secular (and poorly appreciated) Turkey holds the line for Europe. But in the end, Africa simply offers too many attractive traction points for the Salafi jihadists not to engage as the Middle East middle-ages.

Wild Card: Bush has already announced and will sign into existence sometime between now and the end of his administration a new regional U.S. combatant command: AFRICOM, or African Command. The placeholder, the Combined Joint Task Force–Horn of Africa, now sits in a former French Foreign Legion post in Djibouti. It was originally set up as a picket line to trap Al Qaeda operatives as they exited the Gulf for the dark continent. These are the guys who recently helped engineer Ethiopia's intervention in Somalia, and their command represents a serious experiment in combining the "Three D's": diplomacy, development, and defense. AFRICOM will be the future of the fight and the fight of the future.

007
Defense Department: The New Coin of the Realm

Good News: The Army and Marine Corps continue to calibrate their forces and doctrine to adapt to the long-term challenges of counterinsurgency and a return to the frontier-taming functions last witnessed when our Army of the West really was just our Army in our West. With General George Casey coming back from Iraq to become Army chief of staff and General David Petraeus, chief architect of the U.S. military's new counterinsurgency manual, slotting in behind him in Baghdad, that much needed trend can only accelerate. Two other solid moves by Bush: 1) selecting former CIA chief Robert Gates to replace Donald Rumsfeld as secretary of defense (at this point in the fight, it's better that insider agency types run the Pentagon than the outsider neocons) and 2) sliding Admiral "Fox" Fallon over from Pacific Command to Central Command, bringing along his substantial diplomatic experience and stubbornly strategic vision. (He led a PACOM effort to bolster military-to-military ties with China despite disapproval from Rumsfeld's Pentagon.) With AFRICOM standing up in 2008, we're seeing some serious lessons being learned from Iraq and Afghanistan. Failure is a great teacher.

Bad News: The acquisition overhang from Rumsfeld's transformation initiative remains large, meaning we've still got way too many absurdly complex and expensive weapon systems and platforms (e.g., ships, aircraft) in the pipeline. As ongoing, largely ground operations increasingly exhaust the Army and Marine Corps (and their respective reserve components) both in personnel and equipment, many tough funding cuts loom on the horizon. Rumsfeld never confronted those hard choices, preferring in the end to send his generals to the Hill to beg for more money and let defense contractors stuff emergency supplemental bills with their pet programs. Hopefully, intel-savvy Gates will recognize that a substantial resource shift must ensue, in effect curtailing the Pentagon's obsession with smart weapons and boosting its ability to crank out smarter soldiers. But much depends on how Gates and the Bush administration continue to interpret China's rise in military terms. If you keep hearing the word *hedge,* then expect the Pentagon to keep overstuffing the war-fighting force while starving the nation-building one, and that nasty habit matters plenty if it's your loved ones over in southwest Asia today.

Wild Card: A winner would be Congress somehow stepping up and delivering "Goldwater-Nichols II," or an omnibus restructuring legislation that fixes the broken interagency process (the real cause of our failures in Iraq and Afghanistan) just as the original fixed the dysfunctional interservice rivalries that plagued our military in the post-Vietnam era. Of course, the really bold step would be to create some Cabinet-level department that focuses on transition or failed states. We basically know how to deal with countries in war (Defense) and peace (State). What we lack, though, is a bureaucratic center of gravity that specializes in getting weak states from war to peace. Presidential candidates and a blue-ribbon commission or two are already raising this proposal, so it's out there, waiting for our next massive fuckup to bring it into being.

008
War on Terror: The Legal Underpinnings

Good News: The International Criminal Court was set up in The Hague in 2002 as a permanent version of the UN-sponsored International Criminal Tribunal for the Former Yugoslavia. As an international court of last resort, it's designed to put war criminals on trial for crimes against humanity. With 104 signatory states, the ICC possesses a well-credentialed system for adjudicating and imprisoning such bad actors. What it's missing is a mechanism for bringing them to justice. Oddly enough, the United States possesses a military force with global reach that routinely snatches these guys, only to hide them in secret prisons and put them on secret trial with secret evidence. The U.S. has kept the court at arm's length, fearing its power enough to negotiate bilateral immunity treaties with roughly a hundred states around the world where we anticipate the possibility of future military interventions (since we fear our soldiers and officials will be subject to war-crime accusations). These arrangements will retard the development of global case law. Eventually, Washington will come to its senses.

Bad News: The Bush administration's continuing Dirty Harry take on the Geneva Conventions destroys America's international reputation for the rule of law, providing us with a host of highly questionable practices in the name of "global war," such as the suspension of habeas corpus, the holding of ghost detainees who disappear into the paperwork, the ordering of "extraordinary renditions," by which suspects are deposited with allies who have long histories of torture, and the extraction of confessions by methods right out of the Salem witch trials. If our own Supreme Court can't stomach much of this, how can we expect to win any hearts and minds abroad by mimicking the human-rights abuses of the very same authoritarian regimes (e.g., Saudi Arabia, Egypt) targeted by our lawless enemies, the Salafi jihadists?

Wild Card: Abu Ghraib didn't do it. Gitmo hasn't done it. Short of killing fields being dug up, it's hard to imagine what would dramatically alter the playing field as seen by the Bush-Cheney team. Bush the Decider, after all, basically blew off both the November election and the Iraq Study Group, so it would seem he's not one to be swayed by much when his famous gut tells him otherwise. Our best hope would seem to be for our Supreme Court to step up more aggressively over time—maybe even before Oslo starts handing out Nobel prizes to the whistle-blowers.

009
Afghanipakistan: The Ungovernable

Good News: The Karzai regime muddles along, keeping the bulk of Afghanistan reasonably stable while enabling legitimate economic growth in those pockets not controlled by the druggies. The Musharraf regime does one better in Pakistan, which is growing at a solid clip and finally starting to attract foreign direct investment that underscores its strategic location as connector between the energy-rich southwest-central Asia and the energy-hungry south and east Asia. When you're talking about the parts of both countries that are effectively governed by the center, either situation is arguably described as a slowly modernizing "success story" in the Long War. Hey, when Iraq defines the floor, these two mark—by comparison—the ceiling.

Bad News: The problem is, of course, that neither capital effectively controls the hinterlands, which overlap precipitously along their shared, mountainous border. There the poppy trade booms, prestate tribalism rules, and the Taliban are back in the business of state-sponsored terror, thanks in no small part to a de facto peace treaty with Musharraf's regime. The Pashtun tribes of northwest Pakistan have been ungovernable for as long as history records. While outsiders can effectively ally with them against perceived common enemies, as America did against the Soviets in Afghanistan, none have effectively conquered them. And yet the Taliban are carving out a ministate within these lands, employing their usual brutal techniques. The result is, once again, a secure sanctuary for Al Qaeda's global leadership (to include Osama bin Laden) and a training ground for motivated jihadists.

Wild Card: The next 9/11-like attack on American soil—especially if WMD are involved—could well trigger the gravest consequences for the Taliban's state-within-a-state. Americans might just countenance a limited nuclear strike in an eye-for-an-eye moment of unleashed fury and frustration. Unthinkable? We did it to Japan under far cooler circumstances but for similar reasons—namely, a full-scale invasion seemed prohibitively costly in human life. Is nuking Afghanistan advisable? No, nuking is always a bad idea. But rubble, as they say, makes no trouble, and bombing them back to the Stone Age would be a very short trip.

010
China: The Slated Near-Peer

Good News: China's torrid growth continues, despite all predictions that it must soon end lest it tear the country apart through some combination of the horrific environmental disasters just unfolding, a financial panic caused by a still-rickety banking system, or—Mao forbid!—political unrest among the masses of rural peasants left behind in abject poverty. So long as the foreign direct investment flows (China's the number-one target in the world outside the West) and export volume rises, the Chinese Communist Party, which has staked its regime legitimacy almost entirely on raising income levels, continues to pull off the seemingly impossible: creating a world-class domestic market while whittling down the world's largest state sector. How hard is that? Bill Clinton created more than twenty million new jobs in America across his eight years as president. China's leaders need to generate almost the same number of new jobs every year to keep this juggernaut moving forward.

Bad News: China's military buildup is real, although America's slated to outspend it by roughly $10 trillion over the next two decades, so our lead seems pretty safe. What's so scary right now about China's strategic relationship with the United States, or lack thereof, is that our economic interdependence is very real and rapidly expanding while our security ties remain embryonic at best and highly suspicious at worst. Even if we get past North Korea, the Taiwan situation still divides us strategically, and as China increasingly penetrates the Middle East, Africa, and Latin America with its rather unprincipled investment strategies, opportunities for conflict with U.S. security interests will abound. Given the right breakdown of cooperation over Iran (or failure to get any in places like Sudan, Nigeria, Zimbabwe, Venezuela—

you name it), we could be looking at a resumption of cold-war binary thinking by which Washington hawks calculate every international loss (or even slight) as China's zero-sum gain. Factor in a Democratic-led Congress eager to take on the threat of "cheap Chinese labor" and their underappreciated currency, and what should be globalization's strongest bilateral relationship could easily turn into its worst—even the cause for its demise.

Wild Card: You'll get the same answer from Wall Street CEOs and White House staffers: Nobody wants to see a financial meltdown triggered inside China, because nobody—and I mean nobody—has any idea how bad that could get for the global economy as a whole. Eventually, something has to give in China's still-white-hot economy, so the question really isn't Can a financial panic happen in China? but rather How will America handle it when it does?

011
North Korea: the Persistent Outlier

Good News: The Bush administration has been successful in maintaining a fairly coherent unity of effort with Russia, Japan, China, and South Korea, in that we're all still talking and cooperating and worrying about the same things. Admittedly, we've not accomplished much vis-à-vis Kim Jong Il's regime (the recent deal smells of a Clinton-like "freeze," with the truly hard details—like the actual bombs—left to the future), but the dialogue itself is laying the groundwork for a post-Kim effort to construct an East Asia NATO-like security architecture that cements China's role as the Germany of Asia and ends fears of emerging security rivalries with offshore Japan. (Asia's never enjoyed a stable peace when both China and Japan were powerful.) While Kim's successfully blackmailed us in the past on nukes, his kleptocratic regime's reliance on self-financing through criminal activities does leave it vulnerable to the sort of stringent financial sanctions recently imposed by the U.S. That tactic begins to work when Chinese banks, more interested in maintaining their international credit ratings, start choosing transparency over illicit dealings with Pyongyang. Talk Tokyo and Beijing into a naval blockade and we may set an endgame in motion.

Bad News: The recent Bush deal is a bad deal that should give no one comfort, as it is unlikely to force Kim into giving up his nukes (not when the blackmailing still works for aid), and then there's the unacknowledged second nuclear program that Pyongyang bought from Pakistan years back. We haven't even begun the negotiations on that one yet. Unlike the years-in-the-making danger of a nuclear Iran, Kim's got the necessary missile technology in hand, and he tested his first crude nuke last October. Remembering East Germany's fate, Kim confronts the high likelihood of not just near-term attempts at regime change but the inevitable liquidation of his entire nation as the wrong half of the last divided-state situation to linger beyond the cold war. Despite Ahmadinejad's fiery threats, Iran's mullahs have plenty to live for, while Kim's got everything to lose, making his long-demonstrated siege mentality and willingness to sacrifice millions of his own people to preserve his rule two crucial indicators of his undeterrability. The problem with the slow squeeze we're pursuing is that eventually it'll trigger some reckless act from Kim, which in turn sets in motion the following scary scenario: South Korean and U.S. forces pouring in from the south and sea, Chinese forces entering from the north to prevent refugee flows, and somewhere in that small chaotic space, the world's fourth-largest military armed with some unknown number of nuclear devices and a Götterdämmerung-inducing ideology of racial superiority. No wonder Beijing's not so psyched to get it on.

Wild Card: Beijing's clearly in the driver's seat on this one, which makes the government's not-so-quiet examination of Ceausescu's rapid fall in Romania in late 1989 (hint: Moscow's KGB gave him a push) all the more telling. China's leaders are definitely exploring an exit strategy on this one, the timing of which couldn't be more crucial for the future of Sino-American relations.

012
The White House: The Bush Imperative

Good News: There's about twenty months left in W.'s presidency and his heart's one helluva lot stronger than Cheney's. The Iraq tie-down pretty much means Bush can't start any more wars anywhere else, despite all the tough talk. Much like Jimmy Carter near the end, Bush seems wholly engulfed by the Gulf, but since nobody other than that pesky Hugo Chávez seems intent on pressing our disadvantage, that's probably a good thing. Although this administration has been willfully oblivious to its gargantuan federal deficits up to now (what is it about Republican administrations?),

Bush has somewhat cynically found religion on the subject recently, declaring his new goal of eliminating those deficits somewhere around the end of his successor's first term. Talk about passing the buck! Then again, if Bush's surge strategy in Iraq creates even the slightest semblance of job-not-too-horrendously-done and allows for our troops' effective withdrawal from combat duty there by January 2009, I doubt we'd hear any complaints from the new resident at 1600.

Bad News: Condoleezza Rice is proving to be an even weaker secretary of state than Colin Powell, although at least she talks out of only one side of her mouth. Then again, since Rice's diplomacy consists solely of delivering White House talking points the world over, that is a mean trick. All dissing aside, the real problem with American diplomacy under Bush (if you can call it diplomacy) is that Dick Cheney has been in charge of it all along, and now that über-ally Don Rumsfeld is gone at Defense, we won't even see its muscular version (the Bush Doctrine) employed anymore, leaving us with basically no foreign policy whatsoever. The big problem with this state of affairs is that Bush's postpresidency has started earlier in his second term than any leader since Richard Nixon, leaving America's global leadership adrift at a rather fluid moment in history. I'm not just talking the Long War but the other 95 percent of reality that actually makes the world go round. With Tony Blair leaving office in the UK, there's virtually no adult supervision left anywhere, which is sad because, with a global economy humming as nice as this one is, the world could really take advantage of some visionary leadership right now to tackle a host of compelling global challenges like AIDS, global warming, childhood diseases—you know, the whole Two Bills/Bono agenda!

Wild Card: Bush has said repeatedly that he's on a personal mission to deny Iran nuclear weapons, and Cheney wants nothing more than to go down in history as the man who restored power to the American presidency. Put those two scary dynamics together and you've got the mother of all October surprises come 2008. Washington is naturally all abuzz with this prospect, causing Bush to deny publicly any plans for war. But as we've learned with this administration, it's Deny, deny, deny, and then strike! If and when Bush pulls that trigger, watch the Democratic Congress start impeachment proceedings. That'll make it two-for-two with Boomer presidents, but that only makes sense for a generation who came of age with Watergate.

013
The Rising East: The Degree of Compliance

Good News: The Bush administration has been successful in drawing both Russia and China into multilateral security discussions on Iran and North Korea, and even when both nations routinely water down our proposed responses, they're staying in the conversation, offering their own helpful ideas (like Moscow's proposal to outsource Iran's uranium enrichment) and generally becoming more comfortable coordinating security policies with the West's great powers on issues of shared concern. It may not sound like much, but such routine is what builds up relationships over the long haul. As Washington's relatively successful courtship of rising India has shown, it's the small gestures that matter most, like the United States finally acknowledging New Delhi's standing as a nuclear power. With India and China, we're looking at two big body shops—as in, million-man-plus armies—that logically should someday soon be enlisted for long-term cooperative peacekeeping and nation-building efforts in Africa, where both nations currently deploy tens of thousands of nationals in market-making commercial and developmental activities. You want to do stuff on the cheap? Well, you better find cheap labor.

Bad News: Each of the big players suffers from strategic myopia, meaning none are currently capable of punching their weight internationally at America's side. With Russia, it's their obsession with their so-called near abroad (the Caucasus and Central Asia) and Putin's aggressive push to renationalize the commanding heights of Russia's new economy—namely, the energy sector. The Chinese, despite their ballooning reliance on distant foreign energy sources, still act as though their entire strategic environment boils down to the Taiwan Strait. Ditto for India and Kashmir. South Korea's ready to climb on Oprah's couch over its queer embrace of its long-lost sibling to the north, but don't expect it to climb out of any foxholes anytime soon on our behalf. Toss in glass-jaw Japan and there's not really anybody in the East we can count on in a tight spot.

Wild Card: The truly intriguing wild cards are local disasters that provide the U.S. military the pretext for drawing out these rising states' militaries in cooperative humanitarian responses, the way the 2004 Christmas tsunamis helped the Pentagon reestablish military-to-military ties with Indonesia (as well as triggering the internal solution of Indonesia's Aceh secessionist movement). If there's going to be a global-warming tipping-point disaster, it'll probably unfold in the East Asian littoral.

014
The Aging West: The State of Alliance

Good News: Recent elections and those looming on the horizon are not producing a crop of anti-American leaders among our traditional allies, which is extraordinarily generous on their part given the unprecedented anti-Americanism that's pervaded the vast majority of the world across the Bush administration. With France and the UK in transition, Germany's Angela Merkel has emerged as Europe's most powerful female leader since Margaret Thatcher, to whom the "iron Frau" is most commonly compared. Most important for America, Merkel is intent on keeping the transatlantic relationship strong and bolstering the role of NATO as its preeminent security structure. With Shinzo Abe taking the reins in economically resurgent Japan and pushing for expanded ties with NATO, we're seeing the old West as a whole assume a more forward-leaning security posture. Given the UN's enduring weakness, NATO's imprimatur is as close as America can get to approval by the international community for most overseas military interventions, with our Balkan missions serving as the best model to date.

Bad News: Though NATO is in Afghanistan, the many operational limitations imposed by individual members make its employment consistently suboptimal, and it has done little to bolster U.S. troop efforts to tame the Taliban's growing influence in the south. As for Iraq, the Middle East, much like all of Africa, simply remains a bridge too far for this collection of former colonial powers who aren't much interested in any lengthy return engagements (although the French occasionally pop up in Africa now and then). Other than the Brits (who've already opted out of Bush's surge strategy in Iraq), it is hard to imagine NATO countries taking serious numbers of casualties anywhere outside of Europe (okay, the French and Italian effort in south Lebanon has some merit), not with the EU's growing unease over its "absorption capacity" of new eastern members and popular fears of the invasive species known as *Homo Islamicus*. In a Long War with a high body requirement, it's unrealistic for America to assume that its traditional military allies, all of whom are demographically moribund, will suffice for the quagmire-like interventions that lie ahead.

Wild Card: The globalization wormhole that connects the United Kingdom to Pakistan features substantial two-way traffic whose upshot is a steady stream of radicalized expats landing in British working-class neighborhoods on a daily basis. The West's "stargate" on this, Britain's world-class internal security service, MI-5, cannot possibly uncover every plot, so if that lucky strike hits the right target at the right time, our European friends could suddenly veer into a *Children of Men*–like extreme-lockdown scenario.

015
All the Rest: Other Complications

Good News: Despite all the ominous news, the developing world is not awash in civil strife. Africa, for example, was suffering from sixteen major civil or cross-border conflicts half a decade ago but endures only a half dozen today. Thanks to the commodities boom, infrastructure development there has shifted from being a supply-push aid effort led by the West to a demand-pull construction effort led by the East. In Latin America, the only serious insurgency still operating is the Revolutionary Armed Forces of Colombia (FARC), and the dozen recent elections there produced far more market-friendly leaders than Chávez-like populists. East Asia's relatively quiet, with nasty flare-ups in Sri Lanka and East Timor, and the dominant economic trends there continue to be rapid marketization and long-term integration with China, globalization's premier final assembler of manufactured goods. Best of all, the current oil boom has triggered voluminous "east-east" capital flows, whereby Arab energy producers direct their surplus capital to Asia's infrastructure build-out while Asia's high savings rates are beginning to flow into the Gulf's emerging financial hubs, in addition to its energy sector.

Bad News: The West's stubborn holdout on its agricultural subsidies keeps the WTO's Doha Round from doing what it should to jump-start agricultural markets in developing economies. While China's doing plenty to create infrastructure in many resource-rich states, it's also replicating the profile that European colonial powers once employed: trading low-cost manufactures for even lower-end commodities. Net result? Local producers and small manufacturers tend to be crowded out by China's Wal-Mart-like impact. No wonder rising economic nationalism in Latin America, for example, is increasingly directed at China instead of just the usual culprits in the West.

Wild Card: Anything that torpedoes China's economic juggernaut would have a huge impact throughout the developing world, so probably the nastiest wild card to cue up would be the SARS/avian-flu-after-next that both derails Asian economies while overwhelming the meager public-health capacities of developing economies.

016
The Wildest Card: 2008

The ancient Greek poet Archilochus said, "The fox knows many things, but the hedgehog knows one big thing." Let me submit that we're living through the final months of the hedgehog presidency of one George W. Bush, whose greatest failure has been his lack of strategic imagination.

Now, as the 2008 presidential campaign gears up, let me presume to offer this: avoid hedgehogs. Don't listen to candidates who tell you this whole election boils down to one thing and one thing alone. We need a president with more than one answer to every question, one whose tool kit is as diverse as his—or her—ideology is flexible. We need a deal maker, a compromiser, a closer. We need someone able to finish what others cannot and start that which others dare not.

We need a leader who knows many things, because we've had quite enough of those who know only one big thing.

The Redirection

Seymour M. Hersh

the *New Yorker* | March 5, 2007

Notwithstanding its recently opened diplomatic dialogue with the U.S., Iran, with its bellicose leadership, its shadowy influence on the turmoil in neighboring Iraq, and its stubborn pursuit of nuclear technology, remains one of America's major foreign-policy headaches. Seymour Hersh has spent the past two years writing in the New Yorker *about discussions within the Bush administration regarding possible military action against the Iranian government. In this article, he reports on how the Iran problem has led the U.S. to reorient its anti-terror policy to focus on the threat posed by Shiite Islamic extremists—even if this means supporting certain Sunni groups who may have ties to Al Qaeda.*

A Strategic Shift

In the past few months, as the situation in Iraq has deteriorated, the Bush administration, in both its public diplomacy and its covert operations, has significantly shifted its Middle East strategy. The "redirection," as some inside the White House have called the new strategy, has brought the United States closer to an open confrontation with Iran and, in parts of the region, propelled it into a widening sectarian conflict between Shiite and Sunni Muslims.

To undermine Iran, which is predominantly Shiite, the Bush administration has decided, in effect, to reconfigure its priorities in the Middle East. In Lebanon, the Administration has cooperated with Saudi Arabia's government, which is Sunni, in clandestine operations that are intended to weaken Hezbollah, the Shiite organization that is backed by Iran. The U.S. has also taken part in clandestine operations aimed at Iran and its ally Syria. A by-product of these activities has been the bolstering of Sunni extremist groups that espouse a militant vision of Islam and are hostile to America and sympathetic to Al Qaeda.

One contradictory aspect of the new strategy is that, in Iraq, most of the insurgent violence directed at the American military has come from Sunni forces, and not from Shiites. But, from the Administration's perspective, the most profound—and unintended—strategic consequence of the Iraq war is the empowerment of Iran. Its president, Mahmoud Ahmadinejad, has made defiant pronouncements about the destruction of Israel and his country's right to pursue its nuclear program, and last week its supreme religious leader, Ayatollah Ali Khamenei, said on state television that "realities in the region show that the arrogant front, headed by the U.S. and its allies, will be the principal loser in the region."

After the revolution of 1979 brought a religious government to power, the United States broke with Iran and cultivated closer relations with the leaders of Sunni Arab states such as Jordan, Egypt, and Saudi Arabia. That calculation became more complex after the September 11th attacks, especially with regard to the Saudis. Al Qaeda is Sunni, and many of its operatives came from extremist religious circles inside Saudi Arabia. Before the invasion of Iraq, in 2003, Administration officials, influenced by neoconservative ideologues, assumed that a Shiite government there could provide a pro-American balance to Sunni extremists, since Iraq's Shiite majority had been oppressed under Saddam Hussein. They ignored warnings from the intelligence community about the ties between Iraqi Shiite leaders and Iran, where some had lived in exile for years. Now, to the distress of the White House, Iran has forged a close relationship with the Shiite-dominated government of Prime Minister Nuri al-Maliki.

The new American policy, in its broad outlines, has been discussed publicly. In testimony before the Senate Foreign Relations Committee in January, Secretary of State Condoleezza Rice said that there is "a new strategic alignment in the Middle East," separating "reformers" and "extremists"; she pointed to the Sunni states as centers of moderation, and said that Iran, Syria, and Hezbollah were "on the other side of that divide." (Syria's Sunni majority is dominated by the Alawi sect.) Iran and Syria, she said, "have made their choice and their choice is to destabilize."

Some of the core tactics of the redirection are not public, however. The clandestine operations have been kept secret, in some cases, by leaving the execution or the funding to the Saudis, or by finding other ways to work around the normal congressional appropriations process, current and former officials close to the Administration said.

A senior member of the House Appropriations Committee told me that he had heard about the new strategy, but felt that he and his colleagues had not been adequately briefed. "We haven't got any of this," he said. "We ask for anything going on, and they say there's nothing. And when we ask specific questions they say, 'We're going to get back to you.' It's so frustrating."

The key players behind the redirection are Vice President Dick Cheney, the deputy national-security adviser Elliott Abrams, the departing Ambassador to Iraq (and nominee for United Nations Ambassador), Zalmay Khalilzad, and Prince Bandar bin Sultan, the Saudi national-security adviser. While Rice has been deeply involved in shaping the public policy, former and current officials said that the clandestine side has been guided by Cheney. (Cheney's office and the White House declined to comment for this story; the Pentagon did not respond to specific queries but said, "The United States is not planning to go to war with Iran.")

The policy shift has brought Saudi Arabia and Israel into a new strategic embrace, largely because both countries see Iran as an existential threat. They have been involved in direct talks, and the Saudis, who believe that greater stability in Israel and Palestine will give Iran less leverage in the region, have become more involved in Arab-Israeli negotiations.

The new strategy "is a major shift in American policy—it's a sea change," a U.S. government consultant with close ties to Israel said. The Sunni states "were petrified of a Shiite resurgence, and there was growing resentment with our gambling on the moderate Shiites in Iraq," he said. "We cannot reverse the Shiite gain in Iraq, but we can contain it."

"It seems there has been a debate inside the government over what's the biggest danger—Iran or Sunni radicals," Vali Nasr, a senior fellow at the Council on Foreign Relations, who has written widely on Shiites, Iran, and Iraq, told me. "The Saudis and some in the Administration have been arguing that the biggest threat is Iran and the Sunni radicals are the lesser enemies. This is a victory for the Saudi line."

Martin Indyk, a senior State Department official in the Clinton administration who also served as Ambassador to Israel, said that "the Middle East is heading into a serious Sunni-Shiite Cold War." Indyk, who is the director of the Saban Center for Middle East Policy at the Brookings Institution, added that, in his opinion, it was not clear whether the White House was fully aware of the strategic implications of its new policy. "The White House is not just doubling the bet in Iraq," he said. "It's doubling the bet across the region. This could get very complicated. Everything is upside down."

The Administration's new policy for containing Iran seems to complicate its strategy for winning the war in Iraq. Patrick Clawson, an expert on Iran and the deputy director for research at the Washington Institute for Near East Policy, argued, however, that closer ties between the United States and moderate or even radical Sunnis could put "fear" into the government of Prime Minister Maliki and "make him worry that the Sunnis could actually win" the civil war there. Clawson said that this might give Maliki an incentive to cooperate with the United States in suppressing radical Shiite militias, such as Moqtada al-Sadr's Mahdi Army.

Even so, for the moment, the U.S. remains dependent on the cooperation of Iraqi Shiite leaders. The Mahdi Army may be openly hostile to

American interests, but other Shiite militias are counted as U.S. allies. Both Moqtada al-Sadr and the White House back Maliki. A memorandum written late last year by Stephen Hadley, the national-security adviser, suggested that the Administration try to separate Maliki from his more radical Shiite allies by building his base among moderate Sunnis and Kurds, but so far the trends have been in the opposite direction. As the Iraqi Army continues to founder in its confrontations with insurgents, the power of the Shiite militias has steadily increased.

Flynt Leverett, a former Bush administration National Security Council official, told me that "there is nothing coincidental or ironic" about the new strategy with regard to Iraq. "The Administration is trying to make a case that Iran is more dangerous and more provocative than the Sunni insurgents to American interests in Iraq, when—if you look at the actual casualty numbers—the punishment inflicted on America by the Sunnis is greater by an order of magnitude," Leverett said. "This is all part of the campaign of provocative steps to increase the pressure on Iran. The idea is that at some point the Iranians will respond and then the Administration will have an open door to strike at them."

President George W. Bush, in a speech on January 10th, partially spelled out this approach. "These two regimes"—Iran and Syria—"are allowing terrorists and insurgents to use their territory to move in and out of Iraq," Bush said. "Iran is providing material support for attacks on American troops. We will disrupt the attacks on our forces. We'll interrupt the flow of support from Iran and Syria. And we will seek out and destroy the networks providing advanced weaponry and training to our enemies in Iraq."

In the following weeks, there was a wave of allegations from the Administration about Iranian involvement in the Iraq war. On February 11th, reporters were shown sophisticated explosive devices, captured in Iraq, that the Administration claimed had come from Iran. The Administration's message was, in essence, that the bleak situation in Iraq was the result not of its own failures of planning and execution but of Iran's interference.

The U.S. military also has arrested and interrogated hundreds of Iranians in Iraq. "The word went out last August for the military to snatch as many Iranians in Iraq as they can," a former senior intelligence official said. "They had five hundred locked up at one time. We're working these guys and getting information from them. The White House goal is to build a case that the Iranians have been fomenting the insurgency and they've been doing it all along—that Iran is, in fact, supporting the killing of Americans." The Pentagon consultant confirmed that hundreds of Iranians have been captured by American forces in recent months. But he told me that that total includes many Iranian humanitarian and aid workers who "get scooped up and released in a short time," after they have been interrogated.

"We are not planning for a war with Iran," Robert Gates, the new Defense Secretary, announced on February 2nd, and yet the atmosphere of confrontation has deepened. According to current and former American intelligence and military officials, secret operations in Lebanon have been accompanied by clandestine operations targeting Iran. American military and special-operations teams have escalated their activities in Iran to gather intelligence and, according to a Pentagon consultant on terrorism and the former senior intelligence official, have also crossed the border in pursuit of Iranian operatives from Iraq.

At Rice's Senate appearance in January, Democratic Senator Joseph Biden, of Delaware, pointedly asked her whether the U.S. planned to cross the Iranian or the Syrian border in the course of a pursuit. "Obviously, the president isn't going to rule anything out to protect our troops, but the plan is to take down these networks in Iraq," Rice said, adding, "I do think that everyone will understand that—the American people and I assume the Congress expect the president to do what is necessary to protect our forces."

The ambiguity of Rice's reply prompted a response from Nebraska Senator Chuck Hagel, a Republican, who has been critical of the Administration:

> Some of us remember 1970, Madam Secretary. And that was Cambodia. And when our government lied to the American people and said, "We didn't cross the border going into Cambodia," in fact we did.
>
> I happen to know something about that, as do some on this committee. So, Madam Secretary, when you set in motion the kind of policy that the president is talking about here, it's very, very dangerous.

The Administration's concern about Iran's role in Iraq is coupled with its long-standing alarm over Iran's nuclear program. On Fox News on January 14th, Cheney warned of the possibility, in a few years, "of a nuclear-armed

Iran, astride the world's supply of oil, able to affect adversely the global economy, prepared to use terrorist organizations and/or their nuclear weapons to threaten their neighbors and others around the world." He also said, "If you go and talk with the Gulf states or if you talk with the Saudis or if you talk with the Israelis or the Jordanians, the entire region is worried. . . . The threat Iran represents is growing."

The Administration is now examining a wave of new intelligence on Iran's weapons programs. Current and former American officials told me that the intelligence, which came from Israeli agents operating in Iran, includes a claim that Iran has developed a three-stage solid-fuelled intercontinental missile capable of delivering several small warheads—each with limited accuracy—inside Europe. The validity of this human intelligence is still being debated.

A similar argument about an imminent threat posed by weapons of mass destruction—and questions about the intelligence used to make that case—formed the prelude to the invasion of Iraq. Many in Congress have greeted the claims about Iran with wariness; in the Senate on February 14th, Hillary Clinton said, "We have all learned lessons from the conflict in Iraq, and we have to apply those lessons to any allegations that are being raised about Iran. Because, Mr. President, what we are hearing has too familiar a ring and we must be on guard that we never again make decisions on the basis of intelligence that turns out to be faulty."

Still, the Pentagon is continuing intensive planning for a possible bombing attack on Iran, a process that began last year, at the direction of the president. In recent months, the former intelligence official told me, a special planning group has been established in the offices of the Joint Chiefs of Staff, charged with creating a contingency bombing plan for Iran that can be implemented, upon orders from the president, within twenty-four hours.

In the past month, I was told by an Air Force adviser on targeting and the Pentagon consultant on terrorism, the Iran planning group has been handed a new assignment: to identify targets in Iran that may be involved in supplying or aiding militants in Iraq. Previously, the focus had been on the destruction of Iran's nuclear facilities and possible regime change.

Two carrier strike groups—the Eisenhower and the Stennis—are now in the Arabian Sea. One plan is for them to be relieved early in the spring, but there is worry within the military that they may be ordered to stay in the area after the new carriers arrive, according to several sources. (Among other concerns, war games have shown that the carriers could be vulnerable to swarming tactics involving large numbers of small boats, a technique that the Iranians have practiced in the past; carriers have limited maneuverability in the narrow Strait of Hormuz, off Iran's southern coast.) The former senior intelligence official said that the current contingency plans allow for an attack order this spring. He added, however, that senior officers on the Joint Chiefs were counting on the White House's not being "foolish enough to do this in the face of Iraq, and the problems it would give the Republicans in 2008."

Prince Bandar's Game

The Administration's effort to diminish Iranian authority in the Middle East has relied heavily on Saudi Arabia and on Prince Bandar, the Saudi national-security adviser. Bandar served as the Ambassador to the United States for twenty-two years, until 2005, and has maintained a friendship with President Bush and Vice President Cheney. In his new post, he continues to meet privately with them. Senior White House officials have made several visits to Saudi Arabia recently, some of them not disclosed.

Last November, Cheney flew to Saudi Arabia for a surprise meeting with King Abdullah and Bandar. The *Times* reported that the King warned Cheney that Saudi Arabia would back its fellow-Sunnis in Iraq if the United States were to withdraw. A European intelligence official told me that the meeting also focused on more general Saudi fears about "the rise of the Shiites." In response, "The Saudis are starting to use their leverage—money."

In a royal family rife with competition, Bandar has, over the years, built a power base that relies largely on his close relationship with the U.S., which is crucial to the Saudis. Bandar was succeeded as Ambassador by Prince Turki al-Faisal; Turki resigned after eighteen months and was replaced by Adel A. al-Jubeir, a bureaucrat who has worked with Bandar. A former Saudi diplomat told me that during Turki's tenure he became aware of private meetings involving Bandar and senior White House officials, including Cheney and Abrams. "I assume Turki was not happy with that," the Saudi said. But, he added, "I don't think that Bandar is going off on his own." Although Turki dislikes Bandar, the Saudi said, he shared his goal of challenging the spread of Shiite power in the Middle East.

The split between Shiites and Sunnis goes back to a bitter divide, in the seventh century, over who should succeed the Prophet Muhammad. Sunnis dominated the medieval caliphate and the Ottoman Empire, and Shiites, traditionally, have been regarded more as outsiders. Worldwide, 90 percent of Muslims are Sunni, but Shiites are a majority in Iran, Iraq, and Bahrain, and are the largest Muslim group in Lebanon. Their concentration in a volatile, oil-rich region has led to concern in the West and among Sunnis about the emergence of a "Shiite crescent"—especially given Iran's increased geopolitical weight.

"The Saudis still see the world through the days of the Ottoman Empire, when Sunni Muslims ruled the roost and the Shiites were the lowest class," Frederic Hof, a retired military officer who is an expert on the Middle East, told me. If Bandar was seen as bringing about a shift in U.S. policy in favor of the Sunnis, he added, it would greatly enhance his standing within the royal family.

The Saudis are driven by their fear that Iran could tilt the balance of power not only in the region but within their own country. Saudi Arabia has a significant Shiite minority in its Eastern Province, a region of major oil fields; sectarian tensions are high in the province. The royal family believes that Iranian operatives, working with local Shiites, have been behind many terrorist attacks inside the kingdom, according to Vali Nasr. "Today, the only army capable of containing Iran"—the Iraqi Army—"has been destroyed by the United States. You're now dealing with an Iran that could be nuclear-capable and has a standing army of four hundred and fifty thousand soldiers." (Saudi Arabia has seventy-five thousand troops in its standing army.)

Nasr went on, "The Saudis have considerable financial means, and have deep relations with the Muslim Brotherhood and the Salafis"—Sunni extremists who view Shiites as apostates. "The last time Iran was a threat, the Saudis were able to mobilize the worst kinds of Islamic radicals. Once you get them out of the box, you can't put them back."

The Saudi royal family has been, by turns, both a sponsor and a target of Sunni extremists, who object to the corruption and decadence among the family's myriad princes. The princes are gambling that they will not be overthrown as long as they continue to support religious schools and charities linked to the extremists. The Administration's new strategy is heavily dependent on this bargain.

Nasr compared the current situation to the period in which Al Qaeda first emerged. In the nineteen-eighties and the early nineties, the Saudi government offered to subsidize the covert American CIA proxy war against the Soviet Union in Afghanistan. Hundreds of young Saudis were sent into the border areas of Pakistan, where they set up religious schools, training bases, and recruiting facilities. Then, as now, many of the operatives who were paid with Saudi money were Salafis. Among them, of course, were Osama bin Laden and his associates, who founded Al Qaeda, in 1988.

This time, the U.S. government consultant told me, Bandar and other Saudis have assured the White House that "they will keep a very close eye on the religious fundamentalists. Their message to us was 'We've created this movement, and we can control it.' It's not that we don't want the Salafis to throw bombs; it's *who* they throw them at—Hezbollah, Moqtada al-Sadr, Iran, and at the Syrians, if they continue to work with Hezbollah and Iran."

The Saudi said that, in his country's view, it was taking a political risk by joining the U.S. in challenging Iran: Bandar is already seen in the Arab world as being too close to the Bush administration. "We have two nightmares," the former diplomat told me. "For Iran to acquire the bomb and for the United States to attack Iran. I'd rather the Israelis bomb the Iranians, so we can blame them. If America does it, we will be blamed."

In the past year, the Saudis, the Israelis, and the Bush administration have developed a series of informal understandings about their new strategic direction. At least four main elements were involved, the U.S. government consultant told me. First, Israel would be assured that its security was paramount and that Washington and Saudi Arabia and other Sunni states shared its concern about Iran.

Second, the Saudis would urge Hamas, the Islamist Palestinian party that has received support from Iran, to curtail its anti-Israeli aggression and to begin serious talks about sharing leadership with Fatah, the more secular Palestinian group. (In February, the Saudis brokered a deal at Mecca between the two factions. However, Israel and the U.S. have expressed dissatisfaction with the terms.)

The third component was that the Bush administration would work directly with Sunni nations to counteract Shiite ascendance in the region.

Fourth, the Saudi government, with Washington's approval, would provide funds and logistical aid to weaken the government of President Bashir Assad, of Syria. The Israelis believe that putting such pressure on the Assad government will make it more conciliatory and open to negotiations. Syria is a major conduit of arms to Hezbollah. The Saudi government is also at odds with the Syrians over the assassination of Rafik Hariri, the former Lebanese Prime Minister, in Beirut in 2005, for which it believes the Assad government was responsible. Hariri, a billionaire Sunni, was closely associated with the Saudi regime and with Prince Bandar. (A UN inquiry strongly suggested that the Syrians were involved, but offered no direct evidence; there are plans for another investigation, by an international tribunal.)

Patrick Clawson, of the Washington Institute for Near East Policy, depicted the Saudis' cooperation with the White House as a significant breakthrough. "The Saudis understand that if they want the Administration to make a more generous political offer to the Palestinians they have to persuade the Arab states to make a more generous offer to the Israelis," Clawson told me. The new diplomatic approach, he added, "shows a real degree of effort and sophistication as well as a deftness of touch not always associated with this Administration. Who's running the greater risk—we or the Saudis? At a time when America's standing in the Middle East is extremely low, the Saudis are actually embracing us. We should count our blessings."

The Pentagon consultant had a different view. He said that the Administration had turned to Bandar as a "fallback," because it had realized that the failing war in Iraq could leave the Middle East "up for grabs."

Jihadis in Lebanon

The focus of the U.S.-Saudi relationship, after Iran, is Lebanon, where the Saudis have been deeply involved in efforts by the Administration to support the Lebanese government. Prime Minister Fouad Siniora is struggling to stay in power against a persistent opposition led by Hezbollah, the Shiite organization, and its leader, Sheikh Hassan Nasrallah. Hezbollah has an extensive infrastructure, an estimated two to three thousand active fighters, and thousands of additional members.

Hezbollah has been on the State Department's terrorist list since 1997. The organization has been implicated in the 1983 bombing of a Marine barracks in Beirut that killed two hundred and forty-one military men. It has also been accused of complicity in the kidnapping of Americans, including the CIA station chief in Lebanon, who died in captivity, and a Marine colonel serving on a UN peacekeeping mission, who was killed. (Nasrallah has denied that the group was involved in these incidents.) Nasrallah is seen by many as a staunch terrorist, who has said that he regards Israel as a state that has no right to exist. Many in the Arab world, however, especially Shiites, view him as a resistance leader who withstood Israel in last summer's thirty-three-day war, and Siniora as a weak politician who relies on America's support but was unable to persuade President Bush to call for an end to the Israeli bombing of Lebanon. (Photographs of Siniora kissing Condoleezza Rice on the cheek when she visited during the war were prominently displayed during street protests in Beirut.)

The Bush administration has publicly pledged the Siniora government a billion dollars in aid since last summer. A donors' conference in Paris, in January, which the U.S. helped organize, yielded pledges of almost eight billion more, including a promise of more than a billion from the Saudis. The American pledge includes more than two hundred million dollars in military aid, and forty million dollars for internal security.

The United States has also given clandestine support to the Siniora government, according to the former senior intelligence official and the U.S. government consultant. "We are in a program to enhance the Sunni capability to resist Shiite influence, and we're spreading the money around as much as we can," the former senior intelligence official said. The problem was that such money "always gets in more pockets than you think it will," he said. "In this process, we're financing a lot of bad guys with some serious potential unintended consequences. We don't have the ability to determine and get pay vouchers signed by the people we like and avoid the people we don't like. It's a very high-risk venture."

American, European, and Arab officials I spoke to told me that the Siniora government and its allies had allowed some aid to end up in the hands of emerging Sunni radical groups in northern Lebanon, the Bekaa Valley, and around Palestinian refugee camps in the south. These groups, though small, are seen as a buffer to Hezbollah; at the same time, their ideological ties are with Al Qaeda.

During a conversation with me, the former Saudi diplomat accused Nasrallah of attempting "to hijack the state," but he also objected to the

Lebanese and Saudi sponsorship of Sunni jihadists in Lebanon. "Salafis are sick and hateful, and I'm very much against the idea of flirting with them," he said. "They hate the Shiites, but they hate Americans more. If you try to outsmart them, they will outsmart us. It will be ugly."

Alastair Crooke, who spent nearly thirty years in MI6, the British intelligence service, and now works for Conflicts Forum, a think tank in Beirut, told me, "The Lebanese government is opening space for these people to come in. It could be very dangerous." Crooke said that one Sunni extremist group, Fatah al-Islam, had splintered from its pro-Syrian parent group, Fatah al-Intifada, in the Nahr al-Bared refugee camp, in northern Lebanon. Its membership at the time was less than two hundred. "I was told that within twenty-four hours they were being offered weapons and money by people presenting themselves as representatives of the Lebanese government's interests—presumably to take on Hezbollah," Crooke said.

The largest of the groups, Asbat al-Ansar, is situated in the Ain al-Hilweh Palestinian refugee camp. Asbat al-Ansar has received arms and supplies from Lebanese internal-security forces and militias associated with the Siniora government.

In 2005, according to a report by the U.S.-based International Crisis Group, Saad Hariri, the Sunni majority leader of the Lebanese parliament and the son of the slain former Prime Minister—Saad inherited more than four billion dollars after his father's assassination—paid forty-eight thousand dollars in bail for four members of an Islamic militant group from Dinniyeh. The men had been arrested while trying to establish an Islamic mini-state in northern Lebanon. The Crisis Group noted that many of the militants "had trained in Al Qaeda camps in Afghanistan."

According to the Crisis Group report, Saad Hariri later used his parliamentary majority to obtain amnesty for twenty-two of the Dinniyeh Islamists, as well as for seven militants suspected of plotting to bomb the Italian and Ukrainian embassies in Beirut, the previous year. (He also arranged a pardon for Samir Geagea, a Maronite Christian militia leader, who had been convicted of four political murders, including the assassination, in 1987, of Prime Minister Rashid Karami.) Hariri described his actions to reporters as humanitarian.

In an interview in Beirut, a senior official in the Siniora government acknowledged that there were Sunni jihadists operating inside Lebanon. "We have a liberal attitude that allows Al Qaeda types to have a presence here," he said. He related this to concerns that Iran or Syria might decide to turn Lebanon into a "theatre of conflict."

The official said that his government was in a no-win situation. Without a political settlement with Hezbollah, he said, Lebanon could "slide into a conflict," in which Hezbollah fought openly with Sunni forces, with potentially horrific consequences. But if Hezbollah agreed to a settlement yet still maintained a separate army, allied with Iran and Syria, "Lebanon could become a target. In both cases, we become a target."

The Bush administration has portrayed its support of the Siniora government as an example of the president's belief in democracy, and his desire to prevent other powers from interfering in Lebanon. When Hezbollah led street demonstrations in Beirut in December, John Bolton, who was then the U.S. Ambassador to the UN, called them "part of the Iran-Syria-inspired coup."

Leslie H. Gelb, a past president of the Council on Foreign Relations, said that the Administration's policy was less pro democracy than "pro American national security. The fact is that it would be terribly dangerous if Hezbollah ran Lebanon." The fall of the Siniora government would be seen, Gelb said, "as a signal in the Middle East of the decline of the United States and the ascendancy of the terrorism threat. And so any change in the distribution of political power in Lebanon has to be opposed by the United States—and we're justified in helping any non-Shiite parties resist that change. We should say this publicly, instead of talking about democracy."

Martin Indyk, of the Saban Center, said, however, that the United States "does not have enough pull to stop the moderates in Lebanon from dealing with the extremists." He added, "The president sees the region as divided between moderates and extremists, but our regional friends see it as divided between Sunnis and Shia. The Sunnis that we view as extremists are regarded by our Sunni allies simply as Sunnis."

In January, after an outburst of street violence in Beirut involving supporters of both the Siniora government and Hezbollah, Prince Bandar flew to Tehran to discuss the political impasse in Lebanon and to meet with Ali Larijani, the Iranians' negotiator on nuclear issues. According to a Middle Eastern ambassador, Bandar's mission—which the ambassador said was endorsed by the White House—also aimed "to create problem between the Iranians and

Syria." There had been tensions between the two countries about Syrian talks with Israel, and the Saudis' goal was to encourage a breach. However, the ambassador said, "It did not work. Syria and Iran are not going to betray each other. Bandar's approach is very unlikely to succeed."

Walid Jumblatt, who is the leader of the Druze minority in Lebanon and a strong Siniora supporter, has attacked Nasrallah as an agent of Syria, and has repeatedly told foreign journalists that Hezbollah is under the direct control of the religious leadership in Iran. In a conversation with me last December, he depicted Bashir Assad, the Syrian president, as a "serial killer." Nasrallah, he said, was "morally guilty" of the assassination of Rafik Hariri and the murder, last November, of Pierre Gemayel, a member of the Siniora Cabinet, because of his support for the Syrians.

Jumblatt then told me that he had met with Vice President Cheney in Washington last fall to discuss, among other issues, the possibility of undermining Assad. He and his colleagues advised Cheney that, if the United States does try to move against Syria, members of the Syrian Muslim Brotherhood would be "the ones to talk to," Jumblatt said.

The Syrian Muslim Brotherhood, a branch of a radical Sunni movement founded in Egypt in 1928, engaged in more than a decade of violent opposition to the regime of Hafez Assad, Bashir's father. In 1982, the Brotherhood took control of the city of Hama; Assad bombarded the city for a week, killing between six thousand and twenty thousand people. Membership in the Brotherhood is punishable by death in Syria. The Brotherhood is also an avowed enemy of the U.S. and of Israel. Nevertheless, Jumblatt said, "We told Cheney that the basic link between Iran and Lebanon is Syria—and to weaken Iran you need to open the door to effective Syrian opposition."

There is evidence that the Administration's redirection strategy has already benefited the Brotherhood. The Syrian National Salvation Front is a coalition of opposition groups whose principal members are a faction led by Abdul Halim Khaddam, a former Syrian Vice President who defected in 2005, and the Brotherhood. A former high-ranking CIA officer told me, "The Americans have provided both political and financial support. The Saudis are taking the lead with financial support, but there is American involvement." He said that Khaddam, who now lives in Paris, was getting money from Saudi Arabia, with the knowledge of the White House. (In 2005, a delegation of the Front's members met with officials from the National Security Council, according to press reports.) A former White

House official told me that the Saudis had provided members of the Front with travel documents.

Jumblatt said he understood that the issue was a sensitive one for the White House. "I told Cheney that some people in the Arab world, mainly the Egyptians"—whose moderate Sunni leadership has been fighting the Egyptian Muslim Brotherhood for decades—"won't like it if the United States helps the Brotherhood. But if you don't take on Syria we will be face to face in Lebanon with Hezbollah in a long fight, and one we might not win."

The Sheikh

On a warm, clear night early last December, in a bombed-out suburb a few miles south of downtown Beirut, I got a preview of how the Administration's new strategy might play out in Lebanon. Sheikh Hassan Nasrallah, the Hezbollah leader, who has been in hiding, had agreed to an interview. Security arrangements for the meeting were secretive and elaborate. I was driven, in the back seat of a darkened car, to a damaged underground garage somewhere in Beirut, searched with a handheld scanner, placed in a second car to be driven to yet another bomb-scarred underground garage, and transferred again. Last summer, it was reported that Israel was trying to kill Nasrallah, but the extraordinary precautions were not due only to that threat. Nasrallah's aides told me that they believe he is a prime target of fellow-Arabs, primarily Jordanian intelligence operatives, as well as Sunni jihadists who they believe are affiliated with Al Qaeda. (The government consultant and a retired four-star general said that Jordanian intelligence, with support from the U.S. and Israel, had been trying to infiltrate Shiite groups, to work against Hezbollah. Jordan's King Abdullah II has warned that a Shiite government in Iraq that was close to Iran would lead to the emergence of a Shiite crescent.) This is something of an ironic turn: Nasrallah's battle with Israel last summer turned him—a Shiite—into the most popular and influential figure among Sunnis and Shiites throughout the region. In recent months, however, he has increasingly been seen by many Sunnis not as a symbol of Arab unity but as a participant in a sectarian war

Nasrallah, dressed, as usual, in religious garb, was waiting for me in an unremarkable apartment. One of his advisers said that he was not likely to remain there overnight; he has been on the move since his decision, last

July, to order the kidnapping of two Israeli soldiers in a cross-border raid that set off the thirty-three-day war. Nasrallah has since said publicly—and repeated to me—that he misjudged the Israeli response. "We just wanted to capture prisoners for exchange purposes," he told me. "We never wanted to drag the region into war."

Nasrallah accused the Bush administration of working with Israel to deliberately instigate *fitna,* an Arabic word that is used to mean "insurrection and fragmentation within Islam." "In my opinion, there is a huge campaign through the media throughout the world to put each side up against the other," he said. "I believe that all this is being run by American and Israeli intelligence." (He did not provide any specific evidence for this.) He said that the U.S. war in Iraq had increased sectarian tensions, but argued that Hezbollah had tried to prevent them from spreading into Lebanon. (Sunni-Shiite confrontations increased, along with violence, in the weeks after we talked.)

Nasrallah said he believed that President Bush's goal was "the drawing of a new map for the region. They want the partition of Iraq. Iraq is not on the edge of a civil war—there *is* a civil war. There is ethnic and sectarian cleansing. The daily killing and displacement which is taking place in Iraq aims at achieving three Iraqi parts, which will be sectarian and ethnically pure as a prelude to the partition of Iraq. Within one or two years at the most, there will be total Sunni areas, total Shiite areas, and total Kurdish areas. Even in Baghdad, there is a fear that it might be divided into two areas, one Sunni and one Shiite."

He went on, "I can say that President Bush is lying when he says he does not want Iraq to be partitioned. All the facts occurring now on the ground make you swear he is dragging Iraq to partition. And a day will come when he will say, 'I cannot do anything, since the Iraqis want the partition of their country and I honor the wishes of the people of Iraq.'"

Nasrallah said he believed that America also wanted to bring about the partition of Lebanon and of Syria. In Syria, he said, the result would be to push the country "into chaos and internal battles like in Iraq." In Lebanon, "There will be a Sunni state, an Alawi state, a Christian state, and a Druze state." But, he said, "I do not know if there will be a Shiite state." Nasrallah told me that he suspected that one aim of the Israeli bombing of Lebanon last summer was "the destruction of Shiite areas and the displacement of Shiites from Lebanon. The idea was to have the Shiites of Lebanon and

Syria flee to southern Iraq," which is dominated by Shiites. "I am not sure, but I smell this," he told me.

Partition would leave Israel surrounded by "small tranquil states," he said. "I can assure you that the Saudi kingdom will also be divided, and the issue will reach to North African states. There will be small ethnic and confessional states," he said. "In other words, Israel will be the most important and the strongest state in a region that has been partitioned into ethnic and confessional states that are in agreement with each other. This is the new Middle East."

In fact, the Bush administration has adamantly resisted talk of partitioning Iraq, and its public stances suggest that the White House sees a future Lebanon that is intact, with a weak, disarmed Hezbollah playing, at most, a minor political role. There is also no evidence to support Nasrallah's belief that the Israelis were seeking to drive the Shiites into southern Iraq. Nevertheless, Nasrallah's vision of a larger sectarian conflict in which the United States is implicated suggests a possible consequence of the White House's new strategy.

In the interview, Nasrallah made mollifying gestures and promises that would likely be met with skepticism by his opponents. "If the United States says that discussions with the likes of us can be useful and influential in determining American policy in the region, we have no objection to talks or meetings," he said. "But, if their aim through this meeting is to impose their policy on us, it will be a waste of time." He said that the Hezbollah militia, unless attacked, would operate only within the borders of Lebanon, and pledged to disarm it when the Lebanese Army was able to stand up. Nasrallah said that he had no interest in initiating another war with Israel. However, he added that he was anticipating, and preparing for, another Israeli attack, later this year.

Nasrallah further insisted that the street demonstrations in Beirut would continue until the Siniora government fell or met his coalition's political demands. "Practically speaking, this government cannot rule," he told me. "It might issue orders, but the majority of the Lebanese people will not abide and will not recognize the legitimacy of this government. Siniora remains in office because of international support, but this does not mean that Siniora can rule Lebanon."

President Bush's repeated praise of the Siniora government, Nasrallah said, "is the best service to the Lebanese opposition he can give, because it weakens their position vis-à-vis the Lebanese people and the Arab and Islamic populations. They are betting on us getting tired. We did not get tired during the war, so how could we get tired in a demonstration?"

There is sharp division inside and outside the Bush administration about how best to deal with Nasrallah, and whether he could, in fact, be a partner in a political settlement. The outgoing director of National Intelligence, John Negroponte, in a farewell briefing to the Senate Intelligence Committee, in January, said that Hezbollah "lies at the center of Iran's terrorist strategy. . . . It could decide to conduct attacks against U.S. interests in the event it feels its survival or that of Iran is threatened. . . . Lebanese Hezbollah sees itself as Tehran's partner."

In 2002, Richard Armitage, then the Deputy Secretary of State, called Hezbollah "the A-team" of terrorists. In a recent interview, however, Armitage acknowledged that the issue has become somewhat more complicated. Nasrallah, Armitage told me, has emerged as "a political force of some note, with a political role to play inside Lebanon if he chooses to do so." In terms of public relations and political gamesmanship, Armitage said, Nasrallah "is the smartest man in the Middle East." But, he added, Nasrallah "has got to make it clear that he wants to play an appropriate role as the loyal opposition. For me, there's still a blood debt to pay"—a reference to the murdered colonel and the Marine barracks bombing.

Robert Baer, a former longtime CIA agent in Lebanon, has been a severe critic of Hezbollah and has warned of its links to Iranian-sponsored terrorism. But now, he told me, "we've got Sunni Arabs preparing for cataclysmic conflict, and we will need somebody to protect the Christians in Lebanon. It used to be the French and the United States who would do it, and now it's going to be Nasrallah and the Shiites.

"The most important story in the Middle East is the growth of Nasrallah from a street guy to a leader—from a terrorist to a statesman," Baer added. "The dog that didn't bark this summer"—during the war with Israel—"is Shiite terrorism." Baer was referring to fears that Nasrallah, in addition to firing rockets into Israel and kidnapping its soldiers, might set in motion a wave of terror attacks on Israeli and American targets around the world. "He could have pulled the trigger, but he did not," Baer said.

Most members of the intelligence and diplomatic communities acknowledge Hezbollah's ongoing ties to Iran. But there is disagreement about the extent to which Nasrallah would put aside Hezbollah's interests in favor of Iran's. A former CIA officer who also served in Lebanon called Nasrallah "a Lebanese phenomenon," adding, "Yes, he's aided by Iran and Syria, but Hezbollah's gone beyond that." He told me that there was a period in the late eighties and early nineties when the CIA station in Beirut was able to clandestinely monitor Nasrallah's conversations. He described Nasrallah as "a gang leader who was able to make deals with the other gangs. He had contacts with everybody."

Telling Congress

The Bush administration's reliance on clandestine operations that have not been reported to Congress and its dealings with intermediaries with questionable agendas have recalled, for some in Washington, an earlier chapter in history. Two decades ago, the Reagan administration attempted to fund the Nicaraguan contras illegally, with the help of secret arms sales to Iran. Saudi money was involved in what became known as the Iran-Contra scandal, and a few of the players back then—notably Prince Bandar and Elliott Abrams—are involved in today's dealings.

Iran-Contra was the subject of an informal "lessons learned" discussion two years ago among veterans of the scandal. Abrams led the discussion. One conclusion was that even though the program was eventually exposed, it had been possible to execute it without telling Congress. As to what the experience taught them, in terms of future covert operations, the participants found: "One, you can't trust our friends. Two, the CIA has got to be totally out of it. Three, you can't trust the uniformed military, and four, it's got to be run out of the Vice President's office"—a reference to Cheney's role, the former senior intelligence official said.

I was subsequently told by the two government consultants and the former senior intelligence official that the echoes of Iran-Contra were a factor in Negroponte's decision to resign from the National Intelligence directorship and accept a sub-Cabinet position of Deputy Secretary of State. (Negroponte declined to comment.)

The former senior intelligence official also told me that Negroponte did not want a repeat of his experience in the Reagan administration, when he served as Ambassador to Honduras. "Negroponte said, 'No way. I'm not going down that road again, with the NSC running operations off the books, with no finding.'" (In the case of covert CIA operations, the president must issue a written finding and inform Congress.) Negroponte stayed on as Deputy Secretary of State, he added, because "he believes he can influence the government in a positive way."

The government consultant said that Negroponte shared the White House's policy goals but "wanted to do it by the book." The Pentagon consultant also told me that "there was a sense at the senior-ranks level that he wasn't fully on board with the more adventurous clandestine initiatives." It was also true, he said, that Negroponte "had problems with this Rube Goldberg policy contraption for fixing the Middle East."

The Pentagon consultant added that one difficulty, in terms of oversight, was accounting for covert funds. "There are many, many pots of black money, scattered in many places and used all over the world on a variety of missions," he said. The budgetary chaos in Iraq, where billions of dollars are unaccounted for, has made it a vehicle for such transactions, according to the former senior intelligence official and the retired four-star general.

"This goes back to Iran-Contra," a former National Security Council aide told me. "And much of what they're doing is to keep the agency out of it." He said that Congress was not being briefed on the full extent of the U.S.-Saudi operations. And, he said, "The CIA is asking, 'What's going on?' They're concerned, because they think it's amateur hour."

The issue of oversight is beginning to get more attention from Congress. Last November, the Congressional Research Service issued a report for Congress on what it depicted as the Administration's blurring of the line between CIA activities and strictly military ones, which do not have the same reporting requirements. And the Senate Intelligence Committee, headed by Senator Jay Rockefeller, has scheduled a hearing for March 8th on Defense Department intelligence activities.

Senator Ron Wyden, of Oregon, a Democrat who is a member of the Intelligence Committee, told me, "The Bush administration has frequently failed to meet its legal obligation to keep the Intelligence Committee fully and currently informed. Time and again, the answer has been 'Trust us.'" Wyden said, "It is hard for me to trust the Administration."

Declaring Victory

James Fallows

the *Atlantic Monthly* | September 2006

The Bush administration has eagerly embraced the war on terror as the great cause of our age—and has harshly criticized those who have suggested, as John Kerry did in his 2004 presidential campaign, that the struggle against Islamic extremism is ultimately a law-enforcement issue. Meanwhile, however, five years have passed since the 9/11 attacks, and the U.S. public's enthusiasm for the so-called "long war" is clearly waning. In a recent Gallup poll, for example, only 4 percent of respondents listed terrorism as their primary concern. (The Iraq War topped the list at 69 percent, followed by immigration, fuel prices, health care, the economy, and education.)

In this piece, James Fallows, a veteran reporter on national-security issues, posits that our government's war stance against the terrorist threat may be exactly what Al Qaeda and similar groups are striving for—and that, with Al Qaeda largely contained, the time has come to refocus America's energies.

Osama bin Laden's public statements are those of a fanatic. But they often reveal a canny ability to size up the strengths and weaknesses of both allies and enemies, especially the United States. In his videotaped statement just days before the 2004 U.S. presidential election, bin Laden mocked the Bush administration for being unable to find him, for letting itself become mired in Iraq, and for refusing to come to grips with Al Qaeda's basic reason for being. One example: "Contrary to Bush's claim that we hate freedom, let him explain to us why we don't strike, for example, Sweden?" Bin Laden also boasted about how easy it had become for him "to provoke and bait" the American leadership: "All that we have to do is to send two mujahideen . . . to raise a piece of cloth on which is written 'Al Qaeda' in order to make the generals race there."

Perhaps Al Qaeda's leaders, like most people, cannot turn a similarly cold eye upon themselves. A purely realistic self-assessment must be all the more difficult for leaders who say that their struggle may last for centuries and that their guidance comes from outside this world. But what if

Al Qaeda's leaders could see their faults and weaknesses as clearly as they see those of others? What if they had a Clausewitz or a Sun Tzu to speak frankly to them?

This spring and summer, I talked with some sixty experts about the current state of the conflict that bin Laden thinks of as the "world jihad"—and that the U.S. government has called both the "global war on terror" and the "long war." I wanted to know how it looked from the terrorists' perspective. What had gone better than expected? What had gone worse? Could bin Laden assume, on any grounds other than pure faith, that the winds of history were at his back? Could he and his imitators count on a growing advantage because technology has made it so easy for individuals to inflict mass damage, and because politics and the media have made it so hard for great powers to fight dirty, drawn-out wars? Or might his strategists have to conclude that, at least for this stage of what they envision as a centuries-long struggle, their best days had passed?

About half of the authorities I spoke with were from military or intelligence organizations; the others were academics or members of think tanks, plus a few businesspeople. Half were Americans; the rest were Europeans, Middle Easterners, Australians, and others. Four years ago, most of these people had supported the decision to invade Iraq. Although they now said that the war had been a mistake (followed by what nearly all viewed as a disastrously mismanaged occupation), relatively few said that the United States should withdraw anytime soon. The reasons most of them gave were the need for America to make good on commitments, the importance of keeping the Sunni parts of Iraq from turning into a new haven for global terrorists, and the chance that conditions in Iraq would eventually improve.

The initial surprise for me was how little fundamental disagreement I heard about how the situation looks through bin Laden's eyes. While the people I spoke with differed on details, and while no one put things exactly the way I am about to here, there was consensus on the main points.

The larger and more important surprise was the implicit optimism about the U.S. situation that came through in these accounts—not on Iraq but on the fight against Al Qaeda and the numerous imitators it has spawned. For the past five years the United States has assumed itself to be locked in "asymmetric warfare," with the advantages on the other side. Any of the tens of millions of foreigners entering the country each year could, in theory, be an enemy operative—to say nothing of the millions of potential recruits already here. Any of the dozens of ports, the scores of natural-gas plants and nuclear facilities, the hundreds of important bridges and tunnels, or the thousands of shopping malls, office towers, or sporting facilities could be the next target of attack. It is impossible to protect them all, and even trying could ruin America's social fabric and public finances. The worst part of the situation is helplessness, as America's officials and its public wait for an attack they know they cannot prevent.

Viewing the world from Al Qaeda's perspective, though, reveals the underappreciated advantage on America's side. The struggle does remain asymmetric, but it may have evolved in a way that gives target countries, especially the United States, more leverage and control than we have assumed. Yes, there could be another attack tomorrow, and most authorities assume that some attempts to blow up trains, bridges, buildings, or airplanes in America will eventually succeed. No modern nation is immune to politically inspired violence, and even the best-executed antiterrorism strategy will not be airtight.

But the overall prospect looks better than many Americans believe, and better than nearly all political rhetoric asserts. The essence of the change is this: because of Al Qaeda's own mistakes, and because of the things the United States and its allies have done right, Al Qaeda's ability to inflict direct damage in America or on Americans has been sharply reduced. Its successor groups in Europe, the Middle East, and elsewhere will continue to pose dangers. But its hopes for fundamentally harming the United States now rest less on what it can do itself than on what it can trick, tempt, or goad us into doing. Its destiny is no longer in its own hands.

"Does Al Qaeda still constitute an 'existential' threat?" asks David Kilcullen, who has written several influential papers on the need for a new strategy against Islamic insurgents. Kilcullen, who as an Australian army officer commanded counter-insurgency units in East Timor, recently served as an adviser in the Pentagon and is now a senior adviser on counterterrorism at the State Department. He was referring to the argument about whether the terrorism of the twenty-first century endangers the very existence of the United States and its allies, as the Soviet Union's nuclear weapons did throughout the Cold War (and as the remnants of that arsenal still might).

"I think it does, but not for the obvious reasons," Kilcullen told me. He said the most useful analogy was the menace posed by European anarchists in the nineteenth century. "If you add up everyone they personally killed, it came to maybe 2,000 people, which is not an existential threat." But one of their number assassinated Archduke Franz Ferdinand and his wife. The act itself took the lives of two people. The unthinking response of European governments in effect started World War I. "So because of the reaction they provoked, they were able to kill millions of people and destroy a civilization.

"It is not the people Al Qaeda might kill that is the threat," he concluded. "*Our reaction is* what can cause the damage. It's Al Qaeda plus our response that creates the existential danger."

Since 9/11, this equation has worked in Al Qaeda's favor. That can be reversed.

What Has Gone Wrong for Al Qaeda

Brian Michael Jenkins, a veteran terrorism expert at the RAND Corporation, recently published a book called *Unconquerable Nation: Knowing Our Enemy, Strengthening Ourselves.* It includes a fictional briefing, in Osama bin Laden's mountain stronghold, by an Al Qaeda strategist assigned to sum up the state of world jihad five years after the 9/11 attacks. "Any Al Qaeda briefer would have to acknowledge that the past five years have been difficult," Jenkins says. His fictional briefer summarizes for bin Laden what happened after 9/11: "The Taliban were dispersed, and Al Qaeda's training camps in Afghanistan were dismantled." Al Qaeda operatives by the thousands have been arrested, detained, or killed. So have many members of the crucial Al Qaeda leadership circle around bin Laden and his chief strategist, Ayman al-Zawahiri. Moreover, Jenkins's briefer warns, it has become harder for the remaining Al Qaeda leaders to carry out the organization's most basic functions: "Because of increased intelligence efforts by the United States and its allies, transactions of any type—communications, travel, money transfers—have become more dangerous for the jihadists. Training and operations have been decentralized, raising the risk of fragmentation and loss of unity. Jihadists everywhere face the threat of capture or martyrdom."

Michael Scheuer was chief of the CIA's Osama bin Laden unit from 1995 to 1999 and was a special adviser to it for three years after 9/11 (the CIA disbanded the unit this summer). In a similar mock situation report that

Scheuer has presented at military conferences, a fictional briefer tells his superiors in Al Qaeda: "We must always keep in focus the huge downside of this war. We are, put simply, being hunted and attacked by the most powerful nation in the history of the world. And despite the heavy personnel losses we have suffered, may God accept them as martyrs, the United States has not yet made the full destructiveness of its power felt."

Any assessment of the world five years after 9/11 begins with the damage inflicted on "Al Qaeda Central"—the organization led by bin Laden and al-Zawahiri that, from the late 1990s onward, both inspired and organized the worldwide anti-American campaign. "Their command structure is gone, their Afghan sanctuary is gone, their ability to move around and hold meetings is gone, their financial and communications networks have been hit hard," says Seth Stodder, a former official in the Department of Homeland Security (DHS).

Kilcullen says, "The Al Qaeda that existed in 2001 simply no longer exists. In 2001 it was a relatively centralized organization, with a planning hub, a propaganda hub, a leadership team, all within a narrow geographic area. All that is gone, because we destroyed it." Where bin Laden's central leadership team could once wire money around the world using normal bank networks, it now must rely on couriers with vests full of cash. (I heard this point frequently in interviews, weeks before the controversial news stories revealing that the U.S. government had in fact been tracking international bank transfers. Everyone I spoke with assumed that some sort of tracking was firmly in place—and that the commanders of Al Qaeda had changed their behavior in a way that showed they were aware of it as well.) Where bin Laden's network could once use satellite phones and the Internet for communication, it now has to avoid most forms of electronic communication, which leave an electronic trail back to the user. Bin Laden and al-Zawahiri now send information out through videotapes and via operatives in Internet chat rooms. "The Internet is all well and good, but it's not like meeting face to face or conducting training," says Peter Bergen, author of *The Osama bin Laden I Know.* "Their reliance on it is a sign of their weakness."

Scheuer, Richard Clarke (the former White House terrorism adviser), and others have long complained that following the bombing of the U.S.S. *Cole,* in 2000, the United States should have been prepared to launch a retaliatory raid on Afghanistan immediately after any successor attack—

"the next day!" Scheuer told me—rather than taking several weeks to strike, and that it might well have chased down and eliminated bin Laden and al-Zawahiri if it had concentrated on them throughout 2002 rather than being distracted into Iraq. Nonetheless, most experts agree that the combination of routing the Taliban, taking away training camps, policing the financial networks, killing many Al Qaeda lieutenants, and maintaining electronic and aerial surveillance has put bin Laden and al-Zawahiri in a situation in which they can survive and inspire but not do much more.

"Al Qaeda has taken some very hard blows," Martin van Creveld, a military historian at the Hebrew University of Jerusalem and the author of *The Transformation of War* and other books, told me. "Osama bin Laden is almost irrelevant, from an operational point of view. This is one reason why he has to keep releasing videos."

Does this matter, given bin Laden's elevation to Che Guevara–like symbolic status and his ability to sneak out no fewer than twenty-four recorded messages between 9/11 and the summer of this year? "For bin Laden, it's clearly a consolation prize to become a 'philosophy' rather than an organization," says Caleb Carr, a history professor at Bard College and the author of *The Lessons of Terror.* "They already were a global philosophy, but they used to have a command structure too. It's like the difference between Marxism and Leninism, and they're back to just being Marx." Marc Sageman, author of *Understanding Terror Networks,* says that before 9/11, people attracted to the terrorist cause could come to Afghanistan for camaraderie, indoctrination, and specific operational training. "Now you can't *find* Al Qaeda, so it's difficult to join them," he told me. "People have to figure out what to do on their own."

The shift from a coherent Al Qaeda Central to a global proliferation of "self-starter" terrorist groups—those inspired by bin Laden's movement but not coordinated by it—has obviously not eliminated the danger of attacks. In different ways, the bombings in Madrid in 2004, in Bali and London in 2005, and in Iraq throughout the past three years all illustrate the menace—and, in the view of many people I spoke with, prefigure the threats—that could arise in the United States. But the shift to these successor groups has made it significantly harder for terrorists of any provenance to achieve what all of them would like: a "second 9/11," a large-scale attack on the U.S. mainland that would kill hundreds or thousands of people and terrorize hundreds of millions.

I asked everyone I spoke with some variant of the familiar American question: Why, through nearly five years after 9/11, had there not been another big attack on U.S. soil? People prefaced their replies with reminders that the future is unknowable, that the situation could change tomorrow, and that the reasons for America's safety so far were not fully understood. But most then went on to say that another shocking, 9/11-scale coordinated attack was probably too hard for today's atomized terrorist groups to pull off.

The whole array of "homeland security" steps had made the United States a somewhat more difficult target to attack, most people said. But not a single person began the list of important post-9/11 changes with these real, if modest, measures of domestic protection. Indeed, nearly all emphasized the haphazard, wasteful, and sometimes self-defeating nature of the DHS's approach.

"It is harder to get into the country—to a fault," says Seth Stodder. Much tougher visa rules, especially for foreign students, have probably kept future Mohammed Attas out of flight schools. But they may also be keeping out future Andrew Groves and Sergey Brins. (Grove, born in Hungary, cofounded Intel; Brin, born in Russia, cofounded Google.) "The student-visa crackdown was to deal with Atta," Stodder says. "It's affecting the commanding heights of our tech economy." Richard Clarke says that the domestic change that has had the biggest protective effect is not any governmental measure but an increased public scrutiny of anyone who "looks Muslim." "It's a terrible, racist reaction," Clarke says, "but it has made it harder for them to operate."

The DHS now spends $42 billion a year on its vast range of activities, which include FEMA and other disaster-relief efforts, the Coast Guard, immigration, and border and customs operations. Of this, about $5 billion goes toward screening passengers at airports. The widely held view among security experts is that this airport spending is largely for show. Strengthened cockpit doors and a flying public that knows what happened on 9/11 mean that commercial airliners are highly unlikely to be used again as targeted flying bombs. "The inspection process is mostly security theater, to make people feel safe about flying," says John Mueller, a political scientist at Ohio State and the author of a forthcoming book about the security-industrial complex. He adds that because fears "are not purely rational, if it makes people feel better, the effort may be worth it."

John Robb, a former clandestine-operations specialist for the Air Force who now writes a blog called "Global Guerrillas," says that it is relatively easy for terrorists to disrupt society's normal operations—think of daily life in Israel, or England under assault from the IRA. But large-scale symbolic shock, of the type so stunningly achieved on 9/11 and advocated by bin Laden ever since, is difficult to repeat or sustain. "There are diminishing returns on symbolic terrorism," Robb told me. "Each time it happens, the public becomes desensitized, and the media pays less attention." To maintain the level of terror, each attack must top the previous one—and in Robb's view, "nothing will ever top 9/11." He allows for the obvious and significant exception of terrorists getting hold of a nuclear weapon. But, like most people I interviewed, he says this is harder and less likely than the public assumes. Moreover, if nuclear weapons constitute the one true existential threat, then countering the proliferation of those weapons themselves is what American policy should address, more than fighting terrorism in general. For a big, coordinated, nonnuclear attack, he says, "the number of people involved is substantial, the lead time is long, the degree of coordination is great, and the specific skills you need are considerable. It's not realistic for Al Qaeda anymore."

Bruce Hoffman, a terrorism expert at Georgetown University and the author of *Inside Terrorism* and other books, says that the 9/11-style spectacular attack remains fundamental to Osama bin Laden's hopes, because of his belief that it would "catapult him back into being in charge of the movement." Robb's fear is that after being thwarted in their quest to blow up the Rose Bowl or the Capitol, today's loosely affiliated terrorists will turn to the smaller-scale attacks on economic targets—power plants, rail lines—that are very hard to prevent and can do tremendous cumulative damage.

The dispersed nature of the new Al Qaeda creates other difficulties for potential terrorists. For one, the recruitment of self-starter cells within the United States is thought to have failed so far. Spain, England, France, and the Netherlands are among the countries alarmed to find Islamic extremists among people whose families have lived in Europe for two or three generations. "The patriotism of the American Muslim community has been grossly underreported," says Marc Sageman, who has studied the process by which people decide to join or leave terrorist networks. According to Daniel Benjamin, a former official on the National Security Council and coauthor of *The Next Attack*, Muslims in America "have been our first line of defense." Even though many have been "unnerved by a law-enforcement approach that might have been inevitable but was still disturbing," the community has been "pretty much immune to the jihadist virus."

Something about the Arab and Muslim immigrants who have come to America, or about their absorption here, has made them basically similar to other well-assimilated American ethnic groups—and basically different from the estranged Muslim underclass of much of Europe. Sageman points out that western European countries, taken together, have slightly more than twice as large a Muslim population as does the United States (roughly 6 million in the United States, versus 6 million in France, 3 million in Germany, 2 million in the United Kingdom, more than a million in Italy, and several million elsewhere). But most measures of Muslim disaffection or upheaval in Europe—arrests, riots, violence based on religion—show it to be ten to fifty times worse than here.

The median income of Muslims in France, Germany, and Britain is lower than that of people in those countries as a whole. The median income of Arab Americans (many of whom are Christians originally from Lebanon) is actually higher than the overall American one. So are their business-ownership rate and their possession of college and graduate degrees. The same is true of most other groups who have been here for several generations, a fact that in turn underscores the normality of the Arab and Muslim experience. The difference between the European and American assimilation of Muslims becomes most apparent in the second generation, when American Muslims are culturally and economically Americanized and many European Muslims often develop a sharper sense of alienation. "If you ask a second-generation American Muslim," says Robert Leiken, author of *Bearers of Global Jihad: Immigration and National Security After 9/11*, "he will say, 'I'm an American and a Muslim.' A second-generation Turk in Germany is a Turk, and a French Moroccan doesn't know what he is."

The point is not that all is comfortable between American Muslims and their fellow citizens. Many measures show that anti-Muslim sentiment is up, as are complaints by Muslims about discrimination and official mistreatment. James Woolsey, a former director of the CIA, points out that while very few American Muslims sympathize with Wahhabi-style extremism, mosques and institutions representing extreme views have begun to appear. Yet what many Western nations fear—widespread terrorist recruitment or activity from among their own population—for now seems less likely in the United States.

An even deeper problem for Al Qaeda and the self-starter groups is an apparent erosion of support where it would be most likely and necessary: in the Arab and Muslim worlds. The difficulty involves what they have done, and what they cannot do.

What they have done is to follow the terrorist's logic of steadily escalating the degree of carnage and violence—which has meant violating the guerrilla warrior's logic of bringing the civilian population to your side. This trade-off has not been so visible to Americans, because most of the carnage is in Iraq. There, insurgents have slaughtered civilians daily, before and after the death this spring of Abu Musab al-Zarqawi, the leader of Al Qaeda in Iraq. But since American troops are also assumed to be killing civilians, the anti-insurgent backlash is muddied.

The situation is different elsewhere. "Like Tourette's syndrome, they keep killing Muslim civilians," says Peter Bergen. "That is their Achilles' heel. Every time the bombs go off and kill civilians, it works in our favor. It's a double whammy when the civilians they kill are Muslims." Last November, groups directed by al-Zarqawi set off bombs in three hotels in Amman, Jordan. Some sixty civilians were killed, including thirty-eight at a wedding. The result was to turn Jordanian public opinion against Al Qaeda and al-Zarqawi, and to make the Jordanian government more openly cooperative with the United States. In October 2002, a suicide bomber from Jemaah Islamiyah (the Indonesian counterpart to Al Qaeda) blew up a nightclub in Bali and killed more than 200 people. Most of them were Australians and other foreigners, and the attack created little backlash among Muslims. A year ago, a second wave of suicide bombings in Bali killed twenty people, fifteen of them Indonesians. "The reaction in Indonesia was extremely negative," Bergen says. Other people described similar reactions to incidents in Egypt, Pakistan, even Saudi Arabia.

If you have a taste for doctrinal dispute, the internal Al Qaeda documents that Bergen included in his book on bin Laden and those available elsewhere make fascinating reading. Fawaz Gerges, of Sarah Lawrence College, who was raised in Lebanon, describes some of these documents in his new book, *Journey of the Jihadist.* He quotes one Egyptian extremist, who is still in prison for his role in the assassination of Anwar Sadat, as saying that Al Qaeda had left the world's Muslims worse off than before 9/11. This man, Mohammed Essam Derbala, told Gerges that jihad for the sake of jihad—which is how he viewed Al Qaeda's efforts—had backfired, and that, as Gerges writes, "It produces the opposite of the desired results: the downfall of the Taliban regime and the slaughter of thousands of young Muslims." In 2005, al-Zawahiri rebuked al-Zarqawi for the extreme brutality of his terrorist campaign within Iraq, in what Bergen has called the "enough with the beheadings!" memo.

Marc Sageman says that those recruited into terrorist groups, from the nineteenth-century anarchists to the present jihadists, are typically "romantic young people in a hurry, with a dream of changing the world." The romance is easiest to maintain during strikes on distant, depersonalized enemies, like the Americans overseas or the Israelis behind their new barriers. But as attacks move into the terrorists' own neighborhoods, and as the victims include recognizable kinsmen or fellow citizens, the romance fades. That is why, Sageman says, "my long-term view is that the militants will keep pushing the envelope and committing more atrocities to the point that the dream will no longer be attractive to young people."

The other part of a battle of ideas is the ability to offer a positive vision, and there Al Qaeda's failure has been complete.

Shibley Telhami, of the University of Maryland, has conducted polls in six Muslim countries since 9/11, gauging popular attitudes toward the United States and toward Al Qaeda. "If their aim was to be the source of inspiration for the Muslim world," Telhami says of Al Qaeda, "they are not that." Telhami's polls, like those from the Pew Global Attitudes Survey, show a steady increase in hostility toward the United States—but no surge of enthusiasm for Taliban-style fundamentalist life. "What we see in the polls," Telhami told me shortly before al-Zarqawi was killed, "is that many people would like bin Laden and Zarqawi to hurt America. But they do not want bin Laden to rule their children." In his polls, people were asked to identify which aspect of Al Qaeda they most sympathized with. Only 6 percent of respondents chose Al Qaeda's advocacy of a puritanical Islamic state.

"The things we have done right have hurt Al Qaeda," says Caleb Carr, who strongly supported the reasoning behind the war in Iraq. By this he means the rout of the Taliban and the continued surveillance of Pakistan. "The things they have done wrong"—meaning the attacks on mosques and markets—"have hurt them worse."

"There is only one thing keeping them going now," he added. "That is our incredible mistakes." The biggest series of mistakes all of these experts have in mind is Iraq.

What Has Gone Right for Al Qaeda

Over the past five years Americans have heard about "asymmetric war," the "long war," and "fourth-generation war." Here is an important but under-discussed difference between all of these and "regular war."

In its past military encounters, the United States was mainly concerned about the damage an enemy could do directly—the Soviet Union with nuclear missiles, Axis-era Germany or Japan with shock troops. In the modern brand of terrorist warfare, what an enemy can do directly is limited. The most dangerous thing it can do is to provoke you into hurting yourself.

This is what David Kilcullen meant in saying that the response to terrorism was potentially far more destructive than the deed itself. And it is why most people I spoke with said that three kinds of American reaction—the war in Iraq, the economic consequences of willy-nilly spending on security, and the erosion of America's moral authority—were responsible for such strength as Al Qaeda now maintained.

"You only have to look at the Iraq War to see how much damage you can do to yourself by your response," Kilcullen told me. He is another of those who supported the war and consider it important to fight toward some kind of victory, but who recognize the ways in which this conflict has helped Al Qaeda. So far the war in Iraq has advanced the jihadist cause because it generates a steady supply of Islamic victims, or martyrs; because it seems to prove Osama bin Laden's contention that America lusts to occupy Islam's sacred sites, abuse Muslim people, and steal Muslim resources; and because it raises the tantalizing possibility that humble Muslim insurgents, with cheap, primitive weapons, can once more hobble and ultimately destroy a superpower, as they believe they did to the Soviet Union in Afghanistan twenty years ago. The United States also played a large role in thwarting the Soviets, but that doesn't matter. For mythic purposes, mujahideen brought down one anti-Islamic army and can bring down another.

If the United States stays in Iraq, it keeps making enemies. If it leaves, it goes dragging its tail. Six months after the start of the Iraq War, bin Laden issued a bitter criticism of the Bush administration ("Bush and his gang, with their heavy sticks and hard hearts, are an evil to all humankind"). After the president was reelected, bin Laden and al-Zawahiri said that the jihad against all Americans should continue until the United States changes its policy toward Muslim countries. "Many believe that the United States, bloodied and exhausted by the insurgency, stripped of its allies, will eventually withdraw," Brian Jenkins writes of the jihadist view. From that perspective, "this defeat alone could bring about the collapse of the United States, just as collapse followed the Soviet defeat in Afghanistan."

Jim Guirard, a writer and former Senate staffer, says that America's response has helped confirm bin Laden's worldview in an unintended way. The Arabic terms often brought into English to describe Islamic extremists —*jihadists* or *mujahideen* for "warriors," plus the less-frequently used *shahiddin* for "martyrs"—are, according to Guirard, exactly the terms Al Qaeda would like to see used. *Mujahideen* essentially means "holy warriors"; the other terms imply righteous struggle in the cause of Islam. The Iraqi clergyman-warlord Muqtada al-Sadr named his paramilitary force the Mahdi Army. To Sunnis and Shiites alike, the Mahdi is the ultimate savior of mankind, equivalent to the Messiah. Branches of Islam disagree about the Mahdi's exact identity and the timing of his arrival on earth, but each time U.S. officials refer to insurgents of the Mahdi Army, they confer legitimacy on their opponent in all Muslims' eyes.

With the advice of Islamic scholars and think-tank officials, Guirard has assembled an alternative lexicon he thinks U.S. officials should use in both English and Arabic. These include *hirabah* ("unholy war") instead of *jihad; irhabists* ("terrorists") instead of *jihadists; mufsidoon* ("evildoers") instead of *mujahideen;* and so on. The long-term effect, he says, would be like labeling certain kinds of battle *genocide* or *war crime* rather than plain *combat*—not decisive, but useful. Conceivably President Bush's frequent use of *evildoers* to describe terrorists and insurgents represented a deliberate step in this direction, intended to steer the Arabic translation of his comments toward the derogatory terms. (I could not confirm whether there was any such plan behind Bush's choice of words, or whether it had made much difference in translations. While granting Guirard's point, for convenience I'll stick with the familiar terms here.)

The fictional Al Qaeda strategist in Brian Jenkins's book tells Osama bin Laden that the U.S. presence in Iraq "surely is a gift from Allah," because it has trapped American soldiers "where they are vulnerable to the kind of warfare the jihadists wage best: lying in wait to attack; carrying out assassinations, kidnappings, ambushes, and suicide attacks; destroying the economy; making the enemy's life untenable." The Egyptian militants profiled in *Journey of the Jihadist* told Fawaz Gerges that they were repelled by Al Qaeda after the 9/11 attacks and deaf to its appeals to undertake jihad against the United States. But that all changed, they said, when the United States invaded Iraq.

Because the general point is familiar, I'll let one more anecdote about the consequences of invading Iraq stand for many that I heard. When Americans think of satellite surveillance and the National Security Agency, they are likely to imagine something out of the TV show *24:* a limitless set of eyes in the sky that can watch everything, all the time. In fact, even today's amply funded NSA can watch only a limited number of sites. "Our overhead imagery is dedicated to force protection in Iraq and Afghanistan," I was told by a former intelligence official who would not let me use his name. He meant that the satellites are tied up following U.S. troops on patrol and in firefights to let them know who might be waiting in ambush. "There are still ammo dumps in Iraq that are open to insurgents," he said, "but we lack the imagery to cover them—let alone what people might be dreaming up in Thailand or Bangladesh." Because so many spy satellites are trained on the countries we have invaded, they tell us less than they used to about the rest of the world.

Documents captured after 9/11 showed that bin Laden hoped to provoke the United States into an invasion and occupation that would entail all the complications that have arisen in Iraq. His only error was to think that the place where Americans would get stuck would be Afghanistan.

Bin Laden also hoped that such an entrapment would drain the United States financially. Many Al Qaeda documents refer to the importance of sapping American economic strength as a step toward reducing America's ability to throw its weight around in the Middle East. Bin Laden imagined this would happen largely through attacks on America's oil supply. This is still a goal. For instance, a 2004 fatwa from the imprisoned head of Al Qaeda in Saudi Arabia declared that targeting oil pipelines and refineries was a legitimate form of economic jihad—and that economic jihad "is one of the most powerful ways in which we can take revenge on the infidels during this present stage." The fatwa went on to offer an analysis many economists would be proud of, laying out all the steps that would lead from a less-secure oil supply to a less-productive American economy and ultimately to a run on the dollar. (It also emphasized that oil wells themselves should be attacked only as a last resort, because news coverage of the smoke and fires would hurt Al Qaeda's image.)

Higher-priced oil has hurt America, but what has hurt more is the economic reaction bin Laden didn't fully foresee. This is the systematic drag on public and private resources created by the undifferentiated need to be "secure."

The effect is most obvious on the public level. "The economy as a whole took six months or so to recover from the effects of 9/11," Richard Clarke told me. "The federal budget never recovered. The federal budget is in a permanent mess, to a large degree because of 9/11." At the start of 2001, the federal budget was $125 billion in surplus. Now it is $300 billion in deficit.

A total of five people died from anthrax spores sent through the mail shortly after 9/11. In *Devils and Duct Tape,* his forthcoming book, John Mueller points out that the U.S. Postal Service will eventually spend about $5 billion on protective screening equipment and other measures in response to the anthrax threat, or about $1 billion per fatality. Each new security guard, each extra checkpoint or biometric measure, is both a direct cost and an indirect drag on economic flexibility.

If bin Laden hadn't fully anticipated this effect, he certainly recognized it after it occurred. In his statement just before the 2004 election, he quoted the finding of the Royal Institute of International Affairs (!) to the effect that the total cost, direct and indirect, to America of the 9/11 attacks was at least $500 billion. Bin Laden gleefully pointed out that the attacks had cost Al Qaeda about $500,000, for a million-to-one payoff ratio. America's deficit spending for Iraq and homeland security was, he said, "evidence of the success of the bleed-until-bankruptcy plan, with Allah's permission."

The final destructive response helping Al Qaeda has been America's estrangement from its allies and diminution of its traditionally vast "soft power." "America's cause is doomed unless it regains the moral high ground," Sir Richard Dearlove, the former director of Britain's secret intelligence agency, MI-6, told me. He pointed out that by the end of the Cold War there was no dispute worldwide about which side held the moral high ground—and that this made his work as a spymaster far easier. "Potential recruits would come to us because they believed in the cause," he said. A senior army officer from a country whose forces are fighting alongside America's in Iraq similarly told me that America "simply has to recapture its moral authority." His reasoning:

> The United States is so powerful militarily that by its very nature it represents a threat to every other nation on earth. The only country that could theoretically destroy every single other country is the United States. The only way we can say that the U.S. is *not* a threat is by looking at intent, and that depends on moral authority. If you're not sure the United States is going to do the right thing, you can't trust it with that power, so you begin thinking, How can I balance it off and find other alliances to protect myself?

America's glory has been its openness and idealism, internally and externally. Each has been constrained from time to time, but not for as long or in as open-ended a way as now. "We are slowly changing their way of life," Michael Scheuer's fictional adviser to bin Laden says in his briefing. The Americans' capital city is more bunkerlike than it was during World War II, he comments; the people live as if terrified, and watch passively as elementary-school children go through metal detectors before entering museums.

"There is one thing above all that bin Laden can feel relieved about," Caleb Carr told me. "It's that we have never stopped to reassess our situation. We have been so busy reacting that we have not yet said, 'We've made some mistakes, we've done serious damage to ourselves, so let's think about our position and strategies.'"

Seizing that opportunity can give America its edge.

Changing the Game

Here is something I never expected. When I began this reporting, I imagined that it would mean a further plunge into current-events gloom. Osama bin Laden and Ayman al-Zawahiri might be under siege, but they had spawned countless imitators. Instead of having one main terrorist group to worry about, the United States now had hundreds. America's explicit efforts to win the "war of ideas" for support from the world's Muslims were being drowned out by the implicit messages from Afghanistan and Iraq and Guantánamo (and from the State Department, as it rejected requests for student visas). Our enemies were thinking in centuries-long terms, while we were living election to election—and with the results of the 2004 presidential election, anti-American sentiment hardened among Muslims worldwide. Sooner or later our enemies would find one of our vulnerable points—and then another, and another.

To some degree, many of these discouraging possibilities are likely to come true. Hostile groups and individuals will keep planning attacks on the United States. Some of the attacks will succeed. Americans—especially those who live in Washington, New York, and other big cities—will share a reality known for many years to residents of cities from London to Jerusalem: that the perils of urban life include the risk of being a civilian casualty of worldwide political tensions.

But the deeper and more discouraging prospect—that the United States is doomed to spend decades cowering defensively—need not come true. How can the United States regain the initiative against terrorists, as opposed to living in a permanent crouch? By recognizing the point that I heard from so many military strategists: that terrorists, through their own efforts, can damage but not destroy us. Their real destructive power, again, lies in what they can provoke us to do. While the United States can never completely control what violent groups intend and sometimes achieve, it can determine its own response. That we have this power should come as good and important news, because it switches the strategic advantage to our side.

So far, the United States has been as predictable in its responses as Al Qaeda could have dreamed. Early in 2004, a Saudi exile named Saad al-Faqih was interviewed by the online publication *Terrorism Monitor.* Al-Faqih, who leads an opposition group seeking political reform in Saudi Arabia, is a longtime observer of his fellow Saudi Osama bin Laden and of the evolution of bin Laden's doctrine for Al Qaeda.

In the interview, al-Faqih said that for nearly a decade, bin Laden and al-Zawahiri had followed a powerful grand strategy for confronting the United States. Their approach boiled down to "superpower baiting" (as John Robb, of the Global Guerrillas blog, put it in an article about the interview). The most predictable thing about Americans, in this view, was that they would rise to the bait of a challenge or provocation. "Zawahiri impressed upon bin Laden the importance of understanding the American mentality," al-Faqih said. He said he believed that al-Zawahiri had at some point told bin Laden something like this:

> The American mentality is a cowboy mentality—if you confront them . . . they will react in an extreme manner. In other words, America with all its resources and establishments will shrink into a cowboy when irritated successfully. They will then elevate you, and this will satisfy the Muslim longing for a leader who can successfully challenge the West.

The United States is immeasurably stronger than Al Qaeda, but against jujitsu forms of attack its strength has been its disadvantage. The predictability of the U.S. response has allowed opponents to turn our bulk and momentum against us. Al Qaeda can do more harm to the United States than to, say, Italy because the self-damaging potential of an uncontrolled American reaction is so vast.

How can the United States escape this trap? Very simply: by declaring that the "global war on terror" is over, and that we have won. "The wartime approach made sense for a while," Dearlove says. "But as time passes and the situation changes, so must the strategy."

As a general principle, a standing state of war can be justified for several reasons. It might be the only way to concentrate the nation's resources where they are needed. It might explain why people are being inconvenienced or asked to sacrifice. It might symbolize that the entire nation's effort is directed toward one goal.

But none of those applies to modern America in its effort to defend itself against terrorist attack. The federal budget reveals no discipline at all about resources: the spending for antiterrorism activities has gone up, but so has the spending for nearly everything else. There is no expectation that Americans in general will share the inconveniences and sacrifice of the 1 percent of the population in uniform (going through airport screening lines does not count). Occasional speeches about the transcendent importance of the "long war" can't conceal the many other goals that day by day take political precedence.

And while a standing state of war no longer offers any advantages for the United States, it creates several problems. It cheapens the concept of war, making the word a synonym for *effort* or *goal.* It predisposes us toward overreactions, of the kind that have already proved so harmful. The detentions at Guantánamo Bay were justified as a wartime emergency. But unlike Abraham Lincoln's declaration of martial law, they have no natural end point.

A state of war encourages a state of fear. "The War on Terror does not reduce public anxieties by thwarting terrorists poised to strike," writes Ian Lustick, of the University of Pennsylvania, in his forthcoming book, *Trapped in the War on Terror.* "Rather, in myriad ways, conducting the antiterror effort as a 'war' fuels those anxieties." John Mueller writes in his book that because "the creation of insecurity, fear, anxiety, hysteria, and overreaction is central for terrorists," they can be defeated simply by a refusal to overreact. This approach is harder in time of war.

A state of war also predisposes the United States to think about using its assets in a strictly warlike way—and to give short shrift to the vast range of their other possibilities. The U.S. military has been responsible for the most dramatic recent improvement in American standing in the Islamic world. Immediately after the invasion of Iraq, the proportion of Indonesians with a favorable view of the United States had fallen to 15 percent, according to the Pew Global Attitudes Survey. After American troops brought ships, cargo planes, and helicopters loaded with supplies for tsunami victims, the overall Indonesian attitude toward the United States was still negative, but some 79 percent of Indonesians said that their opinion of America had improved because of the relief effort. There was a similar turnaround in Pakistan after U.S. troops helped feed and rescue villagers affected by a major earthquake. But in most of the Muslim world, the image of American troops is that of soldiers or marines manning counterinsurgency patrols, not delivering food and water. "The diplomatic component of the war on terror has been neglected so long, it's practically vestigial," a Marine officer told me. "It needs to be regrown." But in time of war, the balance is harder to correct.

Perhaps worst of all, an open-ended war is an open-ended invitation to defeat. *Sometime* there will be more bombings, shootings, poisonings, and other disruptions in the United States. They will happen in the future because they have happened in the past (Oklahoma City; the Unabomber; the Tylenol poisonings; the Washington, D.C.–area snipers; the still-unsolved anthrax mailings; the countless shootings at schools; and so on). These previous episodes were not caused by Islamic extremists; future ones may well be. In all cases they represent a failure of the government to protect its people. But if they occur while the war is still on, they are enemy "victories," not misfortunes of the sort that great nations suffer. They are also powerful provocations to another round of hasty reactions.

War implies emergency, and the upshot of most of what I heard was that the United States needs to shift its operations to a long-term, nonemergency basis. "De-escalation of the rhetoric is the first step," John Robb told me. "It is hard for insurgents to handle de-escalation." War encourages a simple classification of the world into ally or enemy. This polarization gives dispersed terrorist groups a unity they might not have on their own. Last year, in a widely circulated paper for the *Journal of Strategic Studies,* David Kilcullen argued that Islamic extremists from around the world yearn to constitute themselves as a global jihad. Therefore, he said, Western countries should do everything possible to treat terrorist groups individually, rather than "lumping together all terrorism, all rogue or failed states, and all strategic competitors who might potentially oppose U.S. objectives." The friend-or-foe categorization of war makes lumping together more likely.

The United States can declare victory by saying that what is controllable has been controlled: Al Qaeda Central has been broken up. Then the country can move to its real work. It will happen on three levels: domestic protection, worldwide harassment and pursuit of Al Qaeda, and an all-fronts diplomatic campaign.

Domestically, a sustainable post-victory policy would mean shifting from the early, panicky "Code Orange" days, in which everything was threatened and any investment in "security" was justified, to a more practical and triage-minded approach. Four analysts—Mueller, of Ohio State; Lustick, of the University of Pennsylvania; plus Veronique de Rugy, of the American Enterprise Institute; and Benjamin Friedman, of M.I.T.—have written extensively about the mindlessness and perverse effects of much homeland-security spending. In most cases, they argue, money dabbed out for a security fence here and a screening machine there would be far better spent on robust emergency-response systems. No matter how much they spend, state and federal authorities cannot possibly protect every place from every threat. But they could come close to ensuring that if things were to go wrong, relief and repair would be there fast.

Internationally, the effort to pin down bin Laden—to listen to his conversations, keep him off balance, and prevent him from re-forming an organization—has been successful. It must continue. And the international cooperation on which it depends will be easier in the absence of wartime language and friction. The effort to contain the one true existential threat to the United States—that of "loose nukes"—will also be eased by smoother relations with other countries.

Militarily, the United States has been stuck in an awkward middle ground concerning the need for "transformation." Donald Rumsfeld's insistence that the Army, in particular, rely on technology to become leaner and more "efficient" led to steady reductions in the planned size of the ground force that invaded and occupied Iraq. By most accounts, Rumsfeld went too far with that pressure—but not far enough in changing the largest patterns of Pentagon spending. This year's *Quadrennial Defense Review,* which is supposed to represent a bottom-up effort to rethink America's defense needs, says that the nation needs to prepare for a new era of fighting terrorists and insurgents (plus China)—and then offers programs and weapons very much the same as when the enemy was the Soviet Union. "The United States is still trying to use its familiar old instruments against new opponents," says Martin van Creveld, who calls Iraq a "totally unnecessary war." "It was the right army to beat Saddam Hussein," he says, "but the wrong one to occupy the country or deal with Osama bin Laden." Most counterterrorism authorities say that a transformation is also needed in the nation's spy agencies, starting with a much greater emphasis on language training and agents who develop long-term regional expertise in Muslim-dominated parts of the world.

Diplomatically, the United States can use the combination of "hard" and "soft" assets that constitute its unique strength to show a face that will again attract the world. "The only answer to a regime that wages total cold war is to wage total peace." So said Dwight Eisenhower in his State of the Union address in 1958, four months after *Sputnik* was launched. He added, "This means bringing to bear every asset of our personal and national lives upon the task of building the conditions in which security and peace can grow." A similar policy would allow the modern United States to use its diplomatic, economic, intellectual, and military means to reduce the long-term sources of terrorist rage.

America's range of strengths is, if anything, greater than when Eisenhower spoke nearly fifty years ago. The domestic population is more ethnically varied and accepting of outsiders. The university establishment is much larger. The leading companies are more fully integrated into local societies around the world. The nation has more numerous, better-funded, and more broadly experienced charitable foundations. It is much richer in every way. With the passing of the nuclear showdown against the Soviet Union, the country is safer than it was under Eisenhower. We should be able to "wage total peace" more effectively.

Americans still face dangers, as they always have. They have recently lacked leaders to help keep the dangers in perspective. Shaping public awareness—what we mean by "leading"—is what we most remember in our strong presidents: Lincoln's tone as the Civil War came on and as it neared its end; Theodore Roosevelt taking the first real steps toward environmental conservation and coming to terms with new industrial organizations; Franklin Roosevelt in the Depression and the Second World War; Eisenhower managing the showdown with the Soviet Union, but also overseeing the steady expansion of America's transportation, scientific, and educational systems; Kennedy with the race to the moon; and on up to George W. Bush, with his calm focus in the months immediately after 9/11. One of the signals Bush sent in those first days may have had the greatest strategic importance in the long run. That was his immediate insistence that America's Muslims were not the enemy, that they should not be singled out, that they should be seen as part of the nation's solution rather than part of its problem. It is easy to imagine that a different tone would have had damaging repercussions.

Now we could use a leader to help us understand victory and its consequences. We are ready for a message like this one:

> My fellow Americans, we have achieved something almost no one thought possible five years ago. The nation did not suffer the quick follow-up attacks so many people feared and expected. Our troops found the people who were responsible for the worst attack ever on our soil. We killed many, we captured more, and we placed their leaders in a position where they could not direct the next despicable attack on our people—and where the conscience of the world's people, of whatever faith, has turned against them for their barbarism. They have been a shame to their own great faith, and to all other historic standards of decency.

Achieving this victory does not mean the end of threats. Life is never free of dangers. I wish I could tell you that no American will ever again be killed or wounded by a terrorist—and that no other person on this earth will be either. But I cannot say that, and you could not believe me if I did. Life brings risk—especially life in an open society, like the one that people of this land have sacrificed for centuries to create.

We have achieved a great victory, and for that we can give thanks—above all to our troops. We will be at our best if we do not let fear paralyze or obsess us. We will be at our best if we instead optimistically and enthusiastically begin the next chapter in our nation's growth. We will deal with the struggles of our time. These include coping with terrorism, but also recognizing the huge shifts in power and resulting possibilities in Asia, in Latin America, in many other parts of the world. We will recognize the challenges of including the people left behind in the process of global development—people in the Middle East, in Africa, even in developed countries like our own. The world's scientists have never before had so much to offer, so fast—and humanity has never needed their discoveries more than we do now, to preserve the world's environment, to develop new sources of energy, to improve the quality of people's lives in every corner of the globe, to contain the threats that modern weaponry can put into the hands of individuals or small groups.

The great organizing challenge of our time includes coping with the threat of bombings and with the political extremism that lies behind it. That is one part of this era's duty. But it is not the entirety. History will judge us on our ability to deal with the full range of this era's challenges—and opportunities. With quiet pride, we recognize the victory we have won. And with the determination that has marked us through our nation's history, we continue the pursuit of our American mission, undeterred by the perils that we will face.

Different leaders will choose different words. But the message—of realism, of courage, and of optimism despite life's difficulties—is one we need to hear.

The Power of Green

Thomas L. Friedman

the *New York Times Magazine* | April 15, 2007

With the world finally waking up to the seriousness of the global warming threat (in the days leading up to the G-8 summit in the late spring of 2007, even climate-change-skeptic-in-chief George W. Bush has started to make noises about the need to cap global greenhouse emissions), New York Times *columnist Thomas Friedman believes that environmentalism could be the next great direction in American geo-politics. As he puts it, "Green is the new red, white and blue." In this article, he argues that the U.S. needs to become the global leader in a push to "shift our country, and eventually the world, to a largely emissions-free energy infrastructure over the next 50 years."*

Besides ensuring a habitable planet, Friedman theorizes that developing alternative energy sources and promoting energy efficiency—and thereby reducing our dependence on oil—will also encourage the worldwide spread of democracy. He goes on to explore possible approaches to achieving this goal, based on interviews with some of the world's leading experts on emissions-control strategies. As this important essay implies, we don't have a moment to lose.

I.

One day Iraq, our post-9/11 trauma and the divisiveness of the Bush years will all be behind us—and America will need, and want, to get its groove back. We will need to find a way to reknit America at home, reconnect America abroad and restore America to its natural place in the global order—as the beacon of progress, hope and inspiration. I have an idea how. It's called "green."

In the world of ideas, to name something is to own it. If you can name an issue, you can own the issue. One thing that always struck me about the term "green" was the degree to which, for so many years, it was defined by its opponents—by the people who wanted to disparage it. And they defined it as "liberal," "tree-hugging," "sissy," "girlie-man," "unpatriotic," "vaguely French."

Well, I want to rename "green." I want to rename it geostrategic, geo-economic, capitalistic and patriotic. I want to do that because I think that living, working, designing, manufacturing and projecting America in a green way can be the basis of a new unifying political movement for the 21st century. A redefined, broader and more muscular green ideology is not meant to trump the traditional Republican and Democratic agendas but rather to bridge them when it comes to addressing the three major issues facing every American today: jobs, temperature and terrorism.

How do our kids compete in a flatter world? How do they thrive in a warmer world? How do they survive in a more dangerous world? Those are, in a nutshell, the big questions facing America at the dawn of the 21st century. But these problems are so large in scale that they can only be effectively addressed by an America with 50 green states—not an America divided between red and blue states.

Because a new green ideology, properly defined, has the power to mobilize liberals and conservatives, evangelicals and atheists, big business and environmentalists around an agenda that can both pull us together and propel us forward. That's why I say: We don't just need the first black president. We need the first green president. We don't just need the first woman president. We need the first environmental president. We don't just need a president who has been toughened by years as a prisoner of war but a president who is tough enough to level with the American people about the profound economic, geopolitical and climate threats posed by our addiction to oil—and to offer a real plan to reduce our dependence on fossil fuels.

After World War II, President Eisenhower responded to the threat of Communism and the "red menace" with massive spending on an interstate highway system to tie America together, in large part so that we could better move weapons in the event of a war with the Soviets. That highway system, though, helped to enshrine America's car culture (atrophying our railroads) and to lock in suburban sprawl and low-density housing, which all combined to get America addicted to cheap fossil fuels, particularly oil. Many in the world followed our model.

Today, we are paying the accumulated economic, geopolitical and climate prices for that kind of America. I am not proposing that we radically alter our lifestyles. We are who we are—including a car culture. But if we want to continue to be who we are, enjoy the benefits and be able to pass them on to our children, we do need to fuel our future in a cleaner, greener way. Eisenhower rallied us with the red menace. The next president will have to rally us with a green patriotism. Hence my motto: "Green is the new red, white and blue."

The good news is that after traveling around America this past year, looking at how we use energy and the emerging alternatives, I can report that green really has gone Main Street—thanks to the perfect storm created by 9/11, Hurricane Katrina and the Internet revolution. The first flattened the twin towers, the second flattened New Orleans and the third flattened the global economic playing field. The convergence of all three has turned many of our previous assumptions about "green" upside down in a very short period of time, making it much more compelling to many more Americans.

But here's the bad news: While green has hit Main Street—more Americans than ever now identify themselves as greens, or what I call "Geo-Greens" to differentiate their more muscular and strategic green ideology—green has not gone very far down Main Street. It certainly has not gone anywhere near the distance required to preserve our lifestyle. The dirty little secret is that we're fooling ourselves. We in America talk like we're already "the greenest generation," as the business writer Dan Pink once called it. But here's the really inconvenient truth: We have not even begun to be serious about the costs, the effort and the scale of change that will be required to shift our country, and eventually the world, to a largely emissions-free energy infrastructure over the next 50 years.

II.

A few weeks after American forces invaded Afghanistan, I visited the Pakistani frontier town of Peshawar, a hotbed of Islamic radicalism. On the way, I stopped at the famous Darul Uloom Haqqania, the biggest madrasa, or Islamic school, in Pakistan, with 2,800 live-in students. The Taliban leader Mullah Muhammad Omar attended this madrasa as a younger man. My Pakistani friend and I were allowed to observe a class of young boys who sat on the floor, practicing their rote learning of the Koran from texts perched on wooden holders. The air in the Koran class was so thick and stale it felt as if you could have cut it into blocks. The teacher asked an 8-year-old boy to chant a Koranic verse for us, which he did with the elegance of an experienced muezzin. I asked another student, an Afghan refugee, Rahim Kunduz, age 12, what his reaction was to the September 11 attacks, and he said: "Most likely the attack came from Americans inside America. I am pleased that America has had to face pain, because the rest of the world has tasted its pain." A framed sign on the wall said this room was "A gift of the Kingdom of Saudi Arabia."

Sometime after 9/11—an unprovoked mass murder perpetrated by 19 men, 15 of whom were Saudis—green went geostrategic, as Americans started to realize we were financing both sides in the war on terrorism. We were financing the U.S. military with our tax dollars; and we were financing a transformation of Islam, in favor of its most intolerant strand, with our gasoline purchases. How stupid is that?

Islam has always been practiced in different forms. Some are more embracing of modernity, reinterpretation of the Koran and tolerance of other faiths, like Sufi Islam or the populist Islam of Egypt, Ottoman Turkey and Indonesia. Some strands, like Salafi Islam—followed by the Wahhabis of Saudi Arabia and by Al Qaeda—believe Islam should be returned to an austere form practiced in the time of the Prophet Muhammad, a form hostile to modernity, science, "infidels" and women's rights. By enriching the Saudi and Iranian treasuries via our gasoline purchases, we are financing the export of the Saudi puritanical brand of Sunni Islam and the Iranian fundamentalist brand of Shiite Islam, tilting the Muslim world in a more intolerant direction. At the Muslim fringe, this creates more recruits for the Taliban, Al Qaeda, Hamas, Hezbollah and the Sunni suicide bomb squads of Iraq; at the Muslim center, it creates a much bigger constituency of people who applaud suicide bombers as martyrs.

The Saudi Islamic export drive first went into high gear after extreme fundamentalists challenged the Muslim credentials of the Saudi ruling family by taking over the Grand Mosque of Mecca in 1979—a year that coincided with the Iranian revolution and a huge rise in oil prices. The attack on the Grand Mosque by these Koran-and-rifle-wielding Islamic militants shook the Saudi ruling family to its core. The al-Sauds responded to this challenge to their religious bona fides by becoming outwardly more religious. They gave their official Wahhabi religious establishment even more power to impose Islam on public life. Awash in cash thanks to the spike in oil prices, the Saudi government and charities also spent hundreds of millions of dollars endowing mosques, youth clubs and Muslim schools all over the world, ensuring that Wahhabi imams, teachers and textbooks would preach Saudi-style Islam. Eventually, notes Lawrence Wright in *The Looming*

Tower, his history of Al Qaeda, "Saudi Arabia, which constitutes only 1 percent of the world Muslim population, would support 90 percent of the expenses of the entire faith, overriding other traditions of Islam."

Saudi mosques and wealthy donors have also funneled cash to the Sunni insurgents in Iraq. The Associated Press reported from Cairo in December: "Several drivers interviewed by the A.P. in Middle East capitals said Saudis have been using religious events, like the hajj pilgrimage to Mecca and a smaller pilgrimage, as cover for illicit money transfers. Some money, they said, is carried into Iraq on buses with returning pilgrims. 'They sent boxes full of dollars and asked me to deliver them to certain addresses in Iraq,' said one driver. . . . 'I know it is being sent to the resistance, and if I don't take it with me, they will kill me.'"

No wonder more Americans have concluded that conserving oil to put less money in the hands of hostile forces is now a geostrategic imperative. President Bush's refusal to do anything meaningful after 9/11 to reduce our gasoline usage really amounts to a policy of "No Mullah Left Behind." James Woolsey, the former CIA director, minces no words: "We are funding the rope for the hanging of ourselves."

No, I don't want to bankrupt Saudi Arabia or trigger an Islamist revolt there. Its leadership is more moderate and pro-Western than its people. But the way the Saudi ruling family has bought off its religious establishment, in order to stay in power, is not healthy. Cutting the price of oil in half would help change that. In the 1990s, dwindling oil income sparked a Saudi debate about less Koran and more science in Saudi schools, even experimentation with local elections. But the recent oil windfall has stilled all talk of reform.

That is because of what I call the First Law of Petropolitics: The price of oil and the pace of freedom always move in opposite directions in states that are highly dependent on oil exports for their income and have weak institutions or outright authoritarian governments. And this is another reason that green has become geostrategic. Soaring oil prices are poisoning the international system by strengthening antidemocratic regimes around the globe.

Look what's happened: We thought the fall of the Berlin Wall was going to unleash an unstoppable tide of free markets and free people, and for about a decade it did just that. But those years coincided with oil in the $10-to-$30-a-barrel range. As the price of oil surged into the $30-to-$70 range in the early 2000s, it triggered a countertide—a tide of petroauthoritarianism—manifested in Russia, Iran, Nigeria, Venezuela, Saudi Arabia, Syria, Sudan, Egypt, Chad, Angola, Azerbaijan and Turkmenistan. The elected or self-appointed elites running these states have used their oil windfalls to ensconce themselves in power, buy off opponents and counter the fall-of-the-Berlin-Wall tide. If we continue to finance them with our oil purchases, they will reshape the world in their image, around Putin-like values.

You can illustrate the First Law of Petropolitics with a simple graph. On one line chart the price of oil from 1979 to the present; on another line chart the Freedom House or Fraser Institute freedom indexes for Russia, Nigeria, Iran and Venezuela for the same years. When you put these two lines on the same graph you see something striking: the price of oil and the pace of freedom are inversely correlated. As oil prices went down in the early 1990s, competition, transparency, political participation and accountability of those in office all tended to go up in these countries—as measured by free elections held, newspapers opened, reformers elected, economic reform projects started and companies privatized. That's because their petroauthoritarian regimes had to open themselves to foreign investment and educate and empower their people more in order to earn income. But as oil prices went up around 2000, free speech, free press, fair elections and freedom to form political parties and NGOs all eroded in these countries.

The motto of the American Revolution was "no taxation without representation." The motto of the petroauthoritarians is "no representation without taxation": if I don't have to tax you, because I can get all the money I need from oil wells, I don't have to listen to you.

It is no accident that when oil prices were low in the 1990s, Iran elected a reformist Parliament and a president who called for a "dialogue of civilizations." And when oil prices soared to $70 a barrel, Iran's conservatives pushed out the reformers and ensconced a president who says the Holocaust is a myth. (I promise you, if oil prices drop to $25 a barrel, the Holocaust won't be a myth anymore.) And it is no accident that the first Arab Gulf state to start running out of oil, Bahrain, is also the first Arab Gulf state to have held a free and fair election in which women could run and vote, the first Arab Gulf state to overhaul its labor laws to make more of its own people employable and the first Arab Gulf state to sign a free-trade agreement with America.

People change when they have to—not when we tell them to—and falling oil prices make them have to. That is why if we are looking for a Plan B for Iraq—a way of pressing for political reform in the Middle East without going to war again—there is no better tool than bringing down the price of oil. When it comes to fostering democracy among petroauthoritarians, it doesn't matter whether you're a neocon or a radical lib. If you're not also a Geo-Green, you won't succeed.

The notion that conserving energy is a geostrategic imperative has also moved into the Pentagon, for slightly different reasons. Generals are realizing that the more energy they save in the heat of battle, the more power they can project. The Pentagon has been looking to improve its energy efficiency for several years now to save money. But the Iraq war has given birth to a new movement in the U.S. military: the "Green Hawks."

As Amory Lovins of the Rocky Mountain Institute, who has been working with the Pentagon, put it to me: The Iraq war forced the U.S. military to think much more seriously about how to "eat its tail"—to shorten its energy supply lines by becoming more energy efficient. According to Dan Nolan, who oversees energy projects for the U.S. Army's Rapid Equipping Force, it started last year when a Marine major general in Anbar Province told the Pentagon he wanted better-insulated, more energy-efficient tents in the Iraqi desert. Why? His air-conditioners were being run off mobile generators, and the generators ran on diesel, and the diesel had to be trucked in, and the insurgents were blowing up the trucks.

"When we began the analysis of his request, it was really about the fact that his soldiers were being attacked on the roads bringing fuel and water," Nolan said. So eating their tail meant "taking those things that are brought into the unit and trying to generate them on-site." To that end Nolan's team is now experimenting with everything from new kinds of tents that need 40 percent less air-conditioning to new kinds of fuel cells that produce water as a byproduct.

Pay attention: When the U.S. Army desegregated, the country really desegregated; when the Army goes green, the country could really go green.

"Energy independence is a national security issue," Nolan said. "It's the right business for us to be in. . . . We are not trying to change the whole Army. Our job is to focus on that battalion out there and give those commanders the technological innovations they need to deal with today's mission. But when they start coming home, they are going to bring those things with them."

III.

The second big reason green has gone Main Street is because global warming has. A decade ago, it was mostly experts who worried that climate change was real, largely brought about by humans and likely to lead to species loss and environmental crises. Now Main Street is starting to worry because people are seeing things they've never seen before in their own front yards and reading things they've never read before in their papers—like the recent draft report by the United Nations's 2,000-expert Intergovernmental Panel on Climate Change, which concluded that "changes in climate are now affecting physical and biological systems on every continent."

I went to Montana in January and Gov. Brian Schweitzer told me: "We don't get as much snow in the high country as we used to, and the runoff starts sooner in the spring. The river I've been fishing over the last 50 years is now warmer in July by five degrees than 50 years ago, and it is hard on our trout population." I went to Moscow in February, and my friends told me they just celebrated the first Moscow Christmas in their memory with no snow. I stopped in London on the way home, and I didn't need an overcoat. In 2006, the average temperature in central England was the highest ever recorded since the Central England Temperature (C.E.T.) series began in 1659.

Yes, no one knows exactly what will happen. But ever fewer people want to do nothing. Gov. Arnold Schwarzenegger of California summed up the new climate around climate when he said to me recently: "If 98 doctors say my son is ill and needs medication and two say 'No, he doesn't, he is fine,' I will go with the 98. It's common sense—the same with global warming. We go with the majority, the large majority. . . . The key thing now is that since we know this industrial age has created it, let's get our act together and do everything we can to roll it back."

But how? Now we arrive at the first big roadblock to green going down Main Street. Most people have no clue—no clue—how huge an industrial project is required to blunt climate change. Here are two people who do: Robert Socolow, an engineering professor, and Stephen Pacala, an ecology professor, who together lead the Carbon Mitigation Initiative at Princeton, a consortium designing scalable solutions for the climate issue.

They first argued in a paper published by the journal *Science* in August 2004 that human beings can emit only so much carbon into the atmosphere before the buildup of carbon dioxide (CO_2) reaches a level unknown in recent geologic history and the earth's climate system starts to go "haywire."

The scientific consensus, they note, is that the risk of things going haywire—weather patterns getting violently unstable, glaciers melting, prolonged droughts—grows rapidly as CO_2 levels "approach a doubling" of the concentration of CO_2 that was in the atmosphere before the Industrial Revolution.

"Think of the climate change issue as a closet, and behind the door are lurking all kinds of monsters—and there's a long list of them," Pacala said. "All of our scientific work says the most damaging monsters start to come out from behind that door when you hit the doubling of CO_2 levels." As Bill Collins, who led the development of a model used worldwide for simulating climate change, put it to me: "We're running an uncontrolled experiment on the only home we have."

So here is our challenge, according to Pacala: If we basically do nothing, and global CO_2 emissions continue to grow at the pace of the last 30 years for the next 50 years, we will pass the doubling level—an atmospheric concentration of carbon dioxide of 560 parts per million—around midcentury. To avoid that—and still leave room for developed countries to grow, using less carbon, and for countries like India and China to grow, emitting double or triple their current carbon levels, until they climb out of poverty and are able to become more energy efficient—will require a huge global industrial energy project.

To convey the scale involved, Socolow and Pacala have created a pie chart with 15 different wedges. Some wedges represent carbon-free or carbon-diminishing power-generating technologies; other wedges represent efficiency programs that could conserve large amounts of energy and prevent CO_2 emissions. They argue that the world needs to deploy any 7 of these 15 wedges, or sufficient amounts of all 15, to have enough conservation, and enough carbon-free energy, to increase the world economy and still avoid the doubling of CO_2 in the atmosphere. Each wedge, when phased in over 50 years, would avoid the release of 25 billion tons of carbon, for a total of 175 billion tons of carbon avoided between now and 2056.

Here are seven wedges we could chose from: "Replace 1,400 large coal-fired plants with gas-fired plants; increase the fuel economy of two billion cars from 30 to 60 miles per gallon; add twice today's nuclear output to displace coal; drive two billion cars on ethanol, using one-sixth of the world's cropland; increase solar power 700-fold to displace coal; cut electricity use in homes, offices and stores by 25 percent; install carbon capture and sequestration capacity at 800 large coal-fired plants." And the other eight aren't any easier. They include halting all cutting and burning of forests, since deforestation causes about 20 percent of the world's annual CO_2 emissions.

"There has never been a deliberate industrial project in history as big as this," Pacala said. Through a combination of clean power technology and conservation, "we have to get rid of 175 billion tons of carbon over the next 50 years—and still keep growing. It is possible to accomplish this if we start today. But every year that we delay, the job becomes more difficult—and if we delay a decade or two, avoiding the doubling or more may well become impossible."

IV.

In November, I flew from Shanghai to Beijing on Air China. As we landed in Beijing and taxied to the terminal, the Chinese air hostess came on the P.A. and said: "We've just landed in Beijing. The temperature is 8 degrees Celsius, 46 degrees Fahrenheit and the sky is clear."

I almost burst out laughing. Outside my window the smog was so thick you could not see the end of the terminal building. When I got into Beijing, though, friends told me the air was better than usual. Why? China had been host of a summit meeting of 48 African leaders. *Time* magazine reported that Beijing officials had "ordered half a million official cars off the roads and said another 400,000 drivers had 'volunteered' to refrain from using their vehicles" in order to clean up the air for their African guests. As soon as they left, the cars returned, and Beijing's air went back to "unhealthy."

Green has also gone Main Street because the end of Communism, the rise of the personal computer and the diffusion of the Internet have opened the global economic playing field to so many more people, all coming with their own versions of the American dream—a house, a car, a toaster, a microwave and a refrigerator. It is a blessing to see so many people growing out of poverty. But when three billion people move from "low-impact" to "high-impact" lifestyles, Jared Diamond wrote in *Collapse,* it makes it urgent that we find cleaner ways to fuel their dreams. According to Lester Brown, the founder of the Earth Policy Institute, if China keeps growing at 8 percent a year, by 2031 the per-capita income of 1.45 billion Chinese will be the same as America's in 2004. China currently has only one car for every 100 people, but Brown projects that as it reaches American income levels, if it copies American consumption, it will have three cars for every four people, or 1.1 billion vehicles. The total world fleet today is 800 million vehicles!

That's why McKinsey Global Institute forecasts that developing countries will generate nearly 80 percent of the growth in world energy demand between now and 2020, with China representing 32 percent and the Middle East 10 percent. So if Red China doesn't become Green China there is no chance we will keep the climate monsters behind the door. On some days, says the U.S. Environmental Protection Agency, almost 25 percent of the polluting matter in the air above Los Angeles comes from China's coal-fired power plants and factories, as well as fumes from China's cars and dust kicked up by droughts and deforestation around Asia.

The good news is that China knows it has to grow green—or it won't grow at all. On September 8, 2006, a Chinese newspaper reported that China's EPA and its National Bureau of Statistics had re-examined China's 2004 GDP number. They concluded that the health problems, environmental degradation and lost workdays from pollution had actually cost China $64 billion, or 3.05 percent of its total economic output for 2004. Some experts believe the real number is closer to 10 percent.

Thus China has a strong motivation to clean up the worst pollutants in its air. Those are the nitrogen oxides, sulfur oxides and mercury that produce acid rain, smog and haze—much of which come from burning coal. But cleaning up is easier said than done. The Communist Party's legitimacy and the stability of the whole country depend heavily on Beijing's ability to provide rising living standards for more and more Chinese.

So, if you're a Chinese mayor and have to choose between growing jobs and cutting pollution, you will invariably choose jobs: coughing workers are much less politically dangerous than unemployed workers. That's a key reason why China's 10th five-year plan, which began in 2000, called for a 10 percent reduction in sulfur dioxide in China's air—and when that plan concluded in 2005, sulfur dioxide pollution in China had increased by 27 percent.

But if China is having a hard time cleaning up its nitrogen and sulfur oxides—which can be done relatively cheaply by adding scrubbers to the smokestacks of coal-fired power plants—imagine what will happen when it comes to asking China to curb its CO_2, of which China is now the world's second-largest emitter, after America. To build a coal-fired power plant that captures, separates and safely sequesters the CO_2 into the ground before it goes up the smokestack requires either an expensive retrofit or a whole new system. That new system would cost about 40 percent more to build and operate—and would produce 20 percent less electricity, according to a recent MIT study, "The Future of Coal."

China—which is constructing the equivalent of two 500-megawatt coal-fired power plants every week—is not going to pay that now. Remember: CO_2 is an invisible, odorless, tasteless gas. Yes, it causes global warming—but it doesn't hurt anyone in China today, and getting rid of it is costly and has no economic payoff. China's strategy right now is to say that CO_2 is the West's problem. "It must be pointed out that climate change has been caused by the long-term historic emissions of developed countries and their high per-capita emissions," Jiang Yu, a spokeswoman for China's Foreign Ministry, declared in February. "Developed countries bear an unshirkable responsibility."

So now we come to the nub of the issue: Green will not go down Main Street America unless it also goes down Main Street China, India and Brazil. And for green to go Main Street in these big developing countries, the prices of clean power alternatives—wind, biofuels, nuclear, solar or coal sequestration—have to fall to the "China price." The China price is basically the price China pays for coal-fired electricity today because China is not prepared to pay a premium now, and sacrifice growth and stability, just to get rid of the CO_2 that comes from burning coal.

"The 'China price' is the fundamental benchmark that everyone is looking to satisfy," said Curtis Carlson, CEO of SRI International, which is developing alternative energy technologies. "Because if the Chinese have to pay 10 percent more for energy, when they have tens of millions of people living under $1,000 a year, it is not going to happen." Carlson went on to say: "We have an enormous amount of new innovation we must put in place before we can get to a price that China and India will be able to pay. But this is also an opportunity."

V.

The only way we are going to get innovations that drive energy costs down to the China price—innovations in energy-saving appliances, lights and building materials and in non-CO_2-emitting power plants and fuels—is by mobilizing free-market capitalism. The only thing as powerful as Mother

Nature is Father Greed. To a degree, the market is already at work on this project—because some venture capitalists and companies understand that clean-tech is going to be the next great global industry. Take Wal-Mart. The world's biggest retailer woke up several years ago, its CEO Lee Scott told me, and realized that with regard to the environment its customers "had higher expectations for us than we had for ourselves." So Scott hired a sustainability expert, Jib Ellison, to tutor the company. The first lesson Ellison preached was that going green was a whole new way for Wal-Mart to cut costs and drive its profits. As Scott recalled it, Ellison said to him, "Lee, the thing you have to think of is all this stuff that people don't want you to put into the environment is waste—and you're paying for it!"

So Scott initiated a program to work with Wal-Mart's suppliers to reduce the sizes and materials used for all its packaging by 5 percent by 2013. The reductions they have made are already paying off in savings to the company. "We created teams to work across the organization," Scott said. "It was voluntary—then you had the first person who eliminated some packaging, and someone else started showing how we could recycle more plastic, and all of a sudden it's $1 million a quarter." Wal-Mart operates 7,000 huge Class 8 trucks that get about 6 miles per gallon. It has told its truck makers that by 2015, it wants to double the efficiency of the fleet. Wal-Mart is the China of companies, so, explained Scott, "if we place one order we can create a market" for energy innovation.

For instance, Wal-Mart has used its shelves to create a huge, low-cost market for compact fluorescent bulbs, which use about a quarter of the energy of incandescent bulbs to produce the same light and last 10 times as long. "Just by doing what it does best—saving customers money and cutting costs," said Glenn Prickett of Conservation International, a Wal-Mart adviser, "Wal-Mart can have a revolutionary impact on the market for green technologies. If every one of their 100 million customers in the U.S. bought just one energy-saving compact fluorescent lamp, instead of a traditional incandescent bulb, they could cut CO_2 emissions by 45 billion pounds and save more than $3 billion."

Those savings highlight something that often gets lost: The quickest way to get to the China price for clean power is by becoming more energy efficient. The cheapest, cleanest, nonemitting power plant in the world is the one you don't build. Helping China adopt some of the breakthrough efficiency programs that California has adopted, for instance—like rewarding electrical utilities for how much energy they get their customers to save rather than to use—could have a huge impact. Some experts estimate that China could cut its need for new power plants in half with aggressive investments in efficiency.

Yet another force driving us to the China price is Chinese entrepreneurs, who understand that while Beijing may not be ready to impose CO_2 restraints, developed countries are, so this is going to be a global business—and they want a slice. Let me introduce the man identified last year by *Forbes Magazine* as the seventh-richest man in China, with a fortune now estimated at $2.2 billion. His name is Shi Zhengrong and he is China's leading manufacturer of silicon solar panels, which convert sunlight into electricity.

"People at all levels in China have become more aware of this environment issue and alternative energy," said Shi, whose company, Suntech Power Holdings, is listed on the New York Stock Exchange. "Five years ago, when I started the company, people said: 'Why do we need solar? We have a surplus of coal-powered electricity.' Now it is different; now people realize that solar has a bright future. But it is still too expensive. . . . We have to reduce the cost as quickly as possible—our real competitors are coal and nuclear power."

Shi does most of his manufacturing in China, but sells roughly 90 percent of his products outside China, because today they are too expensive for his domestic market. But the more he can get the price down, and start to grow his business inside China, the more he can use that to become a dominant global player. Thanks to Suntech's success, in China "there is a rush of business people entering this sector, even though we still don't have a market here," Shi added. "Many government people now say, 'This is an industry!'" And if it takes off, China could do for solar panels what it did for tennis shoes—bring the price down so far that everyone can afford a pair.

VI.

All that sounds great—but remember those seven wedges? To reach the necessary scale of emissions-free energy will require big clean coal or nuclear power stations, wind farms and solar farms, all connected to a national transmission grid, not to mention clean fuels for our cars and trucks. And the market alone, as presently constructed in the U.S., will not get us those alternatives at the scale we need—at the China price—fast enough.

Professor Nate Lewis, Caltech's noted chemist and energy expert, explained why with an analogy. "Let's say you invented the first cell phone," he said. "You could charge people $1,000 for each one because lots of people would be ready to pay lots of money to have a phone they could carry in their pocket." With those profits, you, the inventor, could pay back your shareholders and plow more into research, so you keep selling better and cheaper cell phones.

But energy is different, Lewis explained: "If I come to you and say, 'Today your house lights are being powered by dirty coal, but tomorrow, if you pay me $100 more a month, I will power your house lights with solar,' you are most likely to say: 'Sorry, Nate, but I don't really care how my lights go on, I just care that they go on. I won't pay an extra $100 a month for sun power. A new cell phone improves my life. A different way to power my lights does nothing.'

"So building an emissions-free energy infrastructure is not like sending a man to the moon," Lewis went on. "With the moon shot, money was no object—and all we had to do was get there. But today, we already have cheap energy from coal, gas and oil. So getting people to pay more to shift to clean fuels is like trying to get funding for NASA to build a spaceship to the moon—when Southwest Airlines already flies there and gives away free peanuts! I already have a cheap ride to the moon, and a ride is a ride. For most people, electricity is electricity, no matter how it is generated."

If we were running out of coal or oil, the market would steadily push the prices up, which would stimulate innovation in alternatives. Eventually there would be a crossover, and the alternatives would kick in, start to scale and come down in price. But what has happened in energy over the last 35 years is that the oil price goes up, stimulating government subsidies and some investments in alternatives, and then the price goes down, the government loses interest, the subsidies expire and the investors in alternatives get wiped out.

The only way to stimulate the scale of sustained investment in research and development of non-CO_2 emitting power at the China price is if the developed countries, who can afford to do so, force their people to pay the full climate, economic and geopolitical costs of using gasoline and dirty coal. Those countries that have signed the Kyoto Protocol are starting to do that. But America is not.

Up to now, said Lester Brown, president of the Earth Policy Institute, we as a society "have been behaving just like Enron the company at the height of its folly." We rack up stunning profits and GDP numbers every year, and they look great on paper "because we've been hiding some of the costs off the books." If we don't put a price on the CO_2 we're building up or on our addiction to oil, we'll never nurture the innovation we need.

Jeffrey Immelt, the chairman of General Electric, has worked for G.E. for 25 years. In that time, he told me, he has seen seven generations of innovation in G.E.'s medical equipment business—in devices like MRIs or CT scans—because health care market incentives drove the innovation. In power, it's just the opposite. "Today, on the power side," he said, "we're still selling the same basic coal-fired power plants we had when I arrived. They're a little cleaner and more efficient now, but basically the same."

The one clean power area where G.E. is now into a third generation is wind turbines, "thanks to the European Union," Immelt said. Countries like Denmark, Spain and Germany imposed standards for wind power on their utilities and offered sustained subsidies, creating a big market for wind-turbine manufacturers in Europe in the 1980s, when America abandoned wind because the price of oil fell. "We grew our wind business in Europe," Immelt said.

As things stand now in America, Immelt said, "the market does not work in energy." The multibillion-dollar scale of investment that a company like G.E. is being asked to make in order to develop new clean-power technologies or that a utility is being asked to make in order to build coal sequestration facilities or nuclear plants is not going to happen at scale—unless they know that coal and oil are going to be priced high enough for long enough that new investments will not be undercut in a few years by falling fossil fuel prices. "Carbon has to have a value," Immelt emphasized. "Today in the U.S. and China it has no value."

I recently visited the infamous Three Mile Island nuclear plant with Christopher Crane, president of Exelon Nuclear, which owns the facility. He said that if Exelon wanted to start a nuclear plant today, the licensing, design, planning and building requirements are so extensive it would not open until 2015 at the earliest. But even if Exelon got all the approvals, it could not start building "because the cost of capital for a nuclear plant today is prohibitive."

That's because the interest rate that any commercial bank would charge on a loan for a nuclear facility would be so high—because of all the risks of lawsuits or cost overruns—that it would be impossible for Exelon to proceed. A standard nuclear plant today costs about $3 billion per unit. The only way to stimulate more nuclear power innovation, Crane said, would be federal loan guarantees that would lower the cost of capital for anyone willing to build a new nuclear plant.

The 2005 energy bill created such loan guarantees, but the details still have not been worked out. "We would need a robust loan guarantee program to jump-start the nuclear industry," Crane said—an industry that has basically been frozen since the 1979 Three Mile Island accident. With cheaper money, added Crane, CO_2-free nuclear power could be "very competitive" with CO_2-emitting pulverized coal.

Think about the implications. Three Mile Island had two reactors, TMI-2, which shut down because of the 1979 accident, and TMI-1, which is still operating today, providing clean electricity with virtually no CO_2 emissions for 800,000 homes. Had the TMI-2 accident not happened, it too would have been providing clean electricity for 800,000 homes for the last 28 years. Instead, that energy came from CO_2-emitting coal, which, by the way, still generates 50 percent of America's electricity.

Similar calculations apply to ethanol production. "We have about 100 scientists working on cellulosic ethanol," Chad Holliday, the CEO of DuPont, told me. "My guess is that we could double the number and add another 50 to start working on how to commercialize it. It would probably cost us less than $100 million to scale up. But I am not ready to do that. I can guess what it will cost me to make it and what the price will be, but is the market going to be there? What are the regulations going to be? Is the ethanol subsidy going to be reduced? Will we put a tax on oil to keep ethanol competitive? If I know that, it gives me a price target to go after. Without that, I don't know what the market is and my shareholders don't know how to value what I am doing. . . . You need some certainty on the incentives side and on the market side, because we are talking about multiyear investments, billions of dollars, that will take a long time to take off, and we won't hit on everything."

Summing up the problem, Immelt of G.E. said the big energy players are being asked "to take a 15-minute market signal and make a 40-year decision and that just doesn't work. . . . The U.S. government should decide: What do we want to have happen? How much clean coal, how much nuclear and what is the most efficient way to incentivize people to get there?"

He's dead right. The market alone won't work. Government's job is to set high standards, let the market reach them and then raise the standards more. That's how you get scale innovation at the China price. Government can do this by imposing steadily rising efficiency standards for buildings and appliances and by stipulating that utilities generate a certain amount of electricity from renewables—like wind or solar. Or it can impose steadily rising mileage standards for cars or a steadily tightening cap-and-trade system for the amount of CO_2 any factory or power plant can emit. Or it can offer loan guarantees and fast-track licensing for anyone who wants to build a nuclear plant. Or—my preference and the simplest option—it can impose a carbon tax that will stimulate the market to move away from fuels that emit high levels of CO_2 and invest in those that don't. Ideally, it will do all of these things. But whichever options we choose, they will only work if they are transparent, simple and long-term—with zero fudging allowed and with regulatory oversight and stiff financial penalties for violators.

The politician who actually proved just how effective this can be was a guy named George W. Bush, when he was governor of Texas. He pushed for and signed a renewable energy portfolio mandate in 1999. The mandate stipulated that Texas power companies had to produce 2,000 new megawatts of electricity from renewables, mostly wind, by 2009. What happened? A dozen new companies jumped into the Texas market and built wind turbines to meet the mandate, so many that the 2,000-megawatt goal was reached in 2005. So the Texas Legislature has upped the mandate to 5,000 megawatts by 2015, and everyone knows they will beat that too because of how quickly wind in Texas is becoming competitive with coal. Today, thanks to Governor Bush's market intervention, Texas is the biggest wind state in America.

President Bush, though, is no Governor Bush. (The Dick Cheney effect?) President Bush claims he's protecting American companies by not imposing tough mileage, conservation or clean power standards, but he's actually helping them lose the race for the next great global industry. Japan has some of the world's highest gasoline taxes and stringent energy efficiency standards for vehicles—and it has the world's most profitable and innovative car company, Toyota. That's no accident.

The politicians who best understand this are America's governors, some of whom have started to just ignore Washington, set their own energy standards and reap the benefits for their states. As Schwarzenegger told me,

"We have seen in California so many companies that have been created that work just on things that have do with clean environment." California's state-imposed efficiency standards have resulted in per-capita energy consumption in California remaining almost flat for the last 30 years, while in the rest of the country it has gone up 50 percent. "There are a lot of industries that are exploding right now because of setting these new standards," he said.

VII.

John Dineen runs G.E. Transportation, which makes locomotives. His factory is in Erie, Pa., and employs 4,500 people. When it comes to the challenges from cheap labor markets, Dineen likes to say, "Our little town has trade surpluses with China and Mexico."

Now how could that be? China makes locomotives that are 30 percent cheaper than G.E.'s, but it turns out that G.E.'s are the most energy efficient in the world, with the lowest emissions and best mileage per ton pulled—"and they don't stop on the tracks," Dineen added. So China is also buying from Erie—and so are Brazil, Mexico and Kazakhstan. What's the secret? The China price.

"We made it very easy for them," said Dineen. "By producing engines with lower emissions in the classic sense (NOx [nitrogen oxides]) and lower emissions in the future sense (CO_2) and then coupling it with better fuel efficiency and reliability, we lowered the total life-cycle cost."

The West can't impose its climate or pollution standards on China, Dineen explained, but when a company like G.E. makes an engine that gets great mileage, cuts pollution and, by the way, emits less CO_2, China will be a buyer. "If we were just trying to export lower-emission units, and they did not have the fuel benefits, we would lose," Dineen said. "But when green is made green—improved fuel economies coupled with emissions reductions —we see very quick adoption rates."

One reason G.E. Transportation got so efficient was the old U.S. standard it had to meet on NOx pollution, Dineen said. It did that through technological innovation. And as oil prices went up, it leveraged more technology to get better mileage. The result was a cleaner, more efficient, more exportable locomotive. Dineen describes his factory as a "technology campus" because, he explains, "it looks like a 100-year-old industrial site, but inside those 100-year-old buildings are world-class engineers working on the next generation's technologies." He also notes that workers in his factory make nearly twice the average in Erie—by selling to China!

The bottom line is this: Clean-tech plays to America's strength because making things like locomotives lighter and smarter takes a lot of knowledge—not cheap labor. That's why embedding clean-tech into everything we design and manufacture is a way to revive America as a manufacturing power.

"Whatever you are making, if you can add a green dimension to it—making it more efficient, healthier and more sustainable for future generations—you have a product that can't just be made cheaper in India or China," said Andrew Shapiro, founder of GreenOrder, an environmental business-strategy group. "If you just create a green ghetto in your company, you miss it. You have to figure out how to integrate green into the DNA of your whole business."

Ditto for our country, which is why we need a Green New Deal—one in which government's role is not funding projects, as in the original New Deal, but seeding basic research, providing loan guarantees where needed and setting standards, taxes and incentives that will spawn 1,000 G.E. Transportations for all kinds of clean power.

Bush won't lead a Green New Deal, but his successor must if America is going to maintain its leadership and living standard. Unfortunately, today's presidential hopefuls are largely full of hot air on the climate-energy issue. Not one of them is proposing anything hard, like a carbon or gasoline tax, and if you think we can deal with these huge problems without asking the American people to do anything hard, you're a fool or a fraud.

Being serious starts with reframing the whole issue—helping Americans understand, as the Carnegie Fellow David Rothkopf puts it, "that we're not 'post-Cold War' anymore—we're pre-something totally new." I'd say we're in the "pre-climate war era." Unless we create a more carbon-free world, we will not preserve the free world. Intensifying climate change, energy wars and petroauthoritarianism will curtail our life choices and our children's opportunities every bit as much as Communism once did for half the planet.

Equally important, presidential candidates need to help Americans understand that green is not about cutting back. It's about creating a new cornucopia of abundance for the next generation by inventing a whole new industry. It's about getting our best brains out of hedge funds and into innovations that will not only give us the clean-power industrial assets to preserve our American dream but also give us the technologies that billions of others need to realize their own dreams without destroying the planet. It's about making America safer by breaking our addiction to a fuel that is powering regimes deeply hostile to our values. And, finally, it's about making America the global environmental leader, instead of laggard, which as Schwarzenegger argues would "create a very powerful side product." Those who dislike America because of Iraq, he explained, would at least be able to say, "Well, I don't like them for the war, but I do like them because they show such unbelievable leadership—not just with their blue jeans and hamburgers but with the environment. People will love us for that. That's not existing right now."

In sum, as John Hennessy, the president of Stanford, taught me: Confronting this climate-energy issue is the epitome of what John Gardner, the founder of Common Cause, once described as "a series of great opportunities disguised as insoluble problems."

Am I optimistic? I want to be. But I am also old-fashioned. I don't believe the world will effectively address the climate-energy challenge without America, its president, its government, its industry, its markets and its people all leading the parade. Green has to become part of America's DNA. We're getting there. Green has hit Main Street—it's now more than a hobby—but it's still less than a new way of life.

Why? Because big transformations—women's suffrage, for instance—usually happen when a lot of aggrieved people take to the streets, the politicians react and laws get changed. But the climate-energy debate is more muted and slow-moving. Why? Because the people who will be most harmed by the climate-energy crisis haven't been born yet.

"This issue doesn't pit haves versus have-nots," notes the Johns Hopkins foreign policy expert Michael Mandelbaum, "but the present versus the future—today's generation versus its kids and unborn grandchildren." Once the Geo-Green interest group comes of age, especially if it is after another 9/11 or Katrina, Mandelbaum said, "it will be the biggest interest group in history—but by then it could be too late."

An unusual situation like this calls for the ethic of stewardship. Stewardship is what parents do for their kids: think about the long term, so they can have a better future. It is much easier to get families to do that than whole societies, but that is our challenge. In many ways, our parents rose to such a challenge in World War II—when an entire generation mobilized to preserve our way of life. That is why they were called the Greatest Generation. Our kids will only call us the Greatest Generation if we rise to our challenge and become the Greenest Generation.

Why Hawks Win

Daniel Kahneman and Jonathan Renshon

Foreign Policy | January/February 2007

Psychologist Daniel Kahneman won the 2002 Nobel Prize in economics for his study of how so-called irrational behavior influences human decision-making. (Examples included "loss aversion"—the fact that people dislike the thought of losing what they already have more than they like the prospect of gaining something of equal value—and the phenomenon by which people will readily give up their part of a shared windfall rather than accept what they perceive to be an unfairly small portion.) In this essay, Kahneman and coauthor Jonathan Renshon, a doctoral student in psychology, provide a fascinating—and somewhat disturbing—insight into why world leaders are invariably more receptive to the advice of hawkish advisors than to the counsel of their more dovish counterparts.

National leaders get all sorts of advice in times of tension and conflict. But often the competing counsel can be broken down into two basic categories. On one side are the hawks: They tend to favor coercive action, are more willing to use military force, and are more likely to doubt the value of offering concessions. When they look at adversaries overseas, they often see unremittingly hostile regimes who only understand the language of force. On the other side are the doves, skeptical about the usefulness of force and more inclined to contemplate political solutions. Where hawks see little in their adversaries but hostility, doves often point to subtle openings for dialogue.

As the hawks and doves thrust and parry, one hopes that the decision makers will hear their arguments on the merits and weigh them judiciously before choosing a course of action. Don't count on it. Modern psychology suggests that policymakers come to the debate predisposed to believe their hawkish advisors more than the doves. There are numerous reasons for the burden of persuasion that doves carry, and some of them have nothing to do with politics or strategy. In fact, a bias in favor of hawkish beliefs and preferences is built into the fabric of the human mind.

Social and cognitive psychologists have identified a number of predictable errors (psychologists call them biases) in the ways that humans judge situations and evaluate risks. Biases have been documented both in the laboratory and in the real world, mostly in situations that have no connection to international politics. For example, people are prone to exaggerating their strengths: About 80 percent of us believe that our driving skills are better than average. In situations of potential conflict, the same optimistic bias makes politicians and generals receptive to advisors who offer highly favorable estimates of the outcomes of war. Such a predisposition, often shared by leaders on both sides of a conflict, is likely to produce a disaster. And this is not an isolated example.

In fact, when we constructed a list of the biases uncovered in 40 years of psychological research, we were startled by what we found: All the biases in our list favor hawks. These psychological impulses—only a few of which we discuss here—incline national leaders to exaggerate the evil intentions of adversaries, to misjudge how adversaries perceive them, to be overly sanguine when hostilities start, and overly reluctant to make necessary concessions in negotiations. In short, these biases have the effect of making wars more likely to begin and more difficult to end.

None of this means that hawks are always wrong. One need only recall the debates between British hawks and doves before World War II to remember that doves can easily find themselves on the wrong side of history. More generally, there are some strong arguments for deliberately instituting a hawkish bias. It is perfectly reasonable, for example, to demand far more than a 50-50 chance of being right before we accept the promises of a dangerous adversary. The biases that we have examined, however, operate over and beyond such rules of prudence and are not the product of thoughtful consideration. Our conclusion is not that hawkish advisors are necessarily wrong, only that they are likely to be more persuasive than they deserve to be.

Vision Problems

Several well-known laboratory demonstrations have examined the way people assess their adversary's intelligence, willingness to negotiate, and hostility, as well as the way they view their own position. The results are sobering. Even when people are aware of the context and possible constraints on another party's behavior, they often do not factor it in when assessing the other side's motives. Yet, people still assume that outside observers grasp the constraints on their own behavior. With armies on high alert, it's an instinct that leaders can ill afford to ignore.

Imagine, for example, that you have been placed in a room and asked to watch a series of student speeches on the policies of Venezuelan leader Hugo Chávez. You've been told in advance that the students were assigned the task of either attacking or supporting Chávez and had no choice in the matter. Now, suppose that you are then asked to assess the political leanings of these students. Shrewd observers, of course, would factor in the context and adjust their assessments accordingly. A student who gave an enthusiastic pro-Chávez speech was merely doing what she was told, not revealing anything about her true attitudes. In fact, many experiments suggest that people would overwhelmingly rate the pro-Chávez speakers as more leftist. Even when alerted to context that should affect their judgment, people tend to ignore it. Instead, they attribute the behavior they see to the person's nature, character, or persistent motives. This bias is so robust and common that social psychologists have given it a lofty title: They call it the fundamental attribution error.

The effect of this failure in conflict situations can be pernicious. A policymaker or diplomat involved in a tense exchange with a foreign government is likely to observe a great deal of hostile behavior by that country's representatives. Some of that behavior may indeed be the result of deep hostility. But some of it is simply a response to the current situation as it is perceived by the other side. What is ironic is that individuals who attribute others' behavior to deep hostility are quite likely to explain away their own behavior as a result of being "pushed into a corner" by an adversary. The tendency of both sides of a dispute to view themselves as reacting to the other's provocative behavior is a familiar feature of marital quarrels, and it is found as well in international conflicts. During the run-up to World War I, the leaders of every one of the nations that would soon be at war perceived themselves as significantly less hostile than their adversaries.

If people are often poorly equipped to explain the behavior of their adversaries, they are also bad at understanding how they appear to others. This bias can manifest itself at critical stages in international crises, when signals are rarely as clear as diplomats and generals believe them to be. Consider the Korean War, just one example of how misperception and a failure to appreciate an adversary's assessment of intentions can lead to hawkish outcomes. In October 1950, as coalition forces were moving rapidly up the Korean Peninsula, policymakers in Washington were debating how far to advance and attempting to predict China's response. U.S. Secretary of State Dean Acheson was convinced that "no possible shred of evidence could have existed in the minds of the Chinese Communists about the non-threatening intentions of the forces of the United Nations." Because U.S. leaders knew that their intentions toward China were not hostile, they assumed that the Chinese knew this as well. Washington was, therefore, incapable of interpreting the Chinese intervention as a reaction to a threat. Instead, the Americans interpreted the Chinese reaction as an expression of fundamental hostility toward the United States. Some historians now believe that Chinese leaders may in fact have seen advancing Allied forces as a threat to their regime.

Carelessly Optimistic

Excessive optimism is one of the most significant biases that psychologists have identified. Psychological research has shown that a large majority of people believe themselves to be smarter, more attractive, and more talented than average, and they commonly overestimate their future success. People are also prone to an "illusion of control": They consistently exaggerate the amount of control they have over outcomes that are important to them—even when the outcomes are in fact random or determined by other forces. It is not difficult to see that this error may have led American policymakers astray as they laid the groundwork for the ongoing war in Iraq.

Indeed, the optimistic bias and the illusion of control are particularly rampant in the run-up to conflict. A hawk's preference for military action over diplomatic measures is often built upon the assumption that victory will come easily and swiftly. Predictions that the Iraq war would be a "cakewalk," offered up by some supporters of that conflict, are just the latest in a long string of bad hawkish predictions. After all, Washington elites treated the first major battle of the Civil War as a social outing, so sure were they that federal troops would rout rebel forces. General Noel de Castelnau, chief of staff for the French Army at the outset of World War I, declared, "Give me 700,000 men and I will conquer Europe." In fact, almost every decision maker involved in what would become the most destructive war in history up to that point predicted not only victory for his side, but a relatively quick and easy victory. These delusions and exaggerations cannot be explained away as a product of incomplete or incorrect information. Optimistic generals will be found, usually on both sides, before the beginning of every military conflict.

If optimism is the order of the day when it comes to assessing one's own chances in armed conflict, however, gloom usually prevails when evaluating another side's concessions. Psychologically, we are receptive not only to hawks' arguments for war but also to their case against negotiated solutions. The intuition that something is worth less simply because the other side has offered it is referred to in academic circles as "reactive devaluation." The very fact that a concession is offered by somebody perceived as hostile undermines the content of the proposal. What was said matters less than who said it. And so, for example, American policymakers would likely look very skeptically on any concessions made by the regime in Tehran. Some of that skepticism could be the rational product of past experience, but some of it may also result from unconscious—and not necessarily rational—devaluation.

Evidence suggests that this bias is a significant stumbling block in negotiations between adversaries. In one experiment, Israeli Jews evaluated an actual Israeli-authored peace plan less favorably when it was attributed to the Palestinians than when it was attributed to their own government. Pro-Israel Americans saw a hypothetical peace proposal as biased in favor of Palestinians when authorship was attributed to Palestinians, but as "even-handed" when they were told it was authored by Israelis.

Double or Nothing

It is apparent that hawks often have the upper hand as decision makers wrestle with questions of war and peace. And those advantages do not disappear as soon as the first bullets have flown. As the strategic calculus shifts to territory won or lost and casualties suffered, a new idiosyncrasy in human decision making appears: our deep-seated aversion to cutting our losses. Imagine, for example, the choice between:

Option A: A sure loss of $890

Option B: A 90 percent chance to lose $1,000 and a 10 percent chance to lose nothing.

In this situation, a large majority of decision makers will prefer the gamble in Option B, even though the other choice is statistically superior. People prefer to avoid a certain loss in favor of a potential loss, even if they risk losing significantly more. When things are going badly in a conflict, the aversion to cutting one's losses, often compounded by wishful thinking, is likely to dominate the calculus of the losing side. This brew of psychological factors tends to cause conflicts to endure long beyond the point where a reasonable observer would see the outcome as a near certainty. Many other factors pull in the same direction, notably the fact that for the leaders who have led their nation to the brink of defeat, the consequences of giving up will usually not be worse if the conflict is prolonged, even if they are worse for the citizens they lead.

U.S. policymakers faced this dilemma at many points in Vietnam and today in Iraq. To withdraw now is to accept a sure loss, and that option is deeply unattractive. The option of hanging on will therefore be relatively attractive, even if the chances of success are small and the cost of delaying failure is high.

Hawks, of course, can cite many moments in recent history when adversaries actually were unremittingly hostile and when force produced the desired result or should have been applied much earlier. The clear evidence of a psychological bias in favor of aggressive outcomes cannot decide the perennial debates between the hawks and the doves. It won't point the international community in a clear direction on Iran or North Korea. But understanding the biases that most of us harbor can at least help ensure that the hawks don't win more arguments than they should.

Part Five:
The 2008 Presidential Race

One of Us

Chris Jones

Esquire | August 2007

The knocks against John McCain as a presidential candidate—his age (if elected he would, at 72, be the oldest president ever inaugurated), his renowned temper, his frayed relationship with the religious right—are well known. On the other hand, there is an essentially human quality to the battle-scarred ex-POW that is immensely attractive in this age of blow-dried, poll-driven politicians. In the following Esquire *profile, written shortly before McCain officially launched his 2008 presidential bid, Chris Jones reflects on the personal appeal of the four-term senator from Arizona as the old warrior heads out on the campaign trail one more time.*

They have stood up and turned their backs on John McCain, about thirty graduating students and faculty of Manhattan's New School university, the sort of progressive institution that awards a master of fine arts in lighting design. About two dozen more are holding up orange signs that read, MCCAIN: OUR COMMENCEMENT IS NOT YOUR PLATFORM. McCain can see every one of them from the stage at Madison Square Garden, where the Class of 2006 has gathered to collect its degrees in front of smiling parents and dozens of unsmiling cops, called in following rumors that the Arizona senator—asked to speak today by the school's president and his old Senate buddy, Bob Kerrey—risks being lacquered with dog shit before he turns the last page of his speech. It's been a tense few minutes, with the expectation that any one of them might, in hindsight, be made historic. Should his assailant's aim be true, John McCain will become the next president of the United States.

He might anyway, this onetime maverick turned front-runner, perhaps the singular hope for the Republicans to keep their hold on the Oval Office. But his taking dog shit to the chest in front of an audience of New York City liberals could clinch it, galvanizing the fractured right wing behind its disrespected war hero, catapulting him through the party primaries (the races that he will always have the most trouble winning), and finally earning him the White House, probably in a center-right landslide over Hillary Clinton. That dog shit could do for McCain what he has never been able to do for himself: make him appear the victim, and this country has always had a thing for saving, as well as for the saved.

McCain is smeared even before he has the chance to speak, principally by a longhaired music student named Jean Rohe. After singing a lovely rendition of Jay Mankita's "Living Planet," Rohe tears into the sad-seeming man seated behind her, buttoned up in his academic robe.

The gown drowns him a little, makes him seem even smaller than he is, with his short-fingered hands folded in his lap and a pair of well-worn black shoes on his feet, pointed inward, leaving him looking like a kid in the front row of a class photo. But in other ways, he looks older than he is, which is sixty-nine, and which would make him the oldest inaugurated president in history. He knows there have been whispers about his health. The surgical scar from a nasty case of skin cancer that runs down the left side of his face—in stretches raised so that it catches the light, and then diving below the surface like a mineral vein—has cut away some of his former handsomeness. And his white hair is thinner than it once was. Despite that, however, and despite his tendency to squint and wince as if there were a bad taste in his mouth, and despite his stiff, robotic movements, permanent reminders of the nightmares of his youth, McCain can still make himself look hale, strong enough to run through a wall.

Not just now, though. "The senator does not reflect the ideals upon which this university was founded," Rohe says, drawing loud cheers. "Not only this," she continues, now taking aim at Kerrey, "but his invitation was a top-down decision that did not take into account the desires and interests of the student body on an occasion that is supposed to honor us above all." Whole sections of the crowd have taken to their feet, and they remain on them until the end of Rohe's speech, poised, it seems, for someone to make front pages and possibly even textbooks.

Almost meekly, McCain steps behind the podium to catcalls and scattered, competing applause, as though rain were trying to wash out thunder. "This is a day to bask in praise," he begins, but when even that line earns him jeers, he knows that precious little of it will be heaped upon him this afternoon.

The body of McCain's speech—a considered, sometimes arcanely eloquent evocation of tolerance and civility—is interrupted by hecklers who are bold, loud, and sometimes obscene. As he talks about the arrogance of his younger days ("It's funny now how less self-assured I feel late in life than I did when I lived in perpetual springtime"), the calculus of going to war ("Whether the cause was necessary or not, whether it was just or not, we should all shed a tear for all that is lost when war claims its wages from us"), or even about selfishness ("There is no honor or happiness in just being strong enough to be left alone"), he is shouted down.

When one man yells, "We're graduating, not voting!" McCain nearly forgets his own message. He thinks to himself, *I wouldn't dream of asking for your goddamn vote,* and he almost blurts it out, but he bites his tongue, as he must these days, and continues with his prepared remarks. From between the curtains drawn to the side of the stage, where McCain's police escort and his staffers (including John Weaver, the lanky, weary political strategist) have stationed themselves, there comes the collective, palpable wish that McCain skip over the remaining several paragraphs of his speech to the last line: "And thank you very much for the privilege of sharing this great occasion with you."

He does not skip ahead. McCain continues on, looking and sounding more and more defeated with each breath, but continuing still and with occasional beauty. ("America and her ideals helped spare me from the weaknesses of my own character. And I cannot forget it.")

Now, finally, mercifully, he is nearing the end, closing with a story of his friendship with a militant anti-Vietnam War activist named David Ifshin, these two young men who had butted heads until their sharpest edges had been softened. "I realized he had not been my enemy but my countryman . . . my countryman . . . and later my friend. His friendship honored me," McCain says. "David remained my countryman and my friend until the day of his death, at the age of forty-seven, when he left a loving wife and three beautiful children—"

At which point, a kid in the crowd points at McCain and cackles.

Weaver hears it. The cops and security guards hear it. A few of the dozens of reporters in attendance hear it. Together, they tense, thinking at once, Here comes the dog shit.

But it does not come. Instead, McCain continues unmolested—physically, at least—wobbling to a tired, tepid finish. "And may God bless you, Class of 2006," he says, trying to sound as though he means it. "The world does indeed await you, and humanity is impatient for your service. Take good care of that responsibility. Everything depends on it.

"And thank you very much for the privilege of sharing this great occasion with you."

McCain takes his seat again, looking smaller than he did when he left it—looking, even without the aid of that dog shit, like a man who needs to be saved after all.

After a few painful minutes, he is rescued, locked away in the back of an elevator, heading for his SUV in the bowels of Madison Square Garden. For the duration of the ride down, McCain is left staring at the vast space between the shoulder blades of some of the biggest cops in New York. It's a quarterback's view of his offensive line.

They clear a path and bundle him into the backseat. A pair of them jump into the front and prepare for a hasty exit. McCain puts on a pair of dark sunglasses and pulls out his phone. He dials up his wife, Cindy, who is waiting anxiously back in Arizona.

"Yeah, it was pretty rough," he tells her, but he does his best to sound upbeat, so that she won't worry. In odd-numbered years, he gets home to Phoenix just about every weekend, which is good and important for both of them. Now he's lucky if he gets back every other weekend. Heading into the fall and the midterm elections, once a month might be all they can hope for.

"I miss you, honey," he says before hanging up.

Weaver is sitting next to him. He asks his boss gently if he heard the student laughing. McCain is quiet. He did not, apparently. "I'm glad I didn't," he says after a long beat. "That could have been very bad."

The SUV threads its way across busy Thirty-fourth Street, guided by a police car on its way to open road and a private, suppertime fundraiser in Darien, Connecticut. He can expect a happier reception there. But it is more than an hour away, and in the back of that truck, it feels as though it will be a long one.

"You did a good job soldiering through," Weaver says.

"Yeah, well, it would've been news if I didn't," McCain says. And there is silence once again.

The senator's ride slips onto the expressway. The pace of escape picks up. The last of Manhattan's skyscrapers disappear in the rearview, giving way first to brown-brick low-rises, and then to single-family homes, and then, finally, to stands of green trees. The mood lightens along with the traffic. Soon, the lead car pulls away, ripping off its sirens in salute, leaving McCain's SUV unattended for the rest of the trip. It feels as though there is room again to breathe. There is room for conversation.

"Do I want to be president?" McCain says. "Sure I do. But the real question is, Do I want to run for it? And do I think I can win?"

Given today's unhappy start—given the absence of history-defining dog shit, for starters—perhaps this afternoon isn't the best time to begin the search for answers. Then again, perhaps it is.

A little less than a week earlier, McCain had given the same speech to a different America. At the invitation of Jerry Falwell, McCain stood before ten thousand polite, well-scrubbed evangelical Christians who had filled a basketball arena at Liberty University in Lynchburg, Virginia, to the tits. The graduating students among them had attended church three times each week for the entirety of their education, during which they had been taught that abortion, homosexuality, socialism, and political correctness were sins to be stamped out.

Like their New School counterparts, they stood when McCain took his place behind the podium, but they did so to greet him with applause. (The only sign held up in the audience read TIE YOR SHOES!, apparently directed toward an apparently absentminded student by his apparently spelling-impaired family.) It was not a raucous ovation; instead, it was an orderly sort of mass appreciation, but still, it felt complete.

It also felt as though McCain's message of civility fell upon more receptive ears than it would at the New School, a bit of a surprise, optimistic somehow, considering how McCain was greeted in parts such as these only six years ago. Back in 2000, when McCain was stopped cold by George Bush in the ugly, bitter South Carolina primary, his defeat was largely Falwell's work.

"I didn't campaign against John McCain; I campaigned for George Bush," Falwell had said a few days earlier. "And after John won New Hampshire, we just had to pull out all the stops." Those pulled stops—which were dusted for fingerprints that could never be traced—included "push polls" suggesting that McCain was the father of an illegitimate black baby and that his wife was a drug addict. ("It was as nasty a thing as I've ever been involved in, and I've been involved in some nasty campaigns,"

Weaver says.) Not long after, a furious McCain cleared his throat in front of a crowd of supporters in Virginia. "That's when he shot us between the eyes," Falwell said.

What McCain said, exactly, was, "Neither party should be defined by pandering to the outer reaches of American politics and the agents of intolerance, whether they be Louis Farrakhan or Al Sharpton on the Left, or Pat Robertson or Jerry Falwell on the Right."

It was a bridge-burning moment. For more than five years, Falwell and McCain did not speak to each other, until last September, when Falwell put a call in to McCain's office in Washington, D.C., and asked for a meeting. It was granted. According to both men, a short time was spent airing out their differences. The rest of their time together was spent making plans for the future, including Falwell's request that McCain come to speak to the students at Liberty. McCain immediately said that he would.

"People always ask me if I'm still mad about what happened in 2000," McCain says now as his SUV continues along the green road to Connecticut. "What in the world is the point of being mad at something that happened six years ago? Did I like it? No. Was I angry at the time? Yes. Did I spend ten wonderful days after I lost feeling sorry for myself? Yes. There's nothing better than feeling sorry for yourself. But there's no point to it, either. I mean, how would it sound if I said, 'Dear citizens of Arizona: I'd like to run for reelection and represent you in the United States Senate. By the way, I'm still pissed off over South Carolina, so I'm sure you'll understand when I spend a lot of my time getting even.' It's over."

But nothing is so simple as that in the life of John McCain. Before his lusty reception at the New School, his visit to Liberty University had been among his most dissected public appearances in months, perhaps years. It was seen as his taking a hard, calculated turn to the Right, embracing those same intolerant agents he had once shunned—and been shunned by—for the cynical sake of political expediency.

If true, McCain's pandering failed to have its desired effect. Falwell stopped short of endorsing his guest, who left for a flight to Salt Lake City even before the students had received their degrees. "Every now and then he gets on this global-warming kick. And there are a lot of other great guys and gals out there," Falwell said, ticking off the holy trinity of George Allen, Mitt Romney, and Bill Frist.

In the days that followed, McCain remained equally noncommittal, refusing to make the jump from like to love.

His SUV pulls up to a mammoth redbrick pile with cedar-shake shingles in Darien, the sort of home where even the nursery has an en suite bath. "Some house," McCain says. In a large reception room, the one with the grand piano in it, McCain's hosts, John and Linda Tavlarios and their children—the boys are each named after an English king—and perhaps thirty or forty of Connecticut's uppermost crust are waiting for him. Together, they have conspired to give McCain about $150,000 for the pleasure of his company.

In exchange, McCain begins expertly working the room, using first names lifted from name tags, before taking his position in front of the fireplace for a short speech. He is skilled at these, seeming both off-the-cuff and practiced, part stand-up comedian and part preacher. "Hillary Clinton wants everyone to have a home," he begins with a jolt. "I want everyone to have a home like this one."

But he turns serious soon enough. For weeks, McCain has plugged the immigration-reform package that he put together with Ted Kennedy and that will be voted on in the Senate next week. He has been attacked for creating a path to what he calls "earned citizenship"—his critics call it amnesty—but now it's his turn to go on the offensive. "Are we a xenophobic, nativist country?" he asks. "Everybody in this room has an ancestor who came here for the same reason these people came here." Taking sips from their glasses of white wine, many of those standing next to the piano nod, suddenly one with the Mexicans.

Now McCain springboards into a tougher sell: Iraq. He was one of the authors of the resolution that allowed President Bush to go to war, and he stands by that. He still believes the cause is right. He's argued that even if Saddam Hussein didn't have weapons of mass destruction, he would have had them one day soon, and he would have used them. He wants you to know that the world is a better place without Hussein's portrait hanging on walls.

He also believes that the war has been botched badly. "I don't blame Bush," he says. "I blame Rumsfeld. It's his failure that we didn't have enough troops in Iraq, because he ignored the advice of the military. We never had enough troops over there from the beginning, and that's where most of our problems come from."

It's a heavy topic for a Friday evening in Darien. Time for another joke, this one about John Kerry's offer to make him vice-president in 2004. "When I was in Vietnam," McCain says, "I was tied up, kept in the dark, fed scraps. Why would I want to do that again?"

His audience suitably primed, he asks for questions; surprisingly, they are not kind, a dissent more telling than the New School's. The first complaint comes from a portly man with a terrific head of slick gray hair. He confesses that after nearly forty-five years as a proud Republican, he recently attended his first Democratic fundraiser; so did his smoking ex-model second wife. He can't understand why Bush is picking fights with everybody and why the old platform of fiscal responsibility—the last six years have seen the most explosive federal-spending spree since the Great Society—has been sacrificed. A woman reclining on a chesterfield sees her opportunity to join the upset chorus. "I don't see why we're telling gays they can't marry," she interrupts. "I thought Republicans stood for keeping government out of our lives."

McCain nods. He knows that with Bush's approval ratings having reached near-record lows, this room is the broad base that the president's been losing. "When you get down to the twenties," McCain likes to say, "you're talking about paid staffers and blood relatives." If he is going to win the White House, these are the people he must coax back into the fold. Moderate Republicans, independents, centrists: He needs every last one of them to see in him what they want to see.

"I understand the frustrations a lot of Republicans feel," McCain says. "We're not representing their hopes and dreams and aspirations. We worry about Ms. Schiavo before we worry about balancing the budget. We're going to take up this Family Marriage Amendment again. Why? The Republicans will vote one way, and the Democrats will vote another, and everybody knows it! It's pointless. I've never seen Washington as polarized as it is today."

Which reminds him . . .

"I would never say this publicly, but some of these talk-show hosts—and I'm not saying they should be taken off the air; they have the right to do what they want to do—I don't think they're good for America."

Which brings him to . . .

"I urge my friends who complain about the influence of the religious Right, get out there and get busy. That's what *they* do! Now, if we believe in the Republican party of Abraham Lincoln and Theodore Roosevelt, the big-tent party, then we have to get out there and show that. The fact is, some of us have sat idly by while those very active people have basically set the agenda for our party. I get attacked every day because I'm working with Ted Kennedy. How can I work with Kennedy? Because I want to get something done!"

And last, full circle . . .

"I think the biggest mistake we could make is to underestimate Hillary Clinton. She's smart and she's tough. She's very disciplined in all ways—unlike her husband—and I think she's formidable. Plus, she already has $20 million in the bank. If we don't get our act together . . ."

There it is. McCain has finally laid it out, the choice this country, in all likelihood, will soon have to make. For all his stubborn coyness about his presidential aspirations—"I'm going to wait until next year to decide"—McCain knows that he will be taking a second run at the White House, and he will probably be taking it against Mrs. Clinton. For him, it's already become more than just another election. He believes that the stakes are even higher than the last time he ran, that his country might be going to pieces, and that he is the one man who might bring it together. He also believes that time is running out, not because he is growing old—or not *just* because he is growing old—but because our politics and even our sense of common identity have degenerated so quickly. The fact is, John McCain believes we are the ones who need saving, not him.

Even with his audience's prodding, he refuses to speak ill of Mrs. Clinton. But in his artful, seasoned way, McCain has given his audience his considered sales pitch for his brand of hawkish, no-bullshit conservatism, marbled with just enough compassion and reason and bipartisanship to set him apart from other Republican breast beaters. Tonight in Connecticut, McCain is of Connecticut. Tomorrow he will be of Delaware, and on Sunday he will be of Maine. McCain's greatest wish is to be all things to all people, impossible to slot on the traditional political spectrum, making it just as impossible—even if his line of thinking does not always coincide with your own—not to find something in him to admire. He will concede New York City and the New School to Hillary. The rest of the country, he believes, can be made his, just as he has come to own this room, the applause as loud as the rancor was this afternoon.

It's well after dark when McCain heads for the airport, where a small plane, six leather seats, and a drawer full of drinks await him.

The plane is a symbol. In 1989, McCain was caught up in the savings-and-loan scandal, one of five senators who had accepted a total of $1.4 million in campaign contributions from Charles Keating, who was being investigated for his role in the collapse of the Lincoln Savings and Loan Association. In exchange for the donations, the senators were to use their influence to take the heat off their benefactor. The Senate Ethics Committee later found that McCain played an insignificant role in the influence-peddling scheme, but he remained stained by the episode, both in public and in private. To cleanse himself, he began working toward sweeping campaign-finance reform. "The system was designed to make good people do bad things and bad people worse," he says today. Along with Democrat Russ Feingold, he wrote 2002's Bipartisan Campaign Reform Act, or the McCain-Feingold Bill, perhaps his greatest success as a legislator.

In some ways, however, McCain again failed. He had fought hard against the accepted method of travel for high-level politicians: corporate jets. Wishing to fly from Washington, D.C., to Memphis, for instance, a senator can hitch a ride on the plane owned by Federal Express. In return, he must pay the equivalent of a first-class ticket (not nearly the cost of the flight) and pretend to listen to the company flack assigned to him, a ready-made sequel to *Snakes on a Plane.* McCain still believes this to be a corrupting practice, and he sought to end it. But his colleagues resisted, and no law was ever adopted. Today, it applies only to McCain.

The instant he steps on a corporate jet, he will be labeled the worst kind of hypocrite, and for a man who claims to lead the straight-talk express, that would be death. So he has effectively denied himself a perk of the job, one more lash in his continued penance for being a member of the Keating Five. He must dip into his own office's coffers for a flight such as this one, a short hop through the night to White Plains, New York.

It isn't all bad. His flights are his respites, occupied by a comforting routine. He reads—at the moment, he is deep into *Cobra II: The Inside Story of the Invasion and Occupation of Iraq*; "It's just devastating," he says—catches some needed sleep, and distracts himself with frivolous things, usually sports. ("I admire Craig Counsell a great deal," he says, talking of the slight Arizona Diamondbacks shortstop who refuses to wear batting gloves. "I think he'll be a big-league manager someday.")

And as usual, there is an odd intimacy among the small group on board, often no more than a couple of longtime aides like Weaver. They share the newspaper, a couple of Heinekens, small talk. Tonight, shortly before touchdown, McCain becomes aware that his hair is standing up. "John," he says to Weaver, "I think my hair is out of place." He announces this out loud because he cannot lift his arms above his shoulders. Weaver, casually dressed and a soft-spoken Texas gentleman, reaches across the aisle and delicately runs his hand across the top of McCain's head, smoothing it. There is a tenderness in the gesture, as there is whenever Weaver straightens McCain's collar or brushes the lint from his jacket. There is tenderness, but there is also a kind of sadness.

At the bottom of the stairs, McCain is greeted by John Sweeney, a hard-right Republican congressman in a tough race for reelection in New York's twentieth district. Sweeney is a bear-sized Irishman with a high forehead and a baritone voice; on behalf of Bush, he helped stop the 2000 recount in Miami, earning him the nickname "Congressman Kickass." But now he is on the verge of getting his own ass kicked, dragged down like every other Republican by his president's approval ratings and a few mistakes of his own, including his appearance at a frat party where he reportedly pushed back too many Keystone Lights. Tonight he has called in the cavalry, and the cavalry has arrived in the form of John McCain.

They man-hug and climb into a car for the ride to the hotel. It is late, and McCain is starting to feel heavy-lidded, but he begins peppering Sweeney with the names of local members of Congress and wonders aloud how each is faring. For every name that McCain rattles off—"How's Sue? How's Walsh? What about Reynolds?"—Sweeney answers with doom.

"I think the whole state's in play," he says.

McCain knows this to be true, and he nods.

A big part of the problem, Sweeney says, is Governor George Pataki: "He's checked out, and everybody knows it. Plus, there's still that big hole in Manhattan. You know what his approval rating is? Twenty-nine."

"Twenty-nine?" McCain says.

Pataki has long been rumored to want to run for the Republican presidential nomination, to run against McCain long before either man will get his chance to run against Hillary Clinton. By Jesus, there will be blood in the sawdust on the floors in New York. In 2000, Pataki worked hard to keep McCain off party ballots across the state. That led to McCain's stopping his campaign bus in front of the Russian consulate in New York City and shouting, "Comrade Pataki, give us our ballots!" McCain eventually won a place in a race that he went on to lose in part because of Pataki—but also, interestingly, because of John Sweeney, who campaigned aggressively for Bush. Sweeney has been forgiven for his sins, after he supported McCain in his fight to rid baseball of steroids and to find better body armor for the troops in Iraq, but Pataki has not.

"I don't know anyone with a twenty-nine," McCain says, "who thinks he can make a run for president."

Following big bites of waffles and bacon the next morning at a buffet in the hotel lobby ("By the way," he says, looking very pleased, "guess who got the game-winning hit against the Braves last night? Craig Counsell"), McCain films a commercial for Sweeney, who watches anxiously from a corner, dreaming of an uptick. Next, he submits to a press conference in front of a bank of cameras, Sweeney hovering over his shoulder, making sure he is in every shot. One of the reporters asks Sweeney why he now seems so close to McCain, despite having taken Bush's side so staunchly only six years ago.

"Well," Sweeney says, "I was wrong."

A fundraiser follows for Congressman Kissass. In a back room, there is a long line of people who have paid $500 to have McCain shake their hands and pose for pictures. One of those in line who has not paid for the privilege is Scott Richards, a forty-year-old Army sergeant from Pleasant Valley dressed in military fatigues, with his wife and four children around him. His truck was blown up when he was delivering a load of fuel in Karsch, Iraq, a blast he very nearly didn't survive, and this morning he received the Purple Heart. Sweeney wanted to present it to Richards along with McCain in front of the cameras, but McCain politely declined: "No fucking way," he said the night before, his gentle way of letting Sweeney know that he will sell out only so much of himself for the cause.

McCain keeps his own collection of medals—a Silver Star, a Bronze Star, the Legion of Merit, a Distinguished Flying Cross, and his own Purple Heart—under wraps, although he is reminded of his exploits as a naval aviator at most of his public appearances, usually during the glowing introductions given by his hosts. On October 26, 1967, he was shot down over Vietnam and held prisoner for more than five years, mostly at the Hanoi

Hilton. As the son and grandson of Navy admirals, he was offered early release, but he refused it. Instead, McCain, who had already broken both of his arms and a leg in ejecting from his plane, was beaten and tortured. After being caught trying to hang himself, he broke down and signed a confession that continues to haunt him: "I am a black criminal and I have performed the deeds of an air pirate." Even now, nearly forty years later, he is reluctant to talk about it, except to say, "I have never considered myself a hero, because I failed in some ways." For him, Vietnam is not the stuff of political capital. Rather, it is the reason why he cannot raise his arms high enough to comb his own hair.

All of which explains why, when McCain congratulates Sergeant Richards on his Purple Heart this morning, he does so out of sight and in whispers.

A less orderly meeting awaits in nearby Brunswick, at the Benevolent & Protective Order of Elks, lodge number 2556, where a picnic has been put together by Joe Bruno, the state-senate majority leader and perhaps New York's most powerful grassroots Republican. Bruno—a strong-jawed, thirty-year senator—and about a thousand of his supporters have been waiting in a steady rain to shake McCain's hand or touch him on the elbow. These folks will do whatever Bruno asks of them, and given the "graciousness of today's visit," he is exactly the sort of man who will one day ask them to vote early and often for John McCain.

To repay the favor, McCain poses for photographs and stops to sign some of his best-selling books, *Faith of My Fathers* and *Character Is Destiny,* which the fortunate few take back from him and clutch to their chests like bibles. After Bruno's Mount Sinai introduction, McCain grabs the microphone and bursts into his routine, telling the same jokes and giving the same "straight talk" about the same hot-button issues, hearing the same laughter and the same generous applause in return. It is like watching the same movie on a different set.

There is something almost rhythmic in watching him when he gets on a roll on the road like this, a steady beat that begins to feel driving. He can feel it, too. You can see that he can. You can see that he loves this, loves the attention, loves the kind words, loves the look that the people give him when he's worked his way through to them. These are not rich folks who have been soaked through waiting for him, and they are not powerful. But they are the sort who take care of their friends, holding up signs that say OUR JOE BRUNO, and in ten minutes McCain has made himself one of them. Even in the rain there is warmth.

He is smiling when he slips back into the car, having been followed the entire way by a deep, adoring mob. Out of sight, he finds a bottle of hand sanitizer, a must-have on the campaign trail. He waves his clean mitts through the window while his car eases out of the crowd and onto the road, on its way to the airport, its passenger on his way to Delaware, where he will do it all over again.

There, he will stand near Dewey Beach, washed clean by the ocean, under blue skies instead of gray, and he will appear beside that state's lone congressman, Mike Castle, who is the chairman of the Republican Main Street Partnership, a collection of the party's moderates. There, Castle will welcome McCain at the Georgetown airport, the way John Sweeney did in White Plains, and the two men will share secrets in the backseat of a black sedan. And there, McCain will hear Castle—the same Mike Castle who wrote the bill to lift the limits on stem-cell research, pro-choice Mike Castle—suggest that he will endorse him in his run for the White House:

"You take a walk in Washington with ninety-five of this country's senators, and nobody would have any idea who they were. Everybody knows who he is. I admire his forthrightness. Some people, you wonder whether they're ideologically driven, whether they're saying what they're saying because they're Right or Left. But he's not like that. When he says something, you're almost always inclined to believe him and to believe that he's correct. I think that makes him very electable. I think there will be other good and viable candidates, but I'm not sure any of them are as qualified to run for president of the United States, and I'm not sure any of them can answer the question of whether they can win against someone like Hillary Clinton."

There it will be again. Not the foreshadowing of elections to come or yet another accounting of the stakes. No, it'll be the same pledge of support that McCain has just received from hard-right John Sweeney and from old-school Joe Bruno, this time from moderate Mike Castle.

The plane is waiting for him. "How ya doin', honey?" McCain says, using the drive to the airport in Albany to call up Cindy again. She tells him about her visit to Annapolis to see their son Jack, one of his seven children by his two wives, and who, like his father, his grandfather, and his great-grandfather, his enrolled at the Naval Academy. Unlike his father, who finished fifth from the bottom of his class, Jack is doing well in school, keeping out of trouble, and looking good in his white uniform. "Was it beautiful?" McCain asks, and Cindy answers yes, it was, and he is even happier now, downright springy. "I don't know what's wrong with that kid," he says after hanging up. "He didn't get a single demerit."

McCain climbs on board with Weaver, who is his own version of buoyant. "That was huge for us," he says of Bruno's show of support.

"Yeah, that was great," McCain says. "We won't have to sue to get on the ballot this time around."

Upstate New York, beachside Delaware, the rain and the sun, the conservatives and the moderates, and by nightfall—when he'll be back in his Crystal City, Virginia, apartment and drop into bed—all of it will feel as though it's McCain's to win or lose, the end of another long day, and the start of everything coming together.

Early Sunday morning, outside the Fox-network studios in Washington, D. C., two polished black SUVs lurch to a halt and double-park. Flanked by a half dozen members of the Secret Service and dressed in cream, Condoleezza Rice steps out and heads inside. She is the first guest on *Fox News Sunday* with Chris Wallace. McCain, who has not yet arrived, will be the second.

Before Rice steps back outside after taping her interview (McCain will go live), two members of her security team sweep the sidewalks. It's impossible to escape their attention.

"You aren't going to try to ask any questions, are you?" one of them doesn't so much ask as he instructs.

Satisfied, the scouts nod to their colleagues. In a rush, Rice and company leap out and make the dash to the SUVs. As they climb in and pull away, one of the truck's rear windows is lowered to reveal the nose of a machine gun. The cracking sound of its cocking lever is louder than the noise of the engines.

Moments later, McCain rounds the corner on foot. By his side is Mark Salter, his longtime chief of staff, a quiet, bespectacled man who looks at his feet when he walks. They have already been busy reviewing the questions that McCain will probably be asked. These days, it's important to be prepared.

"How ya doin', Nancy?" McCain says to the woman holding the makeup brush, submitting to yet another vain effort to try to soften his scar.

In the greenroom, Bill Kristol of the conservative *Weekly Standard* stops by, and he and McCain, taking a hit of coffee, shoot the shit for a while. It is a chummy conversation; if there were any doubts whether this is friendly territory, the photographs on the wall of Bill Frist, Dick Cheney, Colin Powell, and Donald Rumsfeld allay them.

McCain talks to Kristol mostly about immigration reform, about the rival bill coming out of the House of Representatives specifically. "You can't pass laws like that," McCain says. "If a young woman is here illegally, and she gets raped and goes to see rape-crisis counselors, then this would make them guilty of a felony. It enrages me."

Just then, Wallace appears. In the words of Charlie Murphy, dude has a big fucking head. "We're delighted to have you," he says to McCain, passing him a thick book filled with the signatures of his guests. McCain takes a seat with the book on his lap, pulls his ever-present black Sharpie marker out of his jacket pocket, and turns to a clean page.

"Thanks for the interrogation," he begins, before he decides that *interrogation* is spelled wrong. (It is not.) "How do you spell *interrogation*?" he shouts to Salter, who mixes up the number of *r*'s and *g*'s in response. McCain scribbles out his opening salvo and tries again. "That doesn't look right," he says, realizing that he was on target the first time around. "Asshole," he says to Salter, starting a third attempt.

"Oh, God, this is my potato moment," McCain says, and everybody in the room laughs. By the time it passes, he has taken up an entire page of Wallace's book with underscores and arrows and strike-throughs and exclamation points. It looks like a plan for invading Iran.

"*Ermp*," he says, staring at his latest canvas.

It's a quirky, gruff little sound he makes, coming up from the back of his throat, through puffed cheeks, and pushed out of his pursed mouth. It comes out of him whenever he's made an unforced error—after wading into the wrong gaggle of reporters, after giving too frank an answer: *ermp*.

He is called to the set, a hot little box with an expensive view of the Capitol dome. McCain settles into his chair and submits himself to Wallace's rapid-fire questions for twelve minutes. Back in the greenroom, where Salter stands silently, watching his man on TV, it feels like forever.

There are no real surprises, except for a brief, risky detour back into the darkness of South Carolina. The unlikely push comes from a clip of an angry man railing against McCain's stance on the Family Marriage Amendment. Wallace identifies the man as Richard Land. "If he doesn't change his mind and support this amendment," Land says, "he will have a virtually impossible task to win the Republican nomination."

Blowing off the guy in the clip, McCain reaffirms his opposition to the amendment (arguing that marriage is not a federal responsibility), adding, "I've found in my life that when I do what I think is right . . . it always turned out in the end okay. When I do things for political expediency, which I have from time to time, it's always turned out poorly."

Wallace asks for an example of the latter.

"I went down to South Carolina [in 2000] and said that the flag that was flying over the state capitol, which was a Confederate flag—that I shouldn't be involved in it; it was a state issue."

At first, he had taken a far different position, calling the flag "a symbol of racism and slavery" on *Face the Nation.* But John Weaver shit a brick afterward, and that night the two prepared a statement that McCain would read the next day with visible reluctance: "As to how I view the flag, I understand both sides. Some view it as a symbol of slavery. Others view it as a symbol of heritage. Personally, I see the battle flag as a symbol of heritage."

Now, with Wallace staring him down, McCain sums up the episode, the wounds suddenly fresh again: "It was an act of cowardice," he says.

"Act of cowardice on your part?" Wallace says.

"Yes."

Things hang still for a moment, in the studio and in the greenroom, before McCain recovers. "That was a very strong lesson for me," he says. "But I can tell you that I know the difference between right and wrong."

The interview ends, and McCain is in the elevator back down to the street, looking at Salter for approval.

"You were good," Salter says.

"I didn't mean to get into the whole flag thing," McCain says, almost apologetically.

"You were good," Salter says again. "I'd tell you if you weren't."

The elevator stops, and the doors open.

"Who's Richard Land?" McCain asks before leaving.

"Oh, he's just the head of the Southern Baptist Convention," Salter says.

"*Ermp*."

But that little fumble is quickly forgotten by that afternoon, as he takes a solo flight up the rocky coast to Maine. There he is met by another of his staffers, Mike Dennehy, a young guy with a wide smile and a raspy voice. "How ya doin', you little jerk?" McCain says by way of greeting.

McCain has the peculiar habit of expressing affection with invectives, starting with *jerk,* rising on up through *crazy bastard,* and culminating with *asshole*. "If he's not calling you terrible names, he doesn't like you," says Senator Lindsey Graham of South Carolina, one of his best political friends.

He's come to Portland because of a couple of assholes: big, loud Dave Emery, who campaigned for McCain here in 2000 (not easy, given the Bush family's connections to Kennebunkport) and who is now taking a stab at becoming governor; and Greg Stevens, a communications expert who's recovering from what should have been terminal brain cancer. In the way that McCain expects his friends to take care of him, he takes care of his friends, and he greets Emery and Stevens warmly at the local Marriott, where he is swept into a room that's been turned into a makeshift TV studio.

McCain takes a quick glance at the script for the commercial he's about to film for Emery, and he shakes his head. "I can tell just by looking at it, I'll never get that into thirty seconds." Some hurried editing takes place, most of it guided by McCain: "Instead of 'real long hard look,' how about we say 'good look'? And that opening line—'I sure know I can't tell you how to vote'—let's scratch that. Let's just keep it simple: 'I'm John McCain.' That other stuff is kind of hokey."

"You used to say that other stuff all the time," Stevens says.

But today's John McCain isn't yesterday's. He's more polished, more controlled, a little smoother, less ragged seeming. "Smarter," he calls it. "It would be only natural and logical, when I first got this blaze of publicity and attention, that I would be less thoughtful than I should have been and sometimes say stupid things. I still do that, but not nearly with the frequency I used to. It's not that I'm less frank. I've just learned that you have to think a little bit about what you say."

Having done his thinking, he now reads through the script out loud, once, for practice. "The only thing I'd suggest," Stevens says, "is that you try to sound a little happier."

"Got it," McCain says, and he does. The first time he reads the script for tape, he nails it. He's found the right pitch, the right language, and the right intonation, and he's found all of it in 28.5 seconds.

Not accustomed to keeping first takes, the TV crew isn't quite sure what to do next. McCain knows. He's out the goddamn door. Next he will brace himself for another grip-and-grin—get out the hand sanitizer, Dennehy—and then he will give another speech. "The good news is, we have enough money to fund Dave's campaign," he says. "The bad news is, most of it is still in your wallets and purses." Next he will catch a ride back to the airport, lifting off two hours after he landed. [On June 13, Emery would lose his bid in the Republican primary.]

There is a line of sinister black thunderheads between McCain and Manchester, New Hampshire, between him and his dinner, his bed at the Radisson, his night spent watching the Phoenix Suns and the Los Angeles Clippers, and his breakfast with the New Hampshire Federation of Republican Women (who look exactly as foxy as they sound). Even the pilots appear a little nervous about challenging the storm head-on, but McCain is unmoved. "You don't have to worry so long as you're flying with me, boys," he says. "If I was meant to die in a plane crash, it would have happened a long time ago."

Fortunately, McCain's airborne luck holds, and the plane touches down under evening skies that are just beginning to break up. His mood matching the forecast, McCain proposes dinner out. He ends up walking through the doors of an out-of-the-way place called Cotton, upscale without being stuffy. Like every good mafioso, he heads for a booth at the end of a row, where he takes the inside seat, his back flat against the corner. From there, he can see whenever a curious face turns his way.

"It's humbling, it's gratifying, and it still surprises me a bit," he says of his celebrity. "Most of the time, the loser fades into obscurity. But because we ran the kind of campaign that captured the imagination of a lot of people, we've had a lasting impact."

Over meat loaf and all-you-can-eat mashed potatoes, McCain consents to casting back six years, when this was the birthplace of his national presence, the power and the personality. He remembers his collection of good-luck charms, the pockets full of feathers and stones that grew with each stop, and he remembers the people who joined his caravan along the way—the enamored volunteers, the equally enamored reporters—and stayed until the end of the road. He remembers the long rides on the bus in between, the ribald conversations that carried them over the miles, the vodka and the dirty jokes, the laughter that bent him over double until he could barely breathe. (He's laughing so hard now, remembering, that he's hard to understand.) He remembers the feeling that something magical was happening, that if only they could sustain the love and energy with which they charged out of the gate, it might lift them to such great heights. He remembers, especially, a town called Peterborough.

"In the middle of the summer we went there," he says more than a little dreamily, "and we wanted to have a town-hall meeting. I've always liked those. We would have as many as six town-hall meetings a day, ninety minutes each. Anyway, we stopped in Peterborough to have one. And to get people to come, we gave away free ice cream. About twenty people showed up for this ice-cream social with Senator John McCain. Well, the night before the primary, the last town-hall meeting also happened to be in Peterborough. And it was packed. They had to put loudspeakers up for the crowd outside. Fun? You bet that was fun. You could just feel this *momentum*. It just felt like everything was coming together."

The way it felt yesterday, the way it will feel again next week, when his immigration bill will pass, when, after his colleagues vote in favor of cloture—in favor of limiting further debate and voting on this difficult, tempestuous thing—he will stand in front of a gang of reporters alongside an unlikely coalition: senators Graham, Specter, Martinez, and Obama, shoulder to shoulder, and they will heap the praise on him that the students of the New School and hundreds of angry citizens on his office phones did not. And from a side door, in will lumber another senator, big and stooped and white haired, looking like a whaling ship somehow, cruising slowly toward its target: rival and friend John McCain.

Even in that loud, chaotic room, there will be an evident chemistry between them, born of some shared history as Capitol Hill behemoths, but also, rare these obnoxious days, of battles resolved. Without saying a word, Ted Kennedy will slowly dock next to McCain, take the papers that McCain is holding rolled up in his hand, and in his shaky script write triumphantly: 72-23.

McCain will look down at the numbers (later officially revised to 73-25) and smile, almost gratefully, at the sort of lopsided tally that's possible only when Washington, D.C., confuses itself with Brunswick, New York, picnicking in the rain.

And when it forgets, too, about South Carolina, forgets about that moment when everything fell apart: not for McCain's presidential aspirations alone, but also for the country, as though now, over meat loaf and mashed potatoes, 1999 seems the last best time. Because by 2000—by South Carolina, by Michigan, by Arizona—we had already started playing Right versus Left, red state versus blue state, Rush Limbaugh versus Al Franken, the Minutemen versus the Dixie Chicks, Roe Again versus Wade Again, the church versus the state, "Mission Accomplished" versus Abu Ghraib, the Homeland versus the Constitution, Liberty University versus the New School, us versus them, us versus us. John McCain knows this, knows that his reputation was born just when some vital part of the country died, and now we are nearing the days when he must risk it all over again and hope that this time around the finish is different—different for him, different for America. He fears that time is running out for both. He knows that already it may be too late for him, for his wrecked and aging body, and, in his more pessimistic moments, possibly too late for the country. Even to consider running, to do for two years what he has done for the past few days, he must continue to believe that he's the one man who can save us. That's why John McCain would like to tell you a story—and why he would like for you to listen to it—his story of countrymen and friendship, of reconciliation with David Ifshin and with Vietnam, the country that saw to it that he would never again be able to comb his own hair, and he would like to tell you that all wounds can heal, that all memories can be made good, and that every state can be New Hampshire, in the middle of summer, enjoying an ice-cream social with Senator John McCain. And because of who he is—or perhaps because he is saying exactly what you need to hear—you're inclined to believe him and to believe that he's correct.

Rudy Tuesday

Stephen Rodrick

New York magazine | March 5, 2007

New Yorkers who recall the pre-September 11 Rudolph Giuliani with less-than-universal fondness have had a hard time squaring the memory of that notoriously prickly figure with the beloved national icon who emerged from the dust of the World Trade Center disaster. But as Stephen Rodrick points out in this New York *magazine profile, the post-9/11 Rudy is the only version the rest of the country has ever known. His heroic image has already propelled Giuliani to the front of the Republican presidential race (as of this writing, nation-wide polls of likely GOP primary voters had him well ahead of John McCain, Mitt Romney, and Fred Thompson). With that in mind, Rodrick joined the forner mayor of New York City on the campaign trail in an attempt to divine whether his reputation for unflinching leadership is really enough to carry him to the White House.*

This is the sound of a presidential boomlet. Not that it seems like that at the moment. It's Friday evening, January 12, and America's Mayor, copyright pending, finds himself in Wilmington, Delaware, at the crusty Hotel du Pont, for what appears to be a routine stop on the rubber-sole-and-rice-pilaf circuit. Tonight, Rudolph Giuliani is receiving an award at an annual gala held by former governor Pete du Pont, the preppy descendent of the hotel's founder who is best known for conducting an honorable pro-choice 1988 presidential campaign, which, as Rudy must surely know, resulted in zero delegates.

The 300 Republicans arriving for cocktails look desperately in need of them. And with good reason. It's just two days after the speech in which President Bush conceded, sort of, that mistakes were made in Iraq, then unveiled his plan to send 20,000 more troops there. Congress has just reverted to the Democrats, and Hillarymania and Obamamania are sucking up all the political oxygen.

Rudy is cranky, too. The year is barely two weeks old, and it's already off to an epically bad start. Right after New Year's, a 126-page confidential campaign memo concerning a potential Giuliani presidential run fell into the hands of the *Daily News*. His campaign hadn't even begun, and there was already a crisis. It was hard to tell which was more embarrassing: the cataloguing of Rudy's potential weaknesses or the battle plans outlining the courting of GOP moneymen already committed to John McCain. It all suggested a kind of amateurism: *My First Presidential Campaign* brought to you by the folks at Playskool.

A few hours before his speech, Giuliani inadvertently wanders into a sparsely populated press room. He looks older and wearier than the last time we saw him. There's the same dark suit, but the undertaker hunch is a bit more pronounced. When a reporter asks what he's doing here,

Giuliani skips the friendly kibitzing. Instead he snaps, "I'm calling my wife. I need privacy." It's been said that 9/11 softened Rudy's edges. If there really is a kinder, gentler Giuliani, he's not showing it.

Right, 9/11. Out in the dining room, after the salads are served, Delaware congressman Mike Castle takes the microphone. He talks about Rudy and the squeegee men. BlackBerrys continue scrolling. But then Castle tells of the ground-zero tour the mayor gave him and other congressmen in the days after the terror attacks. People start to pay attention. "He attended most of the funerals; he was there in every way possible," says Castle. "I don't think we can ever thank him enough for what he did."

Now Rudy strides to the podium. The room rises. Suits at the cheap tables stand and a banker type sticks his fingers in his mouth and gives a loud whistle.

Initially, Giuliani squanders the goodwill. A bit on immigration lands with a thud. He notes that China has built more than 30 nuclear reactors since we last built one. "Maybe we should copy China."

What? You can see the thought bubbles forming over people's heads: *Can this be the same guy we saw on television? The guy who was so presidential when our actual president was MIA?*

But then Rudy finds his comfort zone. Along with McCain and Mitt Romney, his best-known fellow Republican presidential contenders, Giuliani is out on the thin, saggy pro-surge limb with the president. But Rudy can spin the issue in a way McCain and Romney, not to mention Hillary and Barack Obama, cannot. And now he does just that: Iraq leads to 9/11, which leads to the sacred image of construction workers raising the flag over ground zero.

"I knew what they were standing on top of," Giuliani says. "They were standing on top of a cauldron. They were standing on top of fires 2,000 degrees that raged for a hundred days. And they put their lives at risk raising that flag."

The room is silent. Not a fork hits a plate, not one gold bracelet rattles.

"They put the flag up to say, 'You can't beat us, because we're Americans.'"

The mayor pauses and, as if on cue, an old woman sniffles.

He continues. "And we don't say this with arrogance or in a militaristic way, but in a spiritual way: Our ideas are better than yours."

Applause reverberates off the chandeliers. Millionaires pump fists. Dowagers daub eyes. This is what they came to see! Seemingly every law-enforcement officer in Wilmington appears with a camera. Over and over, Giuliani grips and grins.

It may sound preposterous to a Rudy-savvy New Yorker. But in this ballroom full of lock-jawed Wasps, it sounds like presidential salvation.

Can Rudy Giuliani ride 9/11 all the way to the White House? That appears to be his game plan. Beginning that night in Wilmington, Giuliani spent much of the first two months of the year barnstorming around the country—New Hampshire, South Carolina, California—on his unofficial presidential-campaign rollout tour (unless you count his multiple pseudo-announcements, Giuliani has yet to formally declare his candidacy). In many respects, it's been the standard early-season-campaign drill: Rudy has floated and discarded whole concepts, artfully repositioned his personal history, and studiously avoided all but the most friendly media.

On most issues, his spiel doesn't sound that different from those of McCain and Romney. But there's one exception. Over and over again, wherever he goes, America's Mayor evokes 9/11. And over and over again, wherever he goes, people cheer. Whenever Rudy talks about anything other than the September 11 terror attacks, he's just another Republican presidential hopeful with his particular set of strengths and weaknesses. When he talks about 9/11, he becomes something else: a national hero.

New Yorkers may find that hard to believe. Anyone who lived here at the time remembers the 9/10 Rudy: strong on crime and the economy, yes, but arrogant, bullying, and terrible on race and civil rights. And while it's impossible not to respect what Giuliani did for the city on 9/11 and in the days afterward, New Yorkers have experienced an inevitable September 11 fatigue. The 9/11 story has been told so many times that the Rudy-as-hero narrative, however moving, has lost much of its power. Except for those who have a personal connection to the tragedy, people have generally moved on. Besides, it's common knowledge that a pro-choice, pro-gun-control, pro-gay-rights, thrice-married Catholic northeastern Republican is unelectable, right?

The rest of America sees a far different Rudy. West of the Hudson, the 9/10 Rudy doesn't exist and never did. For them, September 11 was never so much a real day as a distant televised drama. It has more symbolic meaning than actual meaning: It's equal parts Pearl Harbor and resurrection. And guess who plays the role of national savior? Not George Bush. Not John McCain. Not Barack Obama or Hillary Clinton.

Once the rest of the country sees Giuliani up close, the conventional New York wisdom once held, his campaign will surely fold. So far, exactly the opposite has happened. The more Rudy has put himself out there, the higher his numbers have climbed. Last week, a CBS poll showed Giuliani leading McCain by a whopping 21 points while a Quinnipiac survey found Giuliani running five points ahead of Hillary nationally, and dead even in *blue* states.

Yes, Rudy is the new horse in the race and thus, for now, the most compelling. Much of his popularity comes from the fact that he's entered the race just as McCain's ties to George Bush's Iraq policy threaten to render his once inevitable nomination stillborn. At the same time, an idea has taken root that the 70-year-old Arizona senator, cancer survivor, and former POW, who would be the oldest person ever elected president, won't be up to the job.

Giuliani's pro-war stance and his moderate social-issue positions may yet bury him. So could a lack of money, a green campaign staff, his thin political résumé, his trifecta of marriages, and, not least of all, the fact that the 9/11 card, however powerful it is, could simply prove too flimsy to carry him all the way to the White House. With 21 months to go before Election Day, there's still more than enough time for McCain to reassert himself—or any number of other scenarios to play out that don't involve Giuliani's becoming president. Still, no Republican presidential candidate in modern history has held this big a lead a year out and not scored the GOP nomination.

Believe it or not, America's Mayor could be America's next president.

It's nine below zero in Bretton Woods, deep in New Hampshire's North Country. The snow crackles under a cavalcade of SUVs creeping up the driveway of the mammoth Mount Washington Hotel. The hotel once hosted FDR for a pivotal 1944 conference on postwar monetary policy. Now here's Rudy speaking at the Littleton Chamber of Commerce's annual supper. It makes sense, of course. New Hampshire still holds the nation's first primary, and Rudy needs to test his material way, way out of town. On this, Giuliani's first '07 trip to the state, he has his third wife, Judi, in tow. The would-be First Couple looks a bit mismatched as they say hello to a pack of Girl Scouts stationed near the door selling cookies. Judi is all glamour in pearls and a black turtleneck. Rudy is in need of an ear-hair trimmer. But Giuliani proves he's no George Bush the Elder—he whips out a fist-size wad of cash and gives the girls $80 for $70 worth of cookies.

September 11 comes up even faster than Rudy could have expected. One of the scouts tells Giuliani that she lost a cousin that day. Rudy smiles a bit and touches her on the shoulder while Judi gives her a hug. The girl asks how the mayor made it through that day. "With the help of loved ones," he replies. The little girl smiles. Afterward, I ask the girl what her cousin's name was. "I don't know, I never met him," she says. By now, another blonde girl, maybe 11, is tugging on the mayor's sleeve. "You've been my hero since 9/11."

There's more 9/11 bathos—New Hampshire seems awash in it. Holding hands, Rudy and Judi are shuttled into a conference room for photos. When Rudy emerges, Jan Mercieri, the wife of a local fire chief, asks him to autograph *Portraits: 9/11/01*, the *New York Times* book of short biographies of the 9/11 dead. Giuliani signs, Mercieri gets teary, and they embrace. Mercieri is then deluged by the media pack. What did he say? What did he write? What does she think about his stance on abortion? "Those issues don't matter," said Mercieri. "After 9/11, I'd vote for him in a second."

Up on the dais, it's Rudy's turn to raise the subject of the terror attacks. September 11 is proving to be a versatile tool. In Delaware, he used it to invoke heroism. Here, it's all about scaring the bejesus out of country folk. Someone asks him what his management style would be as president if there was another Katrina or terrorist attack.

The secret is to be prepared for anything, Rudy says. Terrorism can happen in New York or Boston or in Shanksville, Pennsylvania, "one of the smallest towns in the United States."

The punchy good cheer of this small town is replaced with grave attention. Rudy notes that he once spoke to the Shanksville high-school graduating class. "But for the grace of God and the bravery of the people who brought that plane down," he says, "those kids wouldn't be with us."

Tonight's attendees, of course, have a far greater chance of being killed on an icy road on the way home tonight than via a plane falling out of the sky. But those are facts; Giuliani is playing on emotion and fear.

After his speech, Rudy never gets a chance to eat. There are too many people wanting pictures, too many people wanting a hug, too many people offering one variation or another of what one woman says: "Thank you for keeping us safe."

Before 9/11, the idea of Rudy Giuliani running for president would have been laughable. That morning, Giuliani had breakfast at the Peninsula Hotel with Bill Simon, a longtime friend. Simon, a business executive and the son of a former Treasury secretary, was contemplating a 2002 California gubernatorial bid. Giuliani agreed to help, but wasn't sure he would be of much assistance. "I could endorse your opponent," joked Giuliani. "That might help you more."

A few minutes later, Giuliani's cell phone rang. As the towers fell, President Bush read a children's story, and Dick Cheney disappeared into a bunker, Rudy Giuliani was in harm's way. By 11 A.M., he was on television asking for calm. That night, he famously proclaimed, "New York is still here. We've undergone tremendous losses and we're going to grieve for them horribly, but New York is going to be here tomorrow morning. And it's going to be here forever."

By the end of that day, Rudy was no longer just a big-city mayor with a mixed record. He was a legend.

September 11 has been Giuliani's alpha and omega ever since. After leaving office, the mayor formed Giuliani Partners, an omnibus security-consulting firm. Giuliani offered his clients his post-9/11 expertise—and his gold-plated name; in return, they paid handsomely and basked in his fame. Mexico City paid Giuliani's firm more than $4 million to help make its city safe. The makers of OxyContin hired Giuliani to beef up their security, and to help persuade the federal government not to curtail access to what came to be called "hillbilly heroin." (Giuliani recently moved to divest himself of the investment-banking arm of Giuliani Partners, Giuliani Capital Advisors, to avoid potential conflicts.)

Giuliani became a rock star on the speaking circuit. At first, he did the events for free. Eventually, he would charge $100,000 an outing. Last year, *Forbes* estimates, Giuliani made $8 million from speaking gigs.

Since 2002, Giuliani has also used his 9/11 fame to help his fellow Republicans, stumping for more than 200 of them, and collecting valuable political chits in return. In a three-day period the weekend before the 2006 elections, as we learned from the leaked campaign memo, Giuliani appeared on behalf of GOP candidates in Florida, Virginia, Maryland, Michigan, Minnesota, New Hampshire, and Pennsylvania.

Everywhere he went, he played the 9/11 card, dismissing the Democrats as squishy on terror. More often than not, it worked. "Ask anyone, and they will tell you that their Giuliani event raised the most money," says Ralph Reed. (Last year, Giuliani campaigned for the former director of the Christian Coalition during his unsuccessful, scandal-marred run for Georgia lieutenant governor.) "People don't forget that."

On *Meet the Press* the Sunday before the 2004 election, Giuliani told Tim Russert that Osama bin Laden "wants George Bush out of the White House." It may have been crude, it may have been crass, but just about everyone allowed it was effective.

Why does 9/11 play so well for Rudy? Our Calvinist streak dictates that the greater the adversity a man overcomes, the more we worship him—and Rudy certainly overcame adversity on 9/11. "Here on the coasts, we make fun of heroes," says presidential historian Douglas Brinkley. "We think it's hokey. But the rest of America craves heroes. To them, Rudy's like Eisenhower. Mothers bring their sons to see him."

Post-9/11 events have only made Giuliani more exalted. The more the war on terror bogs down, the better he looks. September 11 has spawned two wars, cost us 6,000 American lives here and abroad, and produced precious few heroes. Those we got wilted under scrutiny. Donald Rumsfeld turned out to be a nut job, Jessica Lynch may or may not have actually needed to be rescued, and Pat Tillman was killed by friendly fire. There have been no Pattons, no MacArthurs, no Eisenhowers. There is only Rudy.

Outside of New York, there is a still-unsatisfied appetite for revenge (that hunger seems to get stronger, strangely enough, the farther one gets from ground zero). Bin Laden is still at large. Saddam Hussein, it's now tragically clear, had nothing to do with the terror attacks, however awful his other transgressions were. People seem to believe—wish?—that Rudy can somehow bring us justice. Who else could at this point?

To many Americans, Rudy fills the leadership vacuum created by Bush's bungling of the war and Katrina. Joe Trippi, Howard Dean's former campaign manager, recalls running a Democratic focus group for a 2005 mayoral candidate in Los Angeles. "We were asking what they were looking for in a leader," Trippi says. "One guy said, 'Why can't we have someone like Rudy?' Then everyone joined in, saying 'Yeah, we need a Rudy. We need a Rudy.'" Those were Democrats, and this was 2005. "It's still that forceful," says Trippi.

September 11 also gives Giuliani at least some credibility on the signature issue of the campaign: Iraq. So what if Rudy doesn't have a shred of foreign-policy experience? The perception goes something like this: hero of 9/11 = expert in the war on terror = strong commander-in-chief.

September 11 could even help Rudy win over the hard right. Evangelicals see the war on terror as nothing less than a metaphysical battle for the soul of Christianity, with Rudy the Lionheart as their crusader. "Rudy has created great brand equity on terrorism with Christians," says Reed. "They won't give him a pass, but they'll listen on the other issues."

Reed's comment suggests a broader point: 9/11 gives Rudy a kind of golden glow that makes all his positives seem a bit more positive and all his negatives a bit less negative.

Never mind the southern hospitality and softly swaying palmetto trees. South Carolina is the killing fields of Republican presidential politics. Just ask John McCain. He arrived in 2000, fresh from his win in New Hampshire, as the Republican front-runner. Two weeks and a flurry of push-poll attacks later (telephone polling suggesting McCain fathered a black child out of wedlock was the most notorious), he was finished.

Eight years later, on a February Saturday, Rudy Giuliani arrives in Columbia to address the South Carolina Republican Party. Outside Seawell's conference center, there are rumors that a pro-life picket line is going to materialize. It doesn't, another break in a month of breaks for Rudy.

Inside, it's a folksy affair. Chairman Katon Dawson, an excitable auto-parts salesman, gavels the meeting to order. He then asks the county chairs to introduce any guests. Fishing buddies and dads stand up and wave. This takes a while.

Finally, Dawson introduces Giuliani. There's mention of Rudy's crime-busting, budget-balancing ways—and, of course, September 11. "Rudy Giuliani," says Dawson, "is known around the world as a symbol of the resilience of the American spirit."

In seven minutes and change, Giuliani goes to 9/11. "Before September 11, we were playing defense," he says. "President Bush said we can't do that anymore. We have to go on offense. We have to go look for them and stop them before they come here and attack us."

This may be the only place in Christendom where Bush is still popular. Everyone cheers. "The next president of the United States is going to have to continue to deal with this," says Giuliani. "If you don't think you're going to have to deal with it, you're not looking at the real world and you're not going to be able to keep this country safe." There's more clapping (although it's unclear which presidential candidate thinks the war on terror is about to end. Dennis Kucinich?).

Giuliani throws the crowd a few extra chocolates, parroting the White House line of Bush as Truman, a prophet who will be vindicated by history. It's not until Giuliani has deposited as much 9/11 goodwill in the bank as possible that he addresses the real issue of the day. Dawson solicits questions from friendly faces. Eventually, someone asks Giuliani what his approach would be to judicial appointments.

"On the federal judiciary, I would want judges who are strict constructionists," Giuliani answers. "I have a very, very strong view that for this country to work, for our freedoms to be protected, judges have to interpret, not invent, the Constitution."

Down here, of course, constructionist is code for pro-life. Supporting constructionist judges while remaining pro-choice is a Clinton-quality triangulation: It keeps the pro-lifers at bay without a Romney-esque flip on abortion. Half the crowd whoops, half sit on their hands. No one boos, perhaps out of deference to 9/11.

But even 9/11 has its limits. Later, I do a little push-polling of my own. I ask Max Kaster, a local pastor and party chair for Calhoun County, a half-hour south of Columbia, what people down here would think of America's Mayor if they knew he had moved in with a gay couple after separating from his second wife. "Really?" Kaster says. He fiddles with a lapel pin that combines an American flag and a cross. "I think that would roll a lot of people's socks down."

September 11 or no September 11, Rudy's still vulnerable on social issues. No matter how skillful his pandering, there are those on the right who simply won't vote for a pro-choice, pro-gun-control, pro-gay-rights candidate. Giuliani's supporters like to point out that the South is trending more moderate. Still, Rudy is seeking an office that has been held by a centrist southern Democrat or right-leaning Republican southerner or westerner for four decades. The last president from the northeast was JFK.

It's true that 9/11 gives Rudy credibility on Iraq, but not much. If the war continues to go badly—as just about everyone believes it will—Rudy's pro-Bush, pro-surge stance, like McCain's or anyone else's, for that matter, could still derail him.

Rudy's lack of experience is a weakness as well. The highest elected office Giuliani has ever held is mayor, and no one has ever made the leap straight from City Hall to the White House. The chatter among political insiders is that even 9/11 can't cover that up. "There's a reason Giuliani's using 9/11 as an asset," says Bob Shrum, political consultant to a half-dozen Democratic presidential candidates (not to mention David Dinkins). "It's his *only* asset. He's not even running on his mayoral record. He's running on a few weeks. September 11 doesn't change the fact that Rudy has no foreign-policy experience, and his foreign-policy record is limited to having the same position on Iraq as George Bush."

Rudy's campaign team is green in terms of national elections. His inner circle remains the same as that of a decade ago: Peter Powers, a longtime Rudy friend and former chief deputy mayor, lawyer Dennison Young, aide de camp and former chief of staff Anthony Carbonetti, and spokeswoman Sunny Mindel. Outsiders are viewed with skepticism, and Memogate, to their way of thinking, only justified that attitude. (Fingers were quickly pointed at Anne Dickerson, the campaign's head fund-raiser and a former Bushie. She was summarily demoted to consultant.) Naming Mike DuHaime as campaign manager in December didn't particularly impress political pros. Although talented, the 33-year-old DuHaime is not a proven winner. In 2000, he was deputy campaign manager of a failed New Jersey Senate run. In 2004, he ran Bush-Cheney's Northeast campaign, which resulted in no breakthroughs and the switching of New Hampshire from red to blue. In the last cycle, DuHaime was the RNC political director in the year when the GOP gave back Congress.

On the policy side of the campaign, Giuliani insiders speak reverentially about the candidate being put through "Simon University," a series of informal public-policy seminars chaired by Bill Simon. Alas, Simon is perceived in his native California as something of a lightweight. His 2002 California gubernatorial bid was essentially a series of train wrecks punctuated by the release of a photo purporting to show then-Governor Gray Davis receiving a campaign check in his office, an illegal act. The only problem was, the image turned out to be from somebody's home. In New Hampshire, Giuliani hired outgoing state party chairman Wayne Semprini as his state director. Semprini was party chair for only one year, just long enough for his party to lose two congressional seats and the statehouse. In Iowa, Giuliani has been slow out of the gate; his biggest announcement was the support of Congressman Jim Nussle. Like Simon, Nussle's claim to fame was a failed 2006 gubernatorial campaign.

Money-wise, Rudy has lined up some top-shelf donors, including Home Depot founder and former New York Stock Exchange director Kenneth Langone, whose Wall Street connections could bring millions. He also has the support of Roy Bailey, a former finance chair of the Texas Republican Party who provided some of the seed money for Giuliani Partners. Last month, Bailey organized a Houston fund-raiser for Rudy that raised hundreds of thousands of dollars. In California, Bill Simon recently coordinated a series of well-attended fund-raising events as well. But John McCain's alliance with Bush, reluctant though it may have been, locked up GOP rainmakers like Texan Robert Mosbacher and lobbyist Thomas Loeffler a long time ago. And because Rudy was relatively late to the table, he may have missed landing the support of potentially sympathetic high rollers like Henry Kravis. Still, it's early in the game for everyone—no one has yet raised anywhere near the money they'll eventually need—and money flows from poll numbers. Anyone who can get and maintain a lead still has enough time to raise a fortune.

If all of those issues weren't enough, there's also Rudy's temper. Sooner or later, Giuliani will have to endure scrutiny—and lots of it—on issues he doesn't want to talk about. September 11 may well have mellowed Rudy (friends insist it genuinely has), but it remains to be seen if he can avoid being baited into exhibiting the kind of behavior that once made Jimmy Breslin call him "a small man in search of a balcony." Maybe not. In California, I asked Giuliani if he has, in fact, softened. He laughed dismissively, then said, "Is there a mellower version of me? I don't know. Other people are a much better judge of what versions there are of me. I am who I am."

When you see Rudy and Judi together, it's clear the couple is in love (a point they may have made too forcefully in an over-the-top March *Harper's Bazaar* photo spread). And while some people see Judi as too slick for Middle America to embrace, others say she softens him. Regardless, the Judi game is tricky. One way or another, seeing her reminds people of the infamous Donna Hanover affair (Rudy informed the mother of his two children that he was divorcing her via press conference), not to mention the fact that Rudy's first marriage was annulled on the grounds that he unwittingly married his second cousin (his defense was that he thought she was his third cousin).

Even 9/11, Rudy's alleged magic bullet, could prove problematic. At some point, Rudy will inevitably air ads featuring heroic shots of him at ground zero with a voice-over that sounds something like, "On America's darkest day, one man stood tall." But overplaying 9/11 in any way is not without peril. "With most presidents, there's a modesty to their heroism," says Brown University historian and former Clinton speechwriter Ted Widmer. "George H.W. Bush was a war hero, but he didn't talk about it. Eisenhower never used it. You have to be careful not to overinflate it."

Or September 11 could simply lose its power. Right now, 9/11 is about all most voters know about Giuliani. "He's like McCain in 2000," says Mark McKinnon, the former George W. Bush consultant who is now working with McCain. "He's a vessel people are pouring things into." But in time, that could change. "Giuliani has legions of fans in the Republican Party, including President Bush, John McCain, and me," McKinnon is careful to note. "But I think the traditional physics of a presidential Republican primary will be difficult." That's a savvy political pro's way of saying his opponent will get creamed when the press starts looking more closely at him. Then again, McKinnon allows, "Conventional wisdom could go out the door, and the celebrity Rudy justly deserves will allow him to soar above the usual fray, and he'll be president."

In the end, of course, elections are about matchups. Right now, Romney, mired in single digits, is not a factor, which means the bid for the Republican nomination for the moment appears to be a two-man race: Giuliani vs. McCain.

In certain respects, Rudy measures up well in that fight. Yes, the two men hold essentially the same position on Iraq. The difference is that Giuliani is linked with Bush at ground zero in all the macho swaggering ways. McCain is linked to Bush as a bumbling quagmire creator. McCain may have conducted the war better if he had been president and he may have been an articulate critic of the Bush-Rummy fiasco, but voters see him as part of the problem, not part of the solution (assuming a solution exists). To them, McCain is a Washington insider walking lockstep with a hugely unpopular president. For the time being, anyway, Giuliani gets the 9/11 free pass.

In the battle for the hearts and minds of the religious right and social conservatives, neither Rudy nor McCain will ever be accused of being a movement conservative. In 2000, McCain called Jerry Falwell and Pat Robertson "agents of intolerance" for their role in smearing him in South Carolina. He's since made peace with both men, and even spoke at Falwell's Liberty University. Last week, McCain announced that as president he would support the repeal of *Roe v. Wade*. The move was viewed by some observers as the senator's first direct reaction to Giuliani, an explicit statement to the Christian right that he is on their side while Rudy, despite his constructionist-judges talk, is still officially pro-choice. Still, true believers can carry a grudge, and they've never liked McCain. And Rudy can play the 9/11-crusader angle to try to counter his morally wayward ways.

In the end, however, McCain may have the more meaningful advantages. Not only do his fund-raising and campaign operations compare favorably with Giuliani's, but McCain has done this before. He's also got a heroic story of his own, and he can clobber Rudy on the experience issue (four-term senator, ranking member of the Armed Services committee, champion of campaign-finance reform).

But let's say Iraq continues to implode, and McCain proves too tarnished by his association with Bush to survive the fallout. No other credible candidate emerges, and Rudy somehow convinces Republican America that his handling of 9/11 and his stewardship of the country's bluest city qualify him to be their candidate for the highest office in the land. Let's say Rudy wins the nomination. Then what?

Conventional wisdom suggests if a Democrat can't get elected president in 2008, the whole party should just pack it in. Still, Rudy creates problems for all three of the current front-runners. His weakness in the primaries—his centrism—would become a strength in a general election (and he'd only tack further to the middle at that point). Rudy's lack of experience would be mitigated by Hillary's, Obama's, and Edwards's own relatively thin political résumés (leaving aside her time as First Lady, Hillary's got just six years as a senator, while Edwards has only one term, and Obama is in his first term). In some ways, all four candidates are running on image as much as anything. And Rudy's 9/11 pitch is at least as appealing as anything Hillary, Obama, and Edwards are selling.

Still, the defining issue will again be Iraq. If there's no turnaround, there's no Rudy victory, certainly not against Obama (who has opposed the war all along) or Edwards (who now calls his war vote a mistake). Ironically, it's Giuliani's erstwhile 2000 Senate opponent who gives Rudy his best shot. Hillary Clinton's Bush-like refusal to say "I made a mistake" makes her somewhat more vulnerable on Iraq. Rudy, meanwhile, has been careful to leave himself wiggle room on the issue by saying that he recognizes the troop surge may not work (at the same time, to protect his right flank, he's careful to insist that whatever happens in Iraq, the broader war on terror must go on). And despite the fact that she's not the demon she once was to the right, Hillary's very presence on the ballot will still drive many hard-right Republicans straight to the polling place.

Of course, there is a wild card. George Will recently called Rudy the best answer to "the seven-minute question": Which candidate is most capable of analyzing and responding to a global crisis? It may be an awful stereotype, but if there's another terrorist attack in the summer of 2008, a lot of suburban moms who may lean toward Hillary or Obama or Edwards will, in the privacy of the voting booth, pull the lever for Rudy.

It's a mid-February Tuesday, and Giuliani is in California's Central Valley for the opening ceremonies of the World Ag Expo in Tulare, a.k.a. "The Greatest Farm Show on Earth." With the Golden State threatening to move up its presidential primary next year to early February, California suddenly looks a lot more important than it used to. Rudy, in the midst of a week-long trip, has already spoken to Silicon Valley tycoons, keynoted the state Republican convention, and smoked a cigar with Arnold Schwarzenegger.

Today dawns overcast, but eventually the sun pokes through, giving glimpses of an endless blue sky. Amid the almond fields, overalls, and talk of irrigation reform, no place in America seems farther away from that gray, dark pit in lower Manhattan.

Still, five minutes into his speech, Rudy Giuliani, casually dressed in blue blazer, black loafers, and a V-neck sweater, finds his way to September

11. The mayor begins by admitting he doesn't know much about ag policy, but that he's a quick study. What he does know, he says, he learned on 9/11.

"We depend on each other. I always knew that, but that really got into my heart, my soul, in a way I'll never forget, on September 11, 2001," says Giuliani. "You realize how much we depend on each other. We depend on you a lot for food for sustenance."

Rudy's taking 9/11 local again, and he keeps working it. He tells the farmers what they could learn from that day. "We made a mistake on energy. I just met two Marines who were wounded in Fallujah before I came in here. It is very frustrating in a way that goes deep into our heart; we got to send monies to our enemies to protect a lifestyle in America. We can't let it happen with food. The American farmer is the most productive, most innovative farmer in the world."

The crowd cheers. Giuliani continues with his standard "They are at war with us" speech. But today, he adds a new wrinkle. "It was a very, very strange accident of fate or whatever, but I was in London, a half block away from the first bomb that went off a year and a half ago. I was six miles away when the first plane hit the World Trade Center and one mile away when the second plane hit. I've lived through these attacks."

This time, the crowd nods but doesn't clap. The London addendum hit a bum note. It's as if Rudy's trying to make himself out to be the Zelig of terrorism. For the first time, he might have overplayed 9/11.

By now, however, the 9/11 song is so familiar that Rudy quickly finds his way back to the beat. "They believe their perverted ideas are stronger than our belief in democracy, freedom, decency, and the rule of law." He pauses and surveys the room full of fourth-generation Japanese farmers, tractor salesmen, and a lone bagpipe player. "And they're wrong. Absolutely wrong."

There is a standing ovation.

After his speech, Giuliani is golf-carted to a nearby exhibition to try out some of the new farm gadgets. He even screws in a few screws with a new-fangled drill. For no clear reason, a Marine in dress blue is never too far from the mayor's side.

"You're gonna run, right?" asks a worried farmer. "Don't let us down."

"I won't," promises Giuliani.

Then the former mayor of New York, standing in a California farm field surrounded by tractors and a two-story-tall thresher, pulls out a Sharpie, and signs a few more autographs.

The Lessons of the Father

Neil Swidey

the *Boston Globe Magazine* | August 13, 2006

Since his announcement that he's running for U.S. president, a great deal has been written about former Massachusetts governor Mitt Romney's policy U-turns on such issues as abortion (as governor, he publicly supported the right of women to choose—now he's definitively pro-life), same-sex marriage (in the past he's come out in favor of equal rights for gays and lesbians—now he says he favors "traditional marriage"), and gun control (he once backed an assault-weapons ban—now he's a newly minted member of the NRA). In this profile, Boston Globe *reporter Neil Swidey takes a different angle, focusing on how Romney's personality was affected by the experience of living through the failed 1968 presidential campaign of his father, ex-Michigan governor George Romney—in which a single off-the-cuff remark sealed the fate of a once-glittering political career.*

There, you said it. There's no taking it back. Maybe the regret formed in your mind even before the last syllable of the Godforsaken comment had left your lips. Maybe you thought nothing of it until 12 hours later, when a voice woke you out of your REM rebound, demanding to know, "What in the *hell* were you thinking?" Either way, it was too late. We've all said something at some point in our lives that we desperately wanted to take back. In 1976, I was a precocious second-grader listening to my mother explain that she was going to a baby shower for a friend. "Wouldn't it be funny," I asked her, delighted to show off my knowledge of a new word I had picked up, "if she had a *miscarriage* and she had to give back all those baby gifts?" Not funny. All these years later, and I can still recall the look of sadness and disgust frozen on my mother's face. I'm sure she has long since forgotten that comment, but I haven't.

On August 31, 1967, George Romney, the voluble, vigorous three-term governor of Michigan and former automotive executive, walked into a Detroit TV station to be interviewed by a local broadcaster with a lousy hairpiece. For more than a year, Romney had been talked about as the Republicans' best chance for winning the White House in 1968. But the national campaign trail, at first welcoming, had become bumpy. Reporters pressed Romney repeatedly to explain his ever-evolving and often confusing position on military involvement in Vietnam, which he had strongly supported after a visit to South Vietnam in 1965 but later declared a tragic mistake. Polls showed his lead fading.

So, during that August interview, when he was asked to explain his inconsistent position on the war, Romney replied, "Well, you know, when I came back from Vietnam, I had just had the greatest brainwashing that anybody can get."

There, he said it. One word, *brainwashing,* and his presidential campaign would never recover. Worse, that one politically charged word became not just the shorthand for his aborted White House run, but the bumper sticker for his entire life's work. Forget the poor boy who rose, Horatio Alger-style, to national acclaim. Forget the visionary of Detroit, who successfully championed the compact car over what he termed "gas-guzzling dinosaurs." Forget the straight-talking politician who steered Michigan government from financial ruin and pushed through a new state constitution. In the four decades since that interview, there has been a Pavlovian response to the American political trivia question, "Who was George Romney?" Answer: The brainwashed guy.

There's no taking it back.

Think I'm exaggerating? Consider this headline from a national Associated Press obituary in 1995: "George Romney, Who Said Military Brainwashed Him on Vietnam, Dead at 88."

Or this lead paragraph from the *Boston Globe*: "George W. Romney, the three-term Michigan governor whose statement that he'd been brainwashed about the Vietnam War helped scuttle his 1968 presidential hopes, died yesterday at his home in Bloomfield Hills."

Even an AP dispatch from Michigan meant for sentimental local consumption knew which note to hit first: "Former Gov. George W. Romney, whose remark that he was brainwashed into supporting the Vietnam War derailed his presidential bid, was remembered as a man who shaped Michigan's political landscape and automotive history."

Now imagine you're Mitt Romney. Like a lot of boys, you grew up idolizing your dad. But unlike many of them, for you, the glow never wore off. "He was the person who I keyed my life off of," the 59-year-old Massachusetts governor tells me. "He was the person who I looked at as being the definition of a successful human." Yet you have seen your father's remarkable reputation reduced to a single sound bite. Now, as you prepare to make your own run for the presidency, do you think avoiding a fatal slip-up like your father made is going to be on your mind?

"The brainwash thing—has that affected us? You bet," says Jane Romney, Mitt's sister and an actress in Beverly Hills. "You go, 'OK, can't go there. Don't want to get into that.' . . . Mitt is naturally a diplomat, but I think that made him more so. He's not going to put himself out on a limb. He's more cautious, more scripted."

For Mitt, the episode was even harder to make sense of because it happened in the middle of his two-year stint as a Mormon missionary in France. When he left Michigan in 1966, his father was en route to resounding reelection as governor of Michigan and the drumbeat grew louder for his presidential run. When Mitt came home in 1968, his father was already a footnote. Since then, he's heard plenty about his father's fateful interview, but, amazingly, Mitt Romney had never seen the actual footage until I showed it to him last month. Or maybe that's not so amazing. For decades, political writers have invoked the exchange as Exhibit A of the perils of presidential runs. But the narrative they have collectively stitched together makes the interview seem much more dramatic and portentous than it actually was, suggesting that many people who wrote about it may have done so without ever having seen it.

So this is where we are. Forty years after the father's birth, the son was born. Forty years after the father became a governor, the son won his own governorship. And forty years after the father's presidential dream was dashed, along comes the son cueing up to make his own run. On the surface, the two men are near clones. Same business-world pedigree. Same storybook marriage to his high school sweetheart. Same square jaw and large forehead, made larger when he flashes that bright white smile and his eyes recede under a heavy brow. Same central-casting sweep of black hair with a dose of distinguished white at the temples. (Sure, it's talked about entirely too much, but, good Lord, is that a nice head of hair.)

Beneath the surface, however, Romney version 2.0 runs on a different operating system. Whereas George Romney was often zestful, impulsive, hot-tempered, Mitt is analytical, cautious, even-keeled. Michigan reporters loved to cover George because they knew they could always get him worked up enough to deliver a headline. You never hear Beacon Hill reporters talk about Mitt like that.

We can be sure of this much: Unlike most of the governors and senators whose names get bandied about as presidential gold only to melt under the glare of the national spotlight, Mitt Romney is ready for prime time. His steady hand and media savvy running the 2002 Salt Lake City Olympics showed the world that. The lessons of the father have been learned, and learned well, by the son. He is not likely to flub his way to footnote status. But will he remember to breathe? Will he allow himself to go off script? Will he be able to get past that reputation for being so polished that he sometimes seems almost plastic?

His most recent test, stepping forward after twelve tons of Big Dig concrete fell and killed Milena Del Valle, suggests there may be some trouble ahead. On one level, the challenge of getting to the bottom of the Big Dig mess is tailor-made for our CEO-governor. After all, executive competence is precisely the reason that liberal Democratic Catholic Massachusetts gave a conservative Republican Mormon its top job, and Romney has shown reassuring leadership in taking charge of the investigation. No one has talked so confidently about bolts and screws since Henry Phillips named one after himself in the 1930s. But on a deeper level, the Big Dig crisis hints at an emotional deficit in the public Romney. It's a safe bet that either Bill Clinton, with his ability to speak from the heart, or George W. Bush, with his ability to speak from the gut, would have known that shaken citizens needed more from their chief executive in his first comments after the tragedy than a perfunctory apology to the family of the deceased and a lengthy exposition on how the courts would be used to settle an old political score.

Is it possible that Mitt Romney learned the lessons of his father too well?

Mitt was a miracle baby. George and Lenore Romney had two girls and a boy, and the doctors had told Lenore she could not carry another. The couple put in papers to adopt a baby from Switzerland. But while the family was vacationing in the Dakotas, Lenore learned she was pregnant, recalls Jane Romney, who was about nine years old at the time. "Mother was hospitalized immediately. I remember my father's face—the worry and concern," Jane says. "I hadn't seen that before." Imagine, then, the rejoicing that took place when Mitt was born and Mother was healthy.

From an early age, Mitt logged lots of time on his father's lap, listening and questioning. This was a departure for George, who was often described as a man in a hurry. (In golf, he would play three balls at each hole to compress an 18-hole game into six.) "My father took a lot of time with his sons," Jane says. Mitt describes his father as a Teddy Roosevelt character, blunt and larger than life. He began jogging in the 1950s, long before it was in fashion. "He'd get up every morning and go run a couple of miles in Hush Puppies," Mitt says, "because there weren't jogging shoes yet."

Unlike Mitt and his siblings, who grew up in a wealthy suburb of Detroit, their father had known poverty as a child. George was born in a Mormon outpost in Mexico. His grandfather's family had fled there in 1871 in response to U.S. laws against polygamy. (Polygamy in the Romney family ended with Mitt's great-grandfather.) When Mexican rebels seized the territory, George's family bolted for Texas. As a young man, George made his way to Washington, D.C., where he worked as an aide to Democrat David I. Walsh, Massachusetts's first Irish-Catholic senator. A subsequent job with an auto trade group paved the way for his move to Detroit to be an executive with what would eventually become American Motors Corp. After becoming president of that financially troubled company, he boldly bet its future on the compact Rambler. America bit, and American Motors, and George Romney, were hits.

Even though Mitt was the youngest in the family, he was their dad's most able questioner, says his brother, Scott. When their father held family meetings to tell them he was thinking of running for office, Scott recalls: "My sisters, and I would say, 'Gee that sounds fabulous,' while Mitt would say, 'Well, have you thought about this?'"

Around this time, Mitt learned to think more about what he said in front of the press. Campaigning for his father in 1962, the 15-year-old told an Independence Day gathering, "It's really fun to be here in the United States for the Fourth of July for the first time!" (The Romneys had always spent the holiday at their vacation home in Canada, enjoying their own fireworks show.) "That wasn't a great line," Romney recalls with a laugh. "Happened to be true, but it wasn't exactly what the campaign folks were looking for. . . . Yeah, I was not particularly adept at my communications with the media."

Behind the scenes, though, he always knew how to meet his father's passion and temper with cool logic. "Scott would get upset," Jane Romney says. "I'd get quiet and blow later. My sister would just turn and run. But

Mitt talked it through." When it came time for graduate school, Mitt, who aspired to be a car executive like his father, wanted to go to business school. His father, who had dropped out of college and thought business school was a glorified trade school, insisted he go to law school—specifically Harvard. Mitt brokered a compromise, earning a joint degree from Harvard law and business schools.

In that way, Jane says, Mitt is much more like their mother, a stabilizing force with a gift for thinking—and talking—things through. "My dad would get emotional. Mother wouldn't. She would be kicking him under the table to calm him down. And he would say, 'Why are you kicking me under the table?'"

It was a good booking. In the summer of 1967, Jeanne Findlater was the producer of Lou Gordon's *Hot Seat* program on UHF Channel 50 in Detroit, and she had arranged for George Romney to tape an interview. Even though she was a Democrat, Findlater always liked Romney as a governor —and a quotable newsmaker. When he sat down on the spare set, Romney looked a little distracted. His family would explain later that he had just come from the State Fair, where he had spent the afternoon with his grandchildren, and one had gone missing long enough to give the governor a good scare.

Gordon, a political junkie with a probing Mike Wallace approach, was an early practitioner of gotcha journalism. Yet his interview with Romney was cordial and seemingly uneventful. When Gordon got around to asking him about Vietnam, Romney swiveled in his chair, began speaking in a casual tone, and allowed a slight smile.

> *Gordon:* Isn't your position a bit inconsistent with what it was? And what do you propose we do now?
>
> *Romney:* Well, you know, when I came back from Vietnam, I had just had the greatest brainwashing that anybody can get. When you—
>
> *Gordon:* By the generals?
>
> *Romney:* Not only by the generals but also by the diplomatic

> corps over there. They do a very thorough job. Since returning from Vietnam, I've gone into the history of Vietnam all the way back into World War II and before. And, as a result, I have changed my mind. . . ."

Gordon, the pit bull, never even followed up on the brainwashing line. He had no idea what he had. But Jeanne Findlater did. Listening to the interview from the control room, she thought, "Hot dog! That's good stuff; I'll use that." The program would air in a few days, and one of Findlater's duties was to hype it to the press. So she grabbed the audio, dialed up the wire services, hung a couple of phone receivers over the back of a chair, and then hit the play button. "Did you get that?" she asked the wire editors. "Play it again," they said. So she did.

Chuck Harmon, Romney's press secretary, was at his desk the morning after the Gordon program aired. When a reporter called asking about the brainwashed line, Harmon, who hadn't seen the show, stalled long enough to get the transcript. Then his stomach sank. He says he and a few other aides went to Romney, advising him to backtrack and do damage control. But Romney refused.

Coverage began slowly, with an AP story and then a small piece in *The New York Times*. Then it snowballed, as rival campaigns—notably those of Richard Nixon and Lyndon Johnson—delighted in making hay of the comment. How could we trust this guy to sit across the table from the Russians if he couldn't resist pressure from a few American generals and diplomats?

It would take another five months before Romney would drop out of the race. But the ending had already been written. Years later, George Romney downplayed the damage done by that one line. More to blame, he said, was that he got boxed out by Nixon from the right wing of his party and by Nelson Rockefeller, his onetime supporter, from the left. In reality, the remark was probably more of an accelerant than the cause of the fatal fire, exposing how flimsy Romney's national support was. But it was one hell of an accelerant.

The word "brainwash" didn't even exist before the early 1950s. That's when a red-baiting journalist named Edward Hunter introduced it to the West as the translation of what he said Mao Zedong's government called its systematic process of indoctrination. The term gained traction in the United States after American POWs began returning from Korea with horrific reports of their captivity. Early on, the word was reserved exclusively for the Communists' sinister, mystical approach toward thought reform, says Dr. Robert Jay Lifton, a Harvard psychiatrist who is one of the nation's top scholars on the topic. But it didn't take long for a looser meaning to emerge, describing even modest efforts to influence the opinions of others. Romney clearly intended the latter, but in wartime, the word was raw. "The two meanings clashed," Lifton says, "and George Romney appears to have gotten caught in the middle."

Forty years later, from her home in Florida, Findlater concedes, "I really never understood what was wrong with that remark." She knew it was juicy, because here was an older, Republican political leader saying what a lot of young, liberal antiwar activists had argued for years—that the U.S. government was grossly misrepresenting the facts in order to bolster support for a misguided war. But she can't understand how that one comment blew up like it did.

After I read her the lead paragraphs from Romney's obituaries, Findlater lets out a long sigh. "For a long time I just put it out of my mind. But whenever I've heard people talk about it, I've felt terrible. George Romney deserved better than that. He deserved to be understood."

In the winter of 2002, Walt DeVries looked at his TV set and saw his past. Watching Mitt Romney command center stage in Salt Lake took DeVries back to the 1960s, when he was George Romney's chief strategist. "He has the same hand gestures, the same face," DeVries says. "You look at him, and it's like watching George Romney."

Four years later, as the 75-year-old semi-retired political consultant watches the next presidential race begin to take shape, he sees something missing in Mitt. "I see all the similarities with his father, but don't see the risk-taking," says DeVries, who now lives in North Carolina. Where, he wonders, is the daring that George Romney showed in taking on his own party and refusing to back Barry Goldwater in 1964 because of Goldwater's opposition to civil rights? Or in pushing for the politically suicidal creation of a state income tax?

Instead, Mitt Romney has spent the last year recasting some of his more moderate positions, which served him well in Massachusetts, to make them more palatable to the most conservative wing of his party. Politically, those moves make sense. But all those acrobatics may send a troubling message. "When you talked to George Romney," DeVries says, "he would tell you exactly what he thought."

Presidential historian Doris Kearns Goodwin says the Romney relationship brings to mind another father-son presidential duo. George W. Bush saw his father denied reelection because he'd lost the right wing. So tending to that base became the obsessive concern of Bush the younger. "Those are the lessons of winning the election," Goodwin says. "But his father had much more important lessons to impart about governing—building that coalition for the Gulf War, marshaling support."

Perhaps Mitt Romney, in trying to avoid repeating his father's fatal improvisation, may be neglecting some of George Romney's other lessons, notably that his energy, candor and at times utter lack of calculation helped him connect with voters and lawmakers en route to becoming one of the most successful governors in Michigan history.

"Remember, " Goodwin says, "caution can be as much of a problem as free wheelingness."

Mitt Romney, wearing a crisp white shirt, powder-blue tie, and navy slacks, is seated by the fireplace in his office when I hand him my laptop, on which I've cued up a DVD. For the first time, he is about to see the interview that killed his father's campaign. Staring at the screen, Romney, for a moment, channels some of his father's animation. "Imagine how different the world would have been had he been elected president," he says, "instead of Richard Nixon. It would have been very different. There would not have been a Watergate. Who knows . . . what mistakes he would have made. But he was way ahead in the polls. And then *this* happened. And that was it." He gestures to show a sharp drop-off. "Phseuw," he says. "Just disappeared."

As Lou Gordon's image comes up on the screen, Romney chuckles, "Bad toupee!" Then he stares silently, transported back in time. When it's over, Romney shakes his head. So does his communications chief, Eric Fehrnstrom, who'd been watching along and says that in today's controversy-a-day news cycle, "there's no question he would have survived something like that." Romney says that, until now, he had assumed his father's brainwashed line had been more of straight-ahead statement. "But it was a parenthetical comment leading into a discussion about why he had changed his view. . . . It was a word that slips into your head. You're on TV; you don't stop and say, 'No, let me take that back. Let me use this word instead.'"

Then there is what Romney calls the "excessive response of the Fourth Estate." It goes like this: "If John Kerry misspells potato, it's not an issue. It doesn't even get printed. But when Dan Quayle misspells potato, it's like, 'See, he's an idiot.'"

He's right. Candidates, facing the pack journalism coverage of national campaigns, get tagged with identities—the stiff one (Gore), the dumb one ("Dubya"), the aloof one (Kerry), the hothead (Dean). Once formed, the shorthand is hard to recast, since every campaign stop holds the potential for some minor incident or offhand comment to offer yet more evidence for the wisdom of the tag. In his father's case, Romney says, "he was being criticized for the fact that he was a governor, you know, and . . . he'd changed his position on Vietnam, and, 'What do you know, anyway?' and so it sort of fit into that."

Of course, if Romney runs for president, it will also be as a governor relatively inexperienced in foreign affairs, campaigning during an increasingly unpopular war he is on record as supporting. Still, he's not likely to get saddled with the same identity that dragged his dad down, namely the governor in over his head on international relations. That's because Mitt Romney already wowed the world media while running the first post-9/11 Olympics. And a strong case can be made that, on the issue of the horribly mismanaged Iraq war, the skill most needed in the next president is—here's that phrase again—executive competence.

No, the identity Romney has to be wary of getting tagged with is "the airbrushed one," the politician who is so scripted and safe that he has to be nudged to take chances, who has to be reminded to lead emotionally, as well as politically, during a crisis like the Big Dig, who has to be tutored by Rudy Giuliani during a 2002 stop in the North End not to blow off a guy offering to buy him a cannoli, but instead to buy the guy one himself. He's bound to be even more guarded after a recent trip off-script—using the racially loaded phrase "tar baby" to describe the Big Dig—required a morning-after apology.

Then again, if Mitt Romney is a little too cautious, he has every reason to be. While blaming the media is the most predictable move on the part of losing candidates, it happens to be justified when it comes to his father. Who knows if George Romney would have been a great president or a terrible one—or even held up as his party's nominee. It just would have been nice if he'd gotten a fair shot. Had he never sought the presidency, he would be remembered foremost as a great governor and visionary businessman. Instead, outside of Michigan, at least, he's the brainwashed guy.

If Mitt runs and flames out spectacularly, that stain will displace his role as Olympic savior in the lead paragraph of his eventual obituary. But if he wins, well, that changes more than just his obit. Instantly, George Romney becomes not just someone who fathered a president—only 42 other men in American history have done that—but also one of only *three* presidential fathers who himself ran for the highest office in the land. That, of course, would prompt the question about what happened in his race, which would, regrettably, require mentioning that he dropped out after saying he had been brainwashed. But at least, at long last, that Godforsaken clause would have migrated to the end of the story.

The Starting Gate

Jeffrey Goldberg

the *New Yorker* | January 15, 2007

While the Republican presidential candidates strive to distance themselves from President Bush's Iraq policy without trashing it outright, their Democratic rivals are engaging in a tightrope act of their own—namely, how to condemn the prosecution of the Iraq War without appearing to play into their party's fatal image of being "soft" on national security issues. In this article, the New Yorker's *Jeffrey Goldberg examines how the leading Democratic contenders are positioning themselves on Iraq, and what impact their respective stances are likely to have on their prospects in the 2008 primaries.*

Evan Bayh was uncharacteristically dispirited when I met him in the Russell Senate Office Building on a quiet Wednesday before Christmas. For Bayh, who is fifty-one and was first elected to the Senate from Indiana in 1998, December will be recalled as a low moment in an otherwise high-achieving life. Less than two weeks earlier, he had the bad luck to visit New Hampshire on the same weekend that his junior colleague in the Senate Barack Obama, from Illinois, was also visiting. Bayh spoke to a hundred and fifty supporters in a Manchester restaurant; Obama swept through the state trailed by a hundred and fifty reporters. "We originally scheduled the Rolling Stones for this party," the governor, John Lynch, told fifteen hundred people who paid twenty-five dollars apiece to see Obama in a Manchester ballroom. "But we cancelled them when we realized Senator Obama would sell more tickets."

It was not merely this experience, though, which led Bayh to announce, shortly afterward, that he would not seek the 2008 Democratic nomination for president. He did not lack for money—his finance chief, Nancy Jacobson, had already raised more than ten million dollars—or desire. His father, Birch Bayh, was also an Indiana senator, as well as a failed presidential candidate, and Bayh had harbored White House ambitions for years. So his decision, made just two weeks after he formed a presidential exploratory committee, surprised many Democrats.

Bayh suggested that he was deterred by the morass in Iraq and, by extension, the challenges posed by Iran. Liberal Democrats, he said, would not respond to his views about the use of American military power. "You just hope that we haven't soured an entire generation on the necessity, from time to time, of using force because Iraq has been such a debacle," he said. "That would be tragic, because Iran is a grave threat. They're everything we thought Iraq was but wasn't. They are seeking nuclear weapons, they do support terrorists, they have threatened to destroy Israel, and they've threatened us, too."

Bayh believes that the American experience in Iraq is turning some Democrats away from the Party's internationalist tradition, and although that split in the Party is not new—it helped to shape the race in 2004—Bayh appears to think that it has become more intense as the next election draws closer. "While we're rightfully pointing out those errors in Iraq, we've got to say very clearly that Afghanistan was the right war to fight," he said. "There are those kinds of tough steps that occasionally involve the use of force. Lots of Americans wonder whether we Democrats have that in us." Bayh, to be sure, is a pragmatist: he saw that he had little chance of penetrating his party's consciousness in time for a 2008 race. "There are too many Goliaths out there," he said, referring to Obama, Clinton, and

John Edwards, and he added, with more sharpness than usual, "I believe I would be a very strong general-election candidate," suggesting that the dynamics of the Democratic Party left little room for a semi-obscure, non-dazzling senator whose positions, in particular on the Iraq war, have been fairly hawkish.

Twelve months before the Iowa caucuses and the New Hampshire primary, foreign policy, and not abortion, gay rights, tax policy, or voters' church-going habits, is what seems most to separate Democrats from Republicans and, to some extent, from each other. An early test of the Democratic contenders will be how they approach the Iraq war. Clinton, Edwards, and Obama—at this point, the chief competitors—have many views in common. They tend to see China as an economic challenge rather than as a military threat; they are pro-Israel, and support (Bill) Clinton-style engagement to restart the Middle East peace process; they all want more commitment in the fight against AIDS. On Iraq, though, and on the uses of American power, there is less unity.

John Edwards (the 2004 Vice Presidential nominee, who announced his intention to run just after Christmas) has become the candidate of troop withdrawal. When I asked Edwards last week for a concise description of his Iraq position, he said, "Let's start leaving." Hillary Clinton, who has not announced her candidacy but is said to be close to doing so, is a connoisseur of statecraft, the candidate of the Democratic foreign-policy elite. She brings the most experience in foreign policy to the race—much of it gained vicariously, in her husband's White House. Unlike Edwards, she sees the loss of Iraq as potentially catastrophic for American national-security interests.

Obama, who has strongly hinted at a possible candidacy, is the pleaser; he can be rhetorically hawkish, but seems most comfortable when advocating the softer forms of American power. He told me that a quick pullout from Iraq "could result in a spike in deaths," but he does not talk about looming catastrophe if Iraq is not stabilized. His tone is relentlessly measured and sometimes banal; in his best-selling book, *The Audacity of Hope,* a chapter on foreign affairs reads like a tentative primer on the history of American foreign policy. Obama speaks at length of a trip to Iraq, but barely mentions the challenges posed by Iran and North Korea. Still, he would enter the race for president with one clear advantage: he did not support the Iraq war, even at its inception.

Democrats are doubtful about the usefulness of an increase in troop levels. Obama, who does not use the euphemism "surge," favored by the Administration, but, rather, "escalation," said, "I don't know any military expert who says that a modest increase in troop levels is going to make a big difference. Even if you pursue the logic of increased troop levels, you're going to need one hundred thousand more, one hundred and fifty thousand more, orders of magnitude that we don't possess. Twenty thousand troops is not going to make a difference anymore." Clinton says that she has doubts but will withhold judgment until she sees President Bush's actual plan.

Clinton, Edwards, and Obama view themselves as internationalists—eager to keep America engaged in the world and willing to employ force if necessary. And yet, if polls are to be trusted, this outlook separates them from their party's base. A 2005 poll conducted by the Democratic-affiliated Security and Peace Institute found that the top two foreign-policy priorities of Republicans were the destruction of Al Qaeda and a halt to nuclear proliferation; Democrats named the withdrawal of troops from Iraq and the elimination of AIDS. Grassroots Democratic opposition to the Iraq war has been especially potent; it cost Senator Joseph Lieberman the support of Democrats in his primary fight last year. Polls also show that a sizable minority of Democrats now feel that the war in Afghanistan was a mistake—35 percent, according to an MIT survey conducted in November of 2005. Even more noteworthy, only 57 percent of Democrats questioned in the same poll would support the deployment of U.S. troops against a known terrorist camp. A German Marshall Fund poll in June of last year found that 70 percent of Republicans would approve of military action as a last resort to prevent Iran from acquiring nuclear weapons, as opposed to only 41 percent of Democrats. As the *New Republic* editor-at-large Peter Beinart, who has argued for a more assertive Democratic foreign policy, notes in an essay that will appear in a forthcoming collection produced by the Brookings and Hoover Institutions, "America's red-blue divide is no longer chiefly between churched and unchurched. It is between hawk and dove." He is not alone in arguing that Bush has done something that would have seemed impossible in late 2001: he has turned the fight against terrorism into a partisan issue.

"This is an exceedingly strange moment, but a plastic moment," said Jeremy Rosner, a former Clinton administration National Security Council official and now a Democratic pollster. "I tend to think that, once Bush and Iraq are off the screen, someone might be able to rally Democrats to an enlightened internationalism, but the data on that point is mixed right now."

The Democratic Party's base may be dovish, but it accounts for less than 25 percent of the American voting public. It is difficult, therefore, to imagine a serious general-election candidate who does not favor some sort of "enlightened internationalism," with its possible military implications. (Lieberman's ultimate victory as an Independent seemed to demonstrate that dovish voters, even in a liberal state such as Connecticut, cannot by themselves unseat a hawkish senator.) But the Democratic Party's chief problem may be finding a way to arrive at a coherent and persuasive post-Bush foreign policy. Michael E. O'Hanlon, of the Brookings Institution, and Kurt M. Campbell, a former National Security Council official under Bill Clinton, argue in a recent book, *Hard Power: The Politics of National Security,* that Bush administration incompetence, not Democratic foreign-policy wisdom, accounts for the Democrats' success in last November's midterm election. "Without answers of their own to the questions they pose to the Bush administration about how to keep the country safe and secure, Democrats are likely to find current gains in national polls to be fleeting or illusory," they wrote. They might have added that, whether or not the public hopes for a period of international tranquillity, the next president, Democrat or Republican, will inherit an extraordinarily difficult set of problems.

"It's not a great bargain for the next president to take over the mess in Iraq," Obama told me last month. "But there is as much pressure in both the Republican and Democratic camps, because both have genuine concern for the troops and the families and the budget. It won't be good for congressmen of the president's party if we're still spending two billion dollars a week in Iraq in two years."

Obama, like his rivals, would rather not see the Democrats take the blame for what recent events suggest will be an unhappy dénouement in Iraq. But many foreign-policy experts believe that, even without an increase in troop levels in the coming months, Bush may yet succeed in delaying the day of reckoning until the next president takes office. "Bush is going to do anything he can do in his power not to lose," Leslie Gelb, the former president of the Council on Foreign Relations and a onetime State Department official in the Carter administration, said. "The worst challenge the next president will inherit will be to figure out how to lose in Iraq without the appearance or effects of losing. Then, there are these huge problems at either end of Asia—Iran and North Korea. The next president is heading into the biggest, most dangerous set of problems that we've faced since the Cuban missile crisis."

On September 12, 2001, Hillary Clinton gave a speech on the Senate floor in which she sounded much like President Bush, saying that the country should "make very clear that not only those who harbor terrorists but those who in any way give any aid or comfort whatsoever will now face the wrath of our country." She added, "You are either with America in our time of need or you are not."

When we met recently in her office in the Russell building, I mentioned that speech, calling it "pretty pugnacious."

"Well, I *was* pretty pugnacious," she said, laughing. "Post-9/11, that was appropriate language." She has since been critical of Bush's leadership of the war on terror, and in particular his handling of Iraq. She agrees with Gelb that the next president will inherit a set of foreign-policy challenges that will make her husband's 1993 White House transition seem (to borrow a term from the run-up to the Iraq war) like a cakewalk.

Clinton speaks with confidence and directness. On issues of foreign policy and national security, she readily said "I don't know" when she didn't, and she referred frequently, without self-consciousness, to her husband's experience, especially in the Middle East and in the Balkans, perhaps as a way of signaling that nothing prepares a person for four years in the White House like eight years in the White House. She seems to have assimilated data on a comprehensive range of issues. In one conversation, I asked her whether she believed that the best antidote to Islamism might be Islamism itself—in other words, for Muslims to experience periods of Islamist rule to fully grasp its flaws. "Well, I don't see any evidence of that," she said. "You know, if you look around the world, Islamists have had to be defeated by internal military forces, in such places as Algeria and the Philippines, or by external military forces, in places like Afghanistan. We want to be able to continue to export democracy, but we want to deliver it in digestible packages. We want to be smart about this. Take the Palestinians, where we had an election. Don't you think it would have been smart to make sure that the election was run in such a way that everyone knew how to compete? Hamas certainly knew how to compete. They ran a modern election. They knew enough to run only one person in each constituency, unlike Fatah, which we apparently didn't tell. Hamas had a cellphone system to get everyone to the polls. It's not enough to say, 'Let's have an election.' If you're going to do it and install democracy, democracy means rule of law, it means democracy education, democracy means opening up the media."

She went on, "That's what we did during the Cold War. We had a multipronged agenda against Communism and the Soviet Union, we worked with candidates and parties in Europe, we worked to persuade people to be part of our alliance, we used every tool at our disposal." Clinton seemed just moments away from naming individual Hamas precinct captains.

When I asked Clinton to place herself on a foreign-policy continuum in which Brent Scowcroft, President George H. W. Bush's national-security adviser, represents the realists, and Paul Wolfowitz, the former Deputy Defense Secretary, represents the armed idealism of neoconservatives and liberal interventionists, she demurred. "I'm me," she said. "Here's Clinton. I'm not either one of them. I think both of their approaches are not adequate to the task we are facing. I think Wolfowitz's strong feelings and deeply held values come out of the Holocaust, come out of an understanding of the need to expand universal values and create a climate in which people would stand up and fight for those human rights. I think it is real with Wolfowitz, but I think in pursuit of policies people see things that are not real."

She continued, "On the other hand, if you entered the world arena and see it just as a series of Realpolitik transactions, you also miss the larger picture. We can critique the idealists, who have an almost faith-based idealism without adequate understanding or evidence-based decision-making, and we can critique the realists for rejecting the importance of aspiration and values in foreign policy. You know, I find myself, as I often do, in the somewhat lonely middle."

Obama (like Clinton and Bayh) has studiously calibrated his approach to Iraq. Although he cannot be considered one of Congress's foreign-policy experts, it is hard to think of another recent graduate of the Illinois Senate who could speak as comfortably as he does about the arcana of the Middle East. Obama is discomfited by those on the left who, in his view, minimize the threat of terrorism. In his recent book, he even scolds those who put the withdrawal of troops from Iraq, and the improvement of relations with America's allies, ahead of national-security concerns. "The objectives favored by liberals have merit," he writes. "But they hardly constitute a coherent national security policy." He adds that "the threats facing the United States today are real, multiple, and potentially devastating." But when he writes that it's "useful to remind ourselves, then, that Osama bin Laden is not Ho Chi Minh," it's hard to imagine who would confuse the two.

Obama has not yet articulated an overarching national-security world view; the political danger in doing so is that it could alienate him from a wing of his party at a time when he's just becoming widely known. In a conversation last month, he focused on some of the most worrisome issues facing the United States, saying that the possibility of Al Qaeda or another terrorist group obtaining a nuclear weapon was "the No. 1 threat" facing America, and he warned that deterrence theories might not apply to the regimes in Tehran and Pyongyang. "Just because they're state actors doesn't mean they might not act irrationally," he said. "We can't gauge their decision-making process accurately, partly because our intelligence capabilities have been entirely inadequate to the task, and partly due to the nature of the regimes. Whatever you want to say about the Soviets, they were essentially conservative. The North Korean regime and the Iranians are driven more by ideology and fantasy." On the other hand, he is hesitant to describe a scenario in which he would actually use force against those regimes.

"What I don't want to see happen is for Iraq to become an excuse for us to ignore misery or human-rights violations or genocide," Obama said. "We should be engaged in Darfur. We have a self-interest and a stake in preventing hundreds of thousands of people from being slaughtered." (Obama's policy prescription for Darfur, though, is more modest than his rhetoric: he wants to build an "international protective force" in Darfur to buttress the African troops already there.) Democratic Party realism, he said, should reflect the country's moral values. He cited the coup, in 1953, against the Iranian president, Mohammed Mossadegh, aided by the CIA, as an example of American values gone awry. "Iran is a classic case of something biting us on the ankle, when we assisted in overthrowing the democratically elected regime that was replaced by the Shah," he said.

In his less cautious pre-Senate days, Obama expressed his view of the world more bluntly. In a 2002 speech at an antiwar rally in Chicago, he condemned Middle Eastern autocrats, and condemned President Bush (and, it is possible to infer, previous Presidents of both parties) for coddling pro-American dictators in the name of stability. "Let's fight to make sure our so-called allies in the Middle East, the Saudis and the Egyptians, stop oppressing their own people, and suppressing dissent, and tolerating corruption and inequality, and mismanaging their economies, so that their youth grow up without education, without prospects, without hope, the ready recruits of terrorist cells."

I asked Obama if his sympathy for the victims of civil war and ethnic cleansing takes in the mass of Iraqis who are victims, and not the perpetrators, of the current violence. "We absolutely have an obligation to the Iraqi people," he said. "That's why I've resisted calls for an immediate withdrawal."

John Edwards, by contrast, argues that America has fulfilled its commitment to the Iraqi people. "We've been there for a few years," he said. "We've devoted enormous resources, human and otherwise. And now we've reached the place, I think, where the Iraqis are going to have to take responsibility." I asked if he believed that America had a moral responsibility to the Iraqis because the Bush administration chose to topple a dictatorship, only to replace it, albeit inadvertently, with chaos and what looks like civil war.

"My view of Darfur is, we've done nothing but yap. We—as a lot of American families can tell you—we've done a lot more than talk in Iraq. And I think you just reach a place where you have to say, 'We've done our part, and now it's time for them to step up to the plate.' You can't police places forever." When I suggested that Iraqis who "step up to the plate," in the manner that Edwards suggests, are sometimes beheaded, he responded, "But when they're doing it to each other, and America's not there and not fomenting the situation, I think the odds are better of the place stabilizing. I mean, ultimately, that's the judgment."

Edwards unequivocally recommends the immediate withdrawal of forty thousand troops, a position that may help to explain his popularity: in one poll last month in Iowa, Edwards and Obama were tied for first place, each supported by 22 percent of likely Democratic caucus-goers. Iowa's outgoing governor, Tom Vilsack, who is also an announced candidate, was backed by 12 percent of likely caucus-goers, and Hillary Clinton was polling at about 10 percent.

It sometimes seems that Edwards is running in a different election than Obama and Clinton. He is focused on next year's primaries, building support among union members and among Democrats infuriated by the Bush administration's Iraq policy. Obama and Clinton seem focused instead on the general election. Edwards disputes this notion. "Well, I call the surge idea 'the McCain doctrine,'" he said, laughing. When I mentioned how Obama and Clinton have approached the Iraq issue, he said, "They may be trying to run for president, too, you mean?" He insisted that his tack on Iraq was "nonpolitical," and added, "I think the political position is to be cautious. There are consequences to taking positions, but leadership in this situation requires you to make clear what you think should happen in Iraq."

In his announcement speeches, Edwards called for "getting America and the world to break our addiction to oil" but did not mention counterterrorism as a top priority, which sets him apart from the current Democratic field. Rather, he emphasized universal health care, ending poverty, and combating global warming.

I met with Edwards in New York, just after he delivered a speech to the Asia Society about a recent trip he had made to China. During the question-and-answer period, he gave perfunctory responses to a series of questions, and seemed most engaged when the conversation turned to domestic policy. "I could go on all day about this," he said.

When I asked about his relative inexperience in foreign policy, he said, overenthusiastically, "I love this stuff. I think it is the critical thing for the next president of the United States, and whether it is Uganda and Darfur, or the Middle East, or China, or India, or Europe, I just find it fascinating. And I think the president of the United States has to have a very strong, clear vision about how to engage the world."

Edwards is careful not to rule out the use of military force against Iran, but he would much rather talk about other things—his recent interest in Africa, and his antipoverty ideas, which are at the core of his candidacy. Edwards is genial in conversation, but he became almost testy when I brought up his vote, in 2002, in favor of the Iraq-war resolution. Edwards has repudiated his vote, unlike Clinton, who has not renounced her own support for the war despite demands from her backers that she do so. Edwards worries that his vote will be seen as evidence that he was somehow fooled by the Administration into giving it his support. "I was convinced that Saddam had chemical and biological weapons and was doing everything in his power to get nuclear weapons," he said. "There was some disparity in the information I had about how far along he was in that process. I didn't rely on George Bush for that. And I personally think there's some dishonesty in suggesting that members of the United States Senate relied on George Bush for that information, because I don't think it's true. It's great politics. But it's not the truth."

When I asked who was making this suggestion, he said, "I've just heard people say, I can't even tell you who, I've just heard people say, 'Well, you know, George Bush . . . misled us.' You know, it's just—I was there, it's not what happened." (Edwards would not single out anyone, but he appeared to be referring to, among others, his 2004 running mate, John Kerry, who has often said that he was lied to by the Bush administration about W.M.D.s. "We were misled. We were given evidence that was not true," Kerry told a rally of liberal Democrats in June of last year.)

"I was on the Intelligence Committee," Edwards went on, "so I got direct information from the intelligence community. And then I had a series of meetings with former Clinton administration people. And they were all saying the same thing. Everything I was hearing in the Intelligence Committee was the same thing I was hearing from these guys. And there was nary a dissenting voice. And so, for me, the difficult judgment was not about the factual information, which I was convinced was accurate. It was about whether I was going to give authority to this president I didn't trust. That was where the friction was for me. I decided to do it, and I was wrong. I shouldn't have done it."

Hillary Clinton's decision to give Bush her approval in 2002 was influenced by her recent White House experience. "I have respect for presidential decision-making and I saw what the Republican Congress had done to Bill on a range of issues, denying him the authority to deal with Bosnia and Kosovo and second-guessing him on every imaginable issue," she said. "And I don't think that that's good for the country, and I had no problem in giving President Bush the authority to do what he stated he would do and what I was assured privately on many occasions would be done."

Still, Clinton was never an enthusiastic supporter of the war. In a speech to the Senate before casting her vote to support the resolution, she cautioned Bush, saying, "If we were to attack Iraq now, alone or with few allies, it would set a precedent that could come back to haunt us. In recent days, Russia has talked of an invasion of Georgia to attack Chechen rebels. India has mentioned the possibility of a preemptive strike on Pakistan. And what if China were to perceive a threat from Taiwan? So, Mr. President, for all its appeal, a unilateral attack, while it cannot be ruled out, on the present facts is not a good option."

When I asked Clinton if she thought that she had been lied to, she said, "I have to tell you, I think that they believed, as I believed, that there was, at the very least, residual weapons of mass destruction, and whether the Iraqis ever intended to let the inspectors go forward was being answered year by year. There was a lot of evidence that this was not their intention."

Obama wasn't in the Senate at the time of the invasion of Iraq, and in his 2002 Chicago speech he prophesied some of the difficulties that the Bush administration is now experiencing. "I suffer no illusions about Saddam Hussein," he said then. "He is a brutal man. A ruthless man. A man who butchers his own people to secure his own power. The world, and the Iraqi people, would be better off without him. But I also know that Saddam poses no imminent and direct threat to the United States, or to his neighbors." He went on, "I know that even a successful war against Iraq will require a U.S. occupation of undetermined length, at undetermined cost, with undetermined consequences."

A year before the primaries, the Democrats certainly have solid contenders for the presidency, each of whom—some more than others—is struggling to design a credible series of foreign-policy beliefs for a party that has foreign-policy inclinations but no reigning philosophy. Obama and Clinton appear thus far to be the Party's strongest potential candidates, and each brings strengths to the debate. Obama's foresight on Iraq may be one of his most potent weapons, just as Clinton's expertise, and essential centrism, will be an asset to her candidacy. For now, though, Edwards has something that the others lack: a position on Iraq that resonates best with his party.

The Woman in the Bubble

Chris Smith

New York magazine | November 13, 2006

Of all the leading contenders in the upcoming presidential race, no one presents a more complex picture to voters than Hillary Clinton. Besides being the first viable female candidate to seek our nation's highest office, she's also the only former First Lady ever to run for president—leaving open the tantalizing question of what role husband Bill might play in a second Clinton presidency. She's also managed to maintain a somewhat left-wing image even as she's carved out a rather centrist record in the U.S. Senate, including a fairly hawkish position on the Iraq War. What's more, she's earned a reputation during her seven years in the Senate as a hard worker who doesn't hog the limelight, while at the same time maneuvering to cast herself as the front-runner for the Democratic nomination in 2008. Talk about a savvy politician!

In this profile, written prior to her reelection to the Senate—and well before she announced her candidacy for president—Chris Smith reports on Hillary's proto-campaign for the Oval Office.

She is free. For a few minutes, Hillary Rodham Clinton is not New York's junior senator, or the former president's emotionally traumatized wife, or the Democratic Party's presumptive and in some precincts dreaded 2008 presidential nominee, or "Hitlary," the demonic embodiment of everything the right wing hates and fears, or one of the most famous faces in the world. She is simply a suburban woman on a Greenwich Village jaunt, resplendent in a checked brown jacket and knit gold scarf, strolling unnoticed down Downing Street in the sun on a glorious fall Friday afternoon on her way to a quick chat and a hot cup of black tea.

She is walking because she's late, the West Village traffic is terrible, and she doesn't want to stand up an interviewer. Stalled at the corner of Bleecker and Carmine, Clinton had opened the door of her big black van and escaped, hopping down onto the pavement. Now she is suddenly, blissfully, out of the bubble. Her Secret Service agents are scrambling to keep up. Hillary isn't supposed to be the spontaneous Clinton. "Don't you believe it!" she says, grinning and turning onto Bedford and striding into the Blue Ribbon Bakery. "Oh!" she says with a delighted tone. "I've never been here before!"

Clinton settles into a corner table as the startled restaurant staff tries to act as if she drops in all the time. Yesterday afternoon, the Yankees lost Game 2 of their playoff series to the Tigers, so I ask Hill-Rod if she's following the struggles of A-Rod. She is. And for the next five minutes, Clinton's blue eyes dance and her laughter fills the room. She is funny, charming, bitter, clear, persuasive, and insightful, about both baseball and human nature.

She is also, depressingly, off the record. Clinton doesn't say anything remotely controversial or derogatory. But even the Yankees are a complicated subject for Hillary. There's the whole baseball-hat thing, and the authenticity thing, and the Giuliani thing. There's the fact that anything she says, however innocuous, can and will be used against her by multiple enemies. So, best to be off the record. Best to play it safe.

The idle chitchat done, the conversation shifts to Clinton's first term in the Senate. And the curtain immediately comes down. The gears start to whir. Clinton's face sets. "One thing I'm really proud of is working in a bipartisan way to get the health care for the Guard and the Reserves," she says. "I was shocked. When I got on the armed-services committee, and here we are sending these kids, these young men and women, off to Afghanistan and Iraq, and they don't have any insurance. Their families don't have any insurance. And it just seemed to me that it was just such an obvious problem that needed to be righted. And it took three years. But we finally got it done in this last couple of weeks."

She's still pleasant, still expansive. She clearly cares about the work she's done for the state. And much of it is important work. But even Clinton seems bored with what she's saying.

Inside the Blue Ribbon, the four other patrons are being studiously blasé about the celebrity in their midst. Outside, however, a crowd is gathering. The restaurant, right at the intersection of Bedford and Downing, is separated from the sidewalk only by floor-to-ceiling windows. People are staring through the windows. Cell-phone cameras are being aimed. The Secret Service agents are holding back traffic to create space for Clinton's black van and trail cars to park.

Now her aides are telling Clinton it's time to go. "My minders," she says with a sigh. She is apologetic, but she's late for a fund-raiser, the first of three tonight. The van is pulling into position for her getaway. She finishes the tea, hurriedly pops a couple of strawberries into her mouth. Then Hillary Clinton is out the door, waving and offering a chipper "How are you?" to the gawking pedestrians. Back to work. Back to the bubble.

This week, Hillary Clinton will be reelected as senator from New York. She'll win by a landslide, all the more amazing when you think back to who she was six years ago: a carpetbagging First Lady who'd moved to New York to run for office for the first time, trailing Clinton-administration scandals. She and Bill owed millions to defense lawyers. At first, she stumbled as a candidate, was mocked for her "listening tour," then got lucky as Rudy Giuliani self-destructed. But even winning the election was hardly a guarantee she'd succeed in the job: Bill burdened her with one final controversy by pardoning felons at the last minute, and Trent Lott cheerfully wondered if she'd be hit by lightning, underlining Clinton's status as the most polarizing freshman ever to arrive in the U.S. Senate.

But Clinton worked assiduously at playing well with others, including Republicans who'd vilified her and Bill during the White House years. She stood in the back at photo ops. She fetched coffee for her senior colleagues. And she won New York a fair share of pork, especially considering the hostility of the Bush administration. "You can't find anybody on either side of the aisle who would argue she hasn't been an effective senator," says a senior national Republican. "She has been."

Ever since she left the White House, however, there's been a background noise following Clinton, like a persistent hum in a pair of stereo speakers: Hillary '08. Now, the formality of her reelection campaign out of the way, that noise will move to the foreground. The timing couldn't be more fascinating. For the past month, Clinton has watched as the Barack Obama boomlet has swelled. Part of the hype is media infatuation. Part is book-tour manipulation. But beneath the buzz lies a genuine public hunger for change, a fresh face, authenticity. Also feeding Obamamania, on the Democratic left, is a rabid desire for an antiwar 2008 presidential candidate.

These qualities are exactly Clinton's weaknesses. The complaint most often heard about Hillary, even from supporters, is that she has no principles other than ambition, that it's impossible to say what she stands for anymore.

There will never be a single, simple Hillary. But in her six years as New York senator, a genuine, multifaceted Hillary has been on display, in plainer sight than at any other time in her political life. She's less ideologically rigid than her caricature, more obsessed with the details of policy than the media has the attention span for, and true to her faith in government as protector, instigator, and moral force. If Clinton now goes national, the challenge for the candidate and her massive organization will be to turn the unscripted Hillary loose now and then, to trust the human Hillary who's turned up in every remote corner of New York.

Professionally and personally, Clinton has come a vast distance in six years. She's widely hailed as a successful senator, with the potential for greatness. She's a major influence on the philosophical direction of the Democratic Party. At 59, for the first time in her life, Clinton is rich, thanks to her best-selling autobiography. Her daughter is gainfully employed and miraculously sane. And, as best anyone can tell, she's enjoying a period of hard-earned marital peace.

The great mystery isn't who Hillary Clinton is or what she believes. It's why she'd risk giving up the best time of her life to run for president.

The senator is in Harlem, visiting a gleaming charter high school three days before the fifth anniversary of 9/11. The students of Promise Academy are baking bread for a neighborhood senior citizens' residence, an act of kindness organized by a foundation that spreads good deeds in memory of those who died in the terrorist attacks. Clinton plunges right in, kneading dough and decorating the brown paper bags that will hold the loaves. When a sample is finished, Clinton walks around the room offering a taste to everyone, students, teachers, reporters. She is wearing an apron.

This sets off a riot of images and associations in my head: Hillary's infamous "cookie baking" comment on *60 Minutes*. Bill Clinton's campaign visit to a Harlem library when he was first running for the White House. Jack Stanton's campaign visit to Harlem in *Primary Colors* and his dalliance with a fictional librarian. Headband Hillary. Third World microcredit wonk Hillary. Hillary as doting mother to Chelsea.

It's impossible to look at Clinton with anything approaching a clear mind. Some of her political choices have seemed foolish—like refusing to compromise on universal health care—and some transparently cunning, like her support for an anti-flag-burning bill. And some of her private decisions, like staying in her bizarre marriage, have struck me as downright brave. She certainly didn't seem like much fun. But it's strange that Hillary hasn't been able to make my blood boil or heart leap, given the passion she provokes in friends ("She's like a pitcher with a great fastball who insists on nibbling around the corners of the plate," says one frustrated sports-minded pal) and colleagues ("I hope you rip her good"). Maybe it's because I'm not a child of the sixties, but I've never felt she was worth the emotional investment, pro or con.

I've also never seen her in action as senator. One morning in September, two dozen executives of upstate New York credit unions are gathered in the gargantuan marble hallway outside Clinton's Washington office, waiting to pose for pictures with the senator. Suddenly, she pops out of a side door, chewing some kind of lozenge, casual as can be. She sees the assembled bankers, strides over briskly, and begins directing the photos.

When everyone moves around the corner to the Indian Treaty Room for a meeting, Clinton remains firmly in command. She loosens up the group with a joke, then takes questions. The credit-union executives want to talk about fighting legislation pushed by big banks that will make it tougher for credit unions to compete. Clinton listens sympathetically, but she returns, again and again, to asking why the credit unions can't find ways to make more loans to upstate farmers.

This is the side of Clinton that the public rarely gets to see: decisive, analytical, working the angles on behalf of the state. The greatest triumph of her Senate term has been in forcing the Bush administration to live up to its promises of money for victims of the September 11 terrorist attacks. Clinton has had to be determined and diplomatic, and occasionally confrontational, using both her cordial relations with Republicans who used to be enemies and her star power to keep the issue alive.

Six days later, after a weekend at home in Chappaqua, Clinton flies to Binghamton, for a conference on venture capitalism organized by New Jobs for New York.

Campaigning in 2000, Clinton talked of creating 200,000 new jobs for the region north and west of the Hudson. Her legislative proposals never made it out of committee, so instead Clinton has tried to become a rainmaker for the region. NJNY is her signature creation, a hybrid of private enterprise and government largesse, big-money insider connections and wonky policy notions that Clinton helped launch, with former Treasury secretary Roger Altman.

The great surprise of her first term as senator, however, is how Clinton has reveled in the Al D'Amato model of the job. She's become Senator Hillary Pothole. But it isn't just helping farmers hire enough pickers come harvest time. Clinton has developed the crucial retail-politics skills that seemed alien to her in the First Lady years—the warm handshake, the casual banter. Way back in 1993, Lawrence O'Donnell clashed with Clinton. He was Daniel Patrick Moynihan's top staffer on the Senate Finance Committee, which became an enormous roadblock to Clinton's health-care proposal; she was the inflexible crusader who slammed any compromise health-care proposal as "incremental." Today, O'Donnell is a TV writer (*The West Wing*) and a political pundit, and he looks at Senator Clinton with nothing but admiration. "In 2000, her polling got significantly better by Hillary Clinton campaigning," O'Donnell says. "People think that's the way it works; no, it isn't, at all. This time, Hillary is going to win counties upstate that Democrats never win. She is the rare politician who has the ability to change minds. That's the reason I look at her and think she could win a presidential election."

While Clinton hits the pancake breakfasts and union halls upstate, her behind-the-scenes battleship plods onward, its destination far more glamorous than Utica or Lindenhurst. One March afternoon in midtown, Clinton's city insiders assemble at a midtown law firm. Orin Kramer, Roger Altman, Lisa Perry, John Catsimatidis, Fred Hochberg, Robert Zimmerman, Alan Patricof, about 150 heavy hitters in all, gathered for what one of them calls "a pep rally." This is a crowd of pros. They're passionate about Hillary, but they're cold-blooded about restoring Democratic power.

The timing of the meeting was both curious and brilliant. It was already clear that Clinton would be facing only token opposition in her reelection campaign, on both the left and the right. The stated purpose was to discuss her Senate reelection. The part of the program that sent ripples through the room came when Mark Penn, Clinton's most trusted pollster and strategist, narrated a series of slides and charts. The story he told was of Clinton's political strength—against other nationally prominent Democrats, people like John Kerry, John Edwards, and Al Gore. This was as close to an open discussion of the great public unmentionable, the Hillary Race That Must Not Be Named, as any of her prime advisers had ever come. "It struck me as peculiar, because she's not running against any of those people," says one person in attendance. "At least she wasn't then."

The meeting broke up on a short-term, keep-your-eyes-on-the-ball moment: Clinton's staff distributed personalized folders to each donor. "Inside was a sheet tallying your donations and whether you had maxed out," one contributor says. "It felt like getting your grades at the end of the school year! Fortunately I'd given all I could, so I got an A-plus!"

Every major candidate has similar gatherings. But Clinton's organization is different, not just because it's the most professional on the Democratic side. It's the Clinton administration that never disbanded, the East Wing of the White House. Clinton's six years as senator, particularly a senator from New York, have enabled her to broaden and deepen the structure so that it's ready to serve whatever electoral needs may eventually occur to her. There are 32 full-time employees, plus 10 from her Senate office who receive part of their salary from Clinton's political funds; 13 consultants; and a national direct-mail operation, a fierce, permanent campaign with a momentum of its own. Her team is frighteningly disciplined; no one talks out of turn or without prior approval, and even when they do, aides repeat the same anecdotes almost robotically.

The cornerstone of Clinton's empire is called Friends of Hillary. In January 2001—after she'd been elected to the Senate but before she'd been sworn in—Clinton signed papers permitting it to raise money for any future campaign, and in the past six years it's reeled in $48 million (though Clinton will end her romp of a reelection with less in the bank, about $15 million, than many expected). FOH has two headquarters: one in Washington, on the K Street power corridor, and one in the Graybar Building, on Lexington Avenue at 43rd Street. Both are commanded by Patti Solis Doyle, the first person Hillary Clinton hired during the 1992 presidential campaign. But Hillaryland, the playful nickname hung on the predominantly female staff during Clinton's years as First Lady, sprawls far beyond any set of office suites, and includes key New Yorkers like political consultant Howard Wolfson, media guru Mandy Grunwald, and Maureen White, former finance chair of the DNC and wife of investment banker Steve Rattner.

Big as it is, so far the Hillary machine has been impressively quick, efficient, and relentless. The flip side is that Clinton's superstructure also is at the core of her authenticity problems. Everything she does seems stage-managed. Netroots giving Clinton unmitigated grief? Wolfson sees to it that Friends of Hillary hires one of the political blogosphere's sharpest practitioners, Peter Daou. Chattering-class talk that Hillary can't win growing ever louder? James Carville and Mark Penn write an op-ed for the *Washington Post* laying out why she can. Not that she's running for president, mind you.

This is a team of tough, resourceful fighters—and they're a necessity when beating back the Republican attack machine. Yet Hillary's troops give off a pervasive sense of embattlement that contributes to their leader's reputation for coldness. They've nicknamed her "the Warrior," and they mean it as a compliment. But that image, that surface reality, is what turns many people off; there's a great deal more going on inside Clinton.

The most important Friend of Hillary, the one who provides her remarkable story line and much of her considerable momentum in the Democratic Party, is also the most approachable. And, as if Hillary needs it, he's also a Technicolor warning about the perils of life in the White House.

"Hillary want some of this grub?"

Yesterday Bill Clinton was in Africa, Germany, and Switzerland. Today he's in the skybox of Ralph Wilson, the owner of the Buffalo Bills, to catch a game against the Minnesota Vikings. The former president's stepfather is a big Bills fan, one motivation for today's trip.

Bill Clinton is wearing a powder-blue sports jacket and a garish orange tie, and he looks exhausted—and also, somehow, regal. Maybe it's the snow-white hair, but the slimmed-down Clinton is still a commanding presence, even as he scans the skybox steam table, helping himself to some sliced turkey, mixed green salad, avocado, and sausage. He drawls out the question about his wife's appetite to an aide, who scurries into the other half of the stadium suite. Moments later, Hillary is piling up her own plate. The two of them look thrilled to be relaxing in each other's company, screaming like any other wealthy NFL fans at the behemoths crashing into one another on the field below.

Not that politics is ever far from the conversation. "I'm her Westchester caseworker," Bill says, his eyes twinkling. "People come up to me all the time and say, 'Where's my Social Security check?'"

Hillary Clinton has become her own person these past six years. Bill certainly hasn't been invisible during her Senate term, traveling the globe to fight AIDS, among other good works; more ominously, there was his recent blowup on Fox over who lost Osama bin Laden. If Hillary runs, however, there's no way Bill can stay in the background, quietly offering sage advice, even if he's in Botswana. The marquee would be rearranged, but the Hill and Bill Show would be back in town. The prospect of a wife's following her husband into the Oval Office would take on historical and soap-operatic dimensions. A Republican strategist calls Bill a "net asset," pointing to recent approval ratings near 70 percent for the ex-prez. Yet Bill causes Hillary some political problems. He is the face of the Democratic Party, its biggest fund-raising draw. Would she be running to improve on his record, or reinstall him in power? One moment from Hillary's 59th birthday party/fund-raiser at Tavern on the Green last month was emblematic: After a rock band played, Bill and Hillary climbed onstage to shake the musicians' hands and pose for photos. It was Hillary's night, but Bill was the one who grabbed a guitar and stood at the center of the group. Hillary was behind his left shoulder, looking like a backup singer.

"Hill-a-reee! Hill-a-reee!"

"Run for president! We love you!"

The chant follows her the entire route of the Columbus Day parade, all the way up Fifth Avenue, bouncing off the front of Gucci and Abercrombie & Fitch and that giant tilted mirror. Inside the Redken hair salon, stylists have dropped their blow-dryers and customers, dripping mid-shampoo, are lining the second-story picture windows to chant and wave.

"Hill-a-ree!"

No one calls out the names of the other New York Democratic stars, past and present, even though they're all here, marching together, waving with one hand and gripping a City Council banner with the other: Eliot Spitzer, Andrew Cuomo, Geraldine Ferraro, Christine Quinn. The perceived inevitability of her presidential nomination puts other New York politicians in her shadow. Some take it better than others.

Marching about 50 paces behind this show of party unity, flanked by aides carrying red-and-blue-lettered signs shouting MEET CHUCK SCHUMER!, is the state's senior senator. Schumer dashes from one sidewalk to the other, shaking hands, posing for pictures. He's not up for election this year, which doesn't mean Schumer isn't running.

And now, at 61st Street, Schumer is zipping past his fellow Dems, along the west side of the avenue, trailed by his black limo, which pulls into the middle of the reviewing stand's red carpet and blocks the rest of the parade. Spitzer shakes his head and chuckles. "Don't get in Chuck's way!" he says to Clinton.

"You're telling me!" she hollers back, laughing.

Clinton and Schumer dismiss any talk of tension and lavish each other with praise. "She's done a great job, because she's a great listener and she's a great learner," Schumer says. "I think the biggest lesson she learned from the White House years is that you've got to bury the hatchet whenever you can and work together with whoever you can work with. She's accused of having no principles, but I don't buy that. Max Weber had a great quote: 'You can't save your soul and save the city.' I think she's found a very good balance there."

After the parade, Clinton hops into her black van for a short trip to East 73rd Street and Via Quadronno, a sliver of an Italian restaurant, where she sits at a table in the back corner beneath a painting of a flying pig and next to three thrilled British tourists. After ordering a bowl of lentil soup and a glass of fresh grapefruit juice mixed with carbonated water, the senator takes a bite out of the Republicans. "This administration is populated by people who've spent their careers bashing government. They're not just small-government conservatives—they're Grover Norquist, strangle-it-in-the-bathtub conservatives," Clinton says. "It's a cognitive disconnect for them to be able to do something well in an arena that they have so derided and reviled all these years."

Yet even in the wake of two catastrophes of active neglect—the Iraq war and the aftermath of Hurricane Katrina—doesn't it remain hugely difficult for Democrats to win by arguing for themselves as the party of competent government? For the only time in our conversations, Clinton shows real heat. "It's not so long ago that FEMA actually worked!" she says, setting aside her soup. "This is not ancient history! It actually worked in the nineties! It's not so long ago that the VA was a disaster, and it was turned around in the nineties because the right decisions were made. So you can point to two parts of the government that deal with emergencies and take care of our veterans, which most Americans can relate to, and say, 'We know how to do this. We did it before; we can do it again. And so don't be misled.'"

The nineties *we,* of course, weren't just generic Democrats; it was Bill Clinton's time in the White House, and the Veterans Affairs bureau was one of First Lady Hillary Clinton's primary causes after the universal-health-care debacle. But the senator is rolling now. "Let's take the two areas where they claim to be better than Democrats: in foreign policy and national security," Clinton says. "And what do they have to show for it? Even there, they've been an abject failure, putting our country in greater danger and more at risk. So I think you can make a very strong case. Now, you've got to *make* it, and you have to be quite aggressive in making it."

Government works. At bottom, after all these years in public life, that is the core principle to which Hillary Clinton clings: her faith in government to actively spread justice and opportunity, and to reward responsible behavior. That faith has been refined over time. The incrementalism she's practiced for six years—Mark Penn–style government—isn't merely a product of Clinton's place in the minority; she's now a believer in small steps. But the goals remain steady.

Does she still believe in universal health care? "Absolutely," she says, stretching out the syllables. "In fact, I think the argument for it is even stronger today than it was thirteen years ago. So I think it's gonna come back as a very big issue. I'm not offering an alternative—right now."

Ask about any specifics and she remains exasperatingly hard to pin down. "If we take back one or both houses of Congress, we can begin to set an agenda again," Clinton says. "And we can determine how we can create a majority around those agendas. In the '08 elections, no matter who runs, it will be a great time to paint a broader vision of where the country should be. People will either vote for it or they won't. But we can't do any of that right now."

Then I asked her about her vote to allow Bush to invade Iraq. Despite all of her success on her small-bore, Senator Pothole issues, it's liable to be the vote for which she's best remembered. She's elaborated her elaborate reasoning many times—that, at its essence, her yes vote was in favor of presidential authority, and that she believed Bush's promise to allow weapons inspectors to do their job.

What Clinton hasn't discussed much is how she thinks her vote represented her New York constituents, as consistently and vociferously an antiwar state as exists. "Well, I think if you go back and look, [my vote] was not unpopular," Clinton says. "It was unpopular among many of my constituents and supporters, which was very painful. But I think I'm hired to make decisions based on the best information I have at the time."

Bob Kerrey, the Vietnam War vet, former Democratic senator, and current president of the New School, praises Clinton for having learned to play Realpolitik.

"I don't want martyrs who are constantly going to vote their conscience and become ineffective as a consequence," Kerrey says. "Sam Rayburn had this wonderful quote: 'There's two kinds of people in Washington: Those who can count, and those who lose.' Hillary is in the group of people who can count."

Clinton's war vote, agree with it or not, is the most principled stand she's taken as senator. But because it was driven as much by calculation as conviction, it's also the prime example of why many people find it so hard to love her. And why her strongest challenge in 2008 would come from the left.

When Mark Penn did his slide show for donors in March, there was a name missing from his encouraging comparisons between Clinton and other national Democrats: Barack Obama. Of course, back in March Illinois's junior senator was barely on anyone's presidential radar.

Obama's threat to Clinton in 2008 isn't simply stylistic. He'd be a major tactical headache as well, cutting into her popularity with black voters in particular.

Clinton insiders shrug off the idea that a 45-year-old with two years in the Senate under his belt, a man with no foreign-policy experience who'd be running at a time when the country is fighting a disastrous war, makes them nervous. "It will be another person in the race," says Patricof, the New York investment banker and veteran FOH who chairs her Senate campaign's finance committee. "He's new on the scene, he hasn't had much experience in the political world, and she's had a lot more, besides having been in office for six years. We'll have to see. That's what primaries are about. If they happen."

Yet the prospect of an Obama presidential candidacy is one more reason that Clinton '08 isn't the sure thing that conventional wisdom, and the Republicans, like to believe. Lately, there's been increasing Washington talk that what Clinton really should do is stick around and eventually become majority leader. Perhaps the chatter is meant as a compliment. It's fueled in part by anxious Democrats who think Clinton will win the '08 presidential nomination and lose the general election. Clinton's top aides, particularly the women, consider the majority-leader buzz patronizing: You stay here, Mrs. Clinton, and let the men handle the big job.

Clinton smiles thinly. "No, I don't consider it patronizing," she says. "I'm always interested in what people think I should do. It's like watching this movie that I'm in that I had nothing to do with. I've got my life, and then I've got everybody else's opinion of my life." She shakes her head slowly. "But ultimately, I'll decide what I think is the best thing for me to do."

It's Hillary's choice. Perhaps she will calculate she can't win the White House. Or maybe Bill will do something egregious that limits her options. But the strongest reason to believe Hillary won't run for president, or at least hasn't truly made up her mind, is that she loves being a senator. "It's going to be a huge factor in her thinking," says a longtime friend and adviser.

Though Clinton traveled widely as First Lady, she was inevitably isolated. There's a tactile element to her current role that thrills her. Clinton is forever hugging shopkeepers, and dancing little jigs as she waits for official functions to begin. "I adore it," she says of being a senator. "I absolutely adore it. I've been lucky in my life that I've had the opportunity to do a lot of really interesting, satisfying jobs, both in the private sector and the public. But this is just the best experience. I couldn't have a job that I enjoyed more."

Clinton has never been good at the vision thing, and she usually disdains symbolism—two traditional requirements for winning the presidency, if not conducting an exemplary one. "As much as everybody accuses her of wanting to be a candidate from the time she could walk, it really isn't true," says another close adviser. "She was comfortable in the backroom role." Clinton is hardly anonymous as New York's junior senator. But her zone of privacy is enormous when compared with life in the White House.

"If the Democrats make some progress in the midterms, add more members in Congress, I could see her staying," says Susan Thomases, a friend of more than 30 years who talks to Clinton regularly.

If Hillary runs, it will be in part because Bill pushed and her own campaign machinery pulled. But ultimately it will be her call. Clearly, ego will be involved. But, corny as it sounds, Hillary Clinton is a true believer in public service. In these past six years, she's seen government's capacity for good and evil in a fine-grained detail—and experienced her own firsthand ability to move government—that she'd never known before. To Clinton, her political career is about us, not her, and that's why she'd submit herself to a brutal 2008 campaign. Skeptics will never believe it; they'll see a grab for power, the arrogance of a woman who thinks she knows what's best for the little people. Yet central to Clinton's decision will be her judgment of where she can do the most good, for New York and for the nation.

Clinton could, of course, run for president, lose, and have her Senate seat as a fallback. But that's a scenario with nasty political and psychic costs. Just ask John Kerry.

Clinton is walking out of the restaurant now, her path slowed by well-wishers—three men from Britain in town for a Barbra Streisand concert ("I'm going to see her Wednesday night!" she tells them), two women from Costa Rica ("Welcome! I've been to your country!"). After greeting the kitchen staff, she's out the door.

I've chased Clinton from Buffalo to Washington, and she's looser and warmer than I'd expected. I have a better understanding of where she's been creative and where she's been cowardly in the Senate, and why. Clinton is a pragmatic progressive, and after eight years of ruinously inflexible ideology in the White House, her incrementalism would be a quantum improvement. What crafty compromise won't make Clinton is lovable. And we'll never get a completely straight answer from her, at least on the record.

As her steps pick up speed, I ask one more question, to the back of Clinton's expensively blonde head: If I'm a mainstream Democratic voter, why should I hope she's one of the candidates running in '08? Hillary Clinton laughs, loud and hard. "Oh, I'll talk to you about that if I ever make such a decision," she says. "Good try, though! That was clever!" And then she's back inside the black van. Protected, and removed, by the bubble.

The Accidental Populist

Jason Zengerle

the *New Republic* | January 22, 2007

Former North Carolina senator John Edwards may have earned millions as a trial lawyer, but his politics have always been grounded in his mill-town upbringing. It's no surprise, then, that populist economic themes—including the most detailed plan for universal health coverage offered by any candidate—have formed the core of his 2008 presidential bid. Still, early nationwide polls of likely Democratic primary voters have him wallowing in the teens, well behind Hillary Clinton and Barack Obama. In this New Republic *profile, Jason Zengerle catches up with the Edwards campaign and provides a look at how his populist, pro-union message—and its messenger—are going over with the voting public.*

Last October, the United Steelworkers of America went on strike against Goodyear, leading some 13,000 of its members to walk off the job. Once they did, it was only a matter of time before John Edwards went to see them. Like a moth to a flame—or Al Sharpton to a police shooting—Edwards of late seems inexorably drawn to labor strife. As he has laid the groundwork for his 2008 presidential campaign, he has become a fixture at union rallies and on picket lines across the country. Striking janitors at the University of Miami; disgruntled Teamsters at a helicopter plant in Connecticut; beleaguered hotel workers campaigning for better wages and health insurance in Chicago, Los Angeles, even Honolulu—Edwards has visited them all, offering words of encouragement and solidarity at every turn. "When I hear of a group of courageous workers engaged in a historic struggle," he told the janitors in Miami last spring, "it is important to me to show that I am with them."

And so, in early November, about five weeks into the Goodyear strike, Edwards paid a visit to the United Steelworkers (USW) hall in Akron, Ohio. It was a cold Saturday morning just three days before the midterm elections, and USW Local 2 was hosting a rally to support both the strike and Ohio Democratic candidates. Nearly 500 Local 2 members were participating in the strike, and it seemed as if all of them had come to kick off their weekends at the squat, concrete building that sits in the shadow of the tiremaker's world headquarters. Some were taking a break from the picket lines to warm themselves with ten-cent coffee and glazed doughnuts; others were there to inquire about getting much-needed checks from the union's strike benefit fund. As they waited for the rally to start in the hall's central meeting room, large men in windbreakers and varsity-style letterman jackets emblazoned with the USW logo traded gossip about if and when they would be going back to work.

While they did, Edwards huddled with a dozen or so union officials in a small conference room. Although he is now 53, Edwards still has the same slim build, foppish brown hair, and preternaturally youthful face that made him such a bright young thing nearly a decade ago, when he was elected to the Senate from North Carolina. He's also managed to hold on to the same friendly, almost deferential manner—the one he inherited from his father, who said to his son that he could "tell if someone was talking down to me in 30 seconds"; the one he easily could have lost once he became important enough to have his own Secret Service detail. As he made small talk with his hosts, discussing college football and past labor events he had attended, he immediately put them at ease.

After a while, the conversation turned to the meeting's real purpose: preparing Edwards for his speech to the rally. In order to know precisely what words of solidarity to offer, he needed a background briefing—which the union officials eagerly provided, telling him about the perfidy of Goodyear and the terribleness of the strike as he nodded and murmured in agreement. But there was one piece of business even more pressing than what Edwards was going to say: what he was going to wear. He had arrived at the union hall dressed in the standard Saturday uniform for a stumping politician—V-neck sweater, Oxford shirt, and khakis. But that, of course, wouldn't cut it for a labor rally. And so, with the expectant look of a suitor offering his intended a diamond ring, an official handed Edwards a blue USW T-shirt.

There was just one problem. When Edwards put the shirt on, it was huge. Even though he was wearing it over two other pieces of clothing, it fit him like a muumuu, billowing out and away from his body. It clearly had been tailored for the sort of exceptionally large man who tends to belong to an industrial labor union, not for a politician who's a bit of a fitness freak. As Edwards stood awkwardly, the shirt's shoulder seams dangling around his elbows, one of the union officials, a giant with a tremendous gut, slapped him on the back hard enough to knock him forward. "It's OK!" he roared. "It makes you look skinny!"

Like the shirt, Edwards's persona for the 2008 campaign—that of a combative champion of the working class—seems a strange fit. Although Edwards ran for president in 2004 as a populist, he did so as a sunny one—a disposition that appeared a natural extension of his congenitally cheerful personality. He dubbed his political organization the "New American Optimists" and presented himself as the "son of a millworker" whose later success as a lawyer and a senator was a hopeful story about American possibility. His stump speech, which called attention to the "Two Americas," was less an airing of grievances than a buoyant pledge to bridge the divide between rich and poor. And his policy proposals—including incremental reform of health care and micro-initiatives to help the poor—were fiscally friendly as well, showing that his populist heart was governed by a New Democrat brain.

Even when it came to campaign tactics, Edwards played nice. In the Democratic primaries, he abstained from going negative on his opponents —so much so that many assumed he was angling for the number-two spot on the ticket. And, after John Kerry gave him that spot, he didn't adopt the typical running mate's role of attack dog. When he faced off in his vice presidential debate against Dick Cheney—whom Democrats were hoping he would beat like a Darth Vader piñata—Edwards turned in a largely toothless performance. As one Edwards adviser puts it, "He was the smiley, happy candidate."

But now, Edwards is trying to turn that smile into a snarl, or at least a frown of concern. Since losing the vice presidential race in 2004—and subsequently leaving the Senate and Washington—he has spent his time focusing on the forgotten and neglected corners of the United States and, to a lesser extent, the world. Acting as a sort of latter-day Tom Joad, he has visited not just picket lines but homeless shelters, disaster zones, and refugee camps. And, in his current quest for the presidency, he intends to make the plight of the people he has encountered in those places his central issue. Accordingly, he has ditched his past commitment to fiscally restrained Rubinomics and now favors universal health coverage and an expensive raft of other policy initiatives to lift Americans—and even people in other countries—out of poverty. When he officially announced he was running for president in late December, he did so not sitting next to his wife in the comfort of their family home in a Raleigh neighborhood called Country Club Hills—as he had in the 2004 campaign—but standing by himself in the debris-strewn backyard of a hurricane-damaged house in New Orleans's Ninth Ward. "This campaign," he declared, "will be a grass-roots, ground-up campaign, where we ask people to take action."

It's a campaign that seems off to a promising start. Edwards's reinvention has moved him to the left of Hillary Clinton, which, in the Democratic primaries, should be a good location. And, while Barack Obama—presumably the other top-tier Democratic candidate—is also to Clinton's left, he will have to face the questions about experience, or lack thereof, that Edwards dealt with in 2004. The election calendar could also play to Edwards's favor, as he currently leads in public opinion polls of Democrats in Iowa, the site of the first caucus; is strong in South Carolina, which holds the second primary; and is tight with the all-powerful culinary workers union in Nevada, which hosts the second caucus. Indeed, according to *The New York Times*, no less an authority than Clinton herself has told associates that Edwards and Obama are her two biggest obstacles to the nomination.

Still, while Edwards's new incarnation may bring him certain advantages in the race, it's nonetheless a peculiar bit of political positioning. The Democratic primaries have not, after all, been terribly generous to pro-union populists (just ask Dick Gephardt), and it has been a generation or more since a national Democrat has gotten far by campaigning against poverty. Indeed, for all the political calculations that have presumably played into Edwards's shift, it seems as though something else has been at work, as well.

"I can tell you one thing that's changed for me, and it's very significant for me personally," Edwards told me in one of several conversations we had in the weeks before he officially launched his campaign. "When I was running for president before, in 2003, 2004, I spent most of my time thinking about what I could do to be a better candidate." He paused, as if to let this confession sink in. "That's just not what I think about anymore," he went on. "Now what I spend my time thinking about is what I want to do as president of the United States." Often derided as "plastic" and "a lightweight" during his last national campaign, Edwards has, in other words, been searching for his own political essence, both as a source of gravitas and as a rationale for his continued presidential ambitions. And, in his role as a crusader for the working class, he seems to think he has found it.

It's hard to imagine a political defeat more devastating than the one Edwards suffered in November 2004. First, there was the shock of it: On the afternoon of Election Day, when he boarded a plane for Boston to await the official results, the early exit polls had convinced him—and the rest of the Kerry-Edwards campaign—that the Democratic ticket was on its way to victory; it was only a few hours later, after his plane landed, that he learned things didn't look so good. Then there was the frustration: The morning after the election, he participated in a campaign conference call and found himself alone in arguing that Kerry should not concede until the anecdotal reports of voting irregularities in Ohio were cleared up. But the truly crushing blow came immediately after Kerry's concession speech at Faneuil Hall, when Edwards and his wife Elizabeth paid a surreptitious visit to a Boston hospital. A few weeks earlier, she'd discovered a lump on her breast; then, a day after he lost the election, they were told that she had cancer.

John and Elizabeth Edwards have experienced tragedy before: In 1996, their 16-year-old son, Wade, was killed in a car accident. Both of them say that experience helped give them the strength to deal with her illness. Some family friends also believe that her cancer may have helped him better cope with his election defeat. "I never saw him become this morose, bitter person muttering, 'But for Ohio, I'd be on top of the world,'" says Ed Turlington, a North Carolina lawyer who served as the chairman of Edwards's 2004 presidential campaign. "He just threw himself into getting Elizabeth well."

After a few weeks—once Elizabeth had chosen a course of treatment and been given a good prognosis by her doctors—Edwards turned to the question of what he would do next, since his Senate term was up and he was now looking for a job. He had a number of options. Outgoing Democratic National Committee Chairman Terry McAuliffe had pushed him to pursue that post. There were people encouraging him to write a campaign memoir or a book laying out a vision for the future of the Democratic

Party; others wanted him to do a TV talk show. Some investment houses and law firms were interested in having him join them, as well. Around Thanksgiving, Edwards convened a meeting at his Washington house of his inner circle—Elizabeth, people who'd worked for him in the Senate and on his presidential campaign, longtime family friends—to discuss his future options. According to multiple participants, it didn't take him long to dismiss them all. What he wanted to do, he told those assembled, was focus his energies on fighting poverty.

Shortly thereafter, Edwards founded a poverty think tank at the University of North Carolina at Chapel Hill, which he has since used as both a base of operations and a vehicle to familiarize himself with academic research on the issue. Jacob Hacker, a Yale political scientist who attended a two-day seminar at the think tank last year, came away impressed. "It wasn't as if the presentations were by rabble-rousing Democratic activists calling for revolution," Hacker says. "There were some very technical social science discussions, and he seemed very engaged by them." He also conducted his own version of fieldwork. Robert Gordon, a domestic policy adviser to Edwards, recalls a trip they took to a community development corporation in the small town of Washington, North Carolina. "It was a roundtable with regular people like you see in campaigns," Gordon says, "except there were no cameras, and the regular people were really down on their luck. There were a couple of people who'd had pretty serious drug problems, a few who had HIV. There was a woman who'd lived in a homeless shelter and who'd had her kids taken from her." When a minister at the meeting reminded the group that they were sitting next to a man who was almost vice president, Gordon says Edwards interrupted. "He said, 'I might have almost been vice president, but I am no better than anybody in this room.'"

Edwards explains his focus on poverty matter-of-factly. He ran for the Senate, and then the presidency, to "serve." (His successful career as a trial lawyer left him with no real need to make more money: In 2003, his net worth was estimated to be between $12.8 million and $60 million.) Even though he no longer held elected office—and was unsure as to whether he ever would again—he says his commitment to service remained, and poverty was the issue where he thought his service would be most valuable. "It felt to me like there was a huge void in national engagement on this issue," he told me, "and it was something I really cared about, so it was a natural fit." For public consumption, at least, it's as simple as that.

But Edwards's decision to focus on poverty almost certainly involved a political calculation as well. Although he is not someone for whom the presidency has been a lifelong ambition, his 2004 defeat clearly galled him. He may not have been muttering "but for Ohio" while Elizabeth was sick, but, since then, there has been some grumbling "but for Howard Dean's scream." Many in the Edwards camp believe to this day that Dean's televised outburst denied Edwards the momentum he'd earned by finishing a strong second in the Iowa caucuses. The clearest summation of this view can be found in Elizabeth's recent memoir, *Saving Graces:*

> We had always heard that two stories come out of Iowa, and what we wanted was for John to be one of them. If The Scream hadn't happened, Kerry and John would have been the stories coming out of Iowa. . . . Since it did happen, Kerry and The Scream were the stories. And there was no New Hampshire bump.

No New Hampshire bump for Edwards (it went solely to Kerry instead) meant no nomination. Add to this Edwards's displeasure with Kerry's general election campaign—he privately complained that it wasn't aggressive enough in attacking President Bush or competing in some red states—and it appears he felt he was tantalizingly close to the White House or the vice president's office but for other people's mistakes.

And, while focusing on poverty might seem like an odd choice for someone once again eyeing the White House, it makes a certain sense if you view politics the way Edwards does. For a politician of such immense talent, one of the most remarkable things about Edwards is just how politically unformed he is. Prior to his own Senate campaign in 1998, he—unlike most people who make a fortune and then run for office—wasn't even a political junkie: He voted only about half of the time and gave relatively little money in campaign contributions. Since then, Edwards has become a ferocious political animal, preparing himself for campaigns the way he once prepped for trials; but his political knowledge and experience, in many respects, goes back only to the second half of the Clinton administration. And, during that time, of course, questions of authenticity and a candidate's character have dominated presidential campaigns.

This helps explain why Edwards seems to view the presidential campaign less as a contest between ideologies or even policy proposals than as a referendum on each candidate as a person. "Do I have the strength and character to lead this country? I mean, that's the question," he told me. "The judgment should be made on vision, and strength, and character, and who you really are." In 2004, the perception (fair or not) of Edwards was that he was a young politician in a hurry, one defined more by personal ambition than a set of core convictions or a guiding vision for the country. But that's a much harder case to make about someone who has spent the last two years holding poverty seminars and visiting food banks. "Presidential campaigns are primarily about character and sort of a broad sense of priorities and values," says Harrison Hickman, Edwards's pollster. "In that sense, his attention to poverty as an issue defines a lot about where he comes from, about what he thinks the failings of the country are and what he thinks the priorities of the country are."

Nor does Edwards's crusade end at the water's edge. Lack of foreign policy experience was one of his greatest shortcomings in 2004, and, since then, he has been busy trying to make it a strong suit. First, of course, there is Iraq: As a senator, Edwards voted for the resolution authorizing Bush to use force—and defended that vote throughout the last presidential campaign—but, in November 2005, he became one of the first prominent Democrats who supported the war to say his vote had been a mistake. Speaking at an August rally for Democratic Senate candidate (and antiwar champion) Ned Lamont, Edwards reiterated his mea culpa. "I voted for this war. I was wrong. I should not have voted for this war," he told a crowd of several hundred Lamont supporters who had gathered in a courtyard at Yale Medical School. He then added a call for immediate withdrawal of U.S. forces: "We need to make it clear that we're going to leave Iraq, and the best way to make that clear is to obviously start leaving."

More broadly, Edwards—who, as a senator, wasn't a prodigious foreign junketeer—has become something of a globetrotter over the last two years, taking trips to Israel, Russia, China, India, and Uganda, among other exotic locales. And the lesson he has learned from those travels parallels what he has learned in the soup kitchens and union halls he's visited in this country. "We have two responsibilities," he told the Lamontsters. "One of those is to look after the interests of the United States of America. The second responsibility is to look after the interests of humanity."

Undoubtedly aware of the poor track record of foreign policy idealism in Iraq, Edwards tries to couch his call for American global do-goodism in realist terms. "The most important responsibility of the next president," he frequently says, "is to restore America's leadership in the world, because if we don't lead, there is chaos." But, for all the geo-strategic framing, Edwards's desire for increased U.S. engagement with the world sometimes seems to reflect the thinking of someone who has just recently realized how big—and how troubled—the world really is.

"We talk about poverty in America; poverty in America is moderate compared to poverty around the world," Edwards declared at the Lamont rally. He then proceeded to tell a story about how, "just before this past Christmas," he had visited some slums outside of Delhi. Asking the crowd to "picture in your mind for just a minute and be there with me," he described "little narrow alleyways filled with sewage, flies, animals everywhere" and how, amid all this misery, he saw "a little area about twice the size of this stage. There were four blankets laid out on the pavement, and there were probably 15 or 20 children on each blanket." He paused, waiting for his audience to let the picture develop in their minds. "And then I realized," he went on, his voice now tinged with wonder and regret, "these children were in school. This was their school."

It was a powerful story, told in a powerful fashion, but the crowd, while moved, also seemed somewhat puzzled. What was Edwards's point? That, while Lamont battled Joe Lieberman, there were children starving in India? So Edwards spelled it out for them, adding a final line to his tale. "And I walked away from there," he concluded, his voice now practically a whisper, "and I said to myself, 'Where is America?'"

On the second anniversary of one of the worst days of his life—the day that his running mate conceded the election and his wife was diagnosed with cancer—Edwards returned to the place where it all happened. He was in Boston to speak that night at an awards dinner for local community activists, although the trip also served as a convenient excuse to see his oldest daughter, 24-year-old Cate, who's attending Harvard Law School. (Edwards and his wife have two other children, 8-year-old Emma Claire and 6-year-old Jack.) Before the speech, he met me at a seafood restaurant in his hotel for our first interview.

He wasn't in a particularly good mood. He was battling a cold—which seemed to have been exacerbated by the chilly New England weather—and he'd recently tweaked his hamstring, which meant that he'd been unable to go for one of his five-mile runs. When a waiter came to take our order, Edwards curtly informed him, "We're not eating," and asked for an iced tea. But, eventually, as he settled into the interview, he seemed to relax. Still, to most questions I asked, he gave answers that were deeply rehearsed. His comment about the "enormous freedom to choose what I am most interested in doing and spending my time on" sounded a lot like the "enormous freedom [of] being able to do what I am now" that he'd boasted of to a crowd of Democrats in New Hampshire the previous year. The observation he made to me that "China is going to become the largest English-speaking nation on the face of the planet" was one he'd make to Charlie Rose a couple of weeks later. Even his seemingly candid admission that, in the last presidential campaign, he was focused on being a "better candidate" as opposed to a better president was, in fact, a line he's given to numerous reporters.

In all, Edwards seemed at pains to avoid saying anything too candid or potentially controversial. When I asked him for his response to Bill Clinton's contention, as quoted in the *New Yorker*, that he ran for president prematurely in 2004, he dodged: "I think it's the wrong way [for candidates] to think about running for president of the United States . . . to evaluate what's in *their* best interest." (Elizabeth, for her part, is bracingly candid. When I later asked her about Clinton's comment, she shot back, "During the campaign, Bill Clinton was enormously supportive of John, constantly giving him advice and encouraging him in every conceivable way. At no point in my recollection did John ever get off the phone after a conversation with him where he said, 'Bill thinks it's too early for me.' Never. Not once." Was this just Bill trying to talk down a potential rival to Hillary? "I can come to the same supposition anybody else can about why he said that.") Even my mention of the strange coincidence of his being in Boston on the second anniversary of the traumatic day he spent here failed to elicit much of a response. "Is it really?" he asked, before quickly changing the subject to a retelling of his efforts to convince Kerry not to concede—a retelling identical to the one Elizabeth has laid out for public consumption in her book.

Presidential candidates, of course, are given to pat answers—partly because they're so often asked the same questions, partly because being candid carries so many risks. But Edwards's exceptional guardedness seems strange for a candidate who now makes such a fetish of authenticity —for a candidate, in fact, who makes a pointed distinction between guarded, pabulum-spewing politicians and candid, truth-telling leaders. "What happens with politicians," he recently told a public radio interviewer, "is that you're conditioned not to be yourself. You're conditioned to say the same thing over and over and over, because that's the safe route. . . . We need a leader, or leaders, who are willing to be themselves, who'll tell the truth as they see it." Or, as he complained to me about the last presidential campaign, during which he seems to think he acted more like a politician than a leader: "It was just plastic, there was a lot of plasticity to it. You know—young, Southern, dynamic, charismatic, beautiful family, all that. People need to see who I am, what my character is." Which, come to think of it, sounds a lot like something Edwards says in a "behind the scenes" video his campaign recently posted on YouTube: "I actually want the country to see who I am, who I really am. . . . I'd rather be successful or unsuccessful based on who I really am, not based on some plastic Ken doll you put up in front of audiences."

About the only time Edwards seemed to switch off autopilot during the interview was when he talked about poverty. "You should cut me off on this," he warned, "because I spend a lot of time talking about this." And he did. He talked about his various ideas for fighting poverty—raising the minimum wage, strengthening unions, reforming public housing, creating one million federally funded "stepping stone" jobs at nonprofits or government agencies. He talked about just how much he still had to learn and how even he sometimes felt despair about the intractable nature of the problem. "The cultural component of poverty and what feeds the cycle of poverty—I don't think I ever really got it until, like, for the fifteenth time I'm sitting with a 33-year-old, 32-year-old mother who has a 14-year-old who's having the third child," he said. "And you hear that and it's just, 'How will they ever get out?' You know, it's 'What can you do?'" He seemed genuinely offended when I asked him whether he was surprised that Americans' post-Katrina concern about poverty had waned so rapidly. "I think it's very superficial to suggest that there was interest [and] it's gone," he said. "It's not gone. It's still there. It's just not on the surface. . . . It's deeper down."

A few hours later, Edwards went to one of those places where the interest in poverty was anything but buried: the dinner banquet honoring local community activists. It wasn't the hottest political ticket in Boston that night—that honor went to the final big campaign rally for Massachusetts Democratic gubernatorial candidate Deval Patrick, where Barack Obama was giving a speech. But the event seemed like an opportunity for Edwards, since it allowed him to speak to people who were fighting poverty—in other words, his people. He congratulated them for their commitment to "the great moral cause in America today," which, he noted, "is now the cause of my own life." But then Edwards launched into a speech that followed, almost to the letter, the same trajectory as our interview: the same policy proposals, the same observations, even the same revelatory anecdotes. "One of the things that I've been struck by in the work that we've been doing over the last several years is that you sit with a mother, a single mom . . . and her 14-year-old daughter is giving birth to the third child. And it just feeds this cycle of poverty." What had sounded so fresh and genuine to me only hours before already seemed stale and scripted.

Yet it was anything but to the people in the room. When Edwards finished his speech, the vast banquet hall rose as one and gave him a standing ovation. He left the banquet early to have dinner with his daughter, but, as he snuck out through the hotel's kitchen, he was mobbed by some of the waiters and waitresses who'd watched his speech from the wings. "I listened to what you said out there," one told Edwards, her voice breaking. "Thank you so much for saying it. It means a lot. Please keep saying it."

It's a sentiment Edwards hears frequently. Although his spiel may be pat, although his words may be overly rehearsed, he's still saying things that no other candidate in this presidential race seems prepared to say—things that probably need to be said. There's a difference, after all, between spontaneity and sincerity. In his previous profession as a litigating attorney, Edwards was famous for the emotional power of his closing arguments. Other lawyers would pack the courtroom to hear him offer the final brief on behalf of the family of the little girl who'd had her intestines sucked out by a pool drain or the little boy whose parents had been killed by a speeding tractor-trailer. That those closing arguments were rehearsed to the point where Edwards could deliver them in his sleep didn't make the sentiment behind them any less genuine—or, for that matter, less effective. Indeed, that sometimes seems to be Edwards's signal gift—the ability to find the thread of emotional truth even in a line he's recited 20 times before. It's what made him a successful lawyer and makes him a formidable presidential candidate.

This was never more apparent than at the USW hall in Akron, where Edwards stood in his ill-fitting T-shirt as he waited for his turn to address the striking Goodyear workers. The speakers preceding him had offered stiff, stilted words of support to the workers—words that seemed to ring hollow to the crowd, which had grown anxious and restless. When Edwards's turn came, it wasn't hard to sense their skepticism. Here was a millionaire politician with Hollywood good looks who couldn't possibly know the first thing about what these workers were going through. But then Edwards stepped up to the podium, yanked the microphone out of its holder, and launched into his speech.

He began by striking his standard note of solidarity. He said that he had come to Akron on a "personal mission to stand with my brothers and sisters and for those who are standing up for men and women who have worked their entire lives and have earned dignity, and respect, and health care." He said the union was showing "backbone and courage to do what's right." What the workers were fighting for, after all, was a dignity that they already possessed and that their employer was trying to take away from them. "We're talking about standing up to protect what they're entitled to," he said. "That's what this is about."

Edwards went on in this vein for a little longer, casting the strike as part of a larger fight to honor the legacies of those who "have worked to make America what it is today." But, eventually, Edwards brought his speech—and the strike—back to himself. Although he didn't work in a tire factory, although he had every material possession a person could possibly desire, he wanted the striking workers to know that he truly understood their struggle. "I take this very personally," he said, as the crowd grew silent. "My mother and father have health care today because of the union. My brother, my only brother, and his family have health care today because of the union. This is a just and righteous cause. You stood up and made huge concessions for this company in 2003. You did what was right, and it's time to make Goodyear"—he said the company's name with a slight hiss—"do what they're supposed to do."

Before Edwards had even finished his sentence, the crowd began to whoop and cheer. He acknowledged the applause with a grin and a wave. "So I'm proud to be with you," he said, his words now nearly drowned out. The Goodyear strike would drag on for two more months and the USW, in the end, would agree to a contract with some provisions it once considered anathema. But, at that moment, as Edwards stood on the stage and the union hall reverberated with cheers, there was suddenly hope that a better outcome, and maybe even a better life, was possible. The T-shirt may have looked a little ridiculous on Edwards at first, but it turned out to be a perfect fit.

The Conciliator

Larissa MacFarquhar

the *New Yorker* | May 7, 2007

Barack Obama may be trailing Hillary Clinton in the early polls (as of this writing, national surveys of likely Democratic primary voters had him about ten points behind the former First Lady), but he's the clear leader in the charisma sweepstakes. Extremely bright (he was elected president of the Harvard Law Review), unfailingly eloquent, and extraordinarily self-composed, with a family tree tracing back to the American Midwest and east Africa, he's unlike any other presidential candidate this nation has ever seen. Time will tell whether he can overcome his relative lack of experience (he's served just two years in the U.S. Senate, following seven years as a state senator in Illinois) to gain the Democratic nomination in 2008. Win or lose, however, Obama has changed the face of U.S. politics. And yet, as Larissa MacFarquhar points out in this New Yorker *profile, he's a somewhat unlikely agent for change—preferring to focus on a search for common ground among voters, rather than engage in the politics of "us versus them" that Democratic candidates have so often relied on.*

Begin in farm country, late last summer, no particular day. Carmi, Illinois—a town on the Little Wabash River, down in the southern tip of the state, twenty-five miles from Kentucky, population about fifty-five hundred. A group of twelve farmers—burly white men with ruddy complexions and very short hair—sitting around a rectangle of pushed-together tables in a nondescript room, talking with their junior senator, Barack Obama. It was long before Obama decided to run for president, and he wasn't in a rush. He sat at one end of the tables, leaning back in his chair, his knee propped against the table edge. He wore a tie but had removed his jacket and rolled up his shirtsleeves. A young farmer complained about the Jones Act, a 1920 law that he felt was partly responsible for a detrimental consolidation in the barge market. Another farmer had a question about ethanol.

"My question first arose in my mind during the State of the Union address," the farmer said. "President Bush said I'm all for biofuels, and then he started talking about switchgrass. And I'm, like, now wait a minute, we've got a system where we can make ethanol out of corn. I guess cellulosic ethanol"—which can be made from switchgrass—"is more efficient. But we don't know how to do it, and we don't know if farmers are ever going to grow switchgrass, and we don't know if we would even want to grow switchgrass, so why so much emphasis on cellulosic ethanol?"

"Well, I'm not a scientist," Obama said, in a leisurely way, "so I gotta be careful when I start getting into this stuff that I don't wade too deep and then can't get back to shore. Right now cellulosic ethanol is potentially eight times more energy-efficient than corn-based ethanol, because you eliminate the middle step of converting it into sugar before you convert it into ethanol. That's my understanding. I know you're attached to corn, but if somebody came to you and said, you know what, if you take half your fields and grow switchgrass you'll make the same amount of money or more, then—"

"Not really," the farmer interjected. "Because I had a guy come to me before wheat harvest and said do you wanna sell your straw and I said no. I said, 'Don't even talk to me, I don't wanna sell my straw.'"

"Now that's interesting," Obama said. "Why wouldn't you want to sell your straw?"

"Organic matter!" the farmer said, triumphantly.

"Well, but if it's economical to you, if it's a good business decision, you'll be interested."

"If you paid me enough," the farmer conceded.

"If you were paid enough. Now, you know the economics of it better than I do. So we've got to sit down with farmers who are growing the crops and figure out what would make sense. Because, look, I'm not a farmer, and what you just described, I want to keep my straw because it's important, uh—"

"I thought I was the only person who had this idea," the farmer broke in, "and then in *FarmWeek* the guest editorial he said wait a minute, he said what we're talking about is against everything we've preached for the last twenty or thirty years, where we return organic matter to the soil."

"Exactly," Obama said in a soothing tone.

"And all of a sudden we're talking about denuding the ground—"

"Which we shouldn't do. And so," he said, returning to the topic, "the way to think about this is not to impose ideas on farmers that aren't gonna work, by people who don't farm. But we have to create more efficient ethanol if we want to see a significant growth in the market. The fact of the matter is that Brazilian ethanol is substantially cheaper than U.S. ethanol. Now, George Bush wanted to go ahead and let that come in, and myself and Durbin"—Richard Durbin, Illinois's senior senator—"said no, we would continue to support the existing tariff so that we can have the development of a homegrown ethanol market. I want to make sure that whatever is being done is utilizing the fact that we've got some of the richest soil on earth and the best farmers on earth. But the flip side is that farmers need to be engaged and not just put out a hand and say I'm not interested because I'm used to growing corn and beans."

There are three things that Democratic political candidates tend to do when talking with constituents: they display an impressive grasp of the minutiae of their constituents' problems, particularly money problems; they rouse indignation by explaining how those problems are caused by powerful groups getting rich on the backs of ordinary people; and they present well-worked-out policy proposals that, if passed, would solve the problems and put the powerful groups in their place. Obama seldom does any of these things. He tends to underplay his knowledge, acting less informed than he is. He rarely accuses, preferring to talk about problems in the passive voice, as things that are amiss with us rather than as wrongs that have been perpetrated by them. And the solutions he offers generally sound small and local rather than deep-reaching and systemic. Take a recent forum in Las Vegas on health care. Here are Hillary Clinton and Obama speaking about the same subject, preventive care.

"We have to change the way we finance health care, and that's going to mean taking money away from people who make out really well right now, so this is going to be a big political battle," Clinton said. "The insurance companies make money by employing a lot of people to try to avoid insuring you and then, if you're insured, to try to avoid paying for the health care you received." She stood at the front of the stage, declining an invitation to sit down next to the moderator. She spoke energetically but composedly, conveying the impression that she had spent a great deal of time preparing for the event because it was extremely important to her. "A lot of insurance companies will not pay for someone who's pre-diabetic or been diagnosed with diabetes to go to a nutritionist to find out how better to feed themselves, or to go to a podiatrist to have their feet checked," she said. "The insurance companies will tell you this: they don't want to pay for preventive health care because that's like lost money because they're not sure that the patient will still be with them. But if they're confronted with the doctor saying we're going to have to amputate the foot they're stuck with it. That is upside down and backwards!"

Now here is Obama. "We've got to put more money in prevention," he said. "It makes no sense for children to be going to the emergency room for treatable ailments like asthma. Twenty percent of our patients who have chronic illnesses account for 80 percent of the costs, so it's absolutely critical that we invest in managing those with chronic illnesses like diabetes. If we hire a case manager to work with them to insure that they're taking the proper treatments, then potentially we're not going to have to spend thirty thousand dollars on a leg amputation." A young man asked about health care for minorities. "Obesity and diabetes in minority communities are more severe," Obama said, "so I think we need targeted programs, particularly to children in those communities, to make sure that they've got sound nutrition, that they have access to fruits and vegetables and not just Popeyes, and that they have decent spaces to play in instead of being cooped up in the house all day."

In the past couple of months, Obama has hosted health-care forums of his own—in New Hampshire, in Iowa. In these forums, he is tranquil and relaxed, as though on a power-conserve setting. He paces slowly, he revolves, he tilts his head. He comments in a neutral, detached way. He doesn't express sympathy for sickness, or scorn for bureaucracy, or outrage at unfairness. He says that the system is broken and needs to be fixed, but conveys no particular urgency.

This mode of his is often called professorial, and Obama himself likens these forums to the constitutional-law classes that he taught at the University of Chicago. But "professorial" implies that he seems cerebral or didactic, and he doesn't. Despite the criticism he has received for being all inspiration and no policy, Obama has so far stuck to what appears to be an instinct that white papers belong on Web sites, not in speeches. It is surprising, given the recent electoral record of Democratic policy wonks, that he is not given more credit for the astuteness of this approach, but it's true that it's not just strategy—it's who he is. "He doesn't have the handicap that a lot of smart people have, which is that they come across as 'You're not smart enough to talk to me,'" George Haywood, a private investor and a friend of Obama's, says. "Adlai Stevenson, another Illinois guy, had that—he came across as an egghead and it was off-putting to people. Barack is the opposite." Probably one of the reasons for this is that Obama seems not to attach much value to cleverness as such. Even in law school, perhaps the place more than any other where sheer cleverness is prized and love of argument for its own sake is fundamental to the culture, he was not much interested in academic jousting.

No, Obama's detachment, his calm, in such small venues, is less professorial than medical—like that of a doctor who, by listening to a patient's story without emotional reaction, reassures the patient that the symptoms are familiar to him. It is also doctorly in the sense that Obama thinks about the body politic as a whole thing. If you are presenting a problem as something that they have perpetrated on us, then whipping up outrage is natural enough; but if you take unity seriously, as Obama does, then outrage does not make sense, any more than it would make sense for a doctor to express outrage that a patient's kidney is causing pain in his back. There is also, of course, a racial aspect to this. "If you're a black male, you don't have to try hard to impress people with your aggression," Haywood says. "There was a period when black politicians started to be successful, and it was understood that if you wanted to be mainstream you'd better have gray hair. Doug Wilder was an example. David Dinkins. Mayor Bradley in L.A. To be popular with the broader white electorate, you'd better look safe, you'd better not look angry. Now, I don't think Barack made a conscious decision to come across this way, but it is a happy accident. Some people may have seen his speech at the Democratic Convention, or heard that he rocked the house, and they may be disappointed, but the mainstream is not ready for a fire-breathing black man." (It seems likely that, consciously or not, Obama has learned from these examples, and knows that the election of a President Obama wouldn't mean a revolution in race relations, any more than women prime ministers were a sign of flourishing feminism in South Asia. Bigotry has always made exceptions.)

Obama's calm is also a matter of temperament. The first thing almost everybody who knows Obama says about him is how extremely comfortable he is with himself. "He was almost freakishly self-possessed and centered," Christopher Edley, Jr., one of Obama's professors at Harvard Law School, who is now a dean at Berkeley, says. There *is* something freakish about Obama's self-possession—it's conspicuous, it draws attention to itself, like the unnatural stillness of someone able to lower his blood pressure at will. He doesn't strive for an Everyman quality: he is relaxed but never chummy, gracious rather than familiar. His surface is so smooth, his movements so easy and fluid, his voice so consistent and well-pitched that he can seem like an actor playing a politician, too implausibly effortless to be doing it for real. Obama has become known for his open-necked shirts—he may do to the tie what John Kennedy did to the hat—but he never looks casual. "Gore and Bush both have this jokey quality, and I've never seen that in Obama," Robert Putnam, a Harvard political scientist who has spent time with all three politicians, says. "It's not like he's a sobersides, but Bush can be goofy, Gore can be goofy; Obama is not goofy."

What's strange about this is that the serene man his friends describe could not be more different from the person Obama himself describes in his memoir, *Dreams from My Father.* In that book, the young Obama is confused and angry, struggling to figure out who he is, often high, wary of both white condescension and black rage, never trusting himself, always suspicious that his beliefs are just disguised egotism, his emotions just symptoms of his peculiar racial lot. Of course, the book is about his emergence from this state of mind—it's a traditional tale of self-finding which ends, traditionally, with a wedding, in which his confusions are resolved—but the contrast between the Obama of the book and the Obama visible to the world is nonetheless so extreme as to be striking. "He was grounded, comfortable in his own skin, knew who he was, where he came from, why he believed things," Kenneth Mack, a friend of Obama's from Harvard and now a professor there, says. "When I read the book, I was surprised—the confusion and the anger that he described, maybe they were there below the surface, but they were not manifest at all." Asked about this, Obama says, "You know, what puzzles me is why people are puzzled by that. That angry character lasts from the time I was fifteen to the time I was twenty-one or so. I guess my explanation is I was an adolescent male with a lot of hormones and an admittedly complicated upbringing. But that wasn't my natural temperament. And the book doesn't describe my entire life. I could have written an entirely different book, about the joys of basketball and what it's like to bodysurf as the sun's going down on a sandy beach."

Why didn't he write a book about the joys of basketball? Why focus on an aspect of himself that seems so politically unpalatable? When Obama was in law school, just before he wrote *Dreams,* he talked about wanting to be mayor of Chicago, and since people tend for some reason to tolerate—indeed, to delight in—considerably more eccentricity and dubious conduct in mayors than they do in other elected officials, it may be that he wrote the book with that ambition in mind. He probably realized that revealing his druggy past was the best way to defuse the issue in the future. But Obama is a master storyteller, and it's likely that he also knows that the typical story of the political candidate—doing very well in school, followed by doing very well in a profession, meanwhile relishing a good life (victory, revenge, nice house, basketball, whatever)—is not moving or inspiring stuff.

When he was working as a community organizer in Chicago, Obama spoke to a number of black ministers, trying to persuade them to ally themselves with his organization, and in the course of these conversations he discovered that most had something in common. "One minister talked about a former gambling addiction," he writes. "Another told me about his years as a successful executive and a secret drunk. They all mentioned periods of religious doubt . . . the striking bottom and shattering of pride; and then finally the resurrection of self, a self alloyed to something larger. That was the source of their confidence, they insisted: their personal fall, their subsequent redemption. It was what gave them the authority to preach the Good News." Cassandra Butts, a friend of Obama's from law school, remembers, "Barack used to say that one of his favorite sayings of the civil-rights movement was 'If you cannot bear the cross, you can't wear the crown.'"

Obama rose to prominence at the 2004 Democratic Convention, describing his life as a celebration of the America dream: a "skinny kid with a funny name," the product of an improbably idealistic union between an African man and a girl from Kansas, he rose out of obscurity to attend Harvard

Law School and would go on—it was by then clear—to become the third black U.S. senator since Reconstruction. But in another sense his life runs directly counter to the American dream, rejecting the American dreams of his parents and grandparents, in search of something older

Obama's maternal grandfather, Stanley Dunham, grew up a small-time delinquent in El Dorado, Kansas. He didn't know what he wanted to do with himself, but he knew that he wanted to get out of Kansas—out of his parents' house, away from the airless parochialism of the small-town Midwest, where, as his grandson imagined it, "fear and lack of imagination choke your dreams so that you already know on the day that you're born just where you'll die and who it is that'll bury you." After a few false starts and eloping with a restless girl, he did what men of his type iconically do: he moved west. He moved to California, then to Seattle, and then, finally, to the last frontier, as far west as he could go without ending up east again, to Hawaii.

From a starting point eight thousand miles farther east, in Kenya, Obama's other grandfather, Hussein Onyango, moved in the same direction for similar reasons. Discontented and ambitious, he left his father's village, curious about the new white people settling in a nearby town. He took to wearing European clothing and adopted European notions about hygiene and property with a convert's fervor. During the Second World War, he travelled to Europe as a cook for the British Army.

The children of these two men, Obama's parents, one generation removed from their native places, were freer than their fathers. Obama's mother, Ann, married first a man from Kenya and then, when that man left, a man from Indonesia, and when the second marriage fell apart, she briefly returned home to Hawaii to start a master's in anthropology, and then left again for Indonesia, to spend several years doing field work. She gave her son, then thirteen, the choice whether to come with her or stay behind at his school in Hawaii, and he chose to stay.

Obama's father was expelled from school, and his father cut him off, but he managed to obtain a scholarship to attend college in America. He left his pregnant wife and his son to study econometrics at the University of Hawaii. There he met Ann Dunham, married her, and had another child, Barack. He left his second family to return to Kenya to work for the government, where he married another American woman and had two more children with her. After a few years, this third family disintegrated, and, because he was unwilling to accept the unfairness of Kenya's persistent tribalism, so did his government position. Angry and penniless, he started to drink.

"What strikes me most when I think about the story of my family," Obama writes, "is a running strain of innocence, an innocence that seems unimaginable, even by the measures of childhood." Innocence is not, for him, a good quality, or even a redeeming excuse: it is not the opposite of guilt but the opposite of wisdom. In Obama's description of his maternal grandfather, for instance, there is love but also contempt. "His was an American character, one typical of men of his generation, men who embraced the notion of freedom and individualism and the open road without always knowing its price," Obama writes. "Men who were both dangerous and promising precisely because of their fundamental innocence; men prone, in the end, to disappointment." Stanley Dunham's restlessness didn't get him anywhere but far away. He ended up an incompetent, unhappy insurance salesman, his life not very different from the one he might have lived if he'd stayed in Kansas, except that, having travelled all that distance to end up there, he was all the more dissatisfied with it. His daughter saw his dissatisfaction but learned the wrong lesson: the trouble wasn't that he had wandered in a meaningless fashion, wandering for wandering's sake, expecting that a new place meant a new life; the trouble was that he hadn't wandered far enough. She would go farther. "It was this desire of his to obliterate the past, this confidence in the possibility of making the world from whole cloth," Obama writes, "that proved to be his most lasting patrimony."

Obama's mother is, in his portrayal, an American innocent out of Henry James: a young girl who ventures into the world believing that things are as they seem to be; that a person's story begins when she is born and her relations with other people begin when she meets them; that you can leave your home without fear of injury or loneliness because people everywhere are more or less alike. She had no idea what she was getting into when she left Hawaii—no idea that only months before she arrived Indonesia had suffered a failed but brutal coup and the killing of several hundred thousand people. Eventually, somebody told her what had happened, but the knowledge didn't change her. "In a land where fatalism remained a necessary tool for enduring hardship," Obama writes, "she was a lonely witness for secular humanism, a soldier for New Deal, Peace Corps, position-paper liberalism." She had a faith, inherited from her father and resistant to experience, "that rational, thoughtful people could shape their own destiny." She should have counted herself lucky for emerging from the experience with only a second divorce and two bewildered children. "Things could have turned out worse," her son wrote. "Much worse."

Innocence, freedom, individualism, mobility—the belief that you can leave a constricting or violent history behind and remake yourself in a new form of your choosing—all are part of the American dream of moving west, first from the old country to America, then from the crowded cities of the East Coast to the open central plains and on to the Pacific. But this dream, to Obama, seems credulous and shallow, a destructive craving for weightlessness. When Obama, as a young man, went to Kenya for the first time and learned how his father's life had turned out—how he had destroyed his career by imagining that old tribalisms were just pettiness, with the arrogant idea that he could rise above the past and change his society by sheer force of belief—Obama's aunt told him that his father had never understood that, as she put it, "if everyone is family, no one is family." Obama found this striking enough so that he repeated it later on, in italics: *If everyone is family, no one is family.* Universalism is a delusion. Freedom is really just abandonment. You might start by throwing off religion, then your parents, your town, your people and your way of life, and when, later on, you end up leaving your wife or husband and your child, too, it seems only a natural progression.

So when it came time for Obama to leave home he reversed what his mother and father and grandparents had done: he turned around and moved east. First back to the mainland, spending two years of college in California, then farther, to New York. He ended up in Chicago, back in the Midwest, from which his mother's parents had fled, embracing everything they had escaped—the constriction of tradition, the weight of history, the provincial smallness of community, settling for your whole life in one place with one group of people. He embraced even the dirt, the violence, and the narrowness that came with that place, because they were part of its memory. He thought about the great black migration to Chicago from the South, nearly a century before, and the traditions the migrants had made there. "I made a chain between my life and the faces I saw, borrowing other people's memories," he wrote. He wanted to be bound.

Of course, in a sense, by choosing to leave his family and move to a place to which he had no connection, he was doing exactly what his parents had done, but, unlike them, he decided to believe that his choosing self had been shaped by fate and family. There was, at least, something organic, something inescapable about that. "I can see that my choices were never truly mine alone," he wrote, "and that is how it should be, that to assert otherwise is to chase after a sorry sort of freedom." Choosing was the best that he could do. In time, the roots would grow. He married Michelle Robinson, a woman who already owned the memories and the roots, who was by birth the person he was trying to become: the child of an intact, religious black family from the South Side. He took a job organizing a South Side community that was disintegrating but that he hoped, through work and inspiration, to revive. Later, rejecting the agnosticism of his parents and his own skeptical instincts, he became a Christian and joined a church. "I came to realize," he wrote in his second book, *The Audacity of Hope,* that "without an unequivocal commitment to a particular community of faith, I would be consigned at some level to always remain apart, free in the way that my mother was free, but also alone in the same ways that she was ultimately alone."

By the time he arrived at law school, when he was twenty-seven, he had become the man he had imagined. All his life, people had considered him black because he looked black, however confused he might be inside, and now he was no longer confused. His conversion was complete. "If you had met him, you would never get that he was biracial," Kenneth Mack says. "You would never get that he grew up in Hawaii. When I met him, he just seemed like a black guy from Chicago. He seemed like a Midwestern black man."

The victory of freedom over history is not just, of course, an American story about individuals but also a story that America tells about itself. Obama rejects this story even in one of its most persuasive incarnations, the civil-right movement. He calls the "spirit that would grip the nation for that fleeting period between Kennedy's election and the passage of the Voting Rights Act: the seeming triumph of universalism over parochialism and narrow-mindedness" a "useful fiction, one that haunts me . . . evoking as it does some lost Eden." When it seems that history has been defeated, that is only an illusion produced by charisma and rhetoric.

It is, then, not surprising that when it was proposed that America should invade Iraq with the goal of establishing democracy there, Obama knew that it would be a terrible mistake. This was American innocence at its most destructive, freedom at its most deceptive, universalism at its most naïve. "There was a dangerous innocence to thinking that we would be greeted as liberators, or that with a little bit of economic assistance and democratic training you'd have a Jeffersonian democracy blooming in the desert," he says now. "There is a running thread in American history of idealism that can express itself powerfully and appropriately, as it did after World War II with the creation of the United Nations and the Marshall Plan, when we recognized that our security and prosperity depend on the security and prosperity of others. But the same idealism can express itself in a sense that we can remake the world any way we want by flipping a switch, because we're technologically superior or we're wealthier or we're morally superior. And when our idealism spills into that kind of naïveté and an unwillingness to acknowledge history and the weight of other cultures, then we get ourselves into trouble, as we did in Vietnam."

In his view of history, in his respect for tradition, in his skepticism that the world can be changed any way but very, very slowly, Obama is deeply conservative. There are moments when he sounds almost Burkean. He distrusts abstractions, generalizations, extrapolations, projections. It's not just that he thinks revolutions are unlikely: he values continuity and stability for their own sake, sometimes even more than he values change for the good. Take health care, for example. "If you're starting from scratch," he says, "then a single-payer system"—a government-managed system like Canada's, which disconnects health insurance from employment—"would probably make sense. But we've got all these legacy systems in place, and managing the transition, as well as adjusting the culture to a different system, would be difficult to pull off. So we may need a system that's not so disruptive that people feel like suddenly what they've known for most of their lives is thrown by the wayside."

Obama's voting record is one of the most liberal in the Senate, but he has always appealed to Republicans, perhaps because he speaks about liberal goals in conservative language. When he talks about poverty, he tends not to talk about gorging plutocrats and unjust tax breaks; he says that we are our brother's keeper, that caring for the poor is one of our traditions. Asked whether he has changed his mind about anything in the past twenty years, he says, "I'm probably more humble now about the speed with which government programs can solve every problem. For example, I think the impact of parents and communities is at least as significant as the amount of money that's put into education." Obama encourages his crossover appeal. He doesn't often criticize the Bush administration directly; in New Hampshire recently, he told his audience, "I'm a Democrat. I'm considered a progressive Democrat. But if a Republican or a Conservative or a libertarian or a free-marketer has a better idea, I am happy to steal ideas from anybody and in that sense I'm agnostic." "The number of conservatives who've called me—roommates of mine, relatives who are Republicans—who've said, 'He's the one Democrat I could support, not because he agrees with me, because he doesn't, but because I at least think he'll take my point of view into account,'" Michael Froman, a law-school friend who worked in the Clinton administration and is now involved in Obama's campaign, says. "That's a big thing, mainstream Americans feeling like Northeast liberals look down on them."

After Obama's Convention speech, Republican bloggers rushed to claim him, under headings such as "Right Speech, Wrong Convention" and "Barack Obama: A Republican Soul Trapped Inside a Democrat's Body." The Convention speech was uncharacteristically Reaganesque for Obama, being almost uniformly sunny about America, which he called a "magical place"; these days, he tends to be more sombre. Even so, Republicans continue to find him congenial, especially those who opposed the war on much the same conservative grounds that he did. Some of Bush's top fund-raisers are contributing to Obama's campaign. In his election to the U.S. Senate, Obama won 40 percent of the Republican vote; now there is a group called Republicans for Obama, founded by John Martin, a law student and Navy reservist shortly to be posted to Afghanistan, which has chapters in six states. (On its Web site, the group highlights aspects of Obama's biography that aren't usually emphasized, referring to his mother's second husband as an "Indonesian oil manager," and mentioning the year after college that Obama spent working at Business International Corporation.) Of course, not all Republicans like Obama—John Martin receives a steady stream of rude e-mails. "Hi John, Just wanted to let you know that there aren't Republicans for Obama Hussein Barack," one woman wrote. "Please remove me from your mailing list and get over your white guilt." "Some Republicans you scum are!" a man from Hobe Sound, Florida, wrote. "This is someone who has a 100% left wing voting record in the Senate, including rejection of Roberts and Alito and wants to repeal our tax cuts. Screw him! And screw you too!"

In the most widely quoted part of his Convention speech, Obama said, "The pundits like to slice-and-dice our country into Red States and Blue States; Red States for Republicans, Blue States for Democrats. But I've got news for them, too. We worship an awesome God in the Blue States, and we don't like federal agents poking around in our libraries in the Red States." Seasoned observers of Washington tend to dismiss such talk of national unity and bipartisan cooperation as meaningless political boilerplate. Even Obama's allies worry that it sounds a little flaccid. "So much of what he's said he'll do when he's president is about being conciliatory and bipartisan and really listening," a friend says. "All this process-oriented stuff that's not exactly Churchillian rhetoric." But, coming from Obama, the talk about unity isn't boilerplate—he actually means it, and it's substantive, which is to say that it has consequences that make people angry.

Obama is always disappointing people who feel that he gives too much respect or yields too much ground to the other side, rather than fighting aggressively for his principles. "In law school, we had a seminar together and Charles Fried, who is very conservative, was one of our speakers," Cassandra Butts says. "The issue of the Second Amendment came up and Fried is pretty much a Second Amendment absolutist. One of our classmates was in favor of gun control—he'd come from an urban environment where guns were a big issue. And, while Barack agreed with our classmate, he was much more willing to hear Fried out—he was very moved by the fact that Fried grew up in the Soviet bloc, where they didn't have those freedoms. After the class, our classmate was still challenging Fried and Barack was just not as passionate and I didn't understand that." Recently, Obama said that if Bush decided to veto a military spending bill on the ground that it included a timetable for withdrawal from Iraq, he, Obama, would support removing the timetable in order to pass the bill. Liberal bloggers were irate at this capitulation, but the writer Samantha Power, who has worked for Obama on foreign policy, says, "Standing on one side of the room with his arms folded is just not his M.O."

This is, again, partly a matter of temperament. "By nature, I'm not somebody who gets real worked up about things," Obama writes in his second book. "When I see Ann Coulter or Sean Hannity baying across the television screen, I find it hard to take them seriously." He tends to think of his opponents as deluded and ridiculous, rather than as demons. "I've never been a conspiracy theorist," he says. "I've never believed there are a bunch of people out there who are pulling all the strings and pressing all the buttons. And the reason is that the older I get, the more time I spend meeting people in government or in the corporate arena, the more human everybody becomes. What I do believe is that those with money, those with influence, those with control over how resources are allocated in our society, are very protective of their interests, and they can rationalize infinitely the reasons why they should have more money and power than anyone else, why that's somehow good for the society as a whole."

Obama's drive to compromise goes beyond the call of political expediency—it's instinctive, almost a tic. "Barack has an incredible ability to synthesize seemingly contradictory realities and make them coherent," Cassandra Butts says. "It comes from going from a home where white people are nurturing you, and then you go out into the world and you're seen as a black person. He had to figure out whether he was going to accept this contradiction and be just one of those things, or find a way to realize that these pieces make up the whole." In the state senate, this skill served him well—he was unusually dexterous with opponents, and passed bills that at first were judged too liberal to have a chance, such as one that mandated the videotaping of police interviews with suspects arrested for capital crimes. "In our seminar, whether we were arguing about labor or religion or politics, he would sit back like a resource person and then he would say, I hear Jane saying such and such, and Tom seems to disagree on that, but then Tom and Jane both agree on this," Robert Putnam says. (For a couple of years, Obama participated in a seminar about rebuilding community, inspired by Putnam's article "Bowling Alone.") "I don't mean he makes all conflicts go away—that would be crazy. But his natural instinct is not dividing the baby in half—it's looking for areas of convergence. This is part of who he is really deep down, and it's an amazing skill. It's not always the right skill: the truth doesn't always lie somewhere in the middle. But I think at this moment America is in a situation where we agree much more than we think we do. I know this from polling data—we feel divided in racial terms, religious terms, class terms, all kinds of terms, but we exaggerate how much we disagree with each other. And that's why I think he's right for this time." Even when he was very young, Obama was scornful of, as he puts it, "people who preferred the dream to the reality, impotence to compromise."

Sometimes, of course, there is no possibility of convergence—a question must be answered yes or no. In such a case, Obama may stand up for what he believes in, or he may not. "If there's a deep moral conviction that gay marriage is wrong, if a majority of Americans believe on principle that marriage is an institution for men and women, I'm not at all sure he shares that view, but he's not an in-your-face type," Cass Sunstein, a colleague of Obama's at the University of Chicago, says. "To go in the face of people with religious convictions—that's something he'd be very reluctant to do." This is not, Sunstein believes, due only to pragmatism; it also stems from a sense that there is something worthy of respect in a strong and widespread moral feeling, even if it's wrong. "Rawls talks about civic toleration as a modus vivendi, a way that we can live together, and some liberals think that way," Sunstein says. "But I think with Obama it's more like Learned Hand when he said, 'The spirit of liberty is the spirit which is not too sure that it is right.' Obama takes that really seriously. I think the reason that conservatives are O.K. with him is both that he might agree with them on some issues and that even if he comes down on a different side, he knows he might be wrong. I can't think of an American politician who has thought in that way, ever."

Obama is, in fact, committed to respecting the opinions or cultures of others even when religious beliefs aren't involved. "There are universal values that I will fight for," he says. "I think there may have been a time and a place in which genital mutilation was culturally appropriate, but those times are over. I'm not somebody who believes that our foreign policy has to be driven by moral relativism. What I do believe is that we have to apply judgment and a sense of proportion to how change happens in any society—to promote our ideals and our values with some sense of humility."

"Lincoln is a hero of his," Sunstein says—Obama announced his candidacy in front of the Old State Capitol in Springfield in order to draw a connection between himself and that other skinny politician from Illinois—"and in the legal culture Lincoln is famous for believing that there are some principles that you can't compromise in terms of speaking, but, in terms of what you *do,* there are pragmatic reasons and sometimes reasons of principle not to act on them. Alexander Bickel, in *The Least Dangerous Branch,* made this aspect of Lincoln famous, and I don't know if Obama has this directly from Bickel, but if he doesn't he has it from law school." Lincoln, Bickel wrote, "held 'that free government was, in principle, incompatible with chattel slavery.' . . . Yet he was no abolitionist." Should freed slaves become the equals of white men? "The feelings of 'the great mass of white people' would not admit of this," Bickel described Lincoln as thinking, "and hence here also principle would have to yield to necessity." Lincoln wrote, "Whether this feeling accords with justice and sound judgment, is not the sole question, if indeed, it is any part of it. A universal feeling, whether well or ill-founded, can not be safely disregarded."

Obama has staked his candidacy on union—on bringing together two halves of America that are profoundly divided, and by associating himself with Lincoln—and he knows what both of those things mean. He calls America's founding a "grand compromise": compromise, for him, is not an eroding of principle for the sake of getting something done but a principle in itself—the certainty of uncertainty, the fundament of union. "I would save the Union," Lincoln wrote, in a letter to Horace Greeley, the editor of the *New York Tribune*. "If I could save the Union without freeing *any* slave I would do it, and if I could save it by freeing *all* the slaves I would do it; and if I could save it by freeing some and leaving others alone I would also do that." "I like to believe that for Lincoln it was never a matter of abandoning conviction for the sake of expediency," Obama writes. "Rather . . . that we must talk and reach for common understandings, precisely because all of us are imperfect and can never act with the certainty that God is on our side."

Obama sat leaning back in a chair in his office in Washington. He gave the impression that he would be perfectly comfortable sitting in that chair, without moving, all day. As he spoke, he waved his hand in a vague, regal gesture, like somebody absent-mindedly swatting away a fly. He talked about the aftermath of the Iraq war, how he believes that it is crucial to avoid a Vietnam-syndrome-style retreat into isolation.

"There are no countries now with no security implications," he said. "If you have ungoverned spaces, they become havens for terrorists and breeding grounds for pandemics and generate refugees that can destabilize areas that are of great interest to us. Security and humanitarian concerns are all part of one project, which is to create a world in which people see enough opportunity that they end up sharing our interest in maintaining order. . . . I would take some of the troops that we redeploy out of Iraq and use them to bolster NATO forces in Afghanistan. I think we still have the opportunity to succeed there."

Obama has become known for his skepticism about the Iraq war, but he is not a dove, nor is he averse to thinking in international terms. Two of the issues to which he has devoted the most attention since he arrived in the U.S. Senate, avian flu and nuclear nonproliferation, are grand global problems, which, while relatively uncontroversial, are nonetheless risky choices for signature issues, since, in both cases, success is invisible, and failure could mean disaster of world-changing proportions. Still, it seems that this global mode of thinking is comparatively new for him. When the first President Bush invaded Iraq, Obama was in his late twenties and thinking seriously about a career in politics, but friends from that time don't recall his opinion of the war. "I don't want to make claims as if I had been in a position to articulate a clear position on it," he says. "I remember believing that Saddam's invasion justified international action, and had I been forced to articulate a policy I'd like to think that I would have supported it once the international coalition was put together. You know, I was busy in law school at the time, or studying for the bar."

Obama had just returned to his office for an hour or so after voting on the floor of the Senate. He had spent the morning shuttling between the Senate and his office, being briefed on his schedule, chewing gum as he walked. It took him about ten minutes to make the trip each time, a delay sufficiently irritating that Obama's assistant expended considerable effort to avoid it. That day, she had tried to book the Senate's President's Room for a meeting, but Hillary Clinton's assistant had got there ahead of her.

In the office reception area, crowds of people milled about, many of them unscheduled; the office had become something of a tourist attraction. Marian Wright Edelman had marshalled a group of faith leaders, parents, and sample sick children to speak with Obama for a minute or two about children's health. About twenty rotund, middle-aged firefighters arrived and, too many to fit in the office, stood in the hallway, blocking the door. A couple of reporters from the *Chicago Tribune*—two of several people the paper has assigned to cover the Obama beat full time—waited on the sofa for a delayed interview. (The day had begun with a candidates' forum sponsored by a builders' union at which Obama was scheduled to speak after

Senator Joseph Biden, and, as a consequence, a winking press aide told the reporters—we all know what happens when you speak after Joe Biden—Obama was going to be late to everything for the rest of the day.) A white father from Winnetka had brought his two sons, the elder of whom, about nine years old, begged to wait as long as it took to spot Obama for even a second. (After an hour, a receptionist suggested that they come back the following morning.) Two teen-age girls—one, from Lake Elmo, Minnesota, carrying a soda, another, wearing pink tights and carrying a frozen yogurt—stopped by, hoping for a photograph with the Senator. A receptionist gave them a black-and-white portrait from a pile she kept at her desk, and the girls squealed in delight. The girl with the soda snapped a few photographs of the reception area and the empty conference room next to it and signed the guest book. "Where are you? No picture?" she wrote, next to more conventional comments ("Good luck Your Sweet," "My hero!," "Thank you, you rock!").

The moment Obama's Senate schedule ends for the week, he flies somewhere to campaign over the weekend, usually Iowa. "What an unbelievable crowd, I am so grateful to all of you for taking the time out on a Sunday afternoon to be here today." Iowa State University, Ames, Iowa, mid-February. "Let me thank first of all the person who just introduced me, Tom Miller, who is just an outstanding attorney general." Small town after small town, street after street of one- and two-story houses with lawns, then the commercial strip, the same everywhere, McDonald's, Burger King, Holiday Inn, Super 8, Wal-Mart, Kmart, Super Target, and then the smaller regional stores with names that rhyme—Rib Crib, Hobby Lobby, Taco Tico, Prime N' Wine.

"I am Barack Obama and I'm running for president." Algona High School, Algona, Iowa. Early April. "A state senate seat in the area where I lived opened up and some people I knew in the community got involved and asked me if I'd be interested," Obama said. "I did what every black man does when confronted with a major decision like that: I prayed on it, and I asked my wife." (Laughter.) "And after consulting those two higher powers I did what every first-time candidate does, which is to talk to anyone who will listen to you. I'd go to PTA meetings, I'd go to the barbershop, I'd go to softball games, and everywhere I went I'd get the same two questions. First question: Where'd you get that funny name, Barack Obama? Although people would mispronounce it. They would call me Alabama, they called me Yo' Mama." (Laughter.) "But the second question was what led me to run for president. People would ask me, 'You seem like a nice guy, you have a fancy law degree, you make a lot of money, you've got a beautiful, church-going family, why would you want to go into something dirty and nasty like politics?'"

"He's always wanted to be president," Valerie Jarrett, who has been a family friend for years, ever since she hired Michelle Obama to work in Mayor Daley's office, says. (Michelle Obama is now an executive at the University of Chicago Hospitals.) "He didn't always admit it, but oh, absolutely. The first time he said it to me, he said, 'I just think I have some special qualities and wouldn't it be a shame to waste them.' I think it was during the early part of his U.S. senatorial campaign. He said, 'You know, I just think I have something.'"

"Some people who knew of my activism in the community asked me would I be interested in running for that office," Obama said in Ames. "And so I did what every wise man does when confronted with such a decision: I prayed on it, and I asked my wife." (Laughter.) It remains to be seen how well Obama adapts himself to campaigning. It doesn't come altogether naturally to him. Late last year, when he was thinking about whether to run, friends asked him if he was ready for a fight, if the thought got his adrenaline going, and he would say, "Yes—but I don't know if I want the hassle." That's not something you imagine somebody embarking on a presidential campaign saying—not wanting the hassle. "But that's why he's so likable," a friend says. "That's the quality people are seeing in him, they're seeing how campaigning could be a grind." "Bill Clinton was far more into the tactics of politics," David Axelrod, Obama's chief campaign adviser, says. "He was a voracious consumer of polls. Of course, he was so indefatigable that he could do that and still read four books a week and be president of the United States. You wouldn't hire Barack to run your campaign. You might hire Bill Clinton to run your campaign."

This is not the only difference between Obama and Clinton. To compare them is to see that a political natural, as both of them are called, can mean very different things. "Bill Clinton has preternatural ability as a listener," Robert Putnam says. "Everybody always walks away from him thinking, For the first time in my life someone has actually listened to me—that man Bill Clinton is the first person in the world to really understand me. It's almost magical—even Newt Gingrich said something like, Every time I meet him I feel like I have to go rinse my mind out for an hour. Barack is not that good." Putnam's is a common reaction; it seems to be a response to Clinton's passionate political drive, his hunger, the need he is said to have to make everybody love him. Some of this quality, in a more restrained, sublimated form, is present, too, in Hillary Clinton—in her intense desire to win people over, in her exhaustive preparation, in her willingness to give everything she is capable of for every single vote.

This is not Obama's style at all. He doesn't seem hungry. He seems to like people but not to need them. When most politicians speak to a crowd, they give the impression that that is what they live for; Obama at town-hall meetings appears engaged but not fervently so, as if there were several other things that he would be equally happy doing that day. He still has the speechmaking power that he displayed at the 2004 Convention, but for the most part he keeps it in reserve. Even at large rallies these days he doesn't try to overwhelm—his eyes don't flame, his hands remain unclenched and below his shoulders, he doesn't go for a sudden conversion experience. (Sometimes his wife, Michelle, appears onstage with him, and this further dilutes the evangelical tone: the way Obama depicts Michelle in his books and speeches makes her sound like a sitcom wife, rolling her eyes at his excesses, affectionately taking him down a peg if he becomes pompous, humorously scolding him for not picking up his socks, and so her down-to-earth, TV presence undercuts his movie uplift.)

Obama is, obviously, running for president: it's not that he isn't hungry for converts but that his way of courting them is subtle. When his speechwriter, Jon Favreau, who in 2004 wrote speeches for John Kerry, was interviewed for the job, Obama asked him what his theory of speechwriting was. "I didn't have a grand theory in my pocket," Favreau says, "but I told him, When I saw you at the Convention what really struck me was that you told a story from the beginning to the end of that speech—a story about your life, about how it fit in with the larger American story—and it built to a point where people wanted to applaud, rather than using forced applause lines. Democrats just haven't done that. And Barack said, That's exactly what I try to do." That is Obama's theory of speeches, and it seems, also, to be his theory of campaigning: don't try to score huge points at every moment, don't kill yourself for every vote—a campaign is a long, slow story, and you don't want to exhaust your audience or yourself. "One weekend I was with him they were making a big deal about his school in

Indonesia being a madrassa," Valerie Jarrett says. "I said, 'How could they have even run with this story? It's so completely inaccurate!' He said, 'You know, we've contacted the school and the principal's gonna explain what kind of a school it is and we're gonna refute it all. You need to just calm down. This is gonna be fun! Valerie, you're not a guy but let me explain it to you in sport terms. It's like we're in a basketball game, and I'm gonna fumble the ball, and someone's gonna steal the ball, and I'm gonna miss a free throw, but we're gonna win the game. You can't get yourself worked up over every little thing that somebody says about me or you're gonna go crazy.'"

When Christopher Edley first met Obama, in law school, he decided that he would go far, because of his centeredness. Then when, later, he read Obama's first book and saw how Obama had suspected and vivisected himself for so many years, he decided that he would go far because of that. "The capacity for self-reflection is in my experience invaluable for a candidate or a president," he says. (Edley worked in the Carter and Clinton administrations and for Dukakis's campaign.) "It's difficult to describe to someone who hasn't been involved how tough a presidential campaign is. When you spend day after day flying around the country in an aluminum tube at forty thousand feet, it's the easiest thing in the world to lose yourself. And when every misstep becomes a thirty-six-hour media disaster there's every reason to second-guess your instincts, so being sensitive to your strengths and weaknesses and having the courage to come to terms with them is helpful when you're facing a crisis. I've seen candidates who, like a deer frozen in headlights, can't find their way forward and have to be led around by staff. I've also seen candidates who, faced with adversity, turn into the stubbornest of mules and can't adapt or adjust. Most candidates walk into the room asking everybody 'How'm I doing? How'm I doing?,' with no ability to look at themselves in the mirror. So the ability that Barack shows in the book to be brutally self-reflective—this is deep stuff."

"When he's exhausted on day forty of the campaign fund-raising drive, in the grind of it, can he keep it up?" a friend says. "I think sometimes he feels phony to himself. He's going to struggle with being the candidate, being a regular guy who has become a persona named Barack Obama. The persona is going to get larger and larger, and more and more distant from him and the way he used to live his life. We have a real live human being running for president here. He doesn't have much experience in this kind of campaigning, and this is both his strength and his vulnerability."

Some people go into politics with an idea; Obama went in with an example. The only politician he discusses at any length in his first book is the black man who was mayor of Chicago when Obama first moved there, in 1985, Harold Washington. Obama doesn't mention what platform Washington ran on, or what he accomplished in office (though he implies that it wasn't much); he talks about the effect his election had on the black community. When he first arrived in the city, Obama noticed that, all over the South Side, people had hung Washington's picture on their walls. "The night Harold won, let me tell you, people just ran the streets," a barber Obama calls Smitty says. "It was like the day Joe Louis knocked out Schmeling. Same feeling. People weren't just proud of Harold. They were proud of themselves." Washington's victory, Obama saw, had produced in people an almost religious feeling of deliverance. "Like my idea of organizing," he concluded, Washington "held out an offer of collective redemption." It is unlikely that Obama would speak of his own candidacy in these terms—that would be embarrassing. But his talk of unity, his avoidance of blame, and his promise to end the war all seem intended to gesture to a similar prospect of redemption: not only for black people but for white people (for voting for a black man), for Republicans (for embracing unity with a Democrat), and for Americans (for saying to the world that the war was a mistake).

But redemption is brittle. After Harold Washington died suddenly, in his second term, his achievement, such as it was, fell to pieces almost at once. "There was no political organization in place, no clearly defined principles to follow," Obama writes. "The entire of black politics had centered around one man who radiated like a sun." To a man less conservative, this failure might have been crushing—a demonstration of the impossibility of change—but to Obama it seemed only one more proof that charisma is misleading, that revolutions are illusory, that real change is slow. Now that he is running for office himself, it is likely he knows he can be as much harmed as lifted up by celestial expectations, so he tries, in small ways, to discourage them. Obama stands on the ground. If he thought his winning would take a revolution, he wouldn't have run.

Money Chooses Sides

John Heilemann

New York magazine | April 23, 2007

With the 2008 presidential candidates facing the most accelerated primary schedule in history—following January's calendar of caucuses in Iowa and Nevada and primaries in New Hampshire, South Carolina, and Florida, February 5, 2008, is shaping up to be a virtual national primary, with some twenty-three states expected to hold their primaries that day, including California, New York, and Illinois—hitting early fundraising targets has become a more urgent priority than ever. Experts estimate that anyone who wants to be a serious contender will need at least $100 million in the bank by the time February's "Tsunami Tuesday" rolls around, and speculate that the total price tag for the election could easily top $1 billion. In this piece, political correspondent John Heilemann reports from New York City—ground zero for political fundraisers—on how the top Democratic hopefuls fared in the all-important first lap of the money chase.

The investment banker Robert Wolf first met Barack Obama one afternoon in December in a midtown conference room. Obama was in town to deliver a speech at a charity dinner for children in poverty at the Mandarin Oriental —but also to pursue another, less high-minded, but more momentous, objective: to begin the process of attempting to pick Hillary Clinton's pocket.

The conference room belonged to George Soros, the billionaire bête noire of the right. After talking to Soros for an hour about his prospective bid for the White House, Obama walked down the hall and found assembled a dozen of the city's heaviest-hitting Democratic fund-raisers: investment banker Hassan Nemazee, Wall Street power Blair Effron, private-equity hotshot Mark Gallogly, hedge-fund manager Orin Kramer. Most had been big-time John Kerry backers in 2004. Most had a connection to the Clintons. All were officially uncommitted for 2008.

Comparatively speaking, Wolf, now the CEO of UBS Americas, was a buck-raking neophyte. But his prodigious recent efforts (first for Kerry, then for House and Senate Democrats in 2006) had established him as a rising star in the fund-raising firmament. Until a few weeks earlier, the presidential horse he'd planned to ride in 2008 was former Virginia governor Mark Warner. But with Warner's decision to forgo the race, Wolf was up for grabs—and in the sights of every Democrat in the field.

What Wolf, 45, was looking for was a candidate who could change the tenor of our politics. "I'd like my children to soon see a president give a State of the Union address and have both parties applaud," he tells me. But Wolf was looking, too, for a campaign where his presence would be "impactful," for a candidate who would take his calls, listen to his ideas. He wanted to feel the love. And while Wolf refuses to speak ill of Clinton, it's clear he doubted that, no matter how much dough he raised, he'd ever be feeling it from her.

Wolf was wowed by Obama that afternoon: his straightforwardness, his "bold and impressive" early stance against the Iraq war. He handed Obama his card and said, "I'd like to get to know you more." Obama phoned the next day. "When we hung up, he said, 'I'll call you after the holidays,' and I'm thinking, *Yeah, right, he's gonna call me,*" Wolf says. But call Obama did. The next week, they had dinner in Washington, just the two of them, on the night that George W. Bush gave his speech announcing the surge of additional troops into Iraq. "I felt so honored to be sitting down with him for two hours on an occasion like that," Wolf recalls, "knowing that he was going off to be interviewed on television later."

Within ten days, Obama had announced his intention to run and Clinton was officially in. A story in the *Times* reported that Obama had nailed two A-list New York donors: Soros and Wolf. But though Soros's backing was a symbolic coup, it's Wolf who has emerged as Obama's most copious cash collector in the city so far—hosting two high-dollar cocktail parties, making countless calls, harvesting more than $500,000. As Wolf tells me about the soirées he's hosted, he reaches into a meticulously organized scrapbook, takes out a photograph of him and Obama grinning madly, and tells me that I can keep it. "The way Barack has taken this nation with his rock-star status," he says, "it's very exciting!"

The courtship of Robert Wolf is, of course, part of a larger story: How Obama, from a standing start three months ago, built a fund-raising apparatus as powerful as Clinton's. How Obama's people, tapping a national hunger for something new and fresh, along with the unease of many

Democrats about Clinton, ginned up more money for use in the primaries than she did. How they kicked her ass on the Internet and tapped twice as many donors overall. How they even held their own against the Clinton machine in New York. How Obama, that is, won the money primary—or, at least, its first installment—and arguably turned himself into the race's co-front-runner.

New Yorkers have long understood the money primary and its importance in signaling a candidate's plausibility. In a deep-blue city where the Democratic primary has traditionally taken place too late to matter, the battle for cash is the one contest in which New Yorkers (a certain class of New Yorkers) have been able tangibly to influence the selection of the party's nominee. As Julius Genachowski, a high-tech player and law-school friend of Obama's, puts it, "Other states vote; New York invests."

Yet the context in which the money primary is taking place this year is radically different from before. With some two dozen states, including ours, now planning to hold primaries on February 5, the ability to raise vast quantities of early cash is seen by many operatives as essential—not just to create a perception of strength but to build a viable organization. "I say this all the time: It's over on February 5," argues Terry McAuliffe, Clinton's campaign chairman. "To raise money to compete in Texas, California, Florida, New York, Illinois, New Jersey, and Michigan, all on one day—extraordinary!"

Thus the lunatic pace and scale of the campaign now unfolding: a race that seems hopped up on steroids and speed simultaneously. With all three top-tier Democratic candidates having rejected federal spending limits for the primaries, experts reckon the race overall may consume over $1 billion, in excess of the GDP of more than a few small countries. On the Republican side, Rudy Giuliani and Mitt Romney are on the air with advertising (nine months before the first ballots are cast, for heaven's sake). And Democrats are turning out in thousands-strong crowds for Obama, Clinton, and John Edwards—portending a campaign of mind-boggling ferocity and unpredictability.

This sooner-bigger-faster dynamic was supposed to be Clinton's friend. With her purportedly unmatchable capacity to raise stratospheric sums, she seemed to be on an inexorable march to the nomination. But with Obama's show of fund-raising strength—and Edwards's, too—that scenario has flown out the window. "The air of inevitability is gone," says a mega-fund-raiser for Clinton in New York. "Not everyone in the campaign believed this before, but we've got a race on our hands."

The putative Clinton juggernaut was launched on February 6, with a dinner at her house in Washington. In attendance were 70 of Clinton's top-shelf fund-raisers from around the country, including New York financiers Alan Patricof and Steve Rattner. The following day, more than a hundred so-called Hillraisers—donors pledged to pulling in at least $25,000 each—filed into the Hyatt Regency for briefings by Clinton's senior strategists, who offered presentations designed to reinforce her status as the unequivocal, eminently electable, Democratic front-runner.

For weeks already, the Clinton finance team had been working to lock up as many premier bundlers—people proficient at accumulating piles of other people's checks—as possible. Nowhere was the effort more avid than in New York, especially when it came to bundlers flirting with Obama. In short order, the campaign landed Nemazee and Effron, along with PR executive Robert Zimmerman, who'd raised money for Bill Clinton and Al Gore but was keeping his mind open about 2008. "The Obama outreach was sophisticated, cleverly orchestrated; I met with him and was impressed," says Zimmerman. "But it wasn't a hard call. Hillary has the experience and knows how to beat the Republicans, and I can't stress enough how important that is."

Other Clinton fund-raisers, however, rendered their decision more on the basis of personal cost-benefit analyses. "I'll probably be a chicken and go with Hillary," one confided months ago. "Everybody thinks I'm going to. It's easy to explain. I have a long relationship with her, I do like and respect her, I'd be happy if she won. So I can support her, frankly, without pissing off Barack or anyone else. But if I support Barack, I'd piss off a bunch of other folks—and who needs that?"

The Clinton rollout amounted to a show of overwhelming force, the fund-raising equivalent of shock and awe. The list of boldface names behind her was endless: Roger Altman, Fred Hochberg, Stanley Shuman, Carl Spielvogel. Though Clinton proclaimed that she hoped to raise $15 million in the first quarter and $75 million by the end of the year, both record-breaking goals, the consensus in political circles was that these were plainly lowball numbers. Reports in the press stated that the campaign was calling on its upper-echelon bundlers to reap at least $250,000 and as much as $1 million each. One such bundler, New York supermarket magnate John Catsimatidis, boasted to the Web magazine the *Politico*, "She's going to raise more money than all the other candidates put together."

To a great degree, presidential fund-raising is an expectations game: Set them low, then blow them away. But, curiously, the Clinton campaign seemed to be lifting the bar rather than depressing it. "There are a lot of people who give to who they think is going to win; they want to be on the winning team so they can be an ambassador or who the hell knows what," observes a Clinton bundler. "Adopting a we're-gonna-crush-everyone approach was a way to attract as many of those people as possible."

Yet alongside the aura of invincibility, the Clinton team projected something else: a tacit message that it was time for big-dollar Democrats to choose between Obama and Hillary. On the bus or off the bus. No hedging allowed. And apostates would pay a price. For some in the party, the tactic struck a nerve. "It's almost like a shakedown—you're with us or you're not," Jim Neal, a North Carolina investment banker who was on an early conference call with McAuliffe, told the *Times*. "I find the squeeze, this early, to be quite vulgar . . . It's a bullying tactic."

McAuliffe reacts with outsize outrage to suggestions of strong-arming. "Give me one example! One example of one individual who works for this campaign who has ever threatened anyone! It hasn't happened," he tells me. "People rumor about the Hillary Clinton campaign all the time. But I've probably spoken to 15,000 or 20,000 people in this campaign so far, and I haven't had one complaint from one person I've spoken to."

Patricof says the same. "I didn't have to drag anyone kicking and screaming into this," he tells me. "And I would never say, 'You're either with us or against us'—it's not in my vocabulary."

Some Obama backers acknowledge that the widespread accusations of Clintonian heavy-handedness are overblown. "[Clinton finance director] Jonathan Mantz doesn't do that," says an Obama bundler. "In this game, you have a thousand agents out there—who knows what they're saying?" He goes on, "The pressure they exerted comes from trying to create this steamroller effect: 'We have the most resources, the most talent, the most endorsements, so we're going to win.' The dynamic isn't, 'You're with us or against us.' It's, 'You're with us or you're a moron.'"

Even loyal denizens of Clintonworld don't bother to dispute that. They also note the Clintons have elephant memories and value loyalty above all. The result is a realm where threats are unnecessary, because they are implicit: the threat of ostracism, in particular, of being banished from the charmed circle.

"There are some people the Clintons consider Clinton people who have gotten behind Barack," a longtime friend of Bill and Hillary's explains to me. "And there will be total retribution if the opportunity presents itself."

Total retribution? You're joking, right?

"I'm not joking. They're not going to audit somebody's tax return or anything. But once you've been in the Clinton camp, once they think you're part of the team, once you've helped them and they've helped you and you then go somewhere else—I just think it's very hard to crawl back into their good graces. I'm not saying it won't happen. But they won't forget. They may take you back eventually, but they won't forget."

Two weeks after his dinner in Washington with Obama, Robert Wolf found himself supping there with the senator again, in a private room at the Ruth's Chris Steakhouse near Dupont Circle. But this time, their meal was by no means *à deux*. Around the table sat the members of Obama's embryonic New York finance committee: fund manager Jim Torrey (whose daughter is on the staff of this magazine); Provident Group partner Brian Mathis; Citibank executive Michael Froman; private-equity manager Jamie Rubin; and Orin Kramer.

Kramer had yet to sign on to support Obama; he was doing due diligence. But everyone understood what a score bringing him onboard would be. At 61, Kramer was a Clinton stalwart who'd piled up mountainous stacks of cash for Gore and Kerry. "Orin sort of owns New Jersey when it comes to raising money," says Torrey. When the dinner was over, Kramer and the others raced to catch the last shuttle back to New York. At the airport, Froman and Mathis kept prodding him to pull the trigger. "All right, enough already!" Kramer said, pulling out his cell phone and calling Mantz to break the news that he was defecting.

Kramer had been mulling the decision, tortured by conflicting feelings, for weeks. "I ran up against my pain threshold," he said at the time. "I have unalloyed respect for Senator Clinton . . . But despite being a dinosaur, I'm drawn to a different kind of political experience." Moreover, Kramer had concluded, contrary to the conventional wisdom then, that Obama had a chance to win. "The market has mispriced him," Kramer told friends. "The street thinks he's a 5-to-1 underdog, but I think he's undervalued."

Kramer was by no means the only migrant from Clintonworld to Obamaland. "The first part of the calculus was about the civic good," one former Administration official tells me. "Who would be a better president? It's a toss-up—maybe Hillary on the margin. But the likelihood is that whoever you support is going to lose, that's just the odds, so it should matter who'd be the better candidate—I mean, better for the country. And I thought Obama, simply by being a candidate and by virtue of the policies and values he'd espouse as a candidate, had a chance to change the country. The second part is the personal: The Clintons are basically disloyal people. They have a huge track record of jettisoning people far closer to them than I am on the slightest political pretext. Loyalty has to be a two-way street. I don't think they've earned the right to play the loyalty card."

Other Obama bundlers simply found the prospect of plumping for Clinton too depressing to bear. "Hillary has the same problem that Gore and Kerry had," says one. "There are people who believe passionately in her, but a lot have reservations about her electability. I can raise a lot of money for Barack because people are enthusiastic about him. But if I go out and raise money for Hillary, it's like I'm taxing my friends."

One unsurprising aspect of Obama's New York fund-raising network was its ebony hue: the presence of high-profile black bundlers, such as publisher Earl Graves and music executive Andre Harrell. But the most striking element of its composition wasn't racial but generational: Unlike the Clinton side, which was dominated by folks in their fifties, the Obamans were mostly in their forties. "One thing we recognized early on," says David Axelrod, the campaign's chief strategist, "was that there is a substrata of people who in past campaigns weren't allowed to sit at the adult table but who all of a sudden were quite formidable."

Many of Obama's baby bundlers cut their teeth in Bill Clinton's administration. Mathis and Froman both worked in the Treasury Department, while Rubin, son of Bob, had been a staffer at the Federal Communications Commission. There was also Josh Steiner, another Treasury hand and now a partner of Steve Rattner's at the Quadrangle Group. And others had no

Clintonian association, but were emerging fund-raising powerhouses, such as former Goldman Sachs golden boy Eric Mindich.

At the heart of the next-gen cadre were Froman and Mathis, both law-school classmates of Obama's. Together, they recognized that, whereas the Clinton fund-raising corps represented the financial elite tossed up by the LBO and M&A booms of the eighties, they were in a position to mine the vein of freshly minted money spawned by the hedge-fund and private-equity eruptions of the new millennium. The players behind those booms had no loyalties, and owed no debts, to the Clinton dynasty. They were looking for a candidate to call their own.

"In Barack's speech in Selma [earlier this year]," a baby bundler says, "he talked about the Moses generation and the Joshua generation in the civil-rights movement. It's sorta the same story here." He continues, "If we all lined up for Hillary, we wouldn't have even gotten into the anteroom, let alone had seats at the table—there's no more room. It would've been, 'You have an idea? Send us an e-mail and we'll have someone get back to you. Oh, and don't forget to send those checks.' But that's not how it is with Barack. We're already at the table."

Then there was Julius Genachowski, who for years was Barry Diller's go-to guy at InterActiveCorp. Genachowski connected Obama to another pool of money: technology and media. Co-hosting fund-raisers in New York and Washington (with former FCC chairs Reed Hundt and Bill Kennard), he helped raise more than $600,000. And he focused on Obama's Internet operations, persuading the campaign to hire both a private-sector tech wizard and one from the political world. Today, Obama's Web presence is Best in Show—a crucial asset in the dollar derby.

By early March, when Obama hit New York on a fund-raising swing, the sense of momentum was palpable. On a Monday night, Obama crammed in a quartet of parties: two hosted by Wolf, one by Edgar Bronfman Jr., one at the Park Avenue home of music impresario Antonio "LA" Reid. "We had Beyoncé and Patricia Duff, Jay-Z and Jamie Rubin, Jermaine Dupri and Jonathan Soros," Mathis says about the Reid affair. "We raised north of $350,000 in two hours. And that's when it became crystal clear to all of us: We can raise this money."

For all the campaigns, March ended in a flurry. A story in the *Daily News* provoked spasms of fear and trembling for the Obama and Edwards people: Hillary Clinton had apparently raised $10 million in one week. But there were reasons to wonder if the Clinton people were getting twitchy, too: In the last six weeks of the quarter, the campaign had dispatched Bill Clinton to a startling sixteen fund-raisers. Inside the campaign, there were no worries about their final number—it would be gargantuan. But Team Clinton was hearing "rumbles," McAuliffe told me later, about an Obama surge. "I probably made 1,500 calls this quarter," McAuliffe noted. "And there's not a donor I called that Obama didn't call three, four, five times. So I knew he was working hard. I knew he was doing well on the Internet. And I knew someone was going to capture this antiwar stuff like Howard Dean did."

The antiwar stuff was also fueling Edwards's fund-raising efforts. The former North Carolina senator was expected by no one to come close to matching his rivals' tallies—especially in New York, where his populism made him less palatable to many Wall Street donors. Still, on the last day of the quarter, when I visited Brian Mixer, Edwards's New York finance director, in his office near Union Square, Mixer was serene. "We're going to more than double what we did in primary money in New York in the first quarter of 2003," Mixer said with evident satisfaction. "We raised a million then—and we'll do $2.5 million this time."

Leo Hindrey, the former CEO of the YES Network and one of Edwards's prime bundlers, told me, "The Clinton people think they own New York—but what they're finding out is that it's true for the Senate but not for the presidency." Mixer added, "What we've heard is that they tell people, 'If you give money to us, you can't give to anyone else.' We say, 'We understand she's your senator, but why not help us out, too?'" Mixer pauses. "Hey, we're doing fine—there's a lot of money in New York."

Precisely how much would not become clear for another two weeks, the deadline for the campaigns to file detailed reports with the Federal Election Commission. But 24 hours later, Clinton's first-quarter total became public —via the *Drudge Report*, no less. The number was indeed staggering: $36 million. But not as staggering as it appeared. For one thing, it included $10 million left over from her Senate race last year. And of the remaining $26 million, some (though the campaign didn't disclose the figure) had been raised for the general election. By leaking the $36 million figure, the Clinton team was hoping to garner one news cycle in which their results would be seen in the most flattering light. And by not revealing their primary number, they would deny the press the ability to do an immediate comparison with Obama's—which they suspected might be larger than hers.

They were right about that, but they would have to wait awhile to discover just how right. Displaying their own media savvy, Obama's people let anticipation mount for three days before unveiling their numbers. Speculation flooded the political ether: $20 million? $21 million? $23 million?! More, in fact: $25 million, an astonishing figure for a start-up campaign, all the more so because $23.5 million was for the primaries—more than Clinton's total. (By law, the maximum individual donation to presidential candidates is $2,300 for the primaries and the same for the general election, and whereas Obama's fund-raisers, as a rule, collected only primary cash, the Clintonites held many $4,600 events.)

And what of New York? Not surprisingly, the Clinton number was gigantic: more than $8 million. But Obama's was nothing to sneeze at: more than $4 million. Consider, for a start, that Clinton raised next to nothing in Chicago (this in spite of its being her actual hometown). And consider the likelihood that Clinton has tapped out her high-dollar donor base in the city, while Obama's new-money brigade is expanding as contributors are transformed into bundlers.

Ten minutes after the Obama press release hit my in-box, I phoned one of Clinton's most potent fund-raisers in the city.

So: $25 million total, $23.5 million for the primary, 100,000 donors, I said.

"Wow."

Surprised?

"I think everybody will be surprised. Her number was what they always told us it was going to be. But the idea that he would get as far as he got, I don't think anyone thought it was possible."

Seems as though her people let expectations get away from them a bit.

"The last couple weeks, they've been trying to play down our number to spin you guys back to where they wanted you. But it's pretty hard to spin this."

Not that McAuliffe isn't prepared to give it the old college try. It's the Friday after the numbers hit the streets, April 6, and Clinton's chairman and I are sitting in Mantz's tenth-floor office in the campaign's K Street headquarters. The couch is red, the carpet is blue, and McAuliffe's face is alabaster-white. McAuliffe, 50, is justifiably called the greatest fund-raiser in

Democratic history (though critics of the corrupting influence of corporate money in politics hardly consider that an honorific). Also the most maniacal: Famously, he once wrestled a 260-pound alligator to win a $15,000 donation to the Florida Democratic Party. Today, McAuliffe reminds me that, as a kid growing up, he was a boxer. "We're now in a fight," he says. "This is great. I'm actually excited."

I start by asking about the campaign's efforts to foster around Hillary a sheen of invulnerability—efforts that now seem to have backfired. (On top of Obama's haul, the Edwards campaign pulled in $14 million, double its take in the same period four years ago.) I tell McAuliffe that I'd spoken to a Clinton White House veteran, who observed, "It's like they thought they were running the Mondale campaign; they were just going to smother the other guy with money and endorsements."

"Let's just stop right there," McAuliffe says, his voice quickly rising. "So we just finished up the biggest quarter in the history of American politics. She's ahead in the polls. We're taking nothing for granted . . . I've said this from day one, I've said this to Hillary: You've got to earn it. She knows it, her husband knows it, and it's gonna be a long, hard fight."

I mention that I'd been in Chicago the previous day to visit Obama headquarters and that his people had been fairly gloating over a particular statistic: that the database of Clinton donors from her last Senate race contains 250,000 names, yet the campaign had received just 50,000 contributions this quarter—a pretty meager conversion rate. "First of all, that's direct mail," McAuliffe says. "We did only three mailings this quarter, and the response we got back from people is that it's too early. It's just timing. They'll all be there by the end of '07—those 250,000 donors will be back."

McAuliffe's confidence (overconfidence?) strikes me as a less extreme version of some of the wild-eyed claims made by the campaign's bundlers two months earlier. I ask Mantz, who's behind his desk, what he thought when he heard one of his fund-raisers say that Clinton would raise as much as the others put together.

"I love that guy," Mantz deadpans. "Seriously, what I thought was, *How you think this is helpful, I'm not quite sure.*"

There've been mild complaints by some Clinton bundlers that Hillary personally didn't do enough events or make enough phone calls in the first quarter; that she relied too heavily on her surrogates; that, in short, she was complacent. McAuliffe and Mantz allow that Clinton wasn't as active as

Obama. But they argue she was busy attending to her duties in the Senate, wangling endorsements—important work. "And yet she raised more money this quarter than any candidate in history; I'm almost embarrassed to be having this conversation with you!" McAuliffe says. "We were able to do what we wanted to based on the time she gave us. And in the second quarter, she's probably got double the events coming up, a lot more small-donor ones across the country."

Even in New York, Patricof tells me later, Clinton still has plenty of upside potential. "New York's not tapped out for us at all. There's a natural inclination at the beginning to go to your first tier. Now there's going to be greater outreach to new constituencies, new communities, ethnic groups. There are people on my list I still haven't called yet. And I plan to get on the phone with them very, very soon."

That Clinton will knock the cover off the ball in the second quarter is a lead-pipe certainty. For all the ambivalence about her in some quarters, in others there's adulation—and Clinton is disciplined and relentless enough to track down every fan. And McAuliffe and Mantz are right to say that her first-quarter showing was stellar. Mismanaged expectations aside, the real story of the money primary so far isn't that Hillary underperformed. She did not. The real story is about how Obama killed—and what it means for his candidacy and the race ahead.

David Axelrod has an answer at the ready, which isn't surprising, since being on-message comes as naturally for him as breathing. At 52, Axelrod is among the best and most storied consultants in the business; his résumé lists stints with four of the Democratic presidential candidates this year (Obama, Clinton, Edwards, Chris Dodd) as well as Chicago mayor Richard Daley and Illinois congressman Rahm Emanuel. With a caterpillar mustache and a comb-over, he's unfashionable to a fault; today, in his offices in Chicago, he's wearing a red shirt and green corduroys, looking altogether too Christmassy for the first week of April.

"The most gratifying thing about our fund-raising success isn't the bottom line," Axelrod says, "but the number of people who have contributed and the number who are small contributors. The people we're targeting are new to this; they're not constrained by old loyalties. There's a lot of energy in that world, and it gives us enormous potential to grow." When

I ask if he's implying a contrast to Clintonworld, Axelrod offers up a pointed aperçu: "There's a difference between grabbing low-hanging fruit and planting trees."

Obama's finance people know that historically the second and third quarters have seen a falloff in contributions. But whatever happens next on the money front, the political implications of Obama's first quarter are already set in stone. The central question about Obama is whether, for all his charisma and star power, he may simply be a flash in the pan. And that question remains largely unanswered. He has yet to demonstrate anything approaching depth on any area of policy. He has yet to articulate a compelling vision of America's place in the world at a time of clear and present peril. For many people, even those inclined to favor him, he remains something of a cipher. And he has yet to be tested under fire or to prove that he has the fortitude required to withstand the rigors of a presidential campaign—which Clinton has been and does in spades. But Obama's performance in the money primary does demonstrate that he can build an organization, in a breathtakingly short time, that can go toe-to-toe with hers. And that is no small thing. "As someone new to the presidential process, there was a question of, 'Can he hack it?'" says Axelrod. "That question has been answered."

The unanswered question in all of this, of course, is how much, in the end, the money primary actually matters. The history here is singularly unhelpful. In 1995, GOP senator Phil Gramm declared, inspiringly, "I have the most reliable friend you can have in American politics, and that's ready money." Gramm set what was then a presidential fund-raising record—then failed to get past the Iowa caucus. In 2003, Edwards raised the most in the first quarter and Dean the most for the year—then both were trounced by Kerry. On the other hand, Gore set a Democratic record for first-quarter fund-raising in 1999 and went on to win. And Bush blew away his rivals that year, with the same result.

The reason why money is stipulated to matter more than ever this time—and the reason so much more is said to be required—is the accelerated primary schedule. As things now stand, there will be four small-state contests in January: the Iowa and Nevada caucuses, the New Hampshire and South Carolina primaries. Then, on February 5, as many as 24 states, including some of the biggest, will vote in one fell swoop. "We are moving headlong into a quasi-national primary," Axelrod explains. "You've got to build a quasi-national organization from day one. So your operations are more expensive. And the only thing inflating in cost faster than media is health care."

There is, however, an alternative theory, espoused by the Edwards campaign, that the accelerated calendar actually makes money less important. "You have to hit a certain threshold," says Edwards deputy campaign manager Jonathan Prince. "You need enough money to saturate the first four states"—maybe $40 million. "After that, it's all going to be about momentum. If you don't have it, all the money in the world won't be enough to help you. It's not just that no campaign can possibly raise enough to saturate the airwaves on February 5. It's that, even if you could, it wouldn't be nearly enough to counteract the screaming headlines in every local paper and the five-minute pieces every night at the top of the evening news that the candidate with momentum will get."

The Edwards argument is self-serving, to be sure, but far from implausible or lacking in precedent. "In 2000, Gore had momentum, Bradley had more money—which people forget—and Gore won," says Nick Baldick, who ran Edwards's campaign in 2004 and is now focused exclusively on the four early states. "In 2004, we had a favorable calendar, Dean had the money, but Kerry had momentum and that was everything."

Can Edwards be the candidate to seize the early momentum? Quite possibly. While he's clearly the underdog among the big three, his campaign has not only been the most substantive of the lot (see his proposal for universal health care) but also the most strategic and focused. Edwards is virtually living in Iowa, where his organization is deeply rooted. He's tight with organized labor, which will be key in Nevada (because of the large unionized labor force in Las Vegas). And he stands a good chance in South Carolina, which he won in 2004.

I ask Axelrod what he thinks of the Edwards theory about the limited power of money. "It's a theory," he replies. "My theory is, I don't know if they're right, but I'd rather be prepared for either exigency." Yet Axelrod doesn't disagree that the outcome of the early states will be pivotal. "If someone rolls up a bunch of states before February 5, they'll go into that day with a huge amount of momentum. And that's our goal. To go into February 5 and deliver a knockout blow."

That someone will deliver a knockout blow that day is the assumption of all three campaigns. But what if they are wrong? The possibility is tantalizing, and has led at least one Democratic savant to put forward a titillating scenario. "I may be the first idiot foolish enough to say it out loud, but we could be looking at something unheard of in the modern era—someone going into convention with only 30 percent, 40 percent of delegates," Dean's campaign guru, Joe Trippi, said recently. "Edwards, Hillary, and Obama may have enough cash before Iowa even happens to go all the way. The polls are basically all dead heats . . . What could happen is that we're headed for a brokered convention."

The brokered-convention scenario is the political equivalent of the fantasy of a Beatles reunion (back when they were all still alive, that is): "The obsession of nostalgia buffs," as Axelrod puts it. Or maybe not. "I think Trippi is right that it's more likely with this calendar," says Baldick. "I don't think it'll happen, but if there's split victories in the first four states and no one emerges with clear momentum, maybe."

How could it happen? Edwards, who by common consensus needs to win Iowa to survive, doesn't—Obama does. Hillary wins Nevada and New Hampshire. Obama wins South Carolina, where the black vote is potentially huge and Hillary is unloved. Now it's a jump ball on February 5—and Obama and Hillary split the big states between them.

Ah, the lure of fantasy. Which is probably exactly what it is. But more of a fantasy than Obama's beating Clinton in the money primary? We are in uncharted waters here. Things could get very weird.

Until someone can deliver a knockout blow, how about [illegible] the nomination of all three campaigns—but what if they are wrong? The possibility is tantalizing, and has led at least one Democratic consultant to put forward a truly [illegible] scenario. "It may be the first time [illegible] enough to say it, but we could be looking at something unheard of in the modern era—someone coming into the convention with only 40 percent, 30 percent of delegates," Dean's campaign guru, Joe Trippi, said recently. "Edwards, Hillary and Obama may have enough cash before Iowa even happens to go all the way. The polls are basically all dead heats. What could happen is that we're headed for a brokered convention."

The brokered convention scenario is the political equivalent of the fantasy of a Beatles reunion (back when they were all still alive, that is). "This obsession of nostalgic buffs," as Axelrod puts it. Or maybe not. "I think Trippi is right that it's more likely with this calendar," says Baldick. "I don't think it'll happen, but if there are split victories in the first four states and no one emerges with clear momentum, anything . . ."

How could it happen? Edwards, who by common consent needs to win Iowa to survive, does it—Obama does. Hillary wins Nevada and New Hampshire. Obama wins South Carolina, where the black vote is potentially huge and Hillary is eclipsed. Now it's a mere half of February 5—and Obama and Hillary split the big states between them.

Ah, the lure of fantasy. Which is probably exactly what it is. But no more of a fantasy than Obama's beating Clinton in the primary? We are in uncharted waters here. Things could get very weird.

Contributors

Thomas P.M. Barnett is a contributing editor to *Esquire* and a former professor and senior military analyst at the U.S. Naval War College. He is the author of numerous books, including *The Pentagon's New Map: War and Peace in the Twenty-first Century* and *Blueprint for Action: A Future Worth Creating.*

Peter J. Boyer is a staff writer for the *New Yorker* and the author of *Catastrophic Success: How the Bush Administration Remade Our Military to Win New Wars but Not the Peace.*

Carl Cannon is White House correspondent for *National Journal.* He is the author of *The Pursuit of Happiness in Times of War* and coauthor of *Boy Genius: Karl Rove, the Architect of George W. Bush's Remarkable Political Triumphs.*

Elizabeth Drew is a regular contributor to the *New York Review of Books*. She is the author of numerous books, including *Corruption of American Politics: What Went Wrong and Why* and *Fear and Loathing in George W. Bush's Washington.*

James Fallows is a national correspondent for the *Atlantic Monthly* and chairman of the board of The New America Foundation. He is the author of several books including, most recently, *Blind Into Baghdad: America's War in Iraq.*

Ethan Fishman is professor of political science at the University of South Alabama and the author of numerous books, including *The Prudential Presidency: An Aristotelian Approach to Presidential Leadership.*

Max Frankel is a former executive editor of the *New York Times*. He is the author of several books, including *The Times of My Life* and *My Life With The Times.*

Thomas L. Friedman is a columnist for the *New York Times*. He won his third Pulitzer Prize in 2002 for commentary and is the author of several books including, most recently, *The World is Flat: A Brief History of the Twenty-First Century.*

Peter W. Galbraith, a former U.S. Ambassador to Croatia, is currently Senior Diplomatic Fellow at the Center for Arms Control and a principal at the Windham Resources Group. He is the author of *The End of Iraq: How American Incompetence Created a War Without End*

Jeffrey Goldberg is Washington correspondent for the *New Yorker* and the author of *Prisoners: A Muslim and a Jew Across the Middle East Divide.*

John Heilemann is a contributing editor to *New York* magazine.

Seymour M. Hersh is a staff writer for the *New Yorker* magazine and a contributing editor to the *Atlantic Monthly*. Winner of the 1970 Pulitzer Prize for international reporting, he is the author of numerous books including, most recently, *Chain of Command: The Road From 9/11 to Abu Ghraib.*

Chris Jones is a writer at large for *Esquire* and the author of *Too Far From Home: A Story of Life and Death in Space.*

Daniel Kahneman won the 2002 Nobel Prize in economics. He is the Eugene Higgins professor of psychology and professor of public affairs at Princeton University's Woodrow Wilson School of Public and International Affairs.

Larissa MacFarquhar is a staff writer for the *New Yorker*.

Todd S. Purdum is a national editor at *Vanity Fair* and a former Washington correspondent for the *New York Times*. He is the lead author of *A Time of Our Choosing: America's War in Iraq.*

Jonathan Renshon is a doctoral student in the department of government at Harvard University, and the author of *Why Leaders Choose War: The Psychology of Prevention.*

Stephen Rodrick is a contributing editor to *New York* magazine.

David Rose is a contributing editor to *Vanity Fair*.

Jeffrey Rosen is the legal affairs editor at the *New Republic* and the author of *The Supreme Court: The Personalities and Rivalries That Defined America*.

Anthony Shadid is a foreign correspondent for the *Washington Post*. He won a 2004 Pulitzer Prize for his coverage of the U.S. invasion of Iraq, and is the author of *Night Draws Near: Iraq's People in the Shadow of America's War.*

Chris Smith is a contributing editor to *New York* magazine.

Neil Swidey is a staff writer for the *Boston Globe Magazine.*

Matt Taibbi is a contributing editor to *Rolling Stone*.

Michael Wolff is a contributing editor to *Vanity Fair*. He is the author of *Autumn of the Moguls* and *Burn Rate: How I Survived the Gold Rush Years on the Internet.*

Jason Zengerle is a senior editor at the *New Republic*.

Stephen Rodrick is a contributing editor to *New York* magazine.

David Rose is a contributing editor at *Vanity Fair*.

Jeffrey Rosen, legal affairs editor of the *New Republic*, is the author of *The Supreme Court: The Personalities and Rivalries that Defined America*.

Anthony Shadid is a foreign correspondent for the *Washington Post*. He won a 2004 Pulitzer Prize for his coverage of the U.S. invasion of Iraq and its aftermath, and is the author of *Night Draws Near: Iraq's People in the Shadow of America's War*.

Chris Smith is a contributing editor to *New York* magazine.

Neil Swidey is a staff writer for the *Boston Globe Magazine*.

Matt Taibbi is a contributing editor at *Rolling Stone*.

Michael Wolff is a contributing editor to *Vanity Fair*. He is the author of *Autumn of the Moguls* and *Burn Rate: How I Survived the Gold Rush Years on the Internet*.

Jason Zengerle is a senior editor at the *New Republic*.

Permissions

"Untruth and Consequences," by Carl Cannon. Copyright © 2007 by Carl Cannon. Reprinted by permission of the author. Originally appeared in the *Atlantic Monthly*, January-February 2007.

"A Unified Theory of Scandal: The Real Roots of the U.S. Attorney Firings," by Jeffrey Rosen. Copyright © 2007 by Jeffrey Rosen. Originally appeared in the April 23, 2007 issue of the *New Republic*. Reprinted by permission.

"Not Compassionate, Not Conservative," by Ethan Fishman. Copyright © 2006 by Ethan Fishman. Reprinted by permission of the author. Originally appeared in the *American Scholar*, Volume 76, No. 1, Winter 2007.

"The Washington Back Channel," by Max Frankel. Copyright © 2007 by Max Frankel. Reprinted by permission of The New York Times Syndicate. Originally appeared in the *New York Times Magazine*, March 25, 2007.

"Karl Rove's Split Personality," by Todd S. Purdum. Copyright © 2006 by Todd S. Purdum. Reprinted by permission of the author. Originally appeared in *Vanity Fair*, December 2006.

"Southern Discomfort: The Strangest Senate Race of the Year," by Peter J. Boyer. Copyright © 2006 by Peter J. Boyer. Reprinted by permission of the author. Originally appeared in the *New Yorker*, October 30, 2006.

"The Worst Congress Ever," by Matt Taibbi. From *Rolling Stone*, November 2, 2006. Copyright © Men's Journal LLC 2006. All rights reserved. Reprinted by permission.

"Democrats: The Big Surprise," by Elizabeth Drew. Reprinted with permission from the *New York Review of Books*. Copyright © 2007 NYREV, Inc. Originally appeared in the *New York Review of Books*, January 11, 2007.

This is Baghdad. What could be worse?" by Anthony Shadid. Copyright © 2006, The Washington Post. Reprinted with permission. Originally appeared in the *Washington Post*, October 29, 2006.

"Survivor: The White House Edition," by Michael Wolff. Copyright © 2006 by Michael Wolff. Reprinted by permission of the author. Originally appeared in *Vanity Fair*, December 2006.

"The Surge," by Peter W. Galbraith. Reprinted with permission from the *New York Review of Books*. Copyright © 2007 NYREV, Inc. Originally appeared in the *New York Review of Books*, March 15, 2007.

"Neo Culpa," by David Rose. Copyright © 2007 by David Rose. Reprinted by permission of the author. Originally appeared in *Vanity Fair*, January 2007.

"The State of the World," by Thomas P.M. Barnett. Copyright © 2007 by Thomas P.M. Barnett. Originally appeared in *Esquire*, May 2007.

"The Redirection," by Seymour M. Hersh. Copyright © 2007 by Seymour M. Hersh. Reprinted by permission of the author. Originally appeared in the *New Yorker*, May 5, 2007.

"Declaring Victory," by James Fallows. Copyright © 2006 by James Fallows. Reprinted by permission of the author. Originally appeared in the *Atlantic Monthly*, September, 2006.

"The Power of Green," by Thomas L. Friedman. Copyright © 2007 by Thomas L. Friedman. Reprinted by permission of The New York Times Syndicate. Originally appeared in the *New York Times Magazine*, April 15, 2007.

"Why Hawks Win," by Daniel Kahneman and Jonathan Renshon. Reproduced with permission from *Foreign Policy* #158, January/February 2007 (www.foreignpolicy.com). Copyright © 2007, Carnegie Endowment for International Peace.

"One of Us," by Chris Jones. Copyright © 2007 by Chris Jones. Reprinted by permission of the author. Originally appeared in *Esquire*, August 2006.

"Rudy Tuesday," by Stephen Rodrick. Copyright © 2007 by Stephen Rodrick and New York Magazine. Reprinted by permission of *New York* magazine. Originally appeared in *New York* magazine, March 5, 2007.

"The Lessons of the Father," by Neil Swidey. Copyright © 2006 by Globe Newspaper Company. Reprinted by permission. Originally appeared in the *Boston Globe Magazine*, August 13, 2006.

"The Starting Gate," by Jeffrey Goldberg. Reprinted by permission of International Creative Management, Inc. Copyright © 2007 by Jeffrey Goldberg. First appeared in the *New Yorker*, January 15, 2007.

"The Woman in the Bubble," by Chris Smith. Copyright © 2006 by New York Magazine. Reprinted by permission. Originally appeared in *New York* magazine, November 13, 2006.

"The Accidental Populist," by Jason Zengerle. Copyright © 2007 by The New Republic, LLC. Reprinted by permission. Originally appeared in the *New Republic*, January 22, 2007.

"The Conciliator," by Larissa MacFarquhar. Copyright © 2007 by Larissa MacFarquhar. Reprinted by permission of the author. Originally published in the *New Yorker* (www.newyorker.com), May 27, 2007.

"Money Chooses Sides," by John Heilemann. Copyright © 2007 by John Heilemann. Reprinted with the permission of The Wylie Agency, Inc. Originally appeared in *New York* magazine, April 23, 2007.

"The Woman in the Bubble" by Chris Smith. Copyright © 2006 by New York Magazine. Reprinted by permission. Originally appeared in New York magazine, November 13, 2006.

"The Accidental Populist" by Jason Zengerle. Copyright © 2007 by The New Republic, LLC. Reprinted by permission. Originally published in the New Republic, January 22, 2007.

"The Conciliator" by Larissa MacFarquhar. Copyright © 2007 by Larissa MacFarquhar. Reprinted by permission of the author. Originally published in the New Yorker (www.newyorker.com), May 7, 2007.

"Jones Chooses Sides" by John Heilemann. Copyright © 2007 by John Heilemann. Reprinted with the permission of The Wylie Agency, Inc. Originally appeared in New York magazine, April 23, 2007.